D0909660

THE TOKYO WAR CRIMES TRIAL

The Pursuit of Justice

in the Wake

of World War II

Harvard East Asian Monographs 299

THE TOKYO WAR CRIMES TRIAL

The Pursuit of Justice

in the Wake

of World War II

Yuma Totani

Published by the Harvard University Asia Center
and distributed by Harvard University Press
Cambridge (Massachusetts) and London, 2008

Printed in the United States of America

The Harvard University Asia Center publishes a monograph series and, in coordination with the Fairbank Center for Chinese Studies, the Korea Institute, the Reischauer Institute of Japanese Studies, and other faculties and institutes, administers research projects designed to further scholarly understanding of China, Japan, Vietnam, Korea, and other Asian countries. The Center also sponsors projects addressing multidisciplinary and regional issues in Asia.

Library of Congress Cataloging-in-Publication Data

Totani, Yuma
    The Tokyo war crimes trial : the pursuit of justice in the wake of World War II / Yuma Totani.
        p. cm. -- (Harvard East Asian monographs ; 299)
    Includes bibliographical references and index.
    ISBN-13: 978-0-674-02870-8 (cloth : alk. paper)
    ISBN-10: 0-674-02870-8 (cloth : alk. paper)
        1. International Military Tribunal for the Far East. 2. War crime trials--Japan. 3. World War, 1939–1945--Atrocities. I. Title.
    KZ1181.T67 2008
    341.6'90268--dc22

                                                                    2008000815

⊗ Printed on acid-free paper

Last figure below indicates year of this printing

18 17 16 15 14 13 12 11 10 09 08

For my parents and siblings

Acknowledgments

First and foremost, my gratitude goes to the five members of my dissertation committee for their mentorship during my graduate years at the University of California, Berkeley. They are Andrew Barshay, Mary Elizabeth Berry, Irwin Scheiner, David Cohen, and Eric Stover. Their support and guidance were invaluable in enabling me to complete the original version of this book. I am grateful also to Andrew Gordon and Akira Iriye at Harvard University, who provided me with constructive criticism for revision. I received page-by-page editorial advice from Rebecca Suter, a fellow researcher during my postdoctoral year at Harvard University in 2005–06. I cannot thank her enough for her tremendous assistance.

Over the course of my research, I met many Japanese historians, lawyers, and other scholars who took an interest in my work and extended their collegial support. In particular, I would like to thank Hayashi Hirofumi at Kantō Gakuin University, Kasahara Tokushi at Tsuru University, Yoshida Yutaka at Hitotsubashi University, and Ishida Yūji at the University of Tokyo. Many meetings, workshops, and much correspondence with them revealed to me the richness and vitality of Japanese scholarship. My thanks also go to Awaya Kentarō at Rikkyō University, who took the time to discuss our common research interests and shared with me newly acquired archival records.

I was able to complete this book with funding from the Edwin O. Reischauer Institute of Japanese Studies at Harvard University, where I was a postdoctoral fellow for one year. I also received generous institu-

viii   *Acknowledgments*

tional support from the History Department and the College of Liberal Arts at the University of Nevada, Las Vegas, where I am currently a faculty member.

Finally, I would like to express my heartfelt thanks to William M. Hammell at the Harvard University Asia Center, whose editorial guidance helped me bring this book to completion.

Contents

x

Contents

Reference Matter

Figures

Note to the Reader

Throughout this book, both Japanese and Chinese names are given in the traditional manner, that is, the family name precedes the personal name. All translations of Japanese-language sources into English are my own, except in the case of court exhibits that were translated by the Allied war crimes investigators at the time of the Tokyo trial. For the most part, Chinese personal and place names are transliterated using the Wade-Giles system of pinyin, in order to maintain consistency with the common Romanization practice in the historical records cited in this book.

The following abbreviations are used throughout:

AWM
    Australian War Memorial, Canberra, Australia

DA
    Documents on Australian Foreign Policy, 1937–1949

DNZ
    Documents on New Zealand External Relations, Vol. II: The Surrender and Occupation of Japan

FRUS
    Foreign Relations of the United States

NAA
    National Archives of Australia, Canberra, Australia

NARA

National Archives and Records Administration, College Park, MD, U.S.A.

Nuremberg Judgment

"Judgment of the International Military Tribunal for the Trial of German Major War Criminals," in *The Trial of German Major War Criminals, by the International Military Tribunal Sitting at Nuremberg, Germany (Commencing 20th November, 1945)*

Pal's Opinion

International Military Tribunal for the Far East: Dissentient Judgment of Justice Pal

TKK

Tōkyō saiban to kokusai kensatsu kyoku: kaitei kara hanketsu made

Tokyo Judgment

The Tokyo Judgment: The International Military Tribunal for the Far East (I.M.T.F.E), 29 April 1946–12 November 1948

Transcripts

The Tokyo War Crimes Trial

TSM

Tōkyō saiban e no michi: kokusai kensatsu kyoku, seisaku kettei kankei bunsho

TWC

Trials of War Criminals before the Nuernberg Military Tribunals under Control Council Law No. 10

THE TOKYO WAR CRIMES TRIAL

The Pursuit of Justice
in the Wake
of World War II

INTRODUCTION

Why the Tokyo Trial Now?

Soon after Japan's defeat in the Pacific theater, the Allied powers established a special international criminal court at the heart of the bombed-out capital of Japan. The Allies named the new court the International Military Tribunal for the Far East, following its predecessor in Nuremberg (which was referred to simply as the International Military Tribunal, or the IMT). The Far Eastern tribunal is more commonly remembered as the Tokyo trial in popular parlance today. At Nuremberg, the Allied prosecuting agency brought before the court Hermann Göring and 23 other German leaders on charges that they waged aggressive war and committed large-scale atrocities, including mass murder of the European Jews. The prosecutors at Tokyo followed suit. They put on trial a group of 28 wartime Japanese political and military leaders. The principal charge against them was that they had participated in the planning and execution of aggressive war in the Asia-Pacific region, dating back to the invasion of Manchuria in September 1931. The prosecutors also charged that the same group of defendants was answerable for atrocities committed by the Japanese armed forces against millions of civilians and prisoners of war in various theaters of war.

The Japanese people today regard the Tokyo trial as a focal point of the remembrance of World War II. There is good reason for them to linger on, and mull over, the significance of this particular historical event even after the passage of six decades. This trial was the first public event, after Japan's surrender to the Allies, by which the Japanese people gained a unique opportunity for firsthand access to documentation about the disastrous war and to determine the responsibility of their leaders for initiating it. The Tokyo trial, in this respect, marked the starting point of Japan's confrontation with its past, a process that continues to this day. To determine its historical significance has proved to be highly complex, however, because there has been disagreement over the legitimacy of the Tokyo Tribunal as an impartial arbiter of the Japanese war, war crimes, and war guilt. This introductory chapter will briefly sketch out the general contour of the debates that have taken place in the postwar period.

Japanese nationalists—including some of those who joined the defense team at Tokyo—were among the first to launch a thoroughgoing criticism of the Tokyo trial. Questioning the Allied moral authority to prosecute the leaders of the vanquished nation, they charged that the true purpose of this special trial was nothing other than to satisfy the desire of the victorious Allied powers for revenge. In support of this contention, they argued that the laws applied at Tokyo were essentially the arbitrary creation of victor nations. They especially made the point that it was an entirely novel idea to prosecute state leaders for the commission of aggressive war. The law criminalizing any type of war, they argued, did not exist before, during, or after World War II. In their opinion, a tribunal that would allow the retroactive application of new law could only be deemed "victors' justice." This kind of assessment quickly took root in Japan, and remains the standard understanding of the Tokyo trial today.

The Japanese nationalist claim subsequently received unexpected support from the American academy. In his landmark monograph, *Victors' Justice: The Tokyo War Crimes Trial* (1971), Richard Minear treated the Tokyo trial as an early manifestation of the self-righteous foreign policy of the United States that culminated in the Vietnam War. He argued essentially that the trial enabled the United States to impose its logic of justice and entrench American supremacy over Japan, and more broadly, in the postwar Asia-Pacific region.[1] His powerful indictment of American neo-imperialism by way of the Tokyo trial was received favorably, and his book continues to serve as the basic reference on the Tokyo trial in the English-speaking world to this day.

Meanwhile in Japan in the 1980s, certain Japanese historians who had been critical of the Japanese nationalists' assertions began to conduct their own research on the Tokyo trial. They, too, concluded that this trial was a politicized event, but the grounds for so concluding were radically different from the ones given by critics in the 1940s and 1950s. The leading historian, Awaya Kentarō, did not deny the historical significance of putting wartime Japanese leaders on trial. He considered rather that the prosecution of Tōjō and other high-ranking Japanese was a crucial step toward Japan's postwar atonement process. In this regard, he held just the opposite position from that of nationalist critics. His point of criticism lay elsewhere; he found that the Allied powers, and in particular the United States, purposely withheld evidence of certain sensitive war crimes cases. The evidence he found to have been omitted from the prosecutorial effort included that of the "comfort women" system, medical experimentation and bacteriological warfare committed by Unit 731, and atrocities targeted at the Asian civilian populations. Awaya added to this list the exemption of Emperor Hirohito from prosecution. According to his research, the Supreme Commander for the Allied Powers, Gen. Douglas MacArthur, granted special immunity to Hirohito, thereby allowing the wartime head of state to remain above the law. In light of these findings, Awaya concluded that the Tokyo trial was one kind of victors' justice, in the sense that justice was meted out selectively and according to the victors' political expediency.[2] This new interpretation in Japan was soon introduced to the United States, adding greater complexity to trans-Pacific debates on the Tokyo trial. Awaya subsequently modified his position in view of new findings that conflicted with his earlier assessment, but his original contention continues to influence American scholarship today.

Each of the interpretive positions taken by the critics above captures certain elements of truth about the Tokyo trial. But as this book will show, their assertions do not always have sufficient supporting evidence in the actual trial records. Some are, in fact, directly contradicted by historical documents. By way of illustration, the transcripts of court proceedings indicate that the prosecuting agency detailed Japanese war crimes rather than withheld information, including some of the crimes that critics charge were neglected. It is true that there was an American cover-up effort with respect to Unit 731. But the same did not apply to a number of other war crimes cases. Military sexual slavery was one such Japanese wartime offense that the Allied prosecutors sought to substantiate. Similarly, the common belief that MacArthur granted immunity to Hirohito does not stand up to the test of primary documents. As will be shown in this book, MacArthur had no formal or informal power to make decisions regarding the trial of Hirohito. Those who decided the fate of the Japanese emperor were the leaders of the United States and its allies. The decision they made, moreover, was to keep the option of his trial open, *not* to grant him immunity; the Allied governments ruled out the latter possibility at the outset. How should one, then, explain the ultimate failure of the Allies to put him on trial? This book will address this and other puzzling questions about the treatment of Hirohito.

As for the contention that the law applied at Tokyo was without precedent, this also proves difficult to sustain when assessed against the actual content of the trial. Such criticism may be validly advanced with respect to the charges related to aggressive war. With respect to war crimes, however, international criminal tribunals today consider that the Tokyo judgment provided useful precedents that help advance the cause of international humanitarian law. The very trial that has been thoroughly discredited in the eyes of the Japanese public, in other words, is gaining international recognition as an important precursor of international prosecutorial efforts today. As subsequent chapters will show, the International Criminal Tribunal for the former Yugoslavia (ICTY) and the International Criminal Tribunal for Rwanda (ICTR) cite the Tokyo Tribunal's legal opinions in some of their recent judgments. This indicates that this trial has become as an integral part of the historical development of the international justice system rather than a judicial anomaly.

A wide variety of sources on the Tokyo trial come under scrutiny in this book. The sources can be divided into two broad categories. The record of the Tokyo trial itself constitutes one category. This includes the Charter of the Tokyo Tribunal, the Bill of Indictment, 48,288 pages of trial transcripts, 5,184 pieces of court exhibits (available on 48 reels of microfilm), the judgment, five separate dissenting and concurring opinions, internal records of the prosecution (available on about 770 reels of microfilm), the drafts of the judgment and judges' internal memoranda, and records of the defense counsel. This book makes use of published versions of the Charter of the Tribunal, the indictment, trial transcripts, the judgment, and the separate opinions. User-friendly trial records are provided in *The Tokyo War Crimes Trial*, 22 vols. (accompanied by an additional 5-volume finding aid), and *The Tokyo Judgment: The International Military Tribunal for the Far East (I.M.T.F.E), 29 April 1946–12 November 1948*, 2 vols.[3] The court exhibits are not available in published sources. The copies of exhibits used in this book have been gathered from the Australian War Memorial Library in Canberra. The microfilmed versions are also available at the National Archives and Records Administration (NARA) in College Park, Maryland. Some of the internal records of the International Prosecution Section have been reprinted in recent years in Japan; this book makes extensive use of the reprinted version. For a fuller set of the prosecution's records, one would need to go to the archives at College Park, where all of the records are available on microfilm.[4] As for the drafts of the judgments and judges' internal memoranda, a voluminous record can be found at the National Archives of Australia and the Australian War Memorial Library, both located in Canberra. Australia is the logical place to look for these kinds of records, since the president of the Tokyo Tribunal was Australian. With regard to the records of the defense counsel, this book makes use of memoirs, which are available in the form of books and articles written by former defense lawyers, defendants, and court reporters. Some internal defense records made in preparation for the trial had been kept at the Imperial Household Agency since the end of the trial, and were then transferred to the National Archives of Japan in the 1970s. These records are not discussed in this book, however, since the author was unaware of their existence until the completion of this book. The Japanese national archives also have in their possession the records of the interviews that the Japanese Ministry of Justice had conducted with certain former defendants, defense lawyers, and witnesses in the early 1960s. But these sources remain classified and unavailable to researchers unless their duplicates are deposited for public access elsewhere.

Another set of sources consists of various government records kept by the eleven countries that participated in the Tokyo trial. Whereas the first type of source (as described above) documents the legal proceedings, the second type brings to light the larger politico-military circumstances in which the Tokyo trial was planned and carried out. The languages used in these government records vary, because not all the participating countries were English-speaking. This book makes use of records collected only from those countries that use the English language. The Allied records that are analyzed come partly from published sources, such as *Foreign Relations of the United States* (commonly known as the *FRUS* series), *Documents on Australian Foreign Policy, 1937–1949,* and *Documents on New Zealand External Relations,* Vol. II: *The Surrender and Occupation of Japan.* Additional government documents were collected from archives in Australia, India, and the United States.

This book explores the Tokyo trial thematically, although it is loosely structured along chronological lines as well. Chapter 1, "Lessons from Nuremberg," explores the Allied policy for the establishment of the Tokyo Tribunal from a comparative perspective. It elicits commonalities and differences between Nuremberg and Tokyo in their original conceptions. Chapter 2, "The Trial of Emperor Hirohito?," traces Allied policy regarding the treatment of Emperor Hirohito as a war criminal. Chapter 3, "Tōjō and Other Suspects," explores the criteria that the prosecutors applied to determine whom to indict at the Tokyo trial. The four chapters that follow analyze the content of the trial itself. Chapter 4, "Narrative of the War," examines the legal concept of aggressive war as defined at Nuremberg and Tokyo. It then explores the Tokyo Tribunal's central findings on aggressive war charges. Chapter 5, "Leadership Responsibility for War Crimes," gives an overview of the prosecutors' pretrial preparations concerning war crimes charges. Chapter 6, "Nanking and the Death Railway," focuses on two major cases of Japanese-perpetrated mass atrocity: the Rape of Nanking and the Burma-Siam Death Railway. It analyzes the precedents the Tokyo Tribunal established regarding the responsibility of highest-ranking government and military leaders for these atrocities. This chapter also considers the relevance of the Tokyo judgment to current international war crimes trials. Chapter 7, "Documenting Japanese Atrocities," examines a wide variety of evidentiary material that the prosecutors presented in their effort to substantiate the scope of Japanese war crimes. It also discusses the general rulings and verdicts of the Tokyo Tribunal. The next two chapters explore the historiography of the Tokyo trial. Chapter 8, "The First Trial Analysts," examines commentaries that the first generation of trial analysts wrote during and in the immediate aftermath of the trial. Chapter 9, "Pal's Dissent and Its Repercussions," provides an in-depth analysis of one of the dissenting opinions submitted to the Tokyo Tribunal and its impact on postwar Japanese debates on the Tokyo trial. Finally, the concluding chapter, "Beyond Victors' Justice," traces the development of Japanese scholarship in recent decades and considers the future direction of the study of the Tokyo trial.

The remainder of this introductory chapter will provide background information to set out the trial's basic chronology and introduce key trial participants and organizations.

The Tokyo Trial: An Overview

By signing the Instrument of Surrender on September 2, 1945, the Japanese government formally recognized the Allied prerogative to mete out "stern justice" to war criminals. Pursuant to this part of the surrender terms, the Allied powers established the international criminal court in Tokyo in January of 1946. They also created some 50 separate special war crimes courts in the former theaters of war in the Asia-Pacific region, which fell under national jurisdiction of the individual Allied countries.[5]

The prosecutorial effort before the Tokyo Tribunal began on May 3, 1946. This trial turned out to be protracted—far slower than its predecessor at Nuremberg. It was due largely to the extreme difficulty in carrying out simultaneous translation between English and Japanese, the two official languages used in the courtroom (Fig. 0.1). The Nuremberg court had a similar problem with the translation of as many as four languages (English, French, German, and Russian), but the challenges faced by the participants at Tokyo were significantly greater because of the different linguistic roots of the two languages. As the judges subsequently commented in the judgment, "Translations cannot be made from the one language into the other with the speed and certainty which can be attained in translating one Western speech into another." To complicate the matter, some witnesses made statements in Chinese, French, German, Mongolian, and Russian. Their testimony, too, needed to be translated into English and Japanese. Adding to the language problem was "a tendency for counsel and witnesses to be prolix and irrelevant," largely arising from the Japanese lack of familiarity with Anglo-American court techniques such as cross-examination.[6] The trial consumed two

Fig. 0.1 Japanese-English interpreters in the translators' box in the courtroom. Courtesy National Archives, photo no. 238-FE.

and a half years in the end, as opposed to a single year at Nuremberg. The Tokyo Tribunal heard the prosecution's case between June 4, 1946, and January 24, 1947. The defense case lasted for a longer period, between February 24, 1947, and January 12, 1948. The Tribunal adjourned on April 16, 1948, after hearing the rebuttal, sur-rebuttal, and summations of the two parties. The Tribunal reopened the court on November 4 of the same year and delivered the judgment. After giving sentences to the individual defendants on November 12, the Tokyo Tribunal dissolved without any special ceremony to mark its conclusion.

The courtroom at Tokyo was modeled after its European predecessor,[7] but the buildings that contained the two tribunals were quite different (Fig. 0.2). The one at Nuremberg was set within a large building complex known as the Palace of Justice. Previously it had accommodated the appeals court for the region of Nuremberg. At Tokyo, the new court was constructed within the former Japanese military academy at Ichigaya in central Tokyo. The building had housed the war ministry and the army general headquarters during the war. The sturdy, spacious, three-story building with large wings stretching out on two

Fig. 0.2 The courtroom view from above the translators' box. Rear: the spectators' seats in the balcony (the crowded section on the left was reserved for Japanese citizens) and the press seats on the ground floor. Far left: the defendants' dock. Far right: the judges' bench. Center, rear to front: the defense table, the lectern, the prosecution table, and the witness box (facing the spectators). Courtesy National Archives, photo no. 238-FE.

sides was an ideal place for the historic trial to be held. In any event, few other structures with comparable capacities had survived the Allied air raids. The choice of the Ichigaya building also had the benefit of impressing the Japanese public with the fact of defeat and putting a symbolic end to the unquestioned authority of the Japanese military establishment.[8]

Once the site was decided upon, the large auditorium on the second floor of the building was converted into a courtroom; the remaining part underwent major renovations as well. By the time the trial commenced, the former war ministry building was stripped of the black paint that had given it a protective guise during war. The interior was significantly improved, too, thanks to new paint, furniture, carpets, tiles, and repairs. The rooms in the wings of the building were renovated so that they could be used as the offices of the prosecuting agency, defense counsel, court translators, stenographers, typists, and journalists. Some other rooms were used as the documents office, the printing office, the chamber of the tribunal, the secretariat of the tribunal, and other miscellaneous offices and small shops including the barber, laundry, and kiosk that catered to daily needs of the trial participants.[9]

One important yet often underappreciated spatial feature of the court was its location in the capital city. The physical immediacy of the court was essential for the trial to achieve its educational function, that is, to give history lessons to the Japanese public. Had the tribunal been set up in a faraway land, say, in China, the United States, or even The Hague, it would have created immense logistical difficulties—not to mention financial obstacles—for the Japanese press to report regularly and for ordinary Japanese people to observe the actual proceedings in person. The closeness of the courtroom guaranteed that any interested individuals could have easy access to this historic trial and appreciate its fact-finding mission. While the public enthusiasm was not constant, Japanese journalists and certain dedicated individuals frequented the court (Fig. 0.3). Those who were less committed, too, returned when they learned that high-profile witnesses—such as the former prime minister, Tōjō Hideki—were about to testify.[10]

The Tokyo trial had a multinational judge panel and an international prosecuting agency, following the Nuremberg model. Even defense counsel at Tokyo had an "international" appearance, because the United States government supplied some 20 American lawyers as assistance (Fig. 0.4). Their participation helped mitigate some of the basic difficulties that the Japanese defense lawyers faced in court, such as the latter's lack of fluency in English and unfamiliarity with the Anglo-American adversarial system. To a certain degree, the presence of American lawyers also gave the Tokyo trial the appearance of fairness to trial observers. That said, the limited number of American attorneys posed constant challenges to the defense team to prepare its case expeditiously.[11]

The following eleven countries sent judges and prosecutors to the Tokyo trial: Australia, Britain, Canada, China (the Republic of China), France, India, the Netherlands, New Zealand, the Philippines, the Soviet Union, and the United States. Of the eleven countries, Britain, China, the Soviet Union, and the United States jointly had secured Japan's unconditional surrender after the Potsdam Declaration on July 26, 1945.[12] Three British dominions—Australia, Canada, and New Zealand—were not

Fig. 0.3 Japanese spectators, searched for concealed weapons and cameras at the entrance of the war ministry building, July 23, 1946. Courtesy National Archives, photo no. 238-FE.

Fig. 0.4 Some of the Japanese and American defense lawyers at the defense table in the courtroom. Mentioned in this book are Capt. Alfred Brooks, third from left, and William Logan, to his right. Courtesy National Archives, photo no. 238-FE.

party to the Potsdam Declaration, but had been the major military allies of the British and American forces during World War II in both the European and Pacific theaters. France and the Netherlands joined the Allied war effort, too, as their colonies in the Pacific region had faced Japanese invasion and occupation. India and the Philippines had been subject nations of Britain and the United States during war, but won independence in 1947 and 1946 respectively. Like the British dominions, they, too, had made huge military contributions to the Allied war effort against the Axis powers.

The participation of a large number of countries had two far-reaching consequences. First, maintaining unity among the multinational participants became a major problem. This challenge had been present at Nuremberg, where as many as four countries participated (Britain, France, the Soviet Union, and the United States). With seven additional countries, the Allied representatives were bound to have far greater difficulty coordinating work among themselves. As subsequent chapters will show, the tendency toward division often led to miscommunications among the lead prosecutors and complicated the preparation of their cases. The panel of judges was not so successful in nurturing the spirit of unity and mutual respect, either, as reflected in the split judgments between the majority opinion of eight judges, two separate concurring opinions, and three separate dissenting opinions. This outcome stands in sharp contrast with the result of the Nuremberg trial, where the international judges overcame their differences and delivered a unanimous judgment.[13]

Second, the inclusion of a number of lesser powers gave the Tokyo trial an appearance of what one might call a "victims' trial" of the former victimizer (that is, Japan) as opposed to a victors' trial of the vanquished nation.[14] The participation of the Philippines is a case in point. The Philippines was among the victor nations, but its actual war experience was less than victorious. The war memories of most Philippine civilians were of Japanese invasion, atrocities, and war devastation, although this is not to discount the memory of armed resistance led by Filipino guerrilla forces. The same applies to Burma and Indonesia. These nations were not formal participants in the Allied war crimes program, but one assistant from each country joined the Allied prosecution team to help prepare evidentiary material.[15] For these nations,

the Tokyo trial served as an opportunity to voice publicly their grievances against the former victimizer in the international arena.

The participation of these Asian countries also made the Tokyo trial
as much a multiracial as a multinational event, although such a characterization is rarely made in existing historical literature. As a matter of
fact, the Tokyo trial has faced charges of racial and colonial bias in recent
years for the reason that the Allied powers failed to include Korea and
Taiwan in the prosecutorial effort even though these two former Japanese colonies had been victims of the war.[16] This kind of criticism
deserves serious consideration, especially because this single issue has
come to define the way in which historians today determine the success
or failure of the Tokyo trial. As critics point out, it is an indisputable fact
that the wartime Japanese government used a large number of Taiwanese and Korean people in the war effort. Government policy included
enlisting young Korean and Taiwanese men in the Japanese armed
forces, thereby making them unwilling participants in actual combat
against the Allied soldiers. When the war was over, the Allied powers
put an end to decades of colonial injustice by freeing Korea and Taiwan
from Japanese rule as had been promised in the Cairo Declaration (1943)
and the Potsdam Declaration (1945), and subsequently affirmed by the
San Francisco Peace Treaty (1951).[17] At the same time, however, they
proceeded *also* to prosecute a certain number of Korean and Taiwanese
prisoners of war (148 and 173 respectively), primarily for charges that
they committed war crimes against Allied prisoners held at POW
camps.[18] These two contrasting postwar measures indicate that the Allied powers regarded Korea and Taiwan not only as victims of Japanese
colonialism but also as *victimizers* who had assisted Japan's aggression and
atrocities. There is considerable irony in the double historical victim-
hood of these two former Japanese colonies. The tragic fact, however,
is that the Tokyo trial, being a war crimes trial, was ill-equipped to deal
with problems associated with Japanese colonialism.

That said, it is legitimate to ask whether there was any legal recourse
for addressing certain forms of egregious wartime violence that the
Japanese government committed against its colonial subjects. The use
of Korean and Taiwanese women for the comfort women system is
a case in point. One could argue that the concept of crimes against
humanity could have been used to prosecute this type of systematic

atrocity against women from Japanese colonies.[19] As history shows, Allied prosecutors did not explore this possibility and ultimately failed to hold Japanese leaders accountable for organized sexual slavery. This unfortunate omission can validly be considered as one major historical shortcoming of the Tokyo trial. The plight of Korean and Taiwanese women came under rigorous judicial scrutiny only many decades later. In the 1990s, the International Commission of Jurists and the Economic and Social Council of the United Nations conducted inquiries into the comfort women system and established that sexual enslavement of Korean and Taiwanese women constituted a crime against humanity.[20] (As will be discussed in Chapter 7, however, the Allied prosecutors did present evidence of military sexual slavery targeted at women of enemy nationalities, such as Chinese, Dutch, Indonesian, and Vietnamese women.)

An Australian justice, Sir William F. Webb (Fig. 0.5), was the presiding judge at the Tokyo Tribunal. The chief justice of the Supreme Court of Queensland, Australia, Webb was one of the few jurists with extensive experience on matters related to war crimes in the Pacific region in those years. He had served three times as a war crimes investigator for the Australian government between 1943 and 1945. During his first appointment, from July 1943 through March 1944, he conducted large-scale inquiries singlehandedly, tracking down and interviewing 471 witnesses in Australia and in the New Guinea area. His investigations resulted in a 452-page report, accompanied by 100 exhibits, documenting the atrocities committed by the Japanese armed forces against Australian and American service personnel, missionaries, and other civilian populations in the South Pacific following the Japanese invasion in January 1942.[21] Having achieved a reputation as a competent war crimes investigator, he was appointed to lead another war crimes commission in 1944, and again in 1945, immediately after Japan's surrender. The Australian government requested his service as a judge for the new international court at Tokyo in view of these recent achievements.

The defense took issue with Webb's prior experience in war crimes investigations as soon as the trial began. It argued that he must have already formed opinions prejudicial to the accused, and that he should

Fig. 0.5 Sir William F. Webb, President of the Tribunal. Courtesy National Archives, photo no. 238-FE.

therefore be disqualified. His fellow judges rejected the defense motion, however, on grounds that the Tribunal had no authority to make any change to Webb's appointment. Webb, for his part, had initially considered it prudent not to accept the nomination, but he decided to accept his government's request in the end by reasoning that his previous work did not presuppose cases against those specific individuals who were later put on trial at Tokyo.[22]

Incidentally, a similar situation arose at the United Nations–backed war crimes court in Sierra Leone in 2004. Defense counsel in this case argued that the president of the court, Geoffrey Robertson, should be disqualified because of his prior involvement in war crimes investigations. The defense pointed out especially that Robertson—Queen's Counsel and also a leading British human rights lawyer—had written in his book, *Crimes against Humanity: The Struggle for Global Justice*, that the rebels, including one of the accused, committed "grotesque crimes against humanity" during the civil war. This could be interpreted as his already holding an opinion prejudicial to the three commanders of the rebel group—the Revolutionary United Front (RUF)—who were on trial. The Appeals Chamber, in reply, ruled in favor of the defense. But it went on to rule that Robertson would remain in the appeals chamber of the Special Court, where he would have the power to hear other, non-RUF cases.[23] This ruling is harsher than the one the Tokyo Tribunal handed down with respect to Webb's appointment. Yet, the fact that Robertson was allowed to remain on the Special Court rather than ordered to recuse himself suggests that Webb's continued service in the Tokyo Tribunal might not have been completely out of the norm under the practice of international courts in the past or the present.

Once in the courtroom, Webb proved to be a domineering judge, in contrast to others who sat quietly throughout the proceedings. As a matter of principle, only the president of the tribunal was entitled to speak in court on behalf of all judges. (The same principle applied at Nuremberg.) When he spoke, Webb was typically brusque and undiplomatic, or so he was perceived. Many contemporary observers including his fellow judges considered these qualities to be neither helpful nor likable. But his handling of problems arising from the court proceedings was often judicious, as a few examples of his judgeship will show in subsequent chapters.[24]

As for the ten other justices, all had previously held various prominent positions in their home countries as judges, law professors, or legal advisers (Fig. o.6). But few had such extensive experience in war crimes investigations as Webb did. Two exceptions would be Maj. Gen. Myron C. Cramer, the member from the United States, and Henri Bernard, the member from France. Cramer was the former U.S. judge advocate general and had taken part in planning the German war crimes trials. Toward the end of the Tokyo trial, he served as chairman of the committee that drafted the majority opinion. Prior to joining the Tokyo Tribunal, Bernard had been a prosecutor on various courts that tried Nazi war criminals and collaborators. He wrote a separate dissenting opinion at the conclusion of the Tokyo trial, a section of which will be discussed later. Of the eleven judges, the appointment of the Philippine judge Delfin Jaranilla may have been problematic in that he had been a prisoner of war and a survivor of the Bataan Death March. This alone could—and probably should—have called into question his qualifications to serve on the Tokyo Tribunal. The fact that Jaranilla

Fig. 0.6 The eleven justices. Seated, left to right: Lord Patrick (Britain); Myron C. Cramer (U.S.A.); William F. Webb (Australia); Mei Ju-ao (China); and I. M. Zaryanov (U.S.S.R.). Standing, left to right: Radhabinod Pal (India); B. V. A. Röling (Netherlands); E. S. McDougall (Canada); Henri Bernard (France); E. H. Northcroft (New Zealand); and Delfin Jaranilla (Philippines). Courtesy National Archives, photo no. 238-FE.

recommended much harsher verdicts and sentences than did his fellow judges strengthens doubts about his impartiality.[25] (His recommendations, recorded in a separate opinion, were not reflected in the judgment of the Tokyo Tribunal.) The justice representing India, Radhabinod Pal, was also a controversial appointment, although for an entirely different reason. Problems associated with his judgeship are very complex and will be treated separately in Chapter 9.

Holding an international criminal trial is commonplace today, but it was a novelty 60 years ago.[26] The only relevant precedents before the Tokyo trial were the contemporaneous legal proceedings at Nuremberg. This meant that all judges, including Justice Webb, had to improvise in order to tackle new challenges and make the whole process work. As they soon found out, numerous difficulties awaited them that they had never before encountered in domestic courts. First of all, they had to become acquainted with an unfamiliar city, courtroom, and members of the prosecution and the defense. Most defense lawyers and their clients did not speak English, and their arguments had to be heard through interpreters. Once the trial began, the judges had to set out new rules in response to various disputes that arose from unique circumstances of the trial. Major problems included the difficulty of simultaneous translation, the adequate reproduction and distribution of court exhibits for everyone, and the determination of rules regarding the examination of witnesses and the admissibility of evidence. The judges had to do their best to strike the right balance between the need to guarantee the two parties equal opportunity to present their cases on the one hand, and the need to ensure an expeditious trial on the other. Fulfilling both needs was never easy. Finally, the judges had to analyze on a timely basis thousands of admitted court exhibits and more than 48,000 pages of trial transcripts before reaching their judgments.

The prosecuting agency at Tokyo was formally known as the International Prosecution Section (Fig. 0.7). It was made up initially of a group of 39 American lawyers, stenographers, and clerical staff. It then grew into a multinational force of around 500 at its high point.[27] The original group of 39 arrived in Tokyo in early December of 1945, set up their offices in Meiji Building in Tokyo, and began preliminary investigations while awaiting the arrival of the prosecutors from other participating countries. The leader of the American prosecution team was Joseph B. Keenan, a former assistant to the U.S. attorney general and director of the Criminal Division of the Justice Department. President Harry S. Truman appointed him by executive order in November 1945.[28] The American team was soon internationalized as prosecutors from other countries began to arrive two months later. For the most part, each of the Allied prosecution teams consisted of one lead prosecutor and a small number of assistants. The prosecutors from Canada, New Zealand, and the Philippines seem to have come alone, without any accompanying staff.

The arrival of the Allied prosecutors immediately changed the work dynamic of the prosecuting agency even though they brought in much smaller work forces than the American team had. This was because the Allied prosecutors, especially those from Britain and the British dominions, began taking the lead in order to speed up preparation of the indictment. Arthur S. Comyns-Carr, King's Counsel from Britain, and Justice Alan J. Mansfield, a Supreme Court judge of Queensland and former assistant to Webb's third war crimes commission, emerged

Fig. 0.7 Lead attorneys of the International Prosecution Section, October 22, 1946. Seated, left to right: S. A. Golunsky (U.S.S.R.); Arthur S. Comyns-Carr (U.K.); Joseph B. Keenan (U.S.A.); Maj. Gen. W. G. F. Borgerhoff Mulder (Netherlands); and Alan J. Mansfield (Australia). Standing, left to right: Brig. R. H. Quilliam (New Zealand); Henry Chiu (China); Robert Oneto (France); Pedro Lopez (Philippines); and Brig. H. G. Nolan (Canada). Courtesy National Archives, photo no. 238-FE.

as the *de facto* leaders of the International Prosecution Section. The American lead prosecutor lost his prominence as a result (although he tried to maintain his leadership position). Under the guidance of Comyns-Carr and Mansfield, the International Prosecution Section quickly wrapped up investigations, determined the prospective defendants, and completed the final draft of the indictment. The lead prosecutors from eleven countries continued to share the burden of the prosecutorial effort for the rest of the court proceedings.

With the background information in place, we are now ready to begin our historical investigation of the Tokyo trial.

ONE

Lessons from Nuremberg

The United States began developing its plan for the trial of German war criminals in earnest soon after it started sending numerous ground troops to continental Europe for the eventual invasion of Germany. The War Department emerged as the agency in charge, overtaking other competing federal agencies.[1] The prime movers were a handful of innovative and forward-looking officials within the War Department, headed by Secretary of War Henry L. Stimson. One of the central ideas that emerged from the War Department—and that later became the hallmark of the Nuremberg trial—was the prosecution of Nazi leaders for the "crime of aggression"; it was the idea that a war waged against peaceful countries in breach of the General Treaty for the Renunciation of War of 1928—commonly known as the Kellogg-Briand Pact—constituted a crime under international law, and that those who waged such a war could be held individually and criminally responsible. Originally proposed by Stimson's friend and subordinate, Col. William C. Chanler, it was powerful yet controversial legal thinking. The Kellogg-Briand Pact did outlaw war, but it included no clear wording as to whether a war waged in violation of it constituted an international offense. Notwithstanding the ambiguity of the Pact, however, Chanler's proposal captured Stimson's imagination. He thought that the time had come to set a clear precedent regarding the criminality of aggression by prosecuting German Nazi leaders. The proposal eventually won the favor of President Franklin D. Roosevelt, thereby becoming the cornerstone of American policy for postwar trials in Europe.[2]

Truman continued Roosevelt's policy after the latter's untimely death on April 12, 1945. He dispatched Justice Robert H. Jackson to London, where he met with his counterparts from Britain, France, and the Soviet Union to negotiate the protocol of the new international tribunal. The choice of Jackson was by no means accidental. The former attorney general in the Roosevelt administration and an associate justice of the U.S. Supreme Court, Jackson was a known advocate of the idea that the Kellogg-Briand Pact rendered aggressive war an international offense. By having Jackson as the representative at the London Conference—and subsequently at the Nuremberg trial as the lead American prosecutor—Truman took concrete steps to realize the central tenet of the American policy, inherited from Roosevelt, in the prosecutorial effort against German leaders. Initially, the American proposal to include aggressive war charges met with strenuous resistance from the French and Soviet delegations. After weeks of difficult negotiations, Jackson managed to include the crime of aggression in the protocol, although on the condition that jurisdiction would be limited to Axis aggression only. Termed as "crimes against peace," offenses of this type would become chargeable at the prospective international tribunal along with war crimes and crimes against humanity. On August 8, the four delegations jointly issued the Charter of the International Military Tribunal and officially proclaimed the establishment of the Nuremberg Tribunal.[3]

American planning for the Tokyo trial began with some delay, in March 1945. This time, the State-War-Navy Coordinating Committee took the initiative in drafting the basic policy. This committee had been formed at the end of 1944 by the secretaries of the three departments for the purpose of strengthening interdepartmental communication and coordinating policies on matters related to the execution of war. The proposed policy paper on war crimes trials was to be part of various policies that the committee had been developing concerning the treatment of post-surrender Japan. The actual drafting of the paper did not take place immediately, however. Only on August 9 (one week before Japan's acceptance of surrender) did the committee begin to work in earnest on the proposed document; the draft was completed in early September. The United States government presented the final version to the Allied governments in mid-October of 1945.[4]

Titled "Policy of the United States in Regard to the Apprehension and Punishment of War Criminals in the Far East,"[5] the policy document laid out an overall plan for Allied war crimes trials in the Pacific region. It planned for trials at both the international and national levels, involving high- to low-ranking war criminals. The chargeable crimes were the three types of offense that had been indicated in the Nuremberg Charter: (1) crimes against peace, (2) war crimes, and (3) crimes against humanity. This document did not specify in any detail the organizational structure or the procedure for Allied national-level war crimes trials, since they fell under the separate jurisdictions of the individual countries concerned. But it did set out the basic principle that "the procedures and policies contemplated or already being applied in Europe related to the trial and punishment of war crimes will be generally applicable in the Far East."[6]

What later came to be known as the Tokyo Tribunal was envisioned as one of the multiple international courts to be established in the policy document, but in actuality only one international tribunal came into being. Of all the proposed international tribunals, the Tokyo Tribunal was designated exclusively to hear cases concerning those persons whose primary offenses were crimes against peace.[7] By specifying that one international tribunal should focus on aggressive war charges, the framers of the policy document emphasized the continuity of the American position since the London Conference: that violators of the Kellogg-Briand Pact should face prosecution at an international criminal court.

Incidentally, American policy-makers customarily referred to those Japanese whose principal offenses were crimes against peace as "Category 'I.A.' war criminals" or "Class 'A' war criminals." These terms came into use because the definition of crimes against peace appeared in the "A" section of the first paragraph of the American policy document.[8] These terms subsequently gained currency among the people involved in the Far Eastern war crimes trials, whether they were Americans or not. Even ordinary Japanese people on the streets picked up the jargon. They came to refer to all Japanese suspects who were apprehended for the Tokyo trial as *A-kyū senpan* (Class A war criminals). The broad circulation of this term suggests that the Japanese people, too, understood the centrality of aggressive war charges in the Allied war crimes program.

There are also indications, however, that the Japanese people may not have fully comprehended the connection between the term "Class A" and crimes against peace. A comment by one of the accused Japanese at Tokyo, Lt. Gen. Satō Kenryō, suggests such a possibility. When he was arrested as a Class A suspect, he remarked that he felt "very honored to be named Class A." He explained: "It brought me unanticipated joy to learn that someone like me could be considered Class A. I felt as if I was promoted."[9] During World War II, Satō had never held a position in the cabinet, nor had he served in any other top-level offices in the army, whereas most other defendants had. In light of his relatively modest career background, he probably felt that he was not quite "first-rate" and was undeservedly labeled as Class A. As a side note, American policy-makers referred to those persons whose primary offense was *other than* crimes against peace as "Class BC war criminals." The alphabetical letters "BC" came in use because the "B" and "C" sections of the same paragraph in the American policy document gave the definitions of the two other types of offense: war crimes and crimes against humanity respectively. (There is another theory that the B stood for those superior officers who ordered the commission of war crimes, and the C for those who personally perpetrated war crimes.)[10]

The main concern of the American policy document was to outline the administrative steps to be taken for the establishment of international courts. It proposed that MacArthur assume the responsibility for major preparatory work. Specifically, it recommended that he take charge of establishing the international tribunals, appointing judges, prescribing laws and rules of procedure according to the Nuremberg model, and creating a special agency to carry out the war crimes investigation and prosecution under his command.[11] By early September of 1945, Truman had appointed MacArthur to serve as Supreme Commander for the Allied Powers with the task of overseeing the implementation of the terms of surrender.[12] The policy document indicated that MacArthur should establish the international courts in his official capacity as the highest-ranking Allied representative in occupied Japan. The purpose of these recommendations was to expedite the preparatory process of the Far Eastern trials by making use of MacArthur's authority. The same recommendations would also have the benefit of institutionalizing organizational cohesion in the international prosecutorial efforts.

The State-War-Navy Coordinating Committee came up with the plan to use MacArthur's supreme command in view of the lessons Justice Jackson had learned from the London Conference in preceding months. When in London, Jackson had had enormous difficulty coming to agreement with other delegations on the Nuremberg Charter. The negotiation with the Soviet representatives proved particularly challenging, leading him to contemplate the possibility of holding an America-only tribunal or an international tribunal without Soviet participation. He did not pursue either option only because Truman made it clear that his policy was to pursue the establishment of an international court by the four-power collaboration.[13]

When the time came to formulate the basic policy for the trials in the Pacific region, the State-War-Navy Coordinating Committee sought to avoid repeating what Jackson had faced in London. John J. McCloy— the Assistant Secretary of War and a member of the interdepartmental committee—was one such American top official who was sympathetic to Jackson's predicament. When he learned in early September of 1945 that State Department officials leaned toward holding another intergovernmental conference for the establishment of new international courts, McCloy informed Acting Secretary of State Dean Acheson that both War and Navy Department officials preferred to have MacArthur take charge of all preparatory tasks. He stressed that using MacArthur "will save us many of the delays and vexations which Jackson encountered in Germany."[14] When consulted by Acheson, Jackson, too, agreed. He advised that "the difficulty of working out with the other nations . . . an agreement setting forth principles, procedures and definitions would not be too great or time-consuming although . . . it would take appreciatively longer than it would if General MacArthur took the steps mentioned above."[15] He also recommended that there should be "a unified prosecuting staff operating upon a single set of instructions regarding the preparation and presentation of cases."[16] This advice indicated Jackson's skepticism—based on his personal experience at the London Conference—about allowing a multipartite structure in the prosecuting agency. In light of these opinions from Jackson, the State-War-Navy Coordinating Committee eventually agreed on the plan that emphasized organizational cohesion under MacArthur's leadership at the Far Eastern tribunals.

This policy document, however, limited the Supreme Commander's power in one important respect. It required him to obtain separate authorization from his superiors in Washington before establishing the special international tribunal for the trial of Class A war criminals. The pertinent part in the policy document read, "Until further authorization by the Joint Chiefs of Staff, no international court of the trial of persons charged with offenses of the type described in paragraph i.a. above will be established by the Supreme Commander."[17] The purpose of this directive was to ensure ample time for the United States government to initiate negotiations through diplomatic channels and to secure consent from its allies in the establishment of the special tribunal. Until that was done, MacArthur would be debarred from acting independently.

When he received the Washington instructions, MacArthur immediately reacted against this part of the policy document. He feared that seeking a diplomatic path would necessarily delay the commencement of the principal trials in the Pacific theater and compromise their educational function. He particularly opposed delaying the trial of Tōjō and the members of the "Pearl Harbor" cabinet, that is, the cabinet that had authorized the surprise attack on Pearl Harbor. As far as he was concerned, the Tōjō trial was the most important of all trials in the Pacific theater, and "one of the gravest possible psychological mistakes will be made in not permitting the immediate trial of this [Tōjō] group."[18] MacArthur therefore pressed for an early start of the Tōjō trial, although he was not confrontational in challenging American policy on the Class A trials. He simply suggested that Washington officials approach the question of Tōjō's culpability more flexibly. In his opinion, the members of the Tōjō cabinet could be brought before a military commission that would be "composed of United States personnel" since "the offense was solely against the United States." The specific charge would be that "they illegally authorized the assumption by elements of the Japanese armed forces of belligerent rights before making a declaration of war and directed their use against the United States, thus causing the murder of nationals of a country with which their nation was still at peace."[19] In short, the primary offense of the Tōjō cabinet could be downgraded from the A type (crimes against peace) to the B type (war crimes), and the names of Tōjō and his associates could be removed from the list of prospective defendants for the trial before the Tokyo (Class A) Tribunal. In this manner, the Tōjō trial could start immediately under the single jurisdiction of the U.S. Army.

MacArthur's proposal was feasible, but it earned no hearing in Washington. The position of the Truman administration is explained in the letter McCloy sent to MacArthur. Dated November 19, 1945, the pertinent part reads as follows:

> As to the trial of Tojo, I have explained your point of view to all the officials here. The State Department and the President adhere to the position that they wish to call upon the other powers to take part in the trial of Tojo and the Cabinet. They definitely want to make the proffer, at least, to the other powers before turning to an American tribunal and the trial of an American offense. They are aware that we have a good case against Tojo, et al. for Pearl Harbor and are aware of the desirability of expedition but they desire, if undue delays do not develop, to proceed against Tojo on somewhat the same basis as the trials in Nuremberg are laid. As a matter of governmental policy we have set out on a path of establishing international responsibility for the type of conspiracy which resulted in the attacks on Poland by Germany and on Pearl Harbor and the Malay by Japan.[20]

This message shows that the prosecution of crimes against peace at an international court continued to be the top priority for the U.S. government, not only in the European theater but also in the Pacific theater. As McCloy explained, Truman regarded it as a matter of policy to secure rulings that aggressive war constituted a crime under international law. He would not consider the trial of Tōjō at an American military court unless pursuing the original policy goal should prove impracticable.

The United States government began transmitting its policy document to eight of its wartime allies beginning in mid-October of 1945. The contacted countries were Australia, Britain, Canada, China, France, the Netherlands, New Zealand, and the Soviet Union. These eight countries had been signatories to the Instrument of Surrender. (Two additional countries—India and the Philippines—received invitations to participate in the Tokyo trial later on.) Positive replies from the eight governments trickled in after a month of non-response. For example, the British government indicated its support of the American plan, commenting that "His Majesty's Government attach the greatest importance to the earliest possible opening of the trials and they would like to avoid long drawn-out preliminaries such as were involved in connection with the Nuremberg trials." It continued, "They [His Majesty's Government] are there-fore prepared to leave questions of procedure and the arrangements for the staffing of the proposed prosecuting agency to the United States Government."[21] This message shows that the British leaders, too, did not wish to hold another intergovernmental conference after experienc-ing the difficult preparatory process for Nuremberg, and that they wel-comed the suggestion to leave the matter with the United States.

France and the Soviet Union—two other participants in the London Conference—were also receptive to the American proposal. The only thing they quibbled over was whether the American plan contained any provisions that were prejudicial to the equal representation of the judges and prosecutors they would nominate. The Soviet government was par-ticularly insistent, demanding that the United States government clarify the extent of Soviet rights. The U.S.-Soviet discussion became pro-tracted, resulting in the postponement of the Soviet dispatch of its judge and prosecution team to Tokyo. The Soviet government agreed to send its representatives only a few weeks before the commencement of the trial. This kind of diplomatic squabble, however, did not necessarily point to fundamental policy differences between the governments. The Soviet Union expressed no particular opposition to the establishment of the Tokyo Tribunal nor did it object to the use of MacArthur as a unify-ing authority. As long as the United States could promise equal rights of representation, the Soviet government was ready to cooperate.[22]

The countries that had not been party to the London Conference generally supported the American plan as well. Take, for example, Aus-tralia. Soon after receiving the American invitation, the Australian gov-ernment lined up as many as nine jurists for nomination.[23] The Austra-lian government did hold up official nomination for a month or so, just because it preferred "the handling of major war crimes on an inter-allied basis" and did not wish to appear to fall in with the American plan too easily, at least for a while.[24] But Australia set aside its initial caution and became the first Allied country, along with New Zealand, to dispatch its nominees to Japan.

By early January of 1946, all eight contacted governments had trans-mitted the names of judges for the proposed special court. This enabled MacArthur to set up the Class A tribunal with proper authorization. On January 19, he proclaimed the establishment of the International Military

Tribunal for the Far East, and a month later, appointed the nine judges who had been named by the participating governments. Most of the appointed judges had not arrived in Tokyo by that time, but William Webb from Australia and E. H. Northcroft from New Zealand—a Supreme Court judge at Christchurch, New Zealand—were already in Japan.[25]

After securing individual Allied governments' consent through diplomatic channels, the United States government formally submitted its policy document to the Far Eastern Commission for endorsement. Comprised of the representatives of the Allied powers, the Far Eastern Commission was the highest international organ that authorized various policies regarding the occupation of Japan (most of which originated in Washington). In submitting its policy document, the United States accommodated one suggestion that the British government had raised earlier in diplomatic correspondence. While generally agreeing with the American plan, the British leaders had expressed doubts as to "whether the [American] Joint Chiefs of Staff would be the appropriate body to co-ordinate the plans for the holding of the trials and feel that some other body might better be entrusted with this task."[26] In their opinion, an international body such as the Far Eastern Commission, not the United States government, should issue directives to MacArthur if the Tokyo trial were to take on international significance. On April 3, 1946, the Far Eastern Commission adopted the American policy with a few minor amendments.[27] The revised version contained a new provision that allowed the participation of India and the Philippines in the international tribunal. Three weeks later, the United States government transmitted the revised policy document to MacArthur on behalf of the Far Eastern Commission. The new directive superseded the one he had received from his government earlier and became binding upon him thereafter. This process formally established Allied joint control of the war crimes program in the Pacific region.[28]

MacArthur's Discontent

Meanwhile in Tokyo, MacArthur had issued the Charter of the Tokyo Tribunal in order to set out the basic rules for the new court in accordance with the American policy document. The Charter remained generally faithful to the Nuremberg version (on which it was modeled), especially where it concerned the jurisdiction of the Tribunal, laws concerning individual criminal liability, rights of the accused, rules of evidence, and basic rules of trial proceedings.[29] It differed in provisions relating to the organization of the tribunal and the prosecuting agency. Most notably, various powers and responsibilities were concentrated in MacArthur whereas no comparable power center existed at Nuremberg. This feature in the Tokyo Charter reflected one of the central goals of the American policy document: the special tribunal in the Pacific region should have much greater organizational cohesion. Specifically, the Charter gave MacArthur the power to appoint the members of the Tokyo Tribunal from a pool of judges who would be nominated by the participating countries. He was also vested with the power to choose and appoint the president of the tribunal; he picked William Webb. In addition, MacArthur could appoint one chief of counsel from a pool of prosecutors who were to be nominated by the participating countries. The chief of counsel would have the duty to render legal assistance to the Supreme Commander as well as to carry out investigations and trials of Class A war criminals. MacArthur appointed the American lead prosecutor, Joseph Keenan, to take up the post. The lead prosecutors from other participating countries were designated as "associate" counsel, whose role, according to the Tokyo Charter, would be to assist the chief prosecutor. Finally, MacArthur had the power to review the sentences of the convicted and determine whether to approve, reduce, or otherwise alter, but not increase, the sentences.[30]

At Nuremberg, the special prerogatives that the Tokyo Charter gave to MacArthur were distributed among the four participating countries.[31] All four governments had an equal right to nominate *and* appoint one judge and his alternate, for instance. This meant that the judges would be accountable directly to their respective governments, not to a military commander representing the Allied powers in occupied Germany. The participating countries could also appoint one prosecutor each, who would be regarded as chief prosecutor representing his country. This meant that there would be *four* chief prosecutors who would lead four separate prosecution teams at Nuremberg, as opposed to a single chief prosecutor and ten associate prosecutors who would form a unified prosecuting agency at Tokyo. With regard to the president of the tribunal, the judges at Nuremberg selected one from among themselves rather than having a commander of the Allied occupation forces do it.

Finally, the power to review sentences rested with the Allied Control Council, an international organization in occupied Germany that consisted of representatives from the four governments.

It is clear that, when compared with the Nuremberg Charter, the Tokyo Charter vested MacArthur with extensive power and authority. Yet various special prerogatives it gave him were, in fact, largely nominal. For example, he had no actual power to handpick judges as he wished. Theoretically, he had the power to decide the size of the tribunal—between six and eleven judges[32]—and to select judges from a pool of eleven nominated at his own discretion. In practice, however, it was really not an option for him to turn down any of the eleven Allied nominees. Similarly, MacArthur had little power to choose the chief of counsel or the president of the tribunal as he wished. The appointment of Joseph Keenan was not his decision but Truman's. All MacArthur did was to anoint Keenan formally in his capacity as the chief military representative of the Allied powers and in accordance with the rule stipulated in the Tokyo Charter. With respect to the appointment of Webb, it is not clear whether he was MacArthur's personal choice.[33] What is clear, however, is that Webb was hardly MacArthur's yes-man and that he was ready to take a firm stand against the general should he try to interfere with the judges' work. The Supreme Commander's power to review sentences was not limitless either, at least in principle. When the Far Eastern Commission adopted the American plan, it decided that the Supreme Commander had to consult with "the Allied Council for Japan and the Representatives in Japan of the other Powers, members of the Far Eastern Commission" before making decisions on the review.[34]

MacArthur was apparently discontent with the fact that the Charter of the Tokyo Tribunal did not give him much freedom of action. Soon after announcing the establishment of the new court, he began exploring what he could do to gain personal control over it not only in theory but also in practice. In late February of 1946, he came up with the idea that he should make "some sort of inaugural speech" at the beginning of the trial. Such a speech, he seems to have believed, would allow him to assert publicly his supremacy over the new tribunal. The information that MacArthur was contemplating this action soon reached Webb and Northcroft, the two judges who had already arrived in Tokyo. They reacted against the proposal immediately. "Whatever the General might say," Northcroft wrote when later relating this episode to his government in New Zealand, "his presence, under those circumstances, would probably create the impression, especially among the illiterate eastern people, that he was the master of the Court and that the Court was doing his bidding." The judges' opposition was conveyed back to MacArthur, compelling him to rethink whether to pursue the inaugural speech. The judges heard no further word, and—MacArthur probably having given up the idea—the opening speech by the Supreme Commander did not take place after all.[35]

A few weeks after this incident, the judges learned that MacArthur was now considering "giving the Court instructions upon the interpretation of the Charter from time to time as occasion might arise," since "he was the originator of the Charter and was entitled to interpret it." By then, the judges from Australia, Canada, the Netherlands, New Zealand, and the United States had assembled in Tokyo. All of them were alarmed by the suggestion and uniformly opposed to it. They agreed that "we must refuse to entertain any association with General MacArthur upon that matter and that the Charter, like any other formal document or Act of Parliament, must be construed upon its own language." They also agreed that "the Court must be governed by principles of justice and must not be interfered with in any way by the military."[36] After confirming these points, Webb wrote a personal message to MacArthur in order to straighten out the matter:

I have been considerably disturbed because I understand from Mr. Keenan in a conversation on Sunday that you held the view that if any doubt by [word missing] as to interpretation to be placed upon the Charter, it was your intention to direct the tribunal what you intended the charter to mean and that the tribunal would be bound to follow this interpretation. I must make it clear to you that members of the tribunal now in Tokyo as well as myself cannot subscribe to the view that anybody except the tribunal has power to interpret the charter. If your view was correctly stated by Mr. Keenan and you intended to act on it then it is incompatible with my position as a member and President of the tribunal and I shall be compelled to tender my resignation.[37]

Webb emphasized in this message that all judges opposed any meddling by the Supreme Commander in matters pertaining to law, since they believed that there ought to be clear jurisdictional boundaries between the judiciary and the military.

Strong words from Webb prompted MacArthur to arrange a meeting with the justice and to assure him that he was in fact "as jealous of the independence of the Court as would be the members of the Court themselves." Northcroft, who accompanied Webb to the meeting, subsequently concluded, "it appeared that misunderstandings had occurred as to General's point of view or his intentions, and Sir William and I left him completely satisfied that whatever may have been the position previously there was now no fear of any interference."[38] After this confrontation, MacArthur made no other attempt to interfere with the judges, at least not in any overt manner. He would occasionally press the prosecutors and the judges to expedite the court proceedings, but his pressure usually had little immediate effect. In the end, the Tokyo trial turned out to be one of the rare events in occupied Japan that retained little of MacArthur's personal imprint.

Inattentive America

So far, we have seen that the United States generally succeeded in establishing an international court according to its plan. There is, however, one policy area that did not bear fruit. It was the plan to create a unified prosecuting agency that would operate under the direction of a single chief prosecutor. Such an agency did come into existence but only in form; the person who headed it—Joseph Keenan (Fig. 1.1)— failed to live up to the task.

This at least was the shared opinion of the prosecutors from Australia, Britain, Canada, and New Zealand. They became concerned about Keenan's lack of organizational skills soon after they joined the International Prosecution Section. Among the first problems they noticed was Keenan's failure to direct his subordinate staff to search for and secure useful documents systematically from Japanese government offices. What he had done instead before their arrival was to have his many capable American lawyers spend precious days and weeks almost exclusively on the interrogation of war crimes suspects. This was, however, "a long drawn-out business and on the whole [had] been very unproductive," said the New Zealand prosecutor, Brigadier Ronald Henry Quilliam, a criminal lawyer and formerly the deputy adjutant general of the New Zealand Army.[39] Only with the insistence of the prosecutors

Fig. 1.1   Chief Prosecutor Joseph B. Keenan at the lectern. Courtesy National Archives, photo no. 238-FE.

from the British Commonwealth did Keenan pay greater attention to securing documentary evidence as well. "No doubt a great deal had been
accomplished," Quilliam wrote in one of the letters he sent to his government. "[B]ut it seemed to us that what we regarded as the fundamental object of the existence of the organisation had been lost sight of
or had become of minor or secondary importance." The principal goal,
as the Commonwealth prosecutors understood it, should have been to
seek, identify, and collect as many documents with probative value as
possible, link the evidentiary material to individual suspects, and develop
concrete, indictable cases with minimum delay. But none of these tasks
appeared to have been part of the American pretrial preparation scheme.
Keenan had instead instructed his assistants to conduct endless interrogations of war crimes suspects, making them "the slaves of the machine,"[40] a machine that continuously produced massive information
with little sense as to its future use in court.

The failure to secure useful documents at the early stage had a mid-
to long-term detrimental effect on the work of the International Prosecution Section. Quilliam made the following observations two months
after the trial began:

Owing to the lack of any Prosecution Scheme from the beginning and of proper planning (for which Mr Keenan must be held responsible), I have found that valuable evidence has been allowed to be sent back to the States and that essential witnesses have been demobilised and sent home. I have extraordinary difficulty in arranging for these witnesses and for evidence to be brought back here. . . . I have previously criticised the interrogation procedure, and as time goes on it has become apparent that this criticism was more than justified. Months of work were devoted to interrogations which it now transpires can be used hardly at all. On the other hand the failure to carry out at the very beginning the obvious task of investigating Japanese documents has caused many troubles. This task was undertaken belatedly and only after strong pressure had been exerted, and, as appeared to be obvious, it is apparent that the most valuable evidence in the case is contained in these documents. The delay in examining and translating them has caused a great deal of confusion and difficulty.[41]

Quilliam would not go so far as to say that everything the American staff had done was of little use; he was prepared to say that "a lot of very valuable work has been done." Nevertheless, he found that the prosecuting agency continued to suffer from the chief prosecutor's mishandling of useful evidence at the outset. This shortcoming appeared serious enough for him to conclude as early as June of 1946 that "a fundamental error was made in the appointment of Mr. Keenan as Chief Prosecutor, and from this error most of our difficulties have resulted."[42]

Beyond his failure to provide adequate guidelines to those who worked under him, Keenan also impeded the prosecution's work by his repeated absences from Tokyo. His first disappearance occurred in mid-March of 1946. He departed from Tokyo for China, ostensibly to help the Chinese prosecution team with the collection of evidence. No one knew exactly when he was planning to come back or how he wanted the indictment to be prepared.[43] Their chief missing, associate prosecutors had little choice but to wait for his early return. Keenan also absented himself as soon as the trial began. Several days after completing the opening statement on June 4, he vanished from Tokyo without telling anyone except one or two of his senior assistants where he was going. The other Allied prosecutors learned about his departure and the reason for it—"as so often happens," as Quilliam put it—from newspapers. According to news reports, Keenan left for Washington in order to collect further evidence and to take care of other matters related to the Tokyo trial. It was, however, not clear to Quilliam or to any of the other prosecutors in Tokyo what business regarding the trial there was to attend to in Washington.[44]

The chief prosecutor's departure this time did not cause as serious a setback to the prosecution work as it had before, since all members were now in full charge of assigned tasks. Yet Keenan's absences continued to create difficulty. He apparently had a propensity for publicity and—as if to stay in the limelight—he habitually made sensational statements to the press about the progress of the trial or leaked information about policy matters without consulting other members of the prosecuting agency in advance. One such occasion of irresponsible remarks compelled senior American assistant prosecutors to take action against him. They discussed with the Commonwealth prosecutors the possibility of expelling him, concluding that they had "a greater loyalty to the case [before the Tokyo Tribunal] than to Mr Keenan."[45] The American members decided that they would make representations to officials in Washington and to MacArthur in Tokyo in order to secure approval of Keenan's resignation. To their disappointment, no one in Washington or Tokyo was interested in removing Keenan. The chief prosecutor soon returned as if unaware of the rebellious plot against him by his personal assistants. "It is clear that the Americans regard the return of Keenan as little short of a tragedy," Quilliam commented.[46]

During these months of turmoil, the Commonwealth prosecutors came across a disturbing new fact. They learned that Keenan had had a drinking problem for some years. According to the explanation given by the senior American members, he had quit drinking for twelve months prior to his appointment as chief of counsel, but "from the middle of December last, a few days after his arrival in Tokyo, he had been drinking to excess habitually." Allied prosecutors had suspected that he had a problem of this nature but did not have conclusive evidence. They learned the truth only because the senior American staff proposed that he be allowed to stay "if he gave a pledge to abstain totally from alcoholic liquors."[47] It is not clear whether Keenan was asked to make this pledge when he returned to Tokyo.

The chief prosecutor went back to the United States again in December 1946 and did not return for seven months. During those months, the remaining members of the prosecuting agency made no fresh attempt to expel him. They instead learned to appreciate his absence, developed collaborative working relationships among themselves, and began carrying out their work with greater efficiency without the chief prosecutor. They also discovered that Frank S. Tavenner, Jr. (Fig. 1.2), an American lawyer who served as acting chief prosecutor, had admirable leadership qualities. Quilliam happily reported this finding in his letter dated March 25, 1947 to the New Zealand government: "I am very glad to be able to tell you that matters in connection with the conduct of the prosecution are undoubtedly progressing much more satisfactorily than at any other stage. Mr. Tavenner is showing excellent qualities as leader and he has succeeded in obtaining the loyalty of the whole staff."[48] Quilliam confirmed the continued improvement in the prosecution's work two months later. "There is frequent consultation and a real team spirit has developed," he wrote, and "Mr. Tavenner is a very tactful and able leader who is obtaining loyal cooperation from everyone."[49] The irony here is that the associate prosecutors experienced what it was like to work in a truly unified prosecuting agency only when the acting chief prosecutor, and not the actual chief prosecutor, led them.

When Keenan returned to Tokyo after his long leave, the difficulty of his being chief prosecutor resurfaced. He, in fact, occasionally made himself a positive obstacle by interfering with the work of those whom he feared were undermining his authority. He began to feel threatened by the prominence of the Commonwealth prosecutors, even though he had delegated leadership roles to them in preceding months. He became watchful especially of Comyns-Carr from Britain, who had established himself as the brain of the International Prosecution Section (Fig. 1.3). Quilliam found Keenan's guarded attitude somehow "tragic," however, because in reality, Comyns-Carr was one of Keenan's few loyal allies. "[I]ndeed it is one of my criticisms of Carr, who is undoubtedly a very able barrister, that he has not taken a stronger line with Keenan," Quilliam wrote.[50] The chief prosecutor was not aware of Comyns-Carr's loyalty. He was eager to restore his dignity, and if necessary, to do so by pushing aside the Commonwealth prosecutors or anyone else who might steal the limelight from him.

He did just that in October 1947, when Comyns-Carr was about to cross-examine Kido Kōichi (Fig. 1.4). The former Lord Keeper of the

Fig. 1.2 Frank S. Tavenner at the prosecution table. Courtesy National Archives, photo no. 238-FE.

Fig. 1.3 Arthur S. Comyns-Carr at the lectern. Courtesy National Archives, photo no. 238-FE.

Fig. 1.4 Kido Kōichi in the witness box, October 14, 1947. Courtesy National Archives, photo no. 238-FE.

Privy Seal and a personal advisor to Emperor Hirohito between 1940 and 1945, Kido was one of the most important defendants at the Tokyo trial. Being fully aware of this, Keenan decided on the day of cross-examination that he would conduct the cross-examination of Kido himself in place of Comyns-Carr. This decision automatically deprived the British prosecutor of the right to examine the defendant, because the Tokyo Tribunal had previously ruled that no more than one prosecutor could conduct the cross-examination of each accused. Keenan's decision disappointed all members of the prosecuting staff, since they knew that Comyns-Carr had "made a special study of KIDO" and that "it had been understood for at least twelve months that he would cross-examine KIDO."[51] Keenan had, by contrast, made no preparation for this occasion. He concluded the cross-examination without eliciting any new facts against this intelligent and formidable witness.

Keenan made a similar move when it was time to cross-examine Tōjō Hideki (Fig. 1.5), beginning on the last day of December 1947. His original plan was to conduct the cross-examination collaboratively with John Fihelly, an American war crimes investigator who had long been regarded as a Tōjō expert because of his extensive experience in interrogating this particular individual during the pretrial investigation. Keeping in mind the standing one-prosecutor-per-defendant rule, Keenan made a special agreement with defense counsel in advance: the latter would waive the application of this rule with respect to Tōjō and allow both Keenan and Fihelly to cross-examine him. This arrangement fell apart when the time came to examine the accused. The majority of the judges ruled that they would not permit any exception to the one-on-one rule (although Webb was inclined to allow it).[52] Compelled to settle on who was to cross-examine Tōjō, Keenan decided that he had to be the one.

This was hardly a wise move, not just because Fihelly was an expert on matters concerning Tōjō but also because Keenan himself had taken the special trouble of recalling Fihelly from the United States in order to receive assistance from the "old master" (to use Keenan's own words).[53] The chief prosecutor's rash decision in court made meaningless Fihelly's recall to Tokyo as well as the months he had spent in Japan since then. Having no reason to stay on, "Mr Fihelly absented himself from the Court thereafter," Quilliam reported. Shiobara Tokisaburō,

Fig. 1.5 Tōjō Hideki in the witness box, January 7, 1948. Courtesy National Archives, photo no. 238-FE.

one of Tōjō's Japanese defense lawyers, remembered this episode slightly differently. According to his recollection as recorded in 1961, Fihelly "shouted at Keenan, saying 'Keenan, You Fool!' [*Kīnan no baka-yarō*], and went back to the United States."[54] It cannot be ascertained whether Shiobara actually heard Fihelly say this, but this account probably captures Fihelly's inner feelings accurately.

Keenan's cross-examination of Tōjō was one of the lowest points in the prosecutorial effort at Tokyo. Associated Press correspondent Frank L. White commented that this incident turned the Tokyo trial into one of "the most expensive propaganda failures ever charged to American taxpayers."[55] The acute trial observer, Quilliam, used less sensational words, but he, too, assessed the turn of events along the same lines. Keenan, he found, was unable to make effective use of the voluminous incriminatory evidence that the prosecution staff had earlier presented against Tōjō and his cabinet members. He was unable to conduct "purposeful and sustained cross-examination," either, because he was simply not prepared for the task. What he chose to do in order to overcome this problem was, quite astonishingly, to "argue" with Tōjō. "The result was that TOJO came off best," Quilliam wrote. He described the kind of cross-examination Keenan conducted as follows: "Keenan would ask a question vaguely—purposely vaguely, because he was not familiar with his facts—TOJO would ask, 'Do you mean so-and-so?' Keenan would generally say 'yes' and then TOJO would answer. It was this kind of thing which led people to refer to 'TOJO's cross-examination of Keenan.'"[56] Tōjō's testimony did not necessarily help refute the evidence that the prosecution had presented against him earlier, but Keenan's mishandling of this important witness did considerable damage to the educational potential of the Tokyo trial. At least Tōjō managed to refashion himself in the eyes of the Japanese public from a symbol of ignominious defeat to a patriot and defender of Japan. This confrontation between Keenan and Tōjō continues to be one of the favorite episodes of Japanese nationalists, repeatedly told in books and movies on the Tokyo trial to this day.[57]

In fairness, Keenan acted the way he did not simply because he wanted to satisfy his desire to be in the spotlight, but also to help the broader occupation mission—to prevent, apparently, any incriminating evidence against Emperor Hirohito from entering the trial record, with the knowledge that Allied policy was to keep him out of the Tokyo trial. (The next chapter will provide an in-depth discussion of Allied policy on the trial of Hirohito.) Keenan chose to cross-examine key witnesses such as Kido and Tōjō in order to lend material support to this policy. The problem, however, was that his actions did not achieve the desired result, especially when he confronted Kido. During the cross-examination, Keenan pressed the defendant to clarify the extent of Hirohito's power in decision-making circles on the eve of the Pearl Harbor attack. He questioned so insistently that Webb had to intervene and remind him, "Mr. Chief of Counsel, we are not trying the Emperor."[58] Commenting on this part of Kido's cross-examination, Quilliam later wrote, "One would have thought that in these circumstances Keenan would have made every effort to avoid making any reference to the Emperor, but in cross-examining KIDO, he set out to endeavour to exculpate the Emperor. I think he completely failed to do this, and did harm by drawing attention to the Emperor's position."[59]

The number of Keenan's failings raises one perplexing question. Why did Truman send him to Tokyo in the first place? Perhaps he was misinformed and did not know that Keenan had various personal shortcomings such as his drinking problem. However, it would be hard to imagine that Truman was unaware of his appointee's relatively lackluster credentials. Take, for example, Keenan's career background. He had been the director of the criminal division in the Justice Department, which would be a second- or third-tier position in the federal government, as opposed to Jackson's positions as U.S. attorney general and associate judge of the U.S. Supreme Court. Government appointments alone, of course, are not the only criteria by which Keenan's abilities should be measured. However, the decision to send someone who on paper ranked far below Jackson suggests Truman's general indifference to the success of the Tokyo trial. Had Tokyo been as important as Nuremberg, he would have taken great care in his selection of personnel, making sure that someone who matched Jackson—at least in qualifications—would be sent to Tokyo.

Truman's lack of interest can be detected as well in his choice of the American judge for the tribunal. Initially, he nominated John P. Higgins, the chief justice of the state court of Massachusetts. Higgins's credentials, again, were not as distinguished as those of the judges who were appointed for Nuremberg. Francis Biddle, the American member of the Nuremberg Tribunal, had been attorney general during the Roosevelt administration. John J. Parker, who served at Nuremberg as Biddle's alternate, was the presiding judge of the Federal Appeals Court for the Fourth Circuit. It is not hard to see that there is a great gap in stature between a state court judge (Higgins) on the one hand, and the former attorney general and a federal appeals court judge (Biddle and Parker) on the other.[60] It is possible that Higgins possessed an exceptional record as a state court judge and that, for this reason, he was handpicked by Truman for Tokyo. One never had the chance to observe his talents, however. After hearing the prosecution's case for two months, Higgins abruptly resigned, reportedly because he "preferred not to have any responsibility for the Trials" and because he wanted to go back to his court in Massachusetts.[61] Whatever may have been the true reason, Higgins would not—and could not—have resigned so casually had his government attached importance to maintaining American prominence at the Tokyo trial. The embarrassing situation Higgins created was alleviated somewhat when the U.S. government hastily appointed Maj. Myron Cramer, the former judge advocate general. Cramer's appointment immediately provoked criticism, since the Charter had no provision for the replacement of judges. But his participation did help restore the American standing in court, sending the message—both to the Japanese public and to its allies—of the continued commitment of the United States to the Tokyo proceedings.

The poor American selection of the judge and the lead prosecutor stands in contrast to the attitude of the Australian government. To reiterate, Webb was one of the few jurists of his time who had extensive knowledge, experience, and insight into matters related to war crimes. Similarly, the Australian lead prosecutor, Alan Mansfield, was a jurist with undisputed credentials as a war crimes expert. A Supreme Court judge of Queensland in Australia, he had served as Webb's right-hand man in the third Australian war crimes commission in 1945. He personally visited former theaters of war in order to examine and take affidavits from a number of victims and eyewitnesses. These months spent in gathering evidence of atrocities were a critical time for him to acquire firsthand knowledge of Japanese war crimes.[62] Beyond his work as a government-appointed war crimes investigator, Mansfield also served as deputy Australian commissioner for the United Nations War Crimes Commission. Located in London, this commission played a pivotal role in coordinating the identification, apprehension, and trial of numerous war criminals in both theaters (1943–48). During his brief service in London, Mansfield submitted the Australian proposal to name Emperor Hirohito as a major war criminal (see Chapter 2). He also initiated a plan to hold a commission-sponsored exhibition on Japanese war crimes in order to raise the awareness of the European people about the horror of war crimes in the Pacific theater.[63] That the Australian government selected these highly qualified justices attests to how much importance Australia attached to the success of the Tokyo trial. Perhaps what Nuremberg was for Americans, Tokyo was for Australians. As subsequent chapters will show, the Australian participants profoundly shaped the course of the trial and left their deep imprint on its outcome.

TWO

The Trial of Emperor Hirohito?

One major challenge to Allied planning for the Far Eastern trials was determining how to address the culpability of Emperor Hirohito (1901–89). He had been the Sovereign of Japan, the Head of State, and the Supreme Commander of all Japanese armed forces from the day he ascended to the throne in 1926. Between 1931 and 1945, Japan waged war in his name and under his authorization. It ceased fighting and surrendered to the Allied powers in the summer of 1945, again, under Hirohito's direct order (Fig. 2.1). These facts would have been sufficient for the Allies to initiate war crimes investigation against him. However, they withheld action against him and instead treated him as a special case that required treatment separate from that of other war crimes suspects. For the Allied powers, Hirohito was as much a politico-military problem as a legal one because of the immense authority he continued to wield—based on his claim to divinity—over the Japanese people. Decisions regarding his treatment as a war criminal, therefore, had to be made not only in pursuit of justice but also for the maintenance of security in Japan, where the situation was still volatile and unpredictable.

This chapter turns to a series of policy decisions that the Allied powers made from the time of Japan's surrender through the end of occupation (1945–52). Existing studies on this topic have focused predominantly on actions taken by General MacArthur, and on the several months leading up to the commencement of the Tokyo trial. The chapter moves away from the MacArthur-centric approach and broadens the scope of analysis, taking the position that MacArthur was vested with no actual power to make policy regarding the trial of Hirohito. Whatever his personal plan or design might have been, the power to handle this highly sensitive issue rested with the leaders of the Allied governments. They were the ones who incurred the highest responsibility to ensure the security of postwar Japan and, more broadly, the postwar Asia-Pacific region. To understand the policy regarding the future of the Emperor as a war crimes suspect, one thus needs to go beyond MacArthur and to turn to Allied diplomacy.[1]

Initial Policy

The Allied occupation of Japan became an impending reality in early August of 1945 when the Japanese government began to take positive steps to accept unconditional surrender as had been demanded in the Potsdam Declaration of July 26, 1945. The Declaration, jointly issued by Britain, the Republic of China, and the United States, warned Japan that the armed forces of the three powers were now "poised to strike the final blows upon Japan," the consequence of which would be "the inevitable and complete destruction of the Japanese armed forces and, just as inevitably, the utter devastation of the Japanese homeland." It laid out terms of surrender and urged Japan's prompt compliance. The terms indicated included the removal of militaristic elements that had caused Japan's embarkation on world conquest; the Allied occupation of Japan for the purpose of ensuring Japan's full demilitarization; the renunciation of all occupied territories outside Japan proper, including colonial territories; unconditional surrender of all Japanese armed forces in all theaters of war; the meting out of stern justice to all war criminals; the dismantling of military industries; and the establishment of a responsible and peace-loving government "in accordance with the freely expressed will of the Japanese people."[2]

The Japanese government initially took the position that it had no intention to respond to the Potsdam Declaration, but it changed its stance when confronted with an entirely new military situation eleven days later. The first atomic bomb destroyed Hiroshima on August 6, demonstrating that the warning of "the utter devastation of the Japanese homeland" was by no means a rhetorical statement. This was followed by the Soviet declaration of war and invasion of Manchuria on August 8.

Fig. 2.1 The organizational chart of the Japanese government, presented by the prosecution as evidence during the opening session of the trial, June 13, 1946. The Emperor is indicated as the highest organ of the government. Courtesy National Archives, photo no. 238-FE.

The next day, the United States dropped another atomic bomb, on Nagasaki. On August 10, the Japanese government informed Britain, China, the Soviet Union, and the United States, via the Swiss and Swedish governments, of its intention to accept "the declaration made at Potsdam regarding Japanese surrender." The Japanese government added to this communication that it "understood that declaration [the Potsdam Declaration] to mean that the sovereignty of the Emperor of Japan would not be touched" and "[s]ubject to the Japanese Govt's understanding of this point, the unconditional surrender terms at Potsdam are accepted."[3] Apparently concerned about the survival of the Japanese Emperor at the very moment when their own people and homeland were in great peril, the leaders of the Japanese government made a last-ditch effort to read into the Potsdam terms a promise that the Allied powers would permit Hirohito to remain on the throne after surrender. This message triggered intense diplomatic discussions among the four powers in the 24 hours to follow, in particular between Britain

and the United States, which conferred with each other closely in order
to determine an appropriate response.

In Britain, Prime Minister Clement R. Attlee immediately held a
cabinet meeting. Upon its conclusion, he informed his American counterpart that Britain would like to know the U.S. position so that it could
keep its policy "in line" with it. This message points to Britain's posi-
tioning of itself as a junior partner, ready to stand by whatever decision
the United States would make. If they were to offer their own opinions,
however, the British leaders were "inclined to accept the continuation
of the Emperor" and "more precise definition of the reservation was
necessary in light of the Potsdam Declaration."[4]

Meanwhile in Washington, President Truman called a meeting with
Secretary of State James F. Byrnes, Secretary of War Henry L. Stimson,
Secretary of the Navy James V. Forrestal, and Adm. William D. Leahy,
the Chief of Staff to the President. According to Truman's memoir,
he then

> turned to each in turn and asked his opinion on these questions: Were we to
> treat this message from Tokyo as an acceptance of the Potsdam Declaration?
> There had been many in this country who felt that the Emperor was an inte-
> gral part of that Japanese system which we were pledged to destroy. Could we
> continue the Emperor and yet expect to eliminate the warlike spirit in Japan?
> Could we even consider a message with so large a "but" as the kind of un-
> conditional surrender we had fought for?[5]

In the course of the meeting, Truman learned that both Secretary of
War Stimson and Admiral Leahy favored responding positively to the
Japanese message. Stimson held that the Emperor was "the only symbol
of authority which all Japanese acknowledged," while Leahy similarly
considered that the Emperor could be used to secure Japan's surrender.
Secretary of State Byrnes was less inclined to give a reply that might
appear to accommodate the Japanese wish. In his view, "in the present
position it should be the United States and not Japan that should state
conditions." Secretary of the Navy Forrestal took what might be regarded as the middle ground. He recommended "that we might in our
reply indicate willingness to accept, yet define the terms of surrender in
such a manner that the intents and purposes of the Potsdam Declaration
would be clearly accomplished."[6] In a sense, Forrestal's position was the
same as those of Stimson and Leahy, for he, too, regarded the retention

of the Emperor as a practicable course of action. He differed only in recommending that doing so should not compromise the Allied prerogative to implement all the terms set out in the Potsdam proclamation. In sum, three of Truman's four top advisers proposed that the Allied powers reply in such a way as to allow Hirohito to remain on the throne. None of them had personal sympathy for him, but they seemingly found in the Emperor an invaluable military asset that could be exploited for securing Japan's prompt surrender. Secretary Byrnes alone evaluated the situation less in terms of military tactical advantage than in light of the Allied powers' commitment to their stated war aim. He thought that the Allies should adhere to the principle of unconditional surrender as had been contemplated in the Potsdam Declaration. Otherwise, the Japanese leaders might think that there was room to negotiate surrender with the Allies on an equal footing.

Truman's final decision was to respond to the Japanese message along the lines recommended by Forrestal. He instructed Byrnes to draw up a reply accordingly, which the latter promptly did. After receiving Truman's authorization, Byrnes transmitted the draft reply to Britain, China, and the Soviet Union for approval. The pertinent section in the reply read as follows:

From the moment of surrender the authority of the Emperor and the Japanese Government to rule the state shall be subject to the Supreme Commander of the Allied Powers who will take such steps as he deems proper to effectuate the surrender terms.

The Emperor and the Japanese High Command will be required to sign the surrender terms necessary to carry out the provisions of the Potsdam Declaration to issue orders to all the armed forces of Japan to cease hostilities and to surrender their arms, and to issue such other orders as the Supreme Commander may require to give effect to the surrender terms.[7]

The draft reply did not respond directly to the Japanese reading of the Potsdam terms, but only indicated that the Emperor would fall under the control of the Supreme Commander for the Allied Powers from the point of Japan's surrender. This could be interpreted as meaning that Hirohito would continue on the throne. His survival was far from guaranteed, however, since the Allied Commander would have the power to "take such steps as he deems proper to effectuate the surrender terms." Furthermore, the reply was silent about the future of the Emperor—or for that matter, the future of the Japanese imperial institution itself—for the long term. It stated only at the end, "The ultimate form of government of Japan shall, in accordance with the Potsdam declaration, be established by the freely expressed will of the Japanese people."[8] This part of the draft reply reaffirmed what the Potsdam Declaration had indicated earlier: whatever government may come into being in the future, it would have to be the democratic choice of the Japanese people.

Upon receiving the American draft reply, the British government expressed its general concurrence but recommended a more accommodating position vis-à-vis the Emperor. "While agreeing in principle," the British reply read, "we desire to make certain amendments on the ground we doubt if it is wise to ask the Emperor personally to sign the surrender terms." Britain proposed that the Emperor be made to "authorise" the representatives of the Japanese government and military to do the signing, rather than do it himself. "This we believe," the British leaders explained, "will secure the immediate surrender of Japanese in all outlying areas and thereby save American, British and Allied lives." They added that the former prime minister, Winston Churchill (replaced by Attlee after the general elections in July 1945), held the same opinion. He, too, considered that "using the Mikado will save lives in outlying areas."[9] In brief, Britain favored the maximum use of the Emperor's authority for obtaining prompt and complete surrender of Japan. Having witnessed the fierce loyalty of the Japanese to the Emperor, the British leaders predicted that the Emperor's order to surrender would have the immediate effect of bringing the war to a decisive conclusion and preventing further Allied deaths. This policy proposed by Britain fell substantially in line with that of the United States, since Truman also supported the idea of using the Emperor as a tool for securing the Japanese surrender. It was not surprising, then, that the United States government readily incorporated the British suggestion. The relevant part was changed to read, "The Emperor will be required to *authorize* and ensure the signature by the Government of Japan and the Japanese Imperial Headquarters of the surrender terms necessary to carry out the provision of the Potsdam Declaration."[10]

Meanwhile, the British dominions began receiving information separately from the British government concerning the Japanese surrender overture. This prompted Australia to join the four-power negotiation, or at least attempt to do so. Australia was not formally a party to the Potsdam Declaration, but it had been a major ally of Britain and the United States in the war against the Axis powers. In particular, its armed forces played a pivotal role in securing Allied victory in the South Pacific.[11] Given its huge military contribution and sacrifice, the Australian leaders had believed that they should have been consulted at the time of the Potsdam Declaration, or for that matter, with regard to other high-level, politico-military discussions concerning the wars in the European and Pacific theaters. The British government under Churchill had tended to sideline Australia, however, disappointing the latter's expectation to be consulted on equal terms. Discontented, the Australian government felt that its views definitely ought to be taken into account this time when determining the Allied reply to the Japanese government.[12]

The Australian government's primary area of concern was the disposition of the Japanese Emperor and the imperial institution. It believed that the Emperor should be made to admit his personal guilt for the commission of aggressive war and atrocities at the very moment of accepting surrender. Not to make him face responsibility at this critical historical juncture, in Australia's view, would result in allowing a kernel of Japanese militarism to survive in postwar Japan. His survival could, in turn, pose a threat to the future security of the Pacific region. The Australian position is succinctly expressed in the following passage that appeared in one of multiple cables sent to Britain on August 11, 1945:

> If the present system remains unaffected the Japanese people will be unable to appreciate their defeat. The visible dethronement of the system is a primary means of shaking the faith of the Japanese in the heavenly character of the Emperor in whose name they have committed many atrocities. Unless the system goes the Japanese will remain unchanged and recrudescence of aggression in the Pacific will only be postponed to a later generation.[13]

This passage shows that Australian leaders regarded the Japanese Emperor as a great military *threat* whose dethronement was a top priority for the Allies, whereas the British and the United States governments saw him as a potential military *asset*.

Because of its distinct understanding of the Emperor's military significance, Australia had different recommendations as to how the Allied powers should respond to the Japanese message. First, the Japanese government should be made to admit as part of the surrender terms

Hirohito's share of guilt for aggression and atrocities. Put differently, the Allies should take a clear position of *not* promising him exemption from war crimes prosecution. Second, the Allied powers should require the Emperor to accept defeat personally. He should not be allowed to delegate to someone else the task of signing the surrender document, since doing so might give the Japanese people the impression that Hirohito was not directly responsible for starting the war. Third, the disposition of the Japanese imperial institution—as opposed to the disposition of the Emperor, the person—should be left with the Japanese people to resolve at a later time.[14] Of the three "essentials" it proposed as above, the Australian government shared the third with Britain and the United States, that is, the recommendation that the Japanese people should be left to themselves to decide whether to retain or remove the imperial institution. Where the disposition of Hirohito was concerned, however, Australia was firm on the position that he should confront his war guilt at this critical moment in history.

The British government heard the Australian recommendations in full. However, it stopped short of reflecting them when negotiating with the United States. The final version of the four-power reply made no mention of the Emperor's responsibility for war or war crimes, nor did it include any explicit provision that clearly indicated the right of the Allies to put Hirohito on trial. To make things additionally disappointing to the Australian leaders, the four-power reply took a conciliatory stance toward Hirohito by allowing him to enjoy the privilege of not being associated with signing the Instrument of Surrender.

As if suspecting the Australian discontent, British Prime Minister Attlee personally wrote to Australian Prime Minister J. B. Chifley. The message, dated August 12, explained why the four-power reply fell short of incorporating the Australian recommendations. Attlee wrote, "We are impressed by the need of utilizing the Emperor's authority which is we understood absolutely necessary for this purpose to secure the surrender of Japanese forces in the outlying areas." He continued, "To have delayed the reply in order to obtain special reference to the culpability of the Emperor would in my view have been unjustifiable especially if it jeopardized obtaining an all-round surrender." In other words, the urgency of securing Japan's surrender was such that it had to take precedence over the issue of Hirohito's culpability. In Britain's thinking, to mention his responsibility on this occasion was out of the question, since doing so could do irreversible damage to the Allied effort to secure Japan's prompt and total surrender as well as to save many Allied lives. He further wrote, "in view of the fatalistic mentality of the Japanese and their religious beliefs," the failure to use the Emperor's authority could lead to "long and arduous mopping up campaigns against men determined to sell their lives and dearly."[15] In other words, any messages that suggested personal harm to the Emperor might trigger bitter—and possibly indefinite—war. This, from the British viewpoint, was too costly a risk to take.

The Australian government was not entirely satisfied with either the four-power reply or Attlee's after-the-fact explanation, but it realized that the four-power decision did not include any promise of Hirohito's immunity from prosecution. The Australian government hurriedly cabled back to the British government, on August 12, in order to ascertain its reading. "In view of the terms of message to the Japanese Government and of the Potsdam declaration," the Australian message read, "we take it that culpability and trial of the Emperor for war crimes will remain a question for determination by the Allied authorities subsequent to surrender."[16] Viscount Addison, the British Secretary of State for Dominion Affairs, replied on behalf of his government five days later. He affirmed the correctness of the Australian understanding. His message read, "Statements in question do not in themselves prejudice question of the treatment to be given to Emperor Hirohito, which will be a matter for consideration by the Allied Powers."[17] There were thus no assurances, either in the Potsdam terms or in the four-power reply, that might be construed as granting immunity to the Emperor from war crimes prosecution. The four powers simply shelved the matter for later consideration. Having admitted the correctness of the Australian interpretation, Addison made a cautionary remark. The British government believed that the trial of the Emperor would be "a capital political error," since Britain desired "to limit commitment in manpower and other resources by using [the] Imperial Throne as an instrument for the control of the Japanese people."[18] In other words, the British leaders hoped to use the Emperor not only for the immediate purpose of securing Japan's surrender but also for the mid- to long-term purpose of military occupation of Japan. Whether the other Allied governments would go along with the British recommendation was, however, yet to be seen.

The Japanese government accepted the final version of the four-power reply on August 14, 1945.[19] The formal surrender ceremony took place two weeks later on the U.S. battleship *Missouri* at Tokyo Bay. As had been decided, the representatives of the Japanese government and the Japanese armed forces—Shigemitsu Mamoru and Gen. Umezu Yoshijirō respectively—signed the Instrument of Surrender. (The two were subsequently indicted at the Tokyo trial.) Emperor Hirohito was allowed to avoid the surrender ceremony and thus at the scene he was nowhere to be found.

The Australian List

No further discussion concerning the Emperor's future treatment as a war criminal took place in the weeks immediately after Japan's surrender. The United States, in the meanwhile, took action to set in place the position indicated in the four-power reply. A special directive was transmitted from Washington to MacArthur in the fall of 1945, ordering him not to act independently in the absence of conclusive policy concerning the handling of matters related to Hirohito's culpability. The directive in question read, "You will take no action against the Emperor as a war criminal pending the receipt of a special directive concerning his treatment."[20] This directive originated in the working group of the State-War-Navy Coordinating Committee, whose members met in August and September of 1945 in order to draw up the policy document regarding war crimes trials in the Pacific region. One of the immediate problems they confronted was to determine what to recommend in order to reflect in the policy paper the delicate nature of the Emperor's status. After proposing various versions of recommendations, the working group threw them all away, concluding that it was best not to include any concrete plan concerning the prosecution of the Emperor. It was "undesirable to commit the United States to conclusive action one way or the other with respect to the Emperor," as the members of the group put it.[21] Instead they added to the policy paper the above special directive to the Supreme Commander ("You will take no action against the Emperor as a war criminal pending the receipt of a special directive concerning his treatment"). This directive would ensure that MacArthur would act—or *not* act, to be precise—in accordance with the American policy of non-commitment regarding the future treatment of Hirohito as a war criminal.

Soon after the transmission of this directive, a set of additional instructions reached MacArthur from Washington. Approved by the State-War-Navy Coordinating Committee on October 29, 1945, the message indicated no policy change but informed MacArthur that he should begin collecting evidence in secrecy concerning Hirohito's culpability, which would be used to determine the possibility of his trial in the future. The message explained the position of the United States government:

As you know, the subject of whether Hirohito is eventually to be tried as a war criminal is of great interest to the United States. The United States government's position is that Hirohito is not immune from arrest, trial and punishment as a war criminal. It may be assumed that when it appears that the occupation can proceed satisfactorily without him, the question of his trial will be raised. It may also be assumed that if such a proposal will serve a purpose, it may be raised by one or more of our Allies.[22]

This message indicated that the United States did not contemplate any special exemption of Hirohito from criminal prosecution. Its position was rather that his trial would be considered once his retention proved unnecessary for completing occupation missions. Conversely it meant that Hirohito remained on the throne for now but without any guarantee of protection from war crimes prosecution. "It therefore appears clear that in any event we must not delay collecting the evidence," the message continued. "This evidence would appear necessary whether he is eventually to be tried or not, since any decision not to try him should be made in the light of all available facts."[23]

While Washington transmitted its policy to MacArthur in Tokyo, the Australian government began urging the Allied governments to name Hirohito publicly as a major war criminal. The United Nations War Crimes Commission in London became a useful international arena for Australia to make its appeal. Established as an international body for the investigation of war crimes in late 1943, the commission consisted of representatives from nine European governments-in-exile and six other countries.[24] Quite coincidentally, the Australian representative, Lord Wright of Durley, had been serving as chairman of the commission since January 1945. Seizing the opportunity, the Australian government had Lord Wright press the members of the commission to adopt a resolution to name Hirohito as a war criminal. Australia initiated its proposal as early as August 15, 1945, and continued it into March of 1946.[25]

The highlight of the Australian advocacy was the dispatch of Alan Mansfield—then a member of Webb's third war crimes commission— to London as deputy Australian commissioner in December 1945. His main mission was to present the first list of major war criminals, which the Australian War Crimes Office had prepared in the preceding months. As a matter of practice, the United Nations War Crimes Commission received war crimes reports from member states, examined them, and determined whether there were *prima facie* cases to recommend the arrest of the listed individuals. Mansfield presented one such report for the commission's adjudication, a report that proved to be controversial. It named Hirohito along with 61 other former Japanese statesmen, militarists, financiers, and industrialists as major war criminals. It charged Hirohito with crimes against peace and crimes against humanity.[26] Accompanying this list was a long memorandum that explained the Emperor's power and authority in the Japanese political system. Mansfield prepared this document on his own initiative as he found that "the members of the commission were absolutely ignorant of, and possibly disinterested in, Japanese matters," with the exception of the American and British representatives. Although he was not obligated to prepare this type of supplementary material, he reasoned that "before they could have any idea of the actual conditions of the Far East I felt it was necessary to give them a brief summary of Japanese political development over the last hundred years and particularly during the last forty-five years."[27]

When the Australian report was presented at the meeting on January 9, 1946, the member states became divided on the question of whether they had jurisdiction over persons whose principal offenses were unconventional war crimes (that is, crimes against peace and crimes against humanity), and more fundamentally, on the question of whether it was an appropriate body to make any decision regarding a special war crimes suspect such as the Japanese Emperor. Formal and informal discussions ensued, particularly among the representatives of Australia,

Britain, and the United States. Under instructions from their respective governments, the British and American commissioners strenuously resisted the Australian proposal. Their opposition, in turn, compelled Lord Wright to postpone the commission's final decision on the list. After months of prolonged discussion, Lord Wright resolved the matter by deciding to refer the list to other international agencies for adjudication: the International Prosecution Section and the Allied Council for Japan, both established in Tokyo.[28] He wrote that the two agencies were far better equipped than his commission was to handle the controversial list "in view of the fact that the evidence relating to the charges brought against the persons named in the List was available in Tokyo and not in London."[29] This message constituted Lord Wright's admission that the United Nations War Crimes Commission was not competent to make decisions with regard to naming the Japanese Emperor as a major war criminal.

Meanwhile, there was a new development on a related issue at the Far Eastern Commission in Washington. The representatives of the member states met on April 3, 1946, in order to vote on the American policy document concerning the Allied war crimes program in the Pacific region. During the meeting, the New Zealand representative, Sir Carl Berendson, raised the question as to what the Allied policy might be regarding the treatment of the Emperor as a war criminal. He broached the matter in the following manner:

In the directive issued to General MacArthur there is an instruction to him not to take any action on the Emperor without further directive. In terms of this document [the policy document that the Far Eastern Commission adopted], any government representatives of this table can indict a war criminal for trial. I should like to have it understood that I have no grief for the Emperor—I believe he is a war criminal of the deepest dye—but I should like it understood that no action will be taken against the Emperor without a further directive, that this is still the understanding.[30]

In the statement above, Berendson stressed that he personally had no doubt about the culpability of the Japanese Emperor, let alone any sympathy for him. But he indicated his government's willingness to support the American policy currently in force.

The American representative and chairman of the Far Eastern Commission, John McCloy, agreed with Berendson. He replied, "There will be no change in that respect. He's [MacArthur is] governed by a general directive." An off-the-record discussion ensued, deliberating on Berendson's proposal.[31] The member states finally agreed to adopt the existing American policy *verbatim* as the formal policy of the Far Eastern Commission. In other words, the directive, "You will take no action against the Emperor as a war criminal pending the receipt of a special directive concerning his treatment," would remain effective. The United States government transmitted the said directive afresh to MacArthur a few weeks later, this time as part of the Far Eastern Commission's policy document. The existing historical literature on the Tokyo trial interprets this directive from the commission as formal authorization to grant special immunity to Hirohito from war crimes prosecution.[32] Yet the above historical records show that the commission's decision amounted to no more than affirming the existing American policy, that is, not to make any commitment in favor of *or* against the trial of Hirohito.

Soon after the Far Eastern Commission made its decision, the International Prosecution Section based in Tokyo separately made its own— of a sort—on whether to name the Emperor as a major war crimes suspect. On April 8, Mansfield (now in Tokyo as the lead prosecutor for Australia) proposed to vote on whether to include Hirohito in the group of defendants for the Tokyo trial. Keenan opposed him on grounds that "the higher levels would not approve of the Emperor's inclusion." Other members of the prosecution did not support Mansfield's motion, either. Curiously, however, the Allied prosecutors did not move to vote it down; they instead chose to *defer* any conclusive decision because "it was considered inadvisable to take a vote," Quilliam explained.[33] By this course of action, the International Prosecution Section implicitly took the same position as the United Nations War Crimes Commission had: it had no authority to make any policy decisions on matters related to the trial of Hirohito.

The Allied Council for Japan made no decision either, or to be more precise, it never received the Australian list from Lord Wright. MacArthur withheld it, claiming that the Allied Council "lack[ed] authority in the premise." Instead he forwarded it to Washington with a note saying, "The question involved would seem to be one for highest governmental consideration."[34] This remark is crucial, since it indicates that MacArthur, too, understood his own power and authority to be limited on this matter. It is generally believed that MacArthur made the decision to grant Hirohito immunity. Yet his own words, as documented in historical records, show that he deferred the issue of Hirohito's culpability to a higher authority.

The origin of the widespread misconception about MacArthur's power and authority can be traced partly back to the Supreme Commander himself, who often claimed that he did indeed protect the Emperor from war crimes prosecution. In his memoir he wrote:

There had been considerable outcry from some of the Allies, notably the Russians and the British, to include him [Emperor Hirohito] in this category [that is, the category of war criminal]. Indeed, the initial list of those proposed by them was headed by the Emperor's name. Realizing the tragic consequences that would follow such an unjust action, I had stoutly resisted such efforts. When Washington seemed to be veering toward the British point of view, I had advised that I would need at least one million reinforcements should such action be taken. I believed that if the emperor was indicted, and perhaps hanged, as a war criminal, military government would have to be instituted throughout all Japan, and guerrilla warfare would probably break out. The emperor's name had then been stricken from the list.[35]

The claim that MacArthur personally gave his government recommendations regarding the trial of Hirohito is historically true. In late January of 1946, he sent a message to Dwight D. Eisenhower, then Chief of Staff of the U.S. Army, and warned of serious repercussions that Hirohito's trial could entail. He wrote, for example, "His [Hirohito's] indictment will unquestionably cause a tremendous convulsion among the Japanese people, the repercussions of which cannot be overestimated"; "Destroy him and the nation will disintegrate"; and "A vendetta for revenge will thereby be initiated whose cycle may well not be complete for centuries if ever."[36] What is not correct in his recollection is the claim that he succeeded in changing his government's policy. Not only did he not receive any instructions for policy change from Washington, he was explicitly ordered to continue adhering to the existing U.S. directive after the Far Eastern Commission met: namely, that he should "take no action against the Emperor as a war criminal pending the receipt of a special directive concerning his treatment."

What happened to the Australian list in the end? After falling into the hands of MacArthur, the list continued its journey for several months in search of an agency for final adjudication. The list first reached the Joint Chiefs of Staff, to whom MacArthur forwarded it. The Joint Chiefs of Staff then instructed the Joint Civil Affairs Committee, a subordinate policy-making group, to draw up recommendations. The committee examined the list, identified points of controversy, and drew up a draft response. It tentatively concluded that "no new facts have been adduced to suggest revision of the United States policy, approved by the Far Eastern Commission, directing the Supreme Commander to take no action against the Emperor as a war criminal pending receipt of a special directive concerning his treatment." In other words, the committee held that no policy change was necessary in the absence of new evidence. The draft response continued, "Furthermore, major Japanese war criminals were indicted on 29 April 1946 [that is, at the commencement of the Tokyo trial], and the indictment of Hirohito at this late date would therefore come as an anticlimax unless testimony adduced at the Tokyo trial clearly indicates the necessity for his indictment."[37] The committee's position here is that the opportune moment for the Emperor's trial had already passed, but that such a trial might be considered depending on the findings at the ongoing Tokyo trial. This was an implicit admission by the committee that Hirohito's trial remained a possibility under the existing policy.

The draft response was next referred to the State-War-Navy Coordinating Committee for consideration. The interdepartmental committee readily approved it, but could not determine to whom the list should now be transmitted for final disposition. Only on October 22, 1946, did the committee decide to return the list to Tokyo. It instructed MacArthur that the list "be referred to the International Prosecution Section as the agency having competence under your authority and that you report to Lord Wright in due course the action taken in relation to those listed."[38] This instruction was circular, however, since the International Prosecution Section had already concluded long before that it lacked authority to name Hirohito as a war criminal. Returning the list to Tokyo thus brought no complete closure to the question of whether Hirohito could be named as a major war criminal for trial. The fate of the Australian list, in a sense, embodied the basic policy of the Allied governments: they would make no definitive commitment either in support of or against Hirohito's trial, at least for the time being.

The Soviet Initiative

Over the next two years, no discussion concerning the Emperor's trial took place at the intergovernmental level. Instead, in mid-1948 the Far Eastern Commission began considering policy change on its war crimes program in general. The initiative came from the New Zealand representative, G. R. Powles. He put it to the member states that the time had come to end all Allied war crimes trials in the Pacific region. Tentatively, he suggested that the commission adopt a common deadline for the conclusion of all war crimes trials. The date he proposed was June 30, 1949.[39] If approved, this proposal would give blanket immunity to all unindicted suspects after the common deadline. Such a policy change could also affect the Allies' separate policies regarding the treatment of Hirohito if applied without exception. In other words, he might become one of the lucky suspects to escape prosecution.

The members of the Far Eastern Commission were slow to act, deliberating the New Zealand proposal over the course of several months. They finally agreed in early 1949 on two policy documents that grew out of the original proposal. One of them was that "[n]o further trial of Japanese war criminals should be initiated in respect of offenses classified under paragraph 1(a) of the policy decision of the Far Eastern Commission."[40] By this, the commission made the Tokyo trial the first and only Class A trial to be held in the Pacific theater. This could be interpreted as meaning that there was no chance that Hirohito or any other suspects would be put on trial on charges of crimes against peace, at least under the war crimes program sanctioned by the Far Eastern Commission. The second policy decision concerned those suspects whose principal offenses fell under Classes B and C, that is, war crimes and crimes against humanity. The commission recommended the termination of all war crimes investigations against Class BC suspects by the end of June 1949, and the conclusion of all trials by the end of September 1949. Unlike the policy decision regarding Class A trials, however, these deadlines were not mandatory. The commission requested that member states meet the deadlines only "if possible." This meant that they were allowed to continue trials if the recommendation proved impracticable.[41]

The latter policy decision came to take on special significance to Hirohito the following year when the Soviet Union, quite unexpectedly, began advocating his trial on charges of war crimes and crimes against humanity. At the beginning of February 1950, the Soviet government contacted through diplomatic channels the individual member states of the Far Eastern Commission to seek support. The proposal was based on the evidence of Japanese bacteriological warfare that the Soviet Union had secured at its special military tribunal in Khabarovsk in December 1949. This tribunal heard evidence against twelve Japanese army officers who were charged with the preparation and partial introduction of bacteriological warfare against the Soviet, Chinese, and Outer-Mongolian troops. Based primarily on the confession of the accused, the eight-day public hearing brought to light the criminal activities of Unit 731 and Unit 100, the two major bacteriological research units of the Japanese army stationed in northern China. This trial also implicated Hirohito, who had allegedly given secret orders to set up these military units.[42]

The reaction of the contacted governments was uniformly negative. The British Foreign Office described the Soviet suggestion as an "obvious propaganda move."[43] The United States government took the same position, publicly denouncing the proposal as a political act with no sound factual grounds. Its purpose, the American government spokesman charged, was nothing other than skirting criticisms about the Soviet failure to repatriate 376,000 Japanese prisoners of war, rallying the Japanese communists around a new cause, and straining American leadership in Asia, among other things. For these reasons the United States decided not to give any formal reply to the Soviet request.[44] There is irony in the way that the United States resisted the Soviet challenge, since American investigators had had information about Unit 731 and had given protection to its chief scientist, Ishii Shirō.[45] This was, however, not the occasion for the United States to admit its recent cover-up effort, especially when the Soviets were appearing to use Unit 731 and the Emperor to assert their moral leadership in Asia.

The Australian government—which had favored Hirohito's trial earlier—seems also by then to have lost enthusiasm for prosecuting him.[46] Even if they had not, Australia understood that the geopolitical situation in northeast Asia had changed dramatically over the course of the last four years. The year 1949 indeed marked a major turning point in the region. The communist Chinese emerged victorious from the protracted civil war, and declared the founding of the new People's Republic of China, while Chiang Kai-shek's Nationalist government was compelled to retreat to Taiwan. In those changing circumstances, Australia chose to align closely with Britain and the United States.

After being contacted by the Soviet Union, the countries in the Western bloc conferred with one another in order to determine the next course of action. They generally agreed to oppose the Soviet proposal, but the question was how. They could simply ignore it for now, but they might have to review it if and when the Soviet Union formally lodged it with the Far Eastern Commission. This could complicate the closing of the Allied war crimes program, since the standing policy of the commission left the possibility of Hirohito's trial open-ended. David McNicole, the Australian delegate on the Far Eastern Commission, made this point in an informal conversation with his American counterpart. While emphasizing that the Australian government "would prefer not to reopen the war crimes issue," the policy adopted on April 3, 1946, was "not equivalent to a statement that the Emperor should *never* be brought to trial." Therefore, "there is nothing, legally speaking, to prevent the Soviet Union or any other FEC government from proposing that he [the Emperor] be tried now."[47] If the Soviet Union should formally pursue the issue, then, the member states would have to examine new evidence from the Khabarovsk trial and make a policy decision afresh.

The Soviet government followed up the February message by sending reminders to the United States government (but not to other governments, apparently) on May 31 and December 15 of 1950. These reminders elicited no response, since the American position was to continue ignoring them. Interestingly, however, the Soviet Union stopped transmitting further reminders after the end of 1950. It did not bring up the proposal to the Far Eastern Commission, either, contrary to predictions of other member states. The suggestion to put Hirohito on trial eventually evaporated from diplomatic conversations. No other member states of the Far Eastern Commission formally brought up the matter thereafter. (But according to Takeda Kiyoko's study, ex-British Prime Minister Winston Churchill expressed his support for putting Hirohito on trial as late as August 15, 1951.[48]) The time soon came for the Allied powers to withdraw their forces and end the occupation of Japan. On April 28,

1952, Japan regained sovereignty in accordance with the San Francisco Peace Treaty of September 1951, and the Allied war crimes program was no more.

How might one assess the significance of these developments in the last years of occupation? There are two possible interpretations. First, one may conclude that the Allied governments allowed Hirohito *de facto* immunity by continuing to shelve the issue of his culpability indefinitely. This interpretation can be termed as "result-oriented" in that it focuses on the consequence of the Allied policy not to make any conclusive decision about his trial. Second, one may alternatively conclude that the Allied governments transferred to the Japanese people, by default, the power to resolve the final disposition of Hirohito as a war criminal. This interpretation can be termed as "process-oriented" in that it focuses on the historical process in which the Allied governments continued to leave his prosecution an open-ended issue. Both of these interpretations are valid, although the latter might make a stronger case than the former when considered along with the Potsdam Declaration and the four-power reply of August 1945. These two documents had promised, "The ultimate form of government of Japan shall . . . be established *by the freely expressed will of the Japanese people.*" By consistently adopting the policy of non-commitment, the Allied governments may have let the same democratic principle apply to the Emperor's war guilt, leaving with the Japanese people the ultimate power to resolve this complex historical problem on their own. As Chapter 8 will show, certain Japanese came to embrace the idea of democratic empowerment, and made it the foundational principle of postwar Japanese scholarship on Hirohito's culpability.

THREE

Tōjō and Other Suspects

Some 100 Class A suspects under American military custody awaited investigation when the prosecution team arrived in Tokyo in December 1945. The National War Crimes Office of the War Department in Washington drew up lists of suspects, and MacArthur's staff in Tokyo prepared arrest warrants on the basis of these lists.[1] The war crimes suspects were usually kept at the Tokyo Detention Center, where the Imperial Japanese Government used to hold political prisoners. The occupation forces took control of it after the war, renamed it Sugamo Prison (after the name of its location), and held the suspects pending investigation and trial.

The occupation authorities issued the first arrest warrant on September 11, 1945. It included 39 names, including Tōjō Hideki and other members of his wartime cabinet.[2] Tōjō tried to escape the ignominious arrest by attempting suicide before the captors' arrival, but the shot in the chest was not fatal. Found covered in blood, he was promptly taken from his residence for treatment by American military doctors. He recovered quickly and faced war crimes investigation by the International Prosecution Section a few months later. The occupation authorities continued to apprehend Class A suspects until mid-December of 1945. They met no major resistance from either Japanese leaders or the general public, but a handful of suicides were successful. They lost Prince Konoe Fumimaro in this manner; he killed himself by taking poison at home in the early morning of December 16, 1945, the day he was ordered to appear for formal apprehension as a war crime suspect. Konoe had served as prime minister three times between June 1937 and October 1941. Under his leadership, Japan plunged into full-scale war against the Chiang Kai-shek government and, moreover, formed the tripartite military alliance with Germany and Italy. In the aftermath of surrender in 1945, he began to fashion himself as a leader of the new Japan as if oblivious to his personal responsibility for expanding the war in China and precipitating the Japanese military confrontation against the United States in the Pacific. He lost hope for a new leadership role, however, when he learned that the occupation authorities listed him as a major war criminal and were after him.

The members of the International Prosecution Section understood that their primary responsibility was to investigate and try those whom the American military authorities had identified as Class A suspects. On limited occasions, however, on its own initiative it named additional individuals as Class A suspects. For instance, the Soviet prosecutor S. A. Golunsky—who was not able to play any part in the preparation of the indictment due to his late arrival—requested, at the last minute, that five additional names be considered for inclusion. Other lead prosecutors had already decided on a group of 26 defendants by then, but after some deliberation, the majority voted in favor of including two of the five named suspects. These two—Shigemitsu Mamoru and Gen. Umezu Yoshijirō—were promptly arrested and joined the Sugamo detainees.[3] These additions made the total number of defendants 28.

Included in this group were fifteen army officers holding the ranks of general, lieutenant general, and colonel; three navy officers of the ranks of admiral and vice admiral; nine top-ranking career bureaucrats; and one author with no prior government service. Of the 28 defendants, two died of illness while the trial was in progress. They were Adm. Nagano Osami, the former navy minister from 1936 to 1937 and the chief of navy general staff between 1941 and 1944, and Matsuoka Yōsuke, the former foreign minister, who concluded the Axis Alliance in 1940 while serving in the second Konoe cabinet. One other defendant was also removed from the proceedings when the Tokyo Tribunal deemed him mentally unfit to stand trial: Ōkawa Shūmei, an author and a propagandist. Consequently, the actual number of individuals whose cases the Tribunal considered was reduced to 25.

An American war crimes investigator, Solis Horwitz, later wrote about how the defendants had been selected. According to his account, the International Prosecution Section chose defendants so as to have them form a "representative group" as a whole. The group was designed to represent major high-level governmental and military organs that "had played vital roles in Japan's program of aggression,"[4] namely, the cabinet, the Privy Council, the army general staff, the Lord Keeper of the Privy Seal, and the diplomatic corps. The group included four former prime ministers, four foreign ministers, five war ministers, two navy ministers, one finance minister, two education ministers, two overseas ministers, two Greater East Asia ministers, two presidents of the cabinet planning board, three ministers without portfolio, two chiefs of army general staff, one Lord Keeper of the Privy Seal, one president of the Privy Council, and four ambassadors. Most of the selected individuals represented more than one key office of the government. For instance, Kido Kōichi had served as education minister in 1937, home minister in 1939, and Lord Keeper of the Privy Seal between 1940 and 1945. Similarly, Tōjō Hideki had served as war minister between 1940 and 1941, and as prime minister and war minister concurrently between 1941 and 1944. He had also temporarily held the positions of home minister and chief of army general staff during his premiership.

Beyond representing major organs of the wartime Japanese government, the same group of individuals represented the key *phases* of the Japanese war as well. It was "in view of the long period of Japan's aggression," Horwitz explained, that the International Prosecution Section attempted to give "adequate representation" to "each of its important phases."[5] As was the case with the representation of key government organs, all defendants represented more than one key phase of the war. By having the selected individuals represent multiple organizations and events, the International Prosecution Section attempted to cover as broad a field as possible while keeping the number of defendants to a minimum. Ten major phases of war came under its consideration: military aggression in Manchuria since 1931; military aggression in the rest of China since 1937; economic aggression in China and a large part of Asia; corruption and coercion in China and in other occupied territories; general military, productive, and financial preparations for war; military control of the Japanese government and suppression of political opposition;

formation of military alliances with Germany and Italy after Japanese military occupation of French Indochina and Thailand; aggressive war against the Soviet Union; aggressive war against the United States, the Philippines, and the British Commonwealth of Nations; and aggressive war against the Netherlands and Portugal.[6]

In addition to these ten phases, the Allied prosecutors seemed to regard atrocities as constituting another major "phase" or aspect of Japan's war, and had some of the defendants represent it as well. For instance, Gen. Matsui Iwane was one such indictee whose principal offenses were war crimes rather than aggressive war. He was the commander-in-chief of the Central China Area Army that conquered Nanking in December 1937. In the wake of the fall of Nanking, Matsui's forces committed large-scale atrocities against the civilian population and prisoners of war. Lt. Gen. Mutō Akira, too, principally represented the atrocity "phase." He had been a staff officer of Matsui's army at the time of the Rape of Nanking, and the chief of staff to Gen. Yamashita Tomoyuki's army at the time of large-scale atrocities committed by Japanese service personnel in the Philippines in 1944 and 1945.

The idea of selecting a representative group originated in a memorandum that the British lead prosecutor, Arthur Comyns-Carr, submitted to Keenan on February 25, 1946, as a collective proposal from the British Commonwealth prosecutors.[7] They had been with the American prosecution team for a few weeks by then, and were dissatisfied by the fact that the American staff was mired in time-consuming interrogation efforts while making little progress on the actual preparation of the indictment or on narrowing down the list of defendants. The British memorandum was an attempt to set out concrete steps to help the American staff break out of the current stagnation and expedite preparation for the trial.

"Generally speaking," began Comyns-Carr in the memorandum, "the aim of this International Trial is to establish the criminality of certain acts committed by Japan." With this statement, he pointed to the goal of the Tokyo trial: to secure the ruling that planning and waging aggressive war constituted a crime under international law. In light of this understanding, he thought that the International Prosecution Section should not indulge in prolonged war crimes investigation or even try to develop charges against all suspects. It should rather aim at "putting into the dock fifteen, or at the most, twenty men who will be, and will be stated to be, representative of the responsibility for the various criminal acts or Incidents." A small group of defendants would be sufficient for the prosecutors to achieve their main prosecutorial mission. Limiting the number of defendants had practical implications as well. It would mean that the Allied prosecutors could prepare the indictment in a relatively short time and start the trial early. Comyns-Carr believed that an early start was crucial to ensure the maximum educational effect of the trial. He wrote, "[A]t the present moment we understand that the Japanese themselves support the prosecution," but "if the trial is delayed or prolonged, they may swing around in their sympathy and end by regarding as martyrs the men whom at present they wish to see condemned." Predicting the volatility of Japanese public sentiment, he believed that the trial should commence at the earliest possible time. Moreover, he made the point that the Tokyo trial did not enjoy as much prestige or international attention as its predecessor at Nuremberg did. As he put it, "[F]rom the very day on which the Nuremberg Trial is over, world interest, as distinct from the purely Japanese interest, in the whole subject of International Trials, will fall to a vanishing point." To address these problems, he recommended that "it is essential in our view to place all the trained minds and mass of coordinated material under the direction of a Steering Committee, which, subject to your [Keenan's] approval, will direct all available resources to the agreed end in view, that is to say, a speedy trial of a few selected men for broadly stated acts which the nine prosecuting nations regarded as International Crimes."[8]

As it turned out, Keenan was favorably disposed to Comyns-Carr's suggestion. However, other senior American members were opposed to it. Lt. Col. John W. Brabner-Smith, a War Department official who had joined the International Prosecution Section, was the first to voice dissent. He told Keenan that, "if you select 15 persons purely because of their positions you will fail to punish many war criminals in Category A whom we are under a responsibility to punish."[9] In his opinion, the selection criteria should be merit-based and not the individuals' ability to "represent" an organization or incident. Carlisle W. Higgins, a public prosecutor from North Carolina who acted as deputy chief of counsel in the first year at the Tokyo trial, opposed the British proposition for the same reason. He reminded Keenan that the Sugamo detainees and others under house arrest were in confinement because of instructions from their superiors in Washington. He believed that the American prosecutors owed it to the detainees to conduct thorough investigations and determine whether or not their detention was justified. This responsibility could not be met if the chief of counsel were to allow the principle of representation in the selection process as proposed by the Commonwealth prosecutors.[10]

Higgins continued to question the advisability of the British proposal. At a staff meeting at the beginning of March 1946, T. Christmas Humphreys—a Crown Prosecutor of the Old Bailey and an assistant to Comyns-Carr—laid out the basic criteria for determining the representative group. Higgins voiced no objection to the selection scheme itself, but asked Humphreys what might be the policy of the International Prosecution Section regarding the treatment of those suspects who would be dropped from the group of defendants. "If we adopt the method of selecting representative lists and limiting our prosecution to about 20 say," Higgins said, "what do you advise we do with the other 50 in prison?" Humphreys, in response, simply answered that the fate of the remaining ones need not concern the International Prosecution Section. In his understanding, those who were to fall out of the selected group were not prominent enough to come under consideration, or they might be sufficiently prominent but could not be considered for prosecution anyway since "there isn't room for them."[11]

Seeing that Humphreys's answer did not satisfy Higgins, Keenan stepped in. He offered an additional explanation in support of the British proposal. Emphasizing that the practicality issue was the primary concern, he said, "[C]learly we couldn't try 100 at one time and give these men the proper defense and rights to cross-examination." He continued, "If there is a limit and we recognize it then we know we are not going to be able to cover all of them in one proceeding." This comment pointed to the chief prosecutor's view that the International Prosecution Section would have to give up many cases for the simple reason of impracticality. Keenan also reminded Higgins of the fundamental goal of the Tokyo trial. In somewhat muddled words, he explained that the Tokyo trial was designed principally to "establish as a matter of law, as a matter of tradition, and as a matter of fact that those individuals of a Nation who cause the Nation to break the peace of the world in violation of treaties are committing a crime which puts them in the category of Class-A criminals, whose infringements upon the rules of civilization have brought about a world war." He understood that this was "the opinion of General MacArthur, President Truman and so many others."[12] For these reasons, he fully supported the proposal by the Commonwealth members.

Having expressed these opinions, however, Keenan conceded that Higgins had a point about the special duty of the International Prosecution Section vis-à-vis the Sugamo detainees. He admitted that "we do owe a responsibility to the men lodged in Sugamo now and to others who will be added," and that "whatever we have to do with the rest of them we must." He went so far as to say, "It may be that there will have to be more than one trial," and suggested the possibility of "a second or third list" with respect to those Class A suspects who could not be brought to the first trial.[13] This was arguably the first occasion on which anyone in the International Prosecution Section raised the possibility of holding multiple trials of Class A war criminals. Such trials—if they were to take place—would constitute the eastern counterpart of the twelve additional trials that the United States held at Nuremberg under Allied Control Council Law No. 10 between 1946 and 1949.[14] When Keenan broached the matter in March 1945, however, he did not seem to have given it much consideration; rather, he appeared to be trying to dodge Higgins's question by vaguely suggesting the possibility of future trials—thereby failing to offer any concrete explanation on this occasion. Thus leaving the detainee issue up in the air, he proceeded to establish the steering committee that Comyns-Carr had recommended. He appointed the latter as its chairman and had him take charge of redirecting the prosecution's remaining work toward the selection of the proposed representative group. As a result of these decisions, the International Prosecution Section was able to begin determining the defendants expeditiously and to prepare for the trial.

Planning for Successive Class A Trials

Upon completion of the selection process, Commonwealth prosecutors recommended that American authorities assume full responsibility for the remaining Class A suspects at Sugamo, some of whom were to be released immediately and others to stay on for further investigation. The occupation authorities, in turn, freed fifteen detainees between April 1946 and May 1947, but they kept some fifty in custody without making any decisions about their trial or release.[15] The Commonwealth prosecutors learned "with dismay" of the American inaction about a year after the commencement of the Tokyo trial. As Quilliam recalled, they had repeatedly advised Keenan to act on their recommendations immediately lest "it would be a matter of strong criticism if they [the detainees] were to be allowed to remain in custody indefinitely without any action being taken."[16] But the chief prosecutor apparently did not heed their advice.

The news about the prolonged detention reached Gen. MacArthur as well. Learning that many were still in legal limbo at Sugamo, he brought the matter to the attention of the War Department. In his message, dated May 12, 1947, he similarly put blame on Keenan, stating that he had the "understanding and belief that the preparation for trial and prosecution of all class A Japanese war criminal suspects would be the responsibility of the special chief counsel for these cases."[17] MacArthur was silent, however, about his share of the responsibility even though these individuals had been apprehended on his orders. He simply asserted that "[i]t is obvious that the restraint of personal freedoms for unreasonable periods without positive action will not only be contrary to any accepted concept of justice, but will adversely reflect upon the overall mission of the occupation."[18]

MacArthur went on to propose two possible courses of action for the War Department to consider. One of them was to hold additional international trials against the remaining detainees. This would be in keeping with the standing policy of the Far Eastern Commission, according to which those persons whose principal offense fell under category A (that is, crimes against peace) had to be tried by an international tribunal. Personally, MacArthur did not favor this option, because "the cumbersome, slow, costly, and generally unsatisfactory organization prescribed rendered such procedure open to grave criticism." The other possible action, and the one he preferred, was "to grant SCAP [the Supreme Commander for the Allied Powers] authority to proceed against the remaining suspects on the same basis as authorized for class B and C war criminals."[19] This meant that Class A suspects would be brought before the American military commission. The latter proposal would potentially conflict with the basic policy of the Far Eastern Commission. If approved, however, it could resolve the detainee problem quickly, since the fully functioning judicial system under the U.S. Army would be used in place of the nascent, ill-formed international justice system.

The War Department immediately responded to MacArthur's message, but did not commit itself to any concrete plan. It was "impossible to formulate definite policy," the reply read, because the War Department did not have relevant information about the Class A suspects who were presently under American custody.[20] It held that the task for now was to fill this information gap with help from the International Prosecution Section. Keenan—who had left Tokyo and had been back in Washington for some time—apparently was contacted on the matter. He hurriedly sent a cable to Frank Tavenner, the acting chief prosecutor in Tokyo, requesting that Tavenner resume the detainees' screening process and submit the "names and titles of, and brief statements of proposed war crimes charges against, all class A criminals" to Washington as soon as possible. He also requested that "complete dossiers be prepared and ready for my examination" no later than July 27, 1947, when he planned to return to Tokyo.[21]

The sudden request for additional work elicited little enthusiasm among the Allied prosecutors, who were already fully engaged in the substantiation of the high-profile cases before the Tokyo Tribunal. They were not pleased, either, by the fact that Keenan offered no explanation for why the International Prosecution Section should resume the war crimes investigation at this late stage. The Allied prosecutors simply "assumed that the question of a second trial may be under consideration," but with "no positive information."[22] Their discontent can be detected in one of Quilliam's letters to the New Zealand government. He wrote, "So far as assisting with the work of preparing these files is concerned, I feel disposed, but with doubts, to do what is asked, but I intend, as do others, to make it clear that although I am giving this assistance that must not be taken as an indication that my Government is in favor of there being another trial, nor must it be taken as associating my Government with any responsibility for delay and inaction." Quilliam added that a second trial would be a "mistake" in his opinion, given the exceeding prolongation of the present trial.[23]

The reluctance of the associate prosecutors notwithstanding, Keenan was moving ahead with the plan for the additional Class A proceedings.

He returned to Tokyo on August 10, 1947, and held a press conference the following day. He announced that a further trial of remaining major war criminals was now contemplated. "Class 'A' Suspects To Be Tried Soon, Keenan Declares," Associated Press correspondent Frank White reported. His article, as carried in *The Nippon Times* on August 13, 1947, read in part as follows: "An early trial before an 'appropriate lawful tribunal' of a number of so-called Class A Japanese war crimes suspects presently held in Sugamo prison was promised Monday by Chief Prosecutor Joseph B. Keenan." The report continued, "He [Keenan] said the international prosecution section which he heads presently has a staff engaged in an 'acute study' of cases of the suspects in Sugamo—some of whom have been there nearly two years."[24] This news greatly upset the Allied prosecutors, who had not been consulted on the matter in advance. Keenan's public statement gave the impression that all associate prosecutors in the International Prosecution Section were united, that they had already conferred with one another and had approved the plan for successive trials, and that they were now actively taking part in the "acute study" of the suspected Class A war criminals. The associate prosecutors lodged protests with the chief prosecutor, but he retracted neither his statement nor his decision to continue the new screening process.[25] In this manner, Keenan forced the Allied prosecutors into co-operating with the screening process of the Sugamo detainees, even though it was a task that the occupation authorities should have completed months before.

By late October of 1947, the International Prosecution Section had identified 19 individuals for possible trials, and the remaining 31 detainees for release because of insufficient evidence. MacArthur promptly forwarded the names and dossiers of the nineteen to the War Department and freed those who were recommended for release.[26] The conclusive recommendations from Keenan—developed in consultation with other concerned agencies in Tokyo and Washington—reached the War Department separately in January 1948.

Quite paradoxically, Keenan's final advice was not to press charges of crimes against peace against any of the remaining Class A suspects after all. As he put it, "A trial before an international tribunal of any of such suspects would serve as a sharp anti-climax to the proceedings before the International Tribunal for the Far East now rapidly approaching conclusion." He continued, "Subsequent trials for Class A offenses would of necessity be very prolonged and would cover substantially the same ground and required the re-presentation of much of the evidence already adduced in the pending proceeding."[27] In short, he recommended against the continuation of trials because he thought the proceedings would be repetitive and would have little educational value. Rather than proposing the immediate release of the remaining Class A suspects, however, Keenan recommended that the Legal Section of the American occupation forces assume responsibility for them and investigate the charges of war crimes and crimes against humanity. Led by Col. Alva C. Carpenter, the Legal Section had been carrying out a number of war crimes trials in the Philippines, Japan, and China. Having substantial experience in dealing with a wide variety of Class BC cases, this agency would be an appropriate body to assume jurisdiction over the remaining Sugamo detainees. Keenan gave this recommendation probably to satisfy MacArthur, who had suggested the same to the War Department a half year before but failed to secure approval. The War Department was now ready to endorse the identical plan upon its re-submission.

Carpenter quickly put Keenan's recommendation into action. But he soon learned how formidable it would be to develop Class BC charges on the basis of documents that the International Prosecution Section handed over to him: the materials primarily concerned crimes against peace (that is, Class A) and were therefore largely useless. Indeed, "new and independent lines of investigation would have to be opened if there was to be any semblance of legality in the trial of such persons."[28] The best the Legal Section could do was offer to the War Department tentative suggestions for trial and release.

An interim report, submitted to MacArthur in mid-April of 1948, proposed the trial of eight former members of the Pearl Harbor cabinet, one navy officer, and two civilians. The first eight cabinet members would be prosecuted on one or more of the following grounds: (1) that they took part in decisions to authorize war crimes and crimes against humanity; (2) that they committed atrocities themselves or had their subordinates commit them; and (3) that they failed to fulfill the responsibility to take control of Japanese armed forces, thereby failing to prevent or stop atrocities. Carpenter believed that these charges would be "eminently sound," but also noted that "an exact precedent is lacking to sustain" these charges. He thus recommended a stay of the full-fledged investigation until the Tokyo Tribunal handed down its judgment. At Tokyo, four other former members of the Pearl Harbor cabinet were charged with war crimes and crimes against humanity. Carpenter considered that the Legal Section would be able to develop concrete prosecutorial strategies after the Tokyo Tribunal set relevant precedents. The navy officer he recommended for trial was Adm. Toyoda Soemu, the commander-in-chief of the Combined Fleet and the chief of naval general staff in 1945. Carpenter tentatively suggested that this particular individual be charged with war crimes committed by his subordinates, such as the "killing of all survivors of sunken Allied ships and the intentional bombing of hospital ships" in the Indian Ocean in the last year of the war. Further evidence, in his view, "will produce sufficient evidence to charge this suspect with Class B and C crimes." The last two named for possible trial were Kodama Yoshio and Sasakawa Ryōichi. Carpenter identified them as nationalist extremists who had previously been involved in public incitation and violence and war-related business in China. He was not entirely sure if charges against them could stand as yet. It would depend on the evidence to be acquired from further investigation, although, with respect to Kodama, "[i]t is believed that a thorough investigation will develop sufficient evidence to convict this suspect on some legitimate charge." As for Sasakawa, "there is no positive evidence now in hand which would definitely sustain B and C charges against him." Carpenter was reluctant to recommend his release at this stage, however, because he believed that this particular individual "would be a dangerous man" if set free.[29]

The investigation of these suspects continued, culminating in a more concrete set of recommendations from the Legal Section four months later. Titled "Trial of Class A Suspects on B and C Charges" (dated September 25, 1948), the memorandum laid out a revised plan. There would be three separate trials against three individuals: Adm. Toyoda Soemu, Lt. Gen. Tamura Hiroshi, and Kodama Yoshio. Toyoda and Kodama had been named as possible indictees in the April interim report, while Tamura was new. The former chief of the prisoner-of-war information bureau of the war ministry in the last year of the Pacific War, Tamura was considered to be individually responsible for ill-treatment of Allied prisoners of war. (Of the three, the case concerning Kodama was subsequently dropped from the plan seemingly because the Legal Section was unable to secure conclusive evidence against him.) These trials aside, the revised plan also recommended a joint trial of eight former members of the Pearl Harbor cabinet as had been contemplated in the April interim report.[30]

The memorandum set out the timeline for the commencement of the planned trials as well. All trials except the one concerning members of the Pearl Harbor cabinet would begin by October 31, 1948. The date was set in order to comply with the instruction that had been given to MacArthur by Kenneth C. Royall, the Secretary of the Army. Royall had informed MacArthur that he "desired that no trials be commenced in your theater later than 31 Oct 48, and this includes those which involve former class A suspects who might be tried under B and C charges." Explaining the reasons for setting the deadline, Royall said, "It has been my desire for some time that all war crimes trials be concluded at earliest practical date because I do not believe that public opinion will or should support long continuing war crimes trials." The war crimes program in Europe was winding down in those months, including the twelve successive proceedings at Nuremberg. The plan to conclude all war crimes trials in the Pacific region as well by August 31, 1948, had been floated in his department. In those circumstances, Royall considered that the entire war crimes program ought to be completed "this calendar year." He also informed MacArthur that the budgetary plan for 1949 no longer contemplated expenditure for future American trials in the Pacific theater.[31] He allowed special exemption for the joint trial of the eight cabinet ministers, however, in view of the Legal Section's recommendation to wait for the Tokyo judgment. The cabinet trial was set to begin in January of 1949.[32]

With a concrete plan for successive trials in place, Carpenter had the Diplomatic Section of the occupation authorities contact the Allied governments and inquire if they were interested in nominating judges. This was an interesting move given the fact the United States was under no obligation to invite judges from other countries. The proposed trials fell strictly under American military jurisdiction. The occupation authorities extended this courtesy nonetheless, since they considered that other nationals might also have been "victims of the war crimes alleged to have been committed by the accused."[33] Even more interestingly, the Soviet Union was among those countries invited despite the fact it had entered the Allied war effort in the Pacific theater only one week before Japan's surrender. The Diplomatic Section extended its invitation anyway, because "although the evidence expected to be introduced at the three trials does not indicate that any Soviet nationals were victims of the war crimes alleged to have been committed by the accused, the U.S.S.R. may nevertheless have an interest in these cases."[34] Undoubtedly, the relationship between the United States and the Soviet Union was hardly amicable in those years, but the United States continued to maintain the policy of internationalism where the handling of former Class A suspects was concerned.

As of October 23, 1948, MacArthur had already appointed Brigadier J. W. O'Brien of the Australian Army to the Toyoda trial. Similarly, Lt. Col. Francis C. J. Place of the Australian Army and Lt. Col. Alfred D. Yates of the British Army were provided as judges for the cabinet trial. (Britain subsequently withdrew the appointment of Yates.[35]) Other contacted countries showed no interest in participating in the successive trials. Only the Soviet government nominated judges, although after much delay. More than two months had passed since the commencement of the Toyoda and Tamura trials when the Soviet Union sent in its nominees. To complicate the matter, the Russian members did not speak English even though the Legal Section had specifically requested that the nominated judges be fluent in English. Fearing that their appointments would have negative repercussions for the trial proceedings, Carpenter had to turn down the Russian nominees. The judges who presided over the two successive trials, therefore, were Australian and American only.[36]

Meanwhile, the joint trial of the eight cabinet members that was scheduled to begin in January 1949 did not take place after all, due to Carpenter's conclusion that the Tokyo Tribunal did not provide a useful precedent. He did find that "[t]he tribunal's judgment enunciated general principles of law indicating that the cabinet members should be found guilty of criminal negligence in failing to discharge the duties of their offices." But he also noted that the Tokyo Tribunal established only one clear-cut case of criminal negligence among the five former members of the Pearl Harbor cabinet on trial. More discouraging still, the convicted—Shigemitsu Mamoru—received a very lenient penalty:

a seven-year term of imprisonment. This did not seem to Carpenter to be a very promising precedent. In the end, he decided to abandon the proposed cabinet trial entirely and release the eight suspects without charge.[37] The "successive" trials at Tokyo, as a result, were limited to the Tamura and Toyoda trials.

The Japanese public believed—and continues to believe—that Class A suspects were freed from Sugamo Prison instead of made to confront war crimes prosecution because, with the onset of the cold war, the United States had a change of heart in its commitment to the pursuit of justice. This may indeed have been part of the reason. But historical records also suggest that the detainee problem might have been resolved differently had Keenan and MacArthur been much more attentive to fulfilling their respective duties. The combination of three factors discussed in this chapter—namely, (1) Keenan's failure to follow up on the screening process of the detainees in a timely manner; (2) MacArthur's general indifference to Class A issues unless they affected his reputation; and (3) the inattentiveness also of American government officials in Washington about the affairs of major war criminals in the Far Eastern theater—undoubtedly contributed to the American mishandling of the remaining Class A suspects.

Among the eight released, incidentally, was Kishi Nobusuke, the former minister of industry and commerce in the Tōjō cabinet, who quickly returned to the political scene and became prime minister in 1957. The defining incident of his postwar career was the renewal of the U.S.-Japan Security Treaty in 1960. His negotiating partner was the 34th U.S. president, Dwight Eisenhower, the high-ranking American general who had led the war against the Axis powers in the European theater and was also the former superior of General MacArthur in his capacity as Chief of Staff of the U.S. Army. Kishi is remembered to this day for his forceful ratification of the highly unpopular Security Treaty, which many Japanese regarded as Kishi's helping hand to entrench American military, political, and economic domination over Japan. It is perhaps not surprising that the Japanese public responded to the apparent collusion between the former Class A war crimes suspect—who had escaped prosecution by the grace of the United States—and Eisenhower by leading one of the largest popular demonstrations ever to be seen in the history of Japan.

FOUR

Narrative of the War

The notion of aggressive war as an international offense is not as controversial today as it was sixty years ago. But the idea of prosecuting an aggressor still is. Since the time of Nuremberg and Tokyo (Fig. 4.1), the international community has attempted to make crimes against peace a workable legal concept in the international justice system. To date, the attempt has succeeded only in part. The international community generally recognizes the illegality of aggression, but there is little consensus about how or whether legal proceedings should be initiated against those who commit the act. It is, therefore, still to be seen what practical use the precedents from Nuremberg and Tokyo may have in the future.[1] In the absence of a conclusive assessment of these trials' historical significance in this respect, this chapter limits its tasks to exploring how the law pertaining to crimes against peace was put to actual use at Tokyo and comparing this application to the Nuremberg precedent.

At present, three key legal documents codify the illegality of aggression in the body of international law. The first is the Charter of the United Nations, which prohibits a threat to peace, a breach of peace, or an act of aggression. The second is the United Nations General Assembly Resolution 3314 of 1974, which defines "aggression." The third is the Rome Statute of the International Criminal Court (ICC) of 1998, which stipulates that the Court has jurisdiction over the crime of aggression as well as genocide, crimes against humanity, and war crimes.[2] The ICC statute is probably the most significant of the three documents,

Fig. 4.1 Maps presented by the prosecution as evidence during the opening session, June 13, 1946. The maps mark Japan's wartime territories in 1940 and 1941. Courtesy National Archives, photo no. 238-FE.

since it specifies aggression as one of the indictable offenses at the new permanent international criminal court in The Hague. That said, the court's jurisdiction is more theoretical than practical because the member states of the United Nations have not agreed on a legal framework for making this offense chargeable at actual trials. The ICC statute would require amendments if any criminal proceedings were to take place against aggressors. Necessary changes might be made in July of 2009, when the United Nations is scheduled to review the statute.[3]

The idea of outlawing aggressive war has its historical roots in the series of international agreements, conventions, and treaties that have been concluded since the turn of the twentieth century. The first of these is the Hague Conventions of 1899. The signatories agreed to seek peaceful solutions before resorting to the use of force when international controversies arose. The Third Hague Convention of 1907 made agreements to the same effect. The Covenant of the League of Nations of 1919, which was drawn up in the aftermath of World War I, made detailed provisions regarding the prohibition of war as a means for solving international disputes. The Japanese government signed and ratified all of these conventions and agreements. The highlight of the international agreements made prior to World War II was the General Treaty for the Renunciation of War of 1928, commonly known as the Kellogg-Briand Pact or simply as the Pact of Paris. The Pact is considered to be a landmark international agreement, since it not only stated the desirability of avoiding the use of force as a solution to international disputes but also condemned and renounced recourse to war altogether.[4] The relevant articles in the Pact read as follows:

Article I. The High Contracting Parties solemnly declare in the names of their respective peoples that they condemn recourse to war for the solution of international controversies, and renounce it as an instrument of national policy in their relations with one another.

Article II. The High Contracting Parties agree that the settlement or solution of all disputes or conflicts of whatever nature or of whatever origin they may be, which may arise among them, shall never be sought except by pacific means.[5]

Eight countries, including Japan, signed and ratified the Pact, and 56 countries later adhered to its provisions.

A group of forward-looking American policy-makers in the Roosevelt administration in subsequent years held that the Kellogg-Briand Pact made aggressive war a crime under international law and that the Nazi aggressors could be prosecuted for this offense at an international court of justice. This position found codified expression in the Charter of the Nuremberg Tribunal, in which the crime of aggression appeared under the heading of "crimes against peace." (The brief history of American planning for Nuremberg has been discussed in Chapter 1.) Crimes against peace are stipulated in the Nuremberg Charter as follows: "Crimes against peace: namely, planning, preparation, initiation or waging of a war of aggression, or a war in violation of international treaties, agreements or assurances, or participation in a common plan or conspiracy for the accomplishment of any of the foregoing."[6] This provision indicates two types of act that fall under the category of crimes against peace. One of them is the substantive offense of "planning, preparation, initiation or waging of a war of aggression, or a war in violation of existing international treaties, agreements or assurances." The other is the "participation in a common plan or conspiracy" whose objective is to accomplish the planning, preparation, initiation, or waging of aggressive war.

The provision for crimes against peace in the Nuremberg Charter was carried over to the Charter of the Tokyo Tribunal with two minor changes. The alterations did not affect the original definition in any material way, but rather served to clarify certain points of ambiguity in the Nuremberg version.[7] The added words are italicized: "Crimes against peace: namely, the planning, preparation, initiation or waging of a *declared or undeclared* war of aggression, or a war in violation of international *law*, treaties, agreements or assurances, or participation in a common plan or conspiracy for the accomplishment of any of the foregoing."[8] By the insertion of the word "law," the Tokyo Charter stressed the understanding that the criminality of aggressive war had been established by international law, not simply by international treaties, agreements, or assurances that might not have binding power as law. This had been the view of the planners of the Nuremberg Tribunal, but it did not attain its full expression in the Nuremberg Charter. The Charter of the Tokyo Tribunal made a necessary change so as not to leave any ambiguity about the legal status of crimes against peace.

The addition of the phrase "declared or undeclared" highlighted the understanding that the manner in which war commenced was immaterial to determining its legal character. Whether there was a declaration of war or not, international armed conflict could still be brought before an international court for adjudication in order to determine its precise legal designation. The words "declared and undeclared" were added probably in view of the fact that Japan initiated a number of armed attacks without prior warning or declaration of war from the invasion of Manchuria in 1931 through the Pearl Harbor attack in 1941. The defense might have taken up this point and argued that armed conflict without Japan's official recognition of it as "war" did not constitute war in the strict legal sense. This kind of contention could possibly have led the judges to dismiss charges of aggressive war. The defense team indeed advanced this argument with respect to the war in China. It contended that armed clashes in China were all mere "incidents" or localized military disturbances with no legal implications as international armed conflict. This had been the official position of the wartime Japanese government, and the accused at Tokyo continued to advance the same argument. Furthermore, they argued that Chinese captives were not entitled to prisoner-of-war status because no formal state of war ever existed between Japan and China. This, again, had been the official position of the Japanese government during war, and so the defense contended.[9] As will be discussed later, however, the Tokyo Tribunal rejected both contentions on the basis of the findings that the Japanese military attacks in China in fact constituted war, and that the Chinese soldiers under Japanese military control were entitled to prisoner-of-war status.

The International Prosecution Section developed 36 counts of crimes against peace.[10] Five of them were conspiracy counts, and the remaining 31 were substantive counts. The first of the five conspiracy counts—count 1—is the summation of all charges related to crimes against peace. It charged, in essence, that there had existed a common plan or conspiracy to wage a war of aggression in the Asia-Pacific region from 1928 to 1945, and that all 28 accused had taken part in either planning or executing the conspiracy, or both. In the words used in the Bill of Indictment, it was a conspiracy to "wage declared or undeclared war or wars of aggression, and war or wars in violation of international law, treaties, agreements and assurances" in order to "secure [Japan's] military, naval, political and economic domination of East Asia and of the Pacific and Indian Oceans, and of all countries and islands therein and bordering thereon." All defendants, "together with diverse other persons," were accused of having "participated as leaders, organisers, instigators or accomplices in the formation or execution of a common plan or conspiracy."[11] The remaining four conspiracy counts made the identical charge but with one difference. The four altogether alleged the existence of separate conspiracies with separate goals, as opposed to the existence of a single conspiracy with a single goal as defined in count 1. These four counts were in a complementary relationship with the first one. They would come under the consideration of the Tokyo Tribunal only if the prosecution failed to prove the existence of the single conspiracy as alleged in count 1.

What, in any case, does "conspiracy" mean? In Anglo-American criminal law, conspiracy refers to an agreement entered into by two or more persons to commit an unlawful act. The charge of conspiracy can be made in combination with various criminal acts, such as murder, robbery, terrorism, and so on. Both at Nuremberg and at Tokyo, the unlawful act in relation to which the conspiracy charge could be made was restricted to the "planning, preparation, initiation, or waging" of aggressive war. At criminal trials, prosecutors may choose to develop conspiracy counts to supplement substantive counts, especially when they have difficulty securing conclusive evidence of guilt of the accused. Under the doctrine of criminal conspiracy, mere proof that an accused had associated with the common plan would be sufficient to establish his or her individual guilt.

Critics of the Tokyo trial have argued that the Allies were mistaken to develop conspiracy counts, since the 28 selected Japanese had never actually formed a conspiratorial group. Many co-defendants had been political enemies, and some did not even know one another. To bracket these individuals as co-conspirators overlooks these basic facts, critics contend.[12] This type of criticism, however, misses the point in that under the doctrine of criminal conspiracy, whether the defendants had been friends or foes is not an issue. Prosecutors can still develop a conspiracy charge against seemingly disparate individuals by arguing that each of them was instrumental in the accomplishment of a crime. An international law scholar, Okuhara Toshio, makes this point in his analyses of the doctrine of criminal conspiracy.[13] He maintains that while many Japanese understand the term "conspiracy" as meaning "something like a plot," the strict legal meaning of conspiracy is "collusion to commit a crime in which those [who] do not actually take part in executing the crime are held equally responsible." In the latter meaning, "there is no need for the defendants to know each other by sight or even by name." In other words, the selected defendants may not have been acquainted with one another, yet they could still be treated as co-conspirators and put on trial jointly. The failure to comprehend the actual legal meaning of conspiracy, Okuhara maintains, can lead to misunderstandings about the prosecutorial effort at Tokyo.[14]

The remaining 31 counts of crimes against peace charged that the defendants committed the substantive offense of aggression. The counts fell under three subcategories: the planning and preparation of aggressive war; the initiation of aggressive war; and the waging of aggressive war. The prosecution itemized various acts of aggression in a number of separate counts, seemingly because it attempted to clarify for which specific criminal incidents each defendant was being held responsible. Developing many counts also provided for more than one avenue for establishing the defendants' responsibility. The judges of the Tokyo Tribunal, however, did not welcome the prosecution's itemization strategy. Finding that the counts were unnecessarily repetitive, they threw out the overlapping ones and eliminated redundancy in the indictment. Specifically, they decided not to consider the counts that fell under the category of planning and preparation on grounds that these counts were already subsumed under the conspiracy counts. All counts that fell under the category of initiation were discarded as well, since the judges considered the initiation of war as necessarily a part of *waging* war. They saw no good reason why a defendant who might be found guilty of waging war should be cumulatively found guilty of initiation. In the end, more than half of the substantive counts of crimes against peace disappeared from the indictment. The judges considered only five counts of conspiracy and ten substantive counts.[15]

During the trial, the defense challenged all counts of aggressive war by questioning, in principle, the legality of the law pertaining to crimes against peace itself. It argued that neither the Kellogg-Briand Pact nor any other international legal documents had made any war a crime under international law. The truth, the defense argued, was that the concept of crimes against peace was a postwar creation of victor nations. It further held that the application of this novel law constituted a breach of one of the cardinal principles of all laws: no punishment should be meted out for an act against which there was no law, or in Roman adage, *Nullum crimen sine lege, nulla poena sine lege.* The defense also contended that no individual could be prosecuted even if aggressive war had been recognized as an international offense at the time of war. War was waged by the *state*, not by individuals who did nothing other than fulfilling their duty as state officials. The defense, in other words, invoked the act-of-state doctrine in its effort to exculpate the accused.[16]

The Tokyo Tribunal rejected all of the above contentions, but stated the reason for the rejection rather tersely. The judgment simply read that the position of the Tribunal was exactly the same as the one taken by the Nuremberg Tribunal and that it preferred "to express its unqualified adherence to the relevant opinions of the Nuremberg Tribunal rather than by reasoning the matters anew in somewhat different language to open the door to controversy by way of conflicting interpretations of the two statements of opinions."[17] To understand the exact stance of the Tokyo Tribunal, then, one needs to turn to the Nuremberg judgment that had similarly rejected both the ex post facto contention and the act-of-state doctrine.

The judges at Nuremberg prefaced their legal position with the following sentence: "The Charter is not an arbitrary exercise of power on the part of the victorious Nations, but . . . it is the expression of international law existing at the time of its creation."[18] By this statement, the Nuremberg Tribunal took the basic position that the criminality of aggressive war had been an established legal principle and that the Nuremberg Charter simply expressed it in codified form. It then went on to elaborate the finer points of law in consideration of the controversy surrounding the law pertaining to crimes against peace.

First, the judges held that "the Latin maxim, *Nullum crimen sine lege* is not a limitation of sovereignty, but is in general a principle of justice." The rule prohibiting the retroactive application of law, in this regard, was not necessarily an absolute, inviolable rule to which one must rigidly adhere in all circumstances. This principle would be respected only to the extent that doing so would further the cause of justice. They continued, "To assert that it is unjust to punish those who in defiance of treaties and assurances have attacked neighboring states without warning is obviously untrue, for in such circumstances the attacker must know that he is doing wrong, and so far from it being unjust to punish him, it would be unjust if his wrong were allowed to go unpunished."[19] In other words, it would be contrary to the notion of justice if the prohibition of ex post facto law were to be invoked to protect those who had knowingly violated international norms and committed wrong. As far as the case before the Nuremberg Tribunal was concerned, the judges considered that the accused "must have known that they were acting in defiance of all international law when in complete deliberation they carried out their designs of invasion and aggression." "On this view of the case alone," they wrote, "it would appear that the maxim has no application to the present facts."[20]

Second, the judges held that the law pertaining to crimes against peace was not ex post facto in any event, and that the defense challenge on the basis of the retroactive application of law was irrelevant. In their opinion, aggressive war had indeed become a crime under international law since the Pact of Paris of 1928. The judges' reasoning was difficult, however; the pertinent part reads as follows:

> The question is, what was the legal effect of this Pact? The nations who signed the Pact or adhered to it unconditionally condemned recourse to war for the future as an instrument of policy, and expressly renounced it. After the signing of the Pact, any nations resorting to war as an instrument of national policy breaks the Pact. In the opinion of the Tribunal, the solemn renunciation of war as an instrument of national policy necessarily involves the proposition that such a war is illegal in international law; and that those who plan and wage such a war, with its inevitable and terrible consequences, are committing a crime in so doing. War for the solution of international controversies undertaken as an instrument of national policy certainly includes a war of aggression, and such a war is therefore outlawed by the Pact.[21]

In this passage, the judges set out the proposition that waging war in breach of the Pact of Paris was unlawful, and that it was *hence* criminal. This line of argument might be hard to maintain, since critics could still insist that nowhere in the Pact was it indicated that an act committed in violation of it constituted a crime.

The judges must have been aware of the potential logical lapse in the argument above, as they immediately addressed it by advancing the following third argument. "In interpreting the words of the Pact," they wrote, "it must be remembered that international law is not the product of an international legislature, and that such international agreements as the Pact of Paris have to deal with general principles of law, and not with administrative matters of procedure." They continued, "The law of war is to be found not only in treaties, but in the customs and practices of states which gradually obtained universal recognition, and from the general principles of justice applied by jurists and practised by military courts."[22] These passages point to the judges' view that international law grew by custom as well as by codification, and that it did not always have full statutory expression. The legal effect of the Pact of Paris ought to be determined, then, not only in light of what the Pact did or did not state but also in light of customary law.

Finally, the judges held that individuals could not escape criminal prosecution for the commission of aggressive war by invoking the act-of-state doctrine. Articles 7 and 8 of the Nuremberg Charter denied this type of challenge; they stipulated: "The official position of defendants, whether as Heads of State or responsible officials in Government Departments, shall not be considered as freeing them from responsibility or mitigating punishment," and, "The fact that the Defendant acted pursuant to order of his Government or of a superior shall not free him from responsibility, but may be considered in mitigation of punishment if the Tribunal determines that justice so requires."[23] The judges affirmed the validity of these principles and wrote, "Crimes against international law are committed by men, not by abstract entities, and only by punishing individuals who commit such crimes can the provisions of international law be enforced."[24] By this ruling, the judges stressed that no one was free from individual criminal responsibility when he or she committed an international offense. Reaffirming the legal principles stipulated in the Nuremberg Charter, they rejected the impunity that state leaders had historically enjoyed.

In sum, the Nuremberg Tribunal ruled, first, that the principle of non-retroactive application of law could not be invoked for the purpose of protecting those who knowingly committed wrong. Second, the Pact of Paris made aggressive war a crime under international law, and therefore, the criticism of ex post facto law had no relevance to the present case. Third, the lack of codified law regarding the trial of aggressors could not be cited as grounds for dismissing aggressive war charges. Doing so would mean overlooking the effect of customary law. Last, there must be individual responsibility for crimes committed in violation of international law, including crimes against peace. The notion of immunity of state officials could not be invoked as a defense. These legal opinions received full and unequivocal endorsement at the successive trials at Nuremberg.[25] The Tokyo Tribunal, too, adopted them *verbatim*, with no addition or omission. By such strict adherence, the Tokyo Tribunal indicated that all outstanding legal controversies concerning crimes against peace had been resolved at Nuremberg, and that, by extension, any criticisms one might have on points of law may be best directed to the Nuremberg judgment rather than Tokyo. Such a position did not prevent Japanese nationalist critics from challenging the Tokyo trial, however, as will be discussed in Chapter 9.

Conspiracy, Conspiracies, and the Fifteen-Year War

After hearing the cases presented by the prosecution and the defense, the Tokyo Tribunal established that the single conspiracy as alleged in count 1 did indeed exist. Specifically, it found that Japanese leaders had a common plan to wage aggressive war between 1928 and 1945, with the goal of securing Japan's military, political, and economic domination over East Asia, the western and southwestern Pacific, and the Indian Ocean. (There was one qualification to this finding: North and South America were not part of the targeted regions even though the prosecution had alleged so when substantiating count 1.[26]) As a result of the ruling in favor of count 1, the remaining four complementary counts of conspiracy were not considered.

This conclusion by the Tribunal—the finding that successive Japanese leaders took part in a common criminal plan to secure control over the Asia-Pacific region by the use of force over the course of some eighteen years—has been one of the most contested and unpopular legacies of the Tokyo trial. Critics argue that the portrayal of the Japanese war as a product of a conspiracy conflicted with the actual circumstances of the war. By way of illustration, Kojima Noboru—a nonfiction writer and a self-styled historian—remarked that the finding of the single conspiracy was "quite impossible." The truth, as he understood it, was that there were "elements of confusion, of tangled complexity, in Japanese policy-making at this time." He added, "the situation in Japan was very different from that in Nazi Germany, where a single dictator and the group surrounding him were in constant control of policy decisions."[27] Tsunoda Jun, a scholar of diplomatic history and international politics, shared this view, writing that the Allied prosecutors and the majority judges engaged in the "fabrication of history" (*rekishi no gizō*) by upholding the theory of single conspiracy. He deemed it an "absurdity" (*hijōshiki*) that the Tokyo Tribunal took this theory seriously.[28] Outside Japan, Richard Minear advanced a similar criticism. He wrote, "[I]t seems already clear that there was no historical conspiracy even remotely similar to the conspiracy described in the majority judgment." He continued, "The Japanese Government in the period of the indictment was without a unifying planning group, without even a Hitler." By these remarks, Minear did not mean to suggest that no conspiracy ever existed. He rather held that there were "conspiracies and plots galore in the early 1930's" and that "several defendants had been involved."[29] What he took issue with was the historical narrative premised upon the existence of a conspiracy. In his opinion, the conspiracy charge was objectionable since it failed to reflect the complex circumstances in which the wartime Japanese government made its decisions for war.

A Japanese legal scholar, Okuhara Toshio, also considered the Tokyo Tribunal's ruling to be unsatisfactory. His point of criticism, however, was slightly different from those of Kojima, Tsunoda, or Minear. As he understood it, the main problem with the Tokyo judgment was that it established conspiracy on the basis of "the so-called political thought of Ōkawa Shūmei," a leading propagandist and advocate of Japanese military expansion abroad in the 1920s and 1930s. (He was one of the accused but in the initial weeks was declared mentally unfit to stand trial.) Ōkawa's publications were, however, "mere prophecies" (*tannaru yogen*) at best, or works written "from the viewpoint of mere providentialism and for educational purposes" (*tannaru unmeiron to keimōteki kanten*). Put differently, his tracts took on "no character of concrete plans for developing a conspiracy." Nevertheless, the Tokyo Tribunal concluded that Ōkawa's advocacy provided sufficient grounds for establishing the existence of conspiracy as alleged in count 1. Here, in Okuhara's opinion, rested the fundamental problem of the Tokyo judgment on the conspiracy count.[30]

Interestingly, the narrative of war that the Tokyo Tribunal chronicled in the judgment betrayed its own finding of single conspiracy. Instead of telling the story of the Japanese leaders' single-minded pursuit of a grand plan to wage aggressive war over the course of eighteen years, the judges documented a meandering process of formulating, modifying, retracting, and re-formulating various *war plans* throughout the period covered by the indictment. In other words, the Tokyo Tribunal's *general* ruling on the conspiracy charge was inconsistent with the *specific* factual findings it recorded in the judgment. Given this inconsistency, the Tokyo Tribunal might have better ruled that there existed multiple conspiracies of aggressive war, in place of a single conspiracy as charged in count 1.

The Nuremberg Tribunal treated the conspiracy charge in a less controversial manner. At Nuremberg, the prosecution had made a similar

charge of a common plan or conspiracy, which had allegedly existed between around 1921 (when Hitler assumed leadership of the Nazi Party)
and 1945. In the final verdict, the Nuremberg Tribunal established that
a conspiracy indeed existed, but limited this finding by ruling that "the
conspiracy must be clearly outlined in its criminal purpose," and that it
"must not be too far removed from the time of decision and of action."
It further held that documents such as the Nazi Party's 25-point program and Hitler's *Mein Kampf* could not be regarded as proof of criminal conspiracy. These documents only attested to the existence of a
Nazi Party *vision* of conquest, not of a criminal *plan* of war. In the end,
the Tribunal concluded that there were "many separate plans rather
than a single conspiracy embracing them all,"[31] the first of which was
the plan to invade Poland in 1939. In other words, the Tribunal rejected
the prosecution's contention of grand conspiracy and instead established the existence of clearly defined, multiple war plans (= conspiracies). Had the Tokyo Tribunal handed down a similar verdict, it would
have reflected the historical reality of Japan's war-making process more
accurately and might have faced less criticism in later years.

The Tribunal considered ten substantive counts of crimes against
peace. In these counts, the prosecution charged that all defendants were
responsible for waging wars of aggression against China beginning on
September 18, 1931 (count 27), and July 7, 1937 (count 28). All were
also charged with having waged aggressive war since December 7, 1941,
against the United States (count 29), the Philippines (count 30), the British Commonwealth of Nations (count 31), the Netherlands (count 32),
and Thailand (count 34). Certain defendants were further held responsible for having waged aggressive war against France since September
1940 (count 33), the Soviet Union in the summer of 1938 (count 34), and
the Mongolian People's Republic and the Soviet Union in the summer
of 1939 (count 35). In the final judgment, the Tokyo Tribunal upheld
seven of these counts and dismissed the remaining three.

With respect to the two counts related to China, the Tribunal found
that Japan waged a continuous war of aggression against China, starting
with the launch of the unprovoked military attack in Mukden (present-
day Shenyang) on September 18, 1931. This war continued until Japan's
formal acceptance of surrender in September 1945.[32] The Tribunal considered the conflict following the armed clash on the outskirts of Peking

on July 7, 1937, as part of the larger war that had begun with the Mukden Incident. Since the count that covered the war beginning in September 1931 subsumed the one that covered the war starting in July 1937, the Tribunal deemed it unnecessary to consider the latter.[33]

In reaching this ruling, the judges documented in great detail the facts surrounding the Mukden Incident. This points to their awareness that this event weighed greatly in the prosecution's case on crimes against peace. During the trial, the prosecution had framed the Mukden Incident as the first war of aggression by which Japan aimed to secure a foothold in the region of Manchuria (northeastern China) and to wage further expansionist war in neighboring territories. The defense had argued in response that the Mukden Incident was an isolated episode of armed conflict in which the Japanese army acted only in self-defense, and that Japan had no self-aggrandizing ambition or aggressive plan when it executed other military actions thereafter. Given the controversy in court over this episode of armed conflict, it was imperative that the Tokyo Tribunal engage in a thorough analysis of evidence and reach a definitive ruling.

Determining the legal character of the Mukden Incident itself—that is, whether it constituted a war of aggression—was a fairly uncomplicated task for the judges. For one thing, defense witnesses and even certain defendants admitted in court that the garrisoned Japanese army in the region of Manchuria, known as the Kwantung Army, had indeed planned and initiated unprovoked attacks. They testified that the Japanese army caused a railway explosion in order to use it as an excuse to launch attacks on the Chinese forces under the command of the Manchurian warlord, Chang Hsüeh-liang, and bring Manchuria under Japanese military control. The judges also found sufficient evidence to establish that the Chinese forces were actually "caught unprepared" when they came under hostile fire from the Kwantung Army. As they wrote, thousands of Chinese troops were inside the "brightly lit Barracks," defenseless and unprepared for the night attacks. The Kwantung Army confronted only "trifling resistance" in the immediate aftermath of the railway explosion, "mainly from some Chinese troops who were cut off in their attempt to escape." The Tokyo Tribunal further found that Marshal Chang contacted the Japanese consul-general in Mukden and called for the termination of the Japanese attacks at the time of the

incident. His policy at that time was to "act upon the nonresistance principle absolutely." Despite the information that Chang had no desire to
engage in armed conflict, Itagaki Seishirō—one of the accused who had
orchestrated the military action in his capacity as the on-the-spot senior
officer of the Kwantung Army—refused to listen to the consul-general
on grounds of "the right of military command."[34]

The judges also established that Hayashi Kyūjirō, the consul-general,
had telegraphed Foreign Minister Shidehara Kijūrō prior to September
18, informing him of "the news that the Company Commander of a
Japanese Unit at Fushun [east of Mukden] had said that within a week
a big 'Incident' would break out." Morishima Morito, a staff officer
of the Japanese consulate at Mukden, also learned of the plan that
"Kwantung Army units stationed at Fushun would execute a manoeu-
vre which contemplated the occupation of Mukden, leaving Fushun
about 11:30 on the night of 18 September 1931." There was also evidence
that Shidehara "attached so much credence to the information he had
that he complained to the war minister and persuaded the latter to dispatch General Tatekawa to Manchuria to 'stop the plot.'" Tatekawa
Yoshitsugu from the army general staff was duly sent to Mukden, but,
"having no desire to interfere with any proposed 'Incident,'" he did
nothing to stop the plot from being carried out.[35] The proof that credible information about the Kwantung Army's plan to instigate an "incident" had circulated among the Japanese diplomatic corps as well as
the central government at the highest level before September 18 was
sufficient for the judges to reject the defense contention that there was
no premeditated plan of aggressive war on the Japanese side.

These findings led the Tribunal to conclude that "the so-called 'Incident' of 18 September 1931 was planned and executed by the Japanese."[36]
It also found that certain of the defendants, including the accused Itagaki, were individually and criminally accountable for the invasion. After
establishing the Mukden Incident as the starting point of a Japanese war
of aggression, the Tribunal did not dwell on the question of whether
each of the Japanese military actions in China in subsequent years also
constituted aggressive war. This reflected the judges' position that Japanese armed attacks in China for the remaining fourteen years were caus-
ally connected to the occurrence of the Mukden Incident. Put differently, they concluded that Japan and China entered a state of undeclared

war on September 18, 1931, which continued through Japan's surrender in September of 1945.

The Tribunal next considered two counts related to the Soviet Union and Mongolia. The prosecution had charged that Japan waged aggressive war on the borders of Manchukuo on two separate occasions. One of them broke out at Lake Khasan on the eastern border on July 29, 1938. In this conflict, Japanese forces were quickly overwhelmed and defeated by the Soviet Army. Japan formally ended the war by signing an armistice with the Soviet Union on August 10 of the same year. The other took place at Nomonhan on the border between Manchukuo and Outer Mongolia beginning on May 11, 1939. The large-scale conflict at Nomonhan, too, ended in Japan's crushing defeat at the hands of the Mongolian and Russian forces. It was followed by an armistice on September 15, 1939. The defense, in response, had contested the prosecution's charges for both cases. The defense argument converged on the following points. First, the two conflicts were "mere border incidents caused by uncertainty as to the boundaries and resulting in clashes of the opposing frontier guard detachments."[37] In other words, the conflict resulted from the Japanese effort to protect the Manchurian borders, not from an alleged Japanese scheme to commit aggression by invading the Soviet Union or Mongolia. Second, the Tokyo Tribunal had no jurisdiction over the two cases to begin with. The Japanese and Soviet governments had already settled all outstanding issues by concluding armistices. Moreover, the two countries signed a neutrality pact in 1941, thereby putting a formal end to any state of war, if any had existed until that time. There was, therefore, no reason why a third party such as the Tokyo Tribunal should assume jurisdiction and interfere with the standing bilateral agreements.

The judges apparently found neither of the defense contentions convincing. With respect to the first line of argument, the Tribunal established that Japan faced no actual military attacks or imminent threats of attack from the Soviet Union or Mongolia. It held, in essence, that the use of force against another country without military provocation constituted a war of aggression.[38] The Tribunal dismissed the second defense contention on grounds that "[i]n none of the three agreements on which the Defence argument is based, was any immunity granted nor was the question of liability, criminal or otherwise, dealt with." The

Tribunal further wrote, "In a matter of criminal liability whether domestic or international it would be against the public interest for any tribunal to countenance condonation of crime either expressly or by implication."[39] In other words, the judges held that they had a moral as well as legal responsibility to adjudicate the charges of aggression given the seriousness of the offense. Of these two legal opinions, the latter ruling might have been subject to criticism, since both the Nuremberg and Tokyo Charters restricted the applicability of the law pertaining to crimes against peace to the Axis powers alone. Notwithstanding the claim of universality, the legal opinion the Tokyo Tribunal thus had limitations at the level of enforcement.[40]

Next the judges considered the count related to French Indochina. The prosecution's contention had been that Japan and France had been belligerents since September 22, 1940, when Japan sent troops into the northern part of French Indochina and commenced military occupation. This, the prosecution had argued, constituted aggressive war. The defense had contested the validity of such a charge, arguing that the French Vichy government accorded Japan the right of military occupation by a bilateral agreement on August 30, 1940, known as the Matsuoka-Henri Agreement. Thus there could exist no state of war between Japan and France.[41] The defense failed again to convince the Tribunal, however. According to the judgment, the Japanese army entered French territory without securing formal permission from the latter. More specifically, before the Matsuoka-Henri Agreement came into effect, the Japanese government had sent troops across the border of Indochina so as to coerce the governor-general of French Indochina into agreeing to the terms Japan demanded. "Faced with an actual invasion," the Tribunal wrote, "the Governor-General was forced to accept the Japanese demands and signed an agreement on 24th September for military occupation of Tonkin Province, the establishment of air bases and the grant of military facilities in French Indo-China."[42] This finding points to the judges' opinion that the Japanese *threat* to use force was sufficient to establish the subsequent military occupation as constituting a crime against peace.

The Tribunal's ruling on the French case is interesting, since Japan's military occupation of Indochina commenced without the actual initiation of war *per se*. Could the entry of Japanese troops in the French territory be proof of a crime against peace even though they did not launch armed attacks? Legal opinions from Nuremberg may be helpful in answering this question. The International Military Tribunal at Nuremberg faced a similar legal problem with respect to the German seizure of Austria and Czechoslovakia prior to the attack on Poland. As was the case with French Indochina, evidence established that both countries were compelled to allow the German occupation because of the threat of invasion. The Nuremberg Tribunal ruled that these instances of German military advance constituted "[t]he first *acts* of aggression," yet distinguished them from the German invasion of Poland, which they termed "the first *war* of aggression." Such a distinction, though subtle, indicates the ambivalence of the Tribunal about the interpretation of the law pertaining to crimes against peace.[43] The judges at the Ministries Case (*U.S.* v. *Ernst von Weizsäcker et al.*, 1947–49) took a bolder position. They established in unambiguous terms that the German actions against Austria and Czechoslovakia constituted crimes against peace, ruling that "[i]t is not reasonable to assume that an act of war, in the nature of an invasion, whereby conquest and plunder are achieved without resistance, is to be given more favorable consideration than a similar invasion which may have met with some military resistance." Telford Taylor, chief prosecutor for the twelve successive proceedings at Nuremberg, commented positively on the Ministries judgment, writing that it "la[id] at rest the notion that a great power can, with legal impunity, mass such large forces to threaten a weaker country that the latter succumbs without the necessity of a 'shooting war.'"[44] The finding of the Tokyo Tribunal concerning French Indochina fell in line with the opinion of the Ministries Case.

Next followed the judges' findings with respect to the remaining five counts on the war in the Pacific. Established with little controversy was the fact that Japan launched a series of military attacks on cities and ports in Hawai'i, Guam, Wake Island, the Philippines, Hong Kong, Shanghai, and British Malaya on December 7, 1941, and then other Pacific islands in subsequent months. These attacks, the prosecution had held, marked the beginning of Japanese aggressive war against the British Commonwealth of Nations, the Netherlands, the Philippines, Thailand, and the United States. The prosecution had particularly made the point that Japanese state leaders breached the Third Hague Convention of 1907 when they initiated the attack on Pearl Harbor, fully aware that the Convention required prior warning or declaration of war. The willful neglect of this international obligation, in the prosecution's opinion, established the criminality of Japanese military actions against the United States.

The Tribunal established three of the five counts, upholding that Japan planned and waged a war of aggression against the British Commonwealth of Nations, the Netherlands, and the United States.[45] Interestingly, however, it rejected the prosecution's interpretation of the Third Hague Convention of 1907. It ruled that this convention was not a reliable legal document for determining the legal character of the Japanese attack on Pearl Harbor. The convention "undoubtedly imposes the obligation of giving previous and explicit warning before hostilities are commenced," the judges acknowledged, "but it does not define the period which must be allowed between the giving of this warning and the commencement of hostilities." This feature of the convention, as a result, "permit[ted] of a narrow construction and tempt[ed] the unprincipled to try to comply with the obligation thus narrowly constructed while at the same time ensuring that their attacks shall come as a surprise."[46] In the Tribunal's opinion, this was precisely what the Japanese leaders attempted to do in December 1941. According to the Tribunal's findings, the Japanese government developed a plan to deliver a warning to the United States just twenty minutes prior to commencing the attack on Pearl Harbor. This plan allowed "no margin for contingencies," although it technically followed the rules stipulated in the Hague Convention. When the Japanese government actually implemented the plan, the attack on Pearl Harbor took place first, while the delivery of the note to the U.S. Secretary of State, Cordell Hull, came forty minutes later. The responsibility for the delay apparently lay with the Japanese embassy staff in Washington, who did not realize the urgency of the matter and were slow to decode the Japanese warning.[47] In light of these findings, the Tribunal concluded that it was pointless to try to determine the criminality of the Pearl Harbor attack on the basis of whether the Tōjō cabinet had a premeditated plan to violate the Hague Convention.

This finding was a blow to the American prosecution team, since it had long been its goal to establish the intent of the Tōjō cabinet to initiate a sneak attack on Pearl Harbor.[48] While the Tribunal did find Tōjō and certain others guilty of authorizing aggressive war against the United States, the main reason was *not* that they developed a plan of surprise attacks. The Tribunal convicted them rather on grounds that the Tōjō cabinet decided to attack the United States and other powers in the Pacific in order to protect Japan's ill-gotten gains in China from preceding years.

The defense team, for its part, had argued during the trial that Japan was provoked to wage war in the face of the economic blockade orchestrated by the hostile Allied powers and that its war against the United States and other Western powers was purely a war of self-defense. The Tribunal rejected these lines of argument, however. It wrote, "The evidence clearly establishes contrary to the contention of the defense that the acts of aggression against France, and the attacks on Britain, the United States of America and the Netherlands were prompted by the desire to deprive China of any aid in the struggle she was waging against Japan's aggression and to secure for Japan the possessions of her neighbors in the South."[49] This passage summarizes the Tribunal's basic position: that Japan's refusal to give up China was the key to determining the legal character of the Japanese war against the Western powers in the Pacific region.

The causal link that the Tokyo Tribunal established between the wars in China and the Pacific region deserves special attention, since it substantially overlaps with the way in which Japanese historians today comprehend World War II. By illustration, the same causal understanding of war has given rise to terms such as the Fifteen-Year War (*Jūgonen sensō*) and the Asia-Pacific War (*Ajia taiheiyō sensō*). The former term underscores the notion that World War II in the Pacific region began with the Mukden Incident of September 1931 and that the war was waged in China and beyond for fifteen calendar years. The latter term, on the other hand, stresses the link between the wars in China and the Pacific region in spatial terms. By connecting the two distinct geographical spaces, this concept underscores that the root cause of the Pacific War rested with the war on the Chinese continent.[50] The wide circulation of these two concepts in Japan today suggests that although the Tokyo Tribunal may have mishandled the conspiracy counts, its findings on substantive counts stood up to the test of history and came to set the foundation of the postwar Japanese historiography of Word War II.

FIVE

Leadership Responsibility for War Crimes

At both Nuremberg and Tokyo, crimes against peace took center stage in the prosecutorial effort. Hardly less important, however, was the indictment of the same groups of defendants for the commission of atrocities in various theaters of war. The prosecution at Tokyo lodged nineteen counts of war crimes, crimes against humanity, murder, and conspiracy to commit the foregoing three offenses in order to establish the guilt of the accused. They developed these charges on the assumption that all four categories came under the jurisdiction of the Tokyo Tribunal. But the judges ruled that the Charter of the Tribunal allowed charges only of war crimes and crimes against humanity, and threw out all counts related to murder and conspiracy. As a result, only two counts related to atrocities remained in the indictment for the judges' consideration.[1] What, in any case, are war crimes and crimes against humanity?

War crimes, or "conventional war crimes" as they were commonly referred to at the Tokyo trial, are acts committed in violation of laws and customs that govern the conduct of war. The basic legal documents applicable today are the Geneva Conventions of 1949 and the protocols to these conventions, adopted in 1977. These documents did not exist during World War II, but other international conventions, treaties, and agreements provided codified rules of war. The most important document would be the Fourth Hague Convention of 1907, which set out basic rules and customs of war in international armed conflict. This convention remains applicable today. The Geneva Convention of 1929 provided just under 100 rules regarding the proper treatment of prisoners of war. Because of its special focus on the rights and duties of prisoners of war, this document came to be known as the Prisoner of War Convention. Finally, the Red Cross Convention— adopted in the same year—contained rules on the treatment of the sick and wounded in armed conflict.[2] All major powers that fought World War II, including Japan, had been party to one or more of these conventions.

The defense at Tokyo contested the applicability of these conventions, particularly the Prisoner of War Convention, on the grounds that Japan did not ratify it. After the Pearl Harbor attack in December 1941, the Japanese government did give assurances to the Allied governments that Japan would adhere to this convention. Yet the defense explained that these assurances did not legally bind Japan to the rules stipulated in it. Japan's official position, the defense argued, was to apply the Prisoner of War Convention *mutatis mutandis* (*jun'yō suru*), meaning, with necessary modification. This term had been included in the communicated assurances, and supposedly allowed the Japanese government a free hand in determining the degree to which it would respect the rules stipulated in the Prisoner of War Convention. A defense witness, Matsumoto Shun'ichi, supported this interpretation. He had formerly served as chief of the treaties bureau in the foreign ministry during the Pacific War. Matsumoto testified, "It was the intention of Japan with respect to the treatment of prisoners of war that the stipulations of the Geneva Convention be applied so far as circumstances permitted; in other words, unless there were hindrances or obstacles which made its application impracticable."[3] This testimony supported the defense position that the Japanese adherence to the Prisoner of War Convention was only voluntary and conditioned by circumstances.

The prosecution took a different stance on the interpretation of Japan's legal obligation. It contended, first, that the Fourth Hague Convention of 1907, which Japan had ratified, required Japan's adherence not only to codified rules but also to the general principle that prisoners of war should be treated humanely. It went on to argue that Japanese troops might not be held accountable for failing to observe specific provisions in the Prisoner of War Convention for the reason of non-ratification, but that they still had international obligations to treat their captives humanely. At least one defendant supported the prosecution's argument: Tōgō Shigenori (Fig. 5.1), the superior of the defense witness Matsumoto, and the very person who communicated the said assurances to the Allied governments when he served as foreign minister in 1941 and 1942. He testified that Japan assumed international responsibility to observe the Prisoner of War Convention by sending the assurances, and that moreover, the phrase *mutatis mutandis* did not imply that Japan had complete freedom in deciding whether to respect or ignore the convention. He also understood that the Prisoner of War Convention would override Japanese domestic law should there be any conflict between the two. He testified that he had little doubt about the correctness of this understanding, since "neither War nor Navy Ministry ever suggested any other interpretation to me, nor does the War Ministry's reply to our request for a statement of policy suggest it."[4]

The Tribunal ruled that Japan indeed had the duty to treat prisoners of war humanely whether it had ratified the Geneva Convention or not. The pertinent section in the judgment read as follows:

Whatever view may be taken of the assurance or undertaking of the Japanese Government to comply with the Geneva Prisoner of War Convention "mutatis mutandis" the fact remains that under the customary rules of war, acknowledged by all civilized nations, all prisoners of war and civilian internees must be given humane treatment. It is the grossly inhumane treatment by the Japanese military forces . . . that is particularly reprehensible and criminal. A person guilty of such inhumanities cannot escape punishment on the plea that he or his government is not bound by any particular convention. The general principles of the law exist independently of the said conventions. The conventions merely reaffirm the pre-existing law and prescribe detailed provisions for its application.[5]

According to this opinion, the judges did not consider it necessary to determine the exact meaning of *mutatis mutandis*, nor to quibble over which acts were specifically prohibited by codified rules in the existing international conventions. Customary law was binding upon Japan as much as were the international legal documents Japan had ratified. In light of this understanding, the judges concluded that there was no justification for the Japanese armed forces to mete out cruel treatment to those who came under their control. This ruling conformed fully to the judgments of the Nuremberg tribunals and remains valid today.[6]

Fig. 5.1 Tōgō Shigenori in the witness box, December 19, 1947. Courtesy National Archives, photo no. 238-FE.

One may trace the origin of the concept of crimes against humanity at least as far back as the 1907 Hague Convention, but the Charter of the Nuremberg Tribunal was the first to give it clear codified expression.[7] The law pertaining to crimes against humanity provided legal protection from systematic mass atrocity to the civilian population. While this law overlapped to some extent with the law governing conventional war crimes, the scale, pattern, targeted groups, and context of the offenses may make certain civilian-targeted atrocities more appropriately classified as crimes against humanity than as war crimes. A few central features that distinguish crimes against humanity from war crimes may be summarized as follows.[8] First, the law on crimes against humanity extends not only to citizens of enemy countries but also to the belligerent's own nationals. By way of illustration, this law could be applied to prosecute leaders of the German government for crimes committed against

German Jews. The law governing conventional war crimes could not be used in such a case, because the crimes in question were targeted at the perpetrators' own nationals, not against enemy nationals. Only with the law on crimes against humanity did it become possible to charge German leaders for the commission of atrocities against German citizens. Second, persecution of an identifiable group of people for reasons of race, religion, and so on, falls under the category of crimes against humanity. A case in point would be the Nazi persecution of the Jewish people. This type of crime, again, could not be prosecuted as a war crime. Only with the law on crimes against humanity was it possible for the Allied prosecutors to charge the Nazi leaders with persecution of European Jews. Third, crimes against humanity include civilian-targeted atrocities that take place in peacetime as well as in the context of armed conflict. This means that the law on crimes against humanity goes beyond the bounds of conventional rules and customs of war. It gives universal protection from violence to all civilian populations irrespective of whether armed conflict is in progress.

At the time of Nuremberg and Tokyo, the law on crimes against humanity was at a nascent stage and its content was, in a sense, still in the making. Put differently, various features commonly recognized today were not fully expressed in the charters of the two tribunals. The Nuremberg Charter stipulated that all civilians came under the protection of the law on crimes against humanity regardless of nationality. It also included persecution as one type of crime against humanity. The first and second features discussed above were thus articulated. The Charter fell short of stating the third feature, however. Rather, it explicitly required that armed conflict be in progress if civilian-targeted atrocities were to be considered under the category of crimes against humanity.[9] Consequently, it became difficult at Nuremberg to prosecute Nazi leaders for the commission of *prewar* atrocities against German Jews. Such offenses might be covered in the indictment only by applying other supplementary laws such as the doctrine of criminal conspiracy.[10]

The Nuremberg definition of crimes against humanity was carried over to the Charter of the Tokyo Tribunal. The applicability of this law was, therefore, restricted to wartime civilian-targeted atrocities. It appears that the Allied prosecutors at Tokyo did not consider this to be a major constraint, however. They were interested primarily in establishing the responsibility of wartime Japanese leaders for atrocities targeted at Allied nationals. Such offenses could ordinarily be framed as war crimes, thereby requiring no special use of the law on crimes against humanity. The absence of any instance of mass atrocity in the Pacific theater that was comparable to the Holocaust may have further diminished the significance of the concept of crimes against humanity at Tokyo. The prosecution did include the charges of crimes against humanity in the indictment, but only as supplementary to the substantiation of what were essentially war crimes.[11]

The two counts of war crimes and crimes against humanity (which, to reiterate, were in substance war crimes) appear in the Bill of Indictment as counts 54 and 55. The two counts were identical in that they included the charges of both war crimes and crimes against humanity, but they articulated contrasting theories of individual responsibility. Count 54 stated that the accused "ordered, authorised and permitted" their subordinate officers in the government and in theaters of war to commit atrocities repeatedly in breach of rules of war. The meaning of the word "permitted" is somewhat ambiguous,[12] but for now, count 54 will be treated as charging that the defendants directly sanctioned (that is, ordered and authorized) the commission of atrocities. For the sake of identification, let us term this theory of individual responsibility as "direct responsibility."

The underlying notion of responsibility of count 55, on the other hand, was criminal negligence. In the words in the Bill of Indictment, the defendants "deliberately and recklessly disregarded their legal duty to take adequate steps to secure the observance and prevent breaches thereof, and thereby violated the laws of war." One crucial distinction between counts 54 and 55 was that the latter determined an individual's guilt in terms of his or her *knowing inaction*, while the former, in terms of an accused's *sanctioning* of criminal orders. In developing count 55, the Allied prosecutors took special note of certain international legal documents that provided them with supporting theoretical grounds. For instance, they cited in the indictment a stipulation in the Fourth Hague Convention of 1907 that read, "Prisoners of War are *in the power of the hostile Government*, but not of the individual or corps who capture them." This passage indicated that the central government had primary responsibility to ensure the humane treatment of prisoners of war. The

Prisoner of War Convention of 1929 contained exactly the same stipulation, pointing to the overriding responsibility of the government to ensure that laws and customs of war were observed. The Red Cross Convention also stated, "The Commanders-in-Chief of belligerent armies shall arrange the details for carrying out the preceding articles, as well as for cases not provided for, *in accordance with the instructions of their respective Governments* and in conformity with the general principles of the present Convention."[13] This statement, again, underscored that the government, not military commanders in theaters of war, incurred the highest responsibility to ensure proper treatment of the sick and wounded.

The prosecution elaborated its legal opinion concerning count 55 at greater length during its summation. The Australian prosecutor, Lt. Col. Thomas F. Mornane, explained the prosecution's position:

> It is, in our submission . . . clear that it is the Government as a whole which is primarily responsible for the prevention of breaches of these Laws of War. This casts in the first place a duty upon every member of the cabinet and their advisors, and every high officer in the chain of command directly concerned with these matters to satisfy himself that the Laws are being obeyed. Ordinarily no doubt this duty [to prevent breaches of laws of war] could be discharged by satisfying himself that proper machinery had been established for the purpose. But when information reaches him which raises a doubt as to whether they are being flagrantly disregarded, or shows plainly that they are, then a much higher duty devolves upon him.[14]

According to this explanation, responsibility for the day-to-day supervision of the conduct of war rested with the appropriate disciplinary mechanism that had been set in place. But there may have been times when the mechanism failed to ensure the proper conduct of service personnel. On such occasions, the government—or to be more precise, cabinet members, their advisers, and military commanders who jointly formed the policy-making body of the government—incurred a "higher duty" to intervene and rectify the situation.

Mornane continued to explain the content of the higher duty that senior government officials incurred. To start with the members of the cabinet, when they learned about the commission of atrocities by the troops they deployed to theaters of war, they had the responsibility to inform other cabinet members of the fact. There was, according to the prosecution's contention, "a clear duty upon every official who knew about the commission of any of these war crimes to use such power as he possessed to put the matter right at once, at least to the extent of bringing the outrages to an immediate stop." The ones who were informed of atrocities may then "resign unless effective steps [were] taken to prevent their commission."[15] This type of responsibility involving cabinet members may be termed "cabinet responsibility" for now.

Senior military officers in the army or navy also had the duty to act when they learned about the commission of atrocities by subordinate troops. They would not be expected to take action vis-à-vis the cabinet to stop the atrocities, however. The primary responsibility of military officers was to take control of the armed forces under their command, not to press the political leaders in the government to take measures. This type of individual responsibility stemming from the military chain of command can be called "command responsibility," following the common terminology in legal circles today.[16] The prosecution held that the same principle could be applied to senior officials of the war and navy ministries, which were civilian wings of the army and navy. The officials of these ministries took charge of administrative and supervisory tasks regarding the treatment of war prisoners and general law-enforcement in Japanese-occupied territories in the Pacific theater.[17]

In sum, the prosecutors invoked three distinct theories of individual responsibility when developing counts of war crimes against the selected defendants: direct responsibility (count 54), cabinet responsibility (count 55), and command responsibility (count 55). The next two chapters will analyze how the prosecution used these concepts of responsibility, how the defense responded to the charges, and the verdicts the Tokyo Tribunal handed down in the end.

Prosecutorial Strategies

The International Prosecution Section set out to collect evidentiary material far and wide in order to establish the guilt of individual defendants in developing the counts of war crimes. This, however, proved to be extremely difficult. The biggest obstacle was the Japanese government, which had made a concerted effort to destroy confidential documents related to military matters at the end of war so as to prevent incriminating evidence from falling into the hands of Allied investigators. The massive destruction effort had taken place during the two-week hiatus

between Japan's acceptance of surrender and the arrival of Allied occupation forces in Japan. According to the estimate made by the director of
the Japanese Defense Agency's archives in 2003, "as much as 70 percent
of the army's wartime records were burned or otherwise destroyed" as
a result of the coordinated destruction efforts.[18] Such extensive loss inevitably complicated the prosecution's task of establishing links between
widespread Japanese military violence and individual defendants. Allied
prosecutors at Nuremberg were far more fortunate in this respect, since
they had access to a wealth of documents that the Allied forces had captured when they invaded Germany in the last months of the war.

The prosecution introduced certain military records that attested to
the Japanese effort to destroy and conceal incriminating materials. One
document prepared by Miyama Yōzō, the chief of the Correspondence
Section of the First Demobilization Bureau (the former war ministry),
attested that the war ministry dispatched a telegram on August 14, 1945
(the day Japan accepted surrender), instructing all servicemen in the
army that "the confidential documents held by every troop should be
destroyed by fire immediately." The same document also reveals that
the war ministry transmitted the identical order by phone to the troops
in Tokyo and that it directed the troops outside Japan—who received
the telegram—to burn the communication, apparently to ensure that no
trace of the military order would survive the war.[19]

According to another document in evidence, the chief of prisoner of
war camps at Tokyo sent the following message to the Japanese armies
in Korea, Taiwan, Manchuria, China, Hong Kong, Thailand, Borneo,
Malaya, and Java, on August 20, 1945: "Personnel who mistreated prisoners of war and internees or who are held in extremely bad sentiment
by them are permitted to take care of it by immediately transferring or
by fleeing without trace. Moreover, documents which would be un-
favorable for us in the hands of the enemy are to be treated in the same
way as secret documents and destroyed when finished with."[20] Documents such as these indicate awareness at the highest level that criminal
mistreatment had taken place, and that it was *widespread.* (The message
above was sent throughout the Japanese-occupied territories in the Pacific region.) The fact that the International Prosecution Section was able
to secure the above document does suggest that the order to destroy
all incriminating records was not as thoroughly executed as the Japanese

government had planned. Nevertheless, the empire-wide effort to eliminate traces of Japanese war crimes created enormous difficulty for the
Allied prosecutors to prepare their war crimes cases for the Tokyo trial.

The difficulty of securing documentary evidence was compounded
by the fact that the chief prosecutor, Keenan, did not fully appreciate
the importance of doing so. Assuming at the outset that useful Japanese
documents had already been destroyed, he directed his staff to focus
on interrogating war crimes suspects and witnesses with the goal of securing oral evidence from them. Moreover, he made little personal
commitment to preparing charges of war crimes and crimes against
humanity because he understood his primary duty as prosecuting Class
A war crimes (crimes against peace). As a result of Keenan's general
indifference, a number of governmental records that might have established the guilt of the accused for war crimes remained beyond the
reach of the International Prosecution Section. It is only in recent years
that Japanese researchers have brought to light some of the surviving
documents. For example, Yoshimi Yoshiaki, a professor at Chūō University and a leading scholar on the comfort women system, unearthed
from the archives of the Japanese Defense Agency in the early 1990s
pieces of documentary evidence that recorded government sponsorship
of military sexual slavery. He published the documents in the *Asahi
shinbun* on January 11, 1992. This led to the immediate admission by the
Japanese government of military involvement in the comfort women
system.[21] Similarly, a document recording the Tōjō cabinet's decision
to use Chinese captives for slave labor, dated November 27, 1942,
was found and used for the Chinese slave labor lawsuit that started at
the Tokyo District Court on June 28, 1995.[22] Establishing leadership responsibility for war crimes would have been relatively easy had these
kinds of documentation been available to the International Prosecution
Section at the time of the Tokyo trial.

To overcome these challenges posed in part by the Japanese government's obstructionism and in part by Keenan's lack of foresight,
the Allied prosecutors devised a strategic argument that would help
fix responsibility on individual defendants. They argued that the mistreatment of prisoners of war, civilian internees, and other non-interned
civilians in occupied territories was so widespread and followed such
strikingly similar patterns that only one inference was possible: those in

leadership circles must have authorized the commission of war crimes as a general policy of the Japanese war and military occupation. In the words of the Australian lead prosecutor, Alan Mansfield (Fig. 5.2), the prosecution's position was the following: "This similarity of treatment throughout the territories occupied by the Japanese forces will lead to the conclusion that such mistreatment was the result not of the independent acts of the individual Japanese Commanders and soldiers, but of the general policy of the Japanese forces and of the Japanese Government."[23] Treating this as the guiding principle, each national prosecution team separately gathered, selected, and arranged their evidentiary materials. Their shared goal was to demonstrate the recurrence of the same patterns of atrocities throughout the Pacific theater and to compel the judges to infer knowledge on the part of the highest-ranking Japanese government and military leaders. To achieve this, the Allied prosecutors had to seek evidentiary material widely, and to document war crimes thoroughly, so that various common patterns of Japanese-perpetrated atrocities would emerge from the wealth of evidence.

Some fifteen general patterns of Japanese war crimes were listed in an appendix to the indictment. Nine of them concerned war crimes targeted at Allied prisoners of war, military medical personnel, the sick and wounded, and Allied citizens who were held in internment camps. They included murder, torture, rape, and other acts of physical abuse; the use of prisoner-of-war labor for military projects under cruel conditions; refusal to provide proper food, water, clothing, or shelter with sanitary facilities; excessive and illegal punishments; disregard of the rights of the sick and wounded, medical personnel, and nurses; and failure to keep proper records of prisoners of war and to transmit their information to the countries concerned. Five particulars in the list concerned illegal methods of warfare Japan used on land and sea. They were the use of poisonous gas in China; destruction and looting of enemy property without military justification; killing of survivors of torpedoed ships; disregard of rights accorded to military hospital ships; and attacks on neutral ships. One remaining particular enumerated a variety of civilian-targeted atrocities. These included the "[f]ailure to respect family honor and rights, individual life, private property and religious convictions and worship in occupied territories, and deportation

Fig. 5.2   Alan J. Mansfield, Associate Prosecutor from Australia. Courtesy National Archives, photo no. 238-FE.

and enslavement of the inhabitants thereof." It was further explained, "Large numbers of the inhabitants of such territories were murdered, tortured, raped, and otherwise ill-treated, arrested and interned without justification, sent to forced labour, and their property destroyed or confiscated."[24]

During the trial, the International Prosecution Section substantiated all acts listed in the indictment except the use of poison gas.[25] Other than the listed types of war crimes, the prosecutors provided additional evidence concerning other types of war crimes that had been implied but not specifically indicated as separate particulars in the indictment. The additional patterns of civilian-targeted atrocities were: massacres targeted at the civilian populations in Asia and on the Pacific islands on racial, ethnic, political, or economic grounds; deportation and use of numerous Asian civilians as slave laborers; torture and murder perpetrated by the Japanese military police against those who fell into its custody; and sexual enslavement of women who fell under Japanese military control. With respect to mistreatment specifically targeted at prisoners of war, the Allied prosecutors showed that Indian and Chinese prisoners of war were among the prominent ethnic groups that fell victim to torture, murder, and other forms of brutality. Chapters 6 and 7 will provided an in-depth analysis of the prosecution's case.

When collecting evidence of war crimes, most Allied prosecutors relied heavily on resources of the national-level war crimes trials that were held contemporaneously in other parts of the Pacific region. Consequently, the content of the prosecutorial effort at Tokyo was shaped by how the investigations and trials progressed at the national level. The Tokyo trial, in this respect, took on the appearance of the grand summation of the findings made by the Allied national trials leading up to January 1947 (when the International Prosecution Section concluded the presentation of its evidence).

Evidence collected by the Philippine prosecutor, Pedro Lopez, helps illustrate the connection between national and international war crimes investigations. To prepare his case, he extensively used the war crimes investigation reports that the U.S. Army under MacArthur prepared in the aftermath of the retaking of the Philippines in 1945. The judge advocate general of the Army promptly dispatched a team of investigators after the war, who visited the scenes of crimes, took affidavits from eyewitnesses, and filed more than 300 reports of Japanese war crimes with the Legal Section. These reports—14,618 pages worth—were at Lopez's disposal.[26] He also drew upon the records of the two trials that MacArthur's army had held in Manila prior to the Tokyo trial. They were the trials of Gen. Yamashita Tomoyuki and Gen. Homma Masaharu in connection with the Rape of Manila and the Bataan Death March respectively. The prosecutors from other Allied countries similarly made use of sources drawn from national war crimes investigations and trials. For example, the American prosecution member, James Robinson, used the records of the proceedings at the U.S. Navy's military commissions in Guam and Kwajalein when presenting evidence related to Japanese atrocities on central Pacific islands. The Australian prosecutor, Mansfield, used documents from the British war crimes court at Rangoon when presenting evidence concerning Japanese atrocities in Burma. Similarly, the French assistant prosecutor, Roger Depo, introduced the French government's memoranda concerning trials at the French war crimes court at Saigon.[27]

Some other prosecutors conducted war crimes investigations themselves in the former theaters of war. One such example is Lt. Col. J. S.
Sinninghe Damste, a member of the Dutch prosecution team. He was
a lawyer by profession and a former prisoner of war in the Japanese-
occupied Dutch East Indies. Prior to joining the International Prosecution Section, he spent about six weeks traveling across the Dutch East
Indies in order to gather evidence of Japanese war crimes. His assistant,
K. A. de Weerd, continued the investigations after Damste's departure
for Tokyo, subsequently flooding the Dutch prosecution team with
massive war crimes reports that it could hardly digest.[28] The Chinese
prosecutor, Hsiang Che-chun, and some of the American prosecution
staff, too, conducted war crimes investigations in China prior to the
opening of the Tokyo trial. The same applied to the Australian team to
a certain extent, in that Mansfield had been a member of the third Australian war crimes commission before joining the International Prosecution Section.

The link between the Tokyo trial and national war crimes trials is also
evident in the selection of witnesses. Col. Cyril H. D. Wild of the British
Army is a case in point. Fluent in Japanese, Wild had acted as a liaison
officer between Allied prisoners of war and Japanese officers since the
time of the surrender of British forces to Yamashita's army in Singapore
in February 1942. While remaining a Japanese captive, he visited a
number of prisoner-of-war camps in the Burma-Thailand area where the
Japanese undertook a railway construction project by using Allied prisoners of war and the Asian civilian population. When the war was over,
Wild served as a war crimes liaison officer for the Allied Land Forces,
Southeast Asia. Comyns-Carr subsequently called him to testify at Tokyo
in view of his very broad knowledge and personal experience of Japanese
mistreatment of prisoners of war.[29] There were three other British officers who, like Wild, were called to the witness stand because of their
experiences in war crimes investigations as well as their first-hand
knowledge of Japanese atrocities. They were Lt. Col. Nicholas D. J.
Read-Collins of the Royal Artillery, Maj. Cornelius Leenheer of the British Army, and Maj. C. G. Ringer of the British Indian Army. In the
aftermath of war, they served the British war crimes section, which was
affiliated with the Legal Section under MacArthur's occupation forces in
Japan. (The tasks Read-Collins and Leenheer performed for the Dutch

phase will be discussed in Chapter 7.) Similarly, Capt. Fernand Gabrillagues, who testified during the French presentation, was a French army delegate for the war crimes program in Indochina.[30]

The witnesses called by the Commonwealth team used were drawn largely from a pool of individuals whom the third Australian war crimes commission had interviewed in the aftermath of the war. Col. Albert Ernest Coates of the Australian Army Medical Corps was one such person. A surgeon and a medical officer, Coates became a prisoner of war early on. During his captivity, he witnessed the ghastly conditions of the sick and wounded in the Burma-Siam area while assisting them with what little medical care he could offer. He met Webb—then the chairman of the third Australian war crimes commission—in Melbourne in October 1945, revealing that he and his medical associates had kept extensive records of the circumstances of atrocities.[31] Lt. John Charles Van Nooten of the Australian Imperial Forces is another example. He met Mansfield—then an associate investigator of the third Australian war crimes commission—in Morotai in late September 1945. Finding Van Nooten to be one of the "very important witnesses" he examined in those months, Mansfield subsequently brought him to Tokyo in order to take oral evidence on the camp conditions in Ambon. (His role in the British Commonwealth presentation will be discussed in Chapter 7.)[32] Another crucial Australian witness was Warrant Officer William Hector Sticpewich of the Australian Imperial Forces. He survived the "Sandakan Death March," arguably the worst death march that Allied prisoners of war experienced in the Pacific theater in terms of its extremely high death rate. Mansfield interviewed Sticpewich in Morotai in October 1945, and later requested him to testify before the Tokyo Tribunal.[33]

Mansfield and the Synopsis Method

The International Prosecution Section gave its opening statement on June 4, 1946, and began presenting its evidence against the 28 defendants a week later. The prosecution's case was delivered in fifteen separate phases. Most concerned crimes against peace, but at least four were related to war crimes. The first of the four phases began on August 15, 1946. It focused on the atrocities the Japanese armed forces committed in China. This phase served partly to cap the preceding two that substantiated Japanese military aggression in Manchuria and the rest of

China. The lead prosecutor was Hsiang Che-chun, the chief prosecutor of the Shanghai High Court. He was assisted by Henry Chiu, also from China. Others who helped in the presentation of evidence were the Indian lead prosecutor, Govinda Menon, and three American attorneys: David Nelson Sutton, Capt. Arthur Sandusky, and Maj. John F. Hummel. This phase covered the Rape of Nanking and a number of other instances of Japanese-perpetrated atrocities between 1931 and 1945. The presentation was completed on September 5.

The evidence of war crimes related to other parts of the Pacific theater was given after all presentations concerning crimes against peace had been completed. On December 10, 1946, Pedro Lopez began to introduce evidence for the second phase of Japanese war crimes. He had been formally assigned to present evidence related to "crimes against humanity," but the cases he prepared were essentially war crimes, since all victims were either Filipinos or other Allied nationals. An American member, Solis Horwitz, assisted Lopez, but this phase was largely the Philippine prosecutor's one-man show. Six days later, Alan Mansfield picked up where Lopez left off and began presenting the third phase of Japanese war crimes. He took charge of war crimes that the Japanese forces had committed in the Pacific theater between 1941 and 1945 excepting the Philippines, which Lopez had already covered. The team assigned to Mansfield's phase was much larger than the teams that handled the three other phases on war crimes. The composition of the team was markedly multinational, too. It accommodated prosecutors from Australia, Canada, France, the Dutch East Indies, and the United States.

Under Mansfield's leadership, the Allied prosecutors divided the tasks of introducing evidence in accordance with which countries each represented. Mansfield himself formed one loose group with his Australian associate, Lt. Col. Mornane, and the Canadian prosecutor, Brigadier Henry Gratton Nolan. They dealt with cases that had to do primarily with the citizens of the British Commonwealth of Nations and the colonial subjects of the British Empire. Additionally, evidence related to Japanese transportation of prisoners of war by ship across the Pacific Ocean—known as "Hell Ships" due to the extremely cruel conditions that prisoners of war were forced to undergo on board—was introduced.[34] Sinninghe Damste took charge of evidence of Japanese atrocities relating to the Dutch territories in Southeast Asia. The areas he covered were the main islands of present-day Indonesia and surrounding islands: Java, Sumatra, the Celebes, Dutch Borneo, the Lesser Sunda Islands, and Timor. The third group was American, comprised of Cmdr. Charles T. Cole and Capt. James J. Robinson. Cole presented evidence of Japanese atrocities against Allied prisoners of war and civilian internees in China and Japan. Robinson's presentation focused on Japanese crimes against American citizens, in particular the crimes committed on central Pacific islands such as Wake Island, Kwajalein, and Chichijima. The two American members also introduced additional evidence regarding Japanese war crimes in the Philippines and on the high seas. The French lead prosecutor, Robert Oneto, and his assistant, Maj. Roger Depo, formed the fourth sub-team and introduced their evidence after the Americans. The French presentation was relatively small compared to the preceding ones given on behalf of the Philippines, the United States, and the British Commonwealth. This may be an indication either that the war crimes investigation in French Indochina was falling behind, or that the instances of Japanese war crimes were not as great in Indochina as in other Japanese-occupied territories. After the French presentation came the Soviet phase, for which only six pieces of evidence were introduced. This speaks for the relative insignificance of war crimes in the Russian experience of war with Japan. Notably, it was Alan Mansfield who presented the evidence on behalf of the Soviet Union and not the Russians themselves, even though there was no shortage of Soviet staff in the International Prosecution Section.

The fourth and last phase of war crimes proceedings was interposed when Cole and Robinson were presenting their case. Another American member, Gilbert S. Woolworth, was in charge of this phase. His task was to introduce evidence that would help substantiate the individual responsibility of the defendants. He aimed to establish that the Japanese government had the duty to ensure Japan's observance of the laws of war; that certain of the accused authorized the cruel and criminal treatment of enemy nationals in Japanese custody; and that they knew of many instances of ill-treatment because of the numerous protests from foreign governments. The evidence he presented was more supplementary than comprehensive, since other Allied prosecutors had presented some oral and documentary evidence relevant to their own cases. The entire war crimes phase ended on January 17, 1947.

The teams led by Lopez, Mansfield, and Woolworth managed to complete their presentations in only six weeks, between December 10, 1946, and January 17, 1947. This was quite a feat given the fact that the admitted evidence—which was principally documentary—was voluminous enough to match the one-year's worth of transcripts of the Nuremberg trial.[35] This conversely suggests that the Allied prosecutors presented their evidentiary material in a very abbreviated manner. Why did they compress the presentation of such voluminous evidence into such a short time span? Or to put the question differently, did they have to do so? The members of the International Prosecution Section asked these questions themselves just when the phases of crimes against peace were coming to an end.

Realizing that the trial proceedings had become extremely protracted, Keenan one day suggested that it might be wise to cut down the presentation of evidence related to war crimes or even give it up completely. When New Zealand Prosecutor Quilliam learned of this, he suspected that Keenan "had been criticised by General MacArthur and the United States Authorities because of the protracted nature of the proceedings," and consequently "conceived the idea of saving time by dropping these charges."[36] The associate prosecutors, in particular Mansfield, who led the largest team on war crimes, hardly welcomed the suggestion. When asked how much time he might need for his presentation, he informed the chief prosecutor that the estimated required time was ten weeks, but "[i]f a complete historical record of atrocities were presented, the phase would probably last twelve months." He added that he did not plan to spend so many months but that he considered the war crimes phase crucial in the prosecutorial effort. If evidence of atrocity was to be presented at Tokyo at all, "[it] must be dealt with properly," Mansfield said, "and I cannot contemplate that this important phase covering a period of four years and relating to many areas of the Pacific, could be properly presented in less time than ten weeks." He stressed that he was not simply expressing his personal opinion. The position held by the Australian and Dutch governments was that the prisoner-of-war phase was "one of the most important phases of this trial."[37] Keenan, in response, did not want to allow ten weeks for the presentation of this evidence. In the effort to persuade Mansfield not to spend so many weeks, he pointed out that according to the original agreement among the Allied governments, the Tokyo trial was to try those Japanese whose principal offenses were crimes against peace, and not war crimes or crimes against humanity. It would thus be unreasonable to spend so much time on charges that were only secondary to the original purpose of the trial. Mansfield would not budge, however. He replied that he would be the first to adopt a shorter method of presentation if available, but, "if no shorter method can be evolved, I would definitely resist an arbitrary limit being placed on the time for presenting this part of the prosecution case."[38]

Keenan eventually took the matter before all associate prosecutors, seemingly hoping to receive support from them. He was instead confronted with united opposition. Mansfield and Lopez in particular challenged his proposal. According to Quilliam's account, they both "stressed that their Countries and other Countries attached great importance to the offences in respect of treatment of Prisoners of War and civilians," and "further pointed out that following the Charter the Indictment charged these offenses and in Keenan's Opening Address considerable attention had been devoted to them." In other words, it was not only the associate prosecutors who regarded the substantiation of war crimes as a matter of priority. Keenan himself had publicly spoken of it as the centerpiece of the prosecutorial effort at the outset. Mansfield and Lopez also pointed out that the prosecution had already given a significant amount of evidence concerning Japanese atrocities (referring to the evidence related to Japanese war crimes in China). In this light, "to abandon them would be misunderstood and would be harmful" for the overall case made by the International Prosecution Section. Quilliam agreed, and told Keenan that "the discussion was being held six or nine months too late." This was an apt observation, but it "roused Keenan to anger."[39] Finding that virtually all other lead prosecutors stood against him, however, he had no choice but to withdraw his suggestion.

Meanwhile, Mansfield began to contemplate if there were any way at all to shorten the time for presenting the evidence of Japanese war crimes. He himself was aware that the trial had become exceedingly protracted. While opposing Keenan, he felt hard-pressed to expedite the prosecution's case. He found a solution to this dilemma when the Dutch assistant prosecutor, Damste, came up with a method of expeditious presentation.[40] The proposed method—which the judges approved—was as follows.[41] Those prosecutors who took charge of substantiating war crimes would use synopses when presenting evidence. Each synopsis would include summaries of documents to be introduced. The prosecutors would read the synopsis instead of the entire court exhibits. They were free to read extracts or the whole text of the admitted evidence, but doing so would not be required. The use of synopses would not diminish the probative value of the evidentiary material, since the judgment of the Tribunal would be based on the whole of admitted evidence, not on the synopses, regardless of whether it had been read in court. The Tribunal further allowed that the prosecutors would be required to translate only those sections in each document that were to be introduced in evidence. Copies of original documents (from which the prosecution was to select excerpts) had to be distributed to defense counsel as well as to the judges, but they did not have to be translated into Japanese. By this decision, the International Prosecution Section would be able to save much time and labor that they would otherwise have had to spend on onerous translation tasks. The absence of Japanese translation of the English-language documents might handicap the Japanese defense lawyers; there were, however, American defense lawyers who assisted them, and some Japanese lawyers could read English. The judges apparently concluded that the disadvantages that the defendants might incur fell within the range of acceptability. After all, the pressure to expedite the trial was sufficiently great to make these plans practical solutions to a real problem.

With the application of the synopsis method and the selective translation of evidentiary documents, the prosecution was able to present the voluminous documentary evidence in a much shorter time than planned. Mansfield had initially projected that the required minimum time was ten weeks. In the end, Lopez, Mansfield, and Woolworth together presented all of their evidence in six weeks. The defense team, for its part, objected to the use of synopses, but raised no further objections once Mansfield began his phase. It complained only on a few occasions during the Dutch presentation but not because it found the use of synopses prejudicial to the accused. Rather, the defense found that the Dutch prosecutor misrepresented the content of certain court exhibits in the synopses.

The brisk presentation method had a downside, however. It deprived court exhibits of their potential educational impact because each document was reduced to a summary of just a few sentences in the synopses. An abridged account of war crimes could hardly convey to the Japanese spectators in the court gallery the shocking circumstances in which the Japanese armed forces committed war crimes. There were occasions when the Allied prosecutors chose to read out certain parts or the whole of the evidentiary material, but generally they refrained from reading out the court exhibits lest doing so would lead to the undue prolongation of the trial. How this particular method of presentation affected the Tokyo trial's educational mission will be explored further in Chapter 7.

SIX

Nanking and the Death Railway

Of all war crimes committed by the Japanese armed forces, the Rape of Nanking and the Burma-Siam Death Railway were comparatively easy cases to substantiate. A number of contemporaneous witnesses had documented the occurrence of these atrocities, and their records were available to the International Prosecution Section. There were also Japanese government officials and military officers who could testify about the culpability of certain defendants. The exceptional wealth of oral and documentary evidence promised that the International Prosecution Section could make compelling presentations before the Tribunal. This chapter focuses on these two episodes of large-scale war crimes, analyzes the findings of the judges, and considers their historical significance.

The Rape of Nanking

Japan began pursuing military conquest of China following the Mukden Incident in 1931, and launched its armed attack afresh in the vicinity of present-day Beijing in July 1937. Whereas the war zone quickly spread across central and northern China, Shanghai became the main battleground between the Japanese and Chiang Kai-shek's forces. The latter fought with great tenacity in Shanghai, confounding Japan's expectation for an early victory. Only after a long and bitter fight did the Japanese forces overwhelm Chiang's troops. The Japanese army reorganized, combining the Shanghai Expeditionary Force with the Tenth Army to form the Central China Area Army. Gen. Matsui Iwane took command and deployed his troops westward to Nanking—the seat of Chiang Kai-shek's Nationalist government—with the goal of capturing it. Chiang, in the meantime, made a tactical decision to abandon the capital instead of risking another major battle.[1] Consequently, the walled city of Nanking fell into the hands of the Japanese army with little resistance on December 13, 1937.

The Japanese troops began committing acts of violence against the Chinese civilian population as they made their advance in the Shanghai to Nanking stretch.[2] At this early phase of war the Japanese army was already gaining notoriety for sexual violence as well as other forms of cruelty. The Japanese military code explicitly prohibited rape; common articles 86 and 88 of the army and navy criminal regulations stipulated that those who committed rape would be punished by penalties ranging from imprisonment (seven years) to death.[3] Soon after the outbreak of war in 1937, Japanese military authorities attempted to address the outbreak of widespread disciplinary problems by holding a number of courts-martial. However, the Japanese military justice system proved largely ineffective.[4] To complicate this state of affairs, field commanders condoned rape, massacre, arson, and other forms of violence that accompanied the "requisition" effort in Chinese villages, which was in substance the authorization to pillage. Their superiors' implicit approval to loot soon created an environment conducive for Japanese soldiers to defy the military code openly and to commit war crimes with impunity. Even after capturing Nanking, Japanese soldiers continued to inflict violence against Chinese civilians in broad daylight and on a vast scale with the understanding that their military superiors tacitly recognized their entitlement to the spoils of war as rewards for prolonged and exhausting battles.[5]

At the Tokyo trial, the Chinese prosecution team treated large-scale Japanese military violence against civilians and prisoners of war in Nanking as the centerpiece of its presentation on war crimes. It introduced a large number of affidavits, depositions, and statements that had been taken from victims and witnesses. It also presented official reports made by foreign embassies in China and various other records of the atrocities that were kept by foreign residents in Nanking.[6] Documentary evidence aside, about a dozen witnesses were called to the stand to give testimony. This may appear to be a rather small number of witnesses when compared with the much larger number being brought to the international criminal courts today. However, a dozen witnesses was an unusually large number by the standards of the Tokyo Tribunal. The common practice was to limit the number of witnesses and to rely on documentary evidence, seemingly in consideration of the time constraints as well as of logistical problems in locating and bringing witnesses from overseas. When the Allied prosecutors did bring in witnesses, they did so only sparingly. The average number was one or two per episode of war crime, and only for singularly important cases. The exceptionally large group of witnesses for the Nanking portion of the trial attests to the importance the International Prosecution Section attached to this case.

The circumstances of the atrocities as established by the prosecution can be summarized by the following three points. First, the Japanese armed forces committed massacre, rape, looting, and various other inhumane acts against Chinese civilians and disarmed soldiers as soon as they captured Nanking, even though armed resistance had ended at the time of their entry in the city. Atrocities continued on a large scale for at least the initial six weeks, and sporadically thereafter. Second, those Chinese refugees who fled to the Nanking Safety Zone were repeatedly attacked as well. Prior to the Japanese invasion, a group of foreign residents—mostly Germans and Americans who had lived for years in the city as professors, doctors, businessmen, and missionaries—voluntarily formed an International Committee for Establishment of the Safety Zone. They designated a large sector within the city of Nanking as a protected area to ensure the safety of civilians from armed conflict. The Japanese forces disregarded the Safety Zone, however. Despite repeated protests from the International Committee, Japanese soldiers freely entered the protected area, took away Chinese male and female refugees, and carried out summary executions, rape, murder, and other forms of violence. With respect to the scale of rape, John H. D. Rabe—a German businessman who served as chairman of the International Committee—reported at least 20,000 known cases of rape within and outside the Safety Zone in the initial six weeks of Japanese military occupation.[7] Third, the prosecution's evidence showed that some cabinet-level leaders of the central government in Tokyo as well as top military officers of the Central China Area Army were informed of the atrocities committed by the Japanese troops, since they received reports from their diplomatic representatives, journalists, and other sources in China from early on. Of the 28 accused, those implicated by the prosecution's evidence were Matsui Iwane, the commander-in-chief of the Central China Area Army, Mutō Akira, the vice chief of staff of Matsui's army, and Hirota Kōki, the foreign minister of Japan (Fig. 6.1). It was shown that all three had received information about the atrocities committed by the Japanese forces continually and contemporaneously.[8]

What did the defense do when confronted with the prosecution's overwhelming documentary and oral evidence of Japanese-perpetrated war crimes in Nanking? The answer is fairly straightforward: the defense did little to contest it. The failure to challenge the prosecution's evidence was most palpable when witnesses from Nanking appeared in court in person. When survivors of concrete instances of atrocity were called to the stand, the defense usually passed on the opportunity to cross-examine them or asked only a few perfunctory—and mostly immaterial—questions. With their half-hearted attempts at cross-examination, the defense tacitly affirmed the credibility of the prosecution's witnesses. The following two episodes help illustrate the nature of the defense cross-examination, or the lack thereof.[9]

A resident of the city of Nanking, Shang Teh-yi, was called to the witness stand to give testimony on the summary execution that he had survived. At eleven o'clock on the morning of December 16, 1937, Japanese soldiers arrested the witness, his elder brother, his cousin, and five other male neighbors. The captives were bound by rope and forcefully taken to the banks of the Yangtze River along with more than 1,000 other Chinese male civilians. The Japanese soldiers who arrested them were acting presumably under the direction of the Sixteenth Division, commanded by Lt. Nakajima Kesago, of the Shanghai Expeditionary Force. Shang testified that at around four o'clock in the afternoon of that day, the Japanese army began carrying out summary executions of the captured men at the riverbank. They used machine guns, which had been set up within 40 to 50 yards from the captives. The witness survived the massacre because he fell before the firing started. Corpses that tumbled over him shielded him during the shooting. Once the prosecution finished taking testimony from Shang, defense counsel was given the chance to cross-examine the witness. However, neither Japanese nor American defense lawyers came forward to take up the task.

Fig. 6.1 Defendants in the dock. Front row, left to right: Hata Shunroku; Hirota Kōki; and Minami Jirō. Back row, left to right: Hashimoto Kingorō; Koiso Kuniaki; Ōshima Hiroshi; and Matsui Iwane. Courtesy National Archives, photo no. 238-FE.

An American defense lawyer, Capt. Alfred Brooks, simply informed the Tribunal that there would be "[n]o-cross-examination on the part of the defense." The defense, in this manner, voluntarily renounced its right to cross-examine Shang. This can be interpreted as the defense admission that this witness and his testimony were credible.[10]

A survivor of a separate instance of mass execution appeared in court next. He offered testimony that resembled that given by the preceding witness. The 38-year-old witness, Wu Chang-teh, was a grocer and a former city policeman. At the time of the Japanese invasion, he surrendered his arms to the International Committee for the Safety Zone and sought refuge. However, Japanese soldiers forcefully took him and some 300 other disarmed policemen out of the Safety Zone to the western gate of the city. A total of approximately 1,600 males had been gathered. According to Wu's testimony, the Japanese soldiers took these captives outside the gate in groups of about 100 each. The Japanese army then methodically executed them using machine guns. The bullet-riddled bodies were allowed to fall into the canal that ran by the gate. Wu testified that he attempted to escape from the scene of mass execution but that he was shot at and bayoneted from the back. Luckily, he survived because he had played dead and because his bayonet wounds were deep

but not fatal. Wu's testimony was another crucial firsthand account of
mass execution, told by an actual survivor of a massacre.[11] Given the
systematic way in which the massacre was carried out, and given that the
same method of killing was applied in the two instances of mass execution, Wu's testimony could weigh greatly with the judges. But again,
defense counsel declined cross-examination, thereby implicitly admitting
that the witness account was credible.

There were occasions when the defense team attempted to challenge
the prosecution's witnesses, especially those who were not direct victims
of Japanese atrocities. However, such efforts usually ended in failure.
The defense would unwittingly strengthen the credibility of the witnesses, or even draw further incriminating evidence against the defendants. An American defense lawyer, William Logan, committed one such
misstep when cross-examining a prosecution witness, Miner Bates.

An American citizen, Bates had taught history at the University of
Nanking since 1920, and was one of the original members of the International Committee for the Safety Zone. The central issue in his testimony was what he knew about the Japanese authorities' handling of
the information concerning mass atrocities committed by the occupying Japanese armed forces. According to Bates's account, he filed reports and complaints about the atrocities at the Japanese embassy in
Nanking almost daily for the first three weeks of the Japanese occupation. He testified that the embassy people were generally sympathetic
but that they could not take effective action since they were afraid of
the army. As an alternative way to handle the situation, the embassy
staff forwarded Bates's many reports and protests to the Japanese foreign ministry via the diplomatic representative in Shanghai.[12] When
Logan began his cross-examination, he challenged the witness's claim
that the embassy staff in Nanking transmitted Bates's reports to Tokyo.
He attempted to elicit that, contrary to what the witness testified, the
Japanese embassy might not have actually forwarded the messages, and
that Foreign Minister Hirota in Tokyo might not have been informed
of the Japanese military violence in Nanking. In other words, Logan
suggested that Bates's information could be mere hearsay with no basis
to support it. If his testimony could not substantiate the accused Hirota's knowledge, Logan seemed to suggest, the allegation of criminal
negligence against him could not stand.

Logan's line of defense collapsed as soon as he began to initiate it in court, however, since Bates already had further words to add in support of his testimony. Responding to Logan's questioning, he testified that he had personally seen some telegrams that mentioned his protests, sent by the American ambassador to Tokyo, Joseph Grew, to the American embassy in Nanking. The telegrams stated that Ambassador Grew discussed Bates's reports with officials from the Japanese foreign ministry, including its chief, Hirota. Bates further stated, "I should be glad to give you some more evidence from Japanese sources on that." Logan was taken off guard by the unexpected answers that potentially incriminated Hirota. In a flurry, he requested the court stenographer to strike the answers from the trial transcripts and appealed to the Tribunal that the witness should be directed not to "volunteer" additional answers without being asked. Hearing this objection, Justice Webb agreed that "[h]e must, of course, confine his answer to the question," but also said that "he may add any explanation," thereby allowing Bates's statements to stand. In this manner, Logan's cross-examination resulted in unnecessarily extracting a crucial piece of evidence against the accused Hirota.[13]

The cross-examinations by Japanese defense lawyers tended to be more problematic than those conducted by American lawyers, because most of them had little training in the adversarial system and did not fully understand how to carry out cross-examinations effectively.[14] Consider, for instance, the one conducted by Itō Kiyoshi (representing the accused Matsui). He interrogated a prosecution witness, Dr. Hsu Chuan-ying. A 62-year-old resident of Nanking, Hsu had served as deputy chairman of the Red Swastika Society, a charitable organization that buried the massacred people at the time of the atrocities in Nanking. During the examination-in-chief, Hsu gave testimony on forced marches, summary executions, murder, rape, and other crimes that the Japanese soldiers committed that he had heard about or witnessed. When challenging this witness, Itō attempted to make him admit that the Chinese troops, *too*, habitually committed rape and looting. Such admission, Itō seemed to believe, would cancel out the guilt on the part of the Japanese. There was an inherent problem in this line of argument, however, as Justice Webb warned Itō: "I must remind you that rape and the murder of women could never be just reprisals. You are assuming that, if the Japanese did the things said to be done by the witness, they were just reprisal. Rape and murder of women and such like things could never be just reprisals, and it is useless to continue your cross-examination along those lines."[15]

On this occasion, Itō attempted to make the witness admit that Chiang Kai-shek's forces were equally culpable for perpetrating war crimes and to argue that the Japanese forces, in any event, had the right of reprisal for the damages they incurred in fighting Chiang's army. As Webb pointed out, such an admission could not by any stretch constitute a defense. No armed forces were justified in committing sexual violence against women under any circumstances, not to mention by way of reprisal. Itō eventually gave up cross-examining Hsu, since he could not extract the kind of confessional testimony he sought. As Itō motioned to leave the lectern, he complained to the Tribunal, saying, "As far as my competency is concerned, I cannot get the facts or the truth from this witness, and so I regret that I'll have to terminate here." This statement did not please Webb, who promptly warned him: "You must not reflect on the witness. We may have to deal with you if you do."[16]

There were some adept lawyers among the American defense team, but even they did not fare well during the Nanking phase. Take, for example, the cross-examination conducted by Capt. Alfred Brooks. He examined John Magee, an American priest of the Episcopal Church, who lived in Nanking between 1912 and 1940. Magee was a member of the International Committee for the Safety Zone, and also recorded some of the Nanking atrocities on film. (This visual evidence was not presented at the Tokyo trial.) While on the witness stand, Magee gave testimony about various episodes of atrocity that the Japanese forces committed in and around Nanking in the initial months of occupation. He witnessed some of them and received reports on a number of other cases from victims and witnesses. The stories he told the Tribunal were all harrowing, such as the one that he had heard from a fifteen-year-old rape victim and that he related in court:

I took this girl to the hospital at some time in February 1938. I talk to her then at length and then saw her many times after that. She was from the city of Wufu, about sixty miles from Nanking. Japanese soldiers came to her home—her father was a shop-keeper—accused her brother of being a soldier, and killed him. The girl said her brother was not a soldier. They killed her brother's wife because she resisted rape; they killed her older sister because she resisted rape.

In the meantime her old father and mother were kneeling before them, and they killed them, all of these people being killed with a bayonet. The girl fainted. They carried her to some barracks of some kind where they kept her for two months. The first month she was raped repeatedly, daily. They had taken her clothes away from her and locked her in a room. After that she became so diseased, they were afraid of her, and she was sick there for a whole month.[17]

The cruelties the Japanese soldiers inflicted on this victim and her family members are beyond description. Yet recent Japanese scholarship shows that Japanese troops committed this kind of indiscriminate murder and rape of civilians on a vast scale in various combat zones during the war in China.[18]

When confronted with shocking episodes of Japanese war crimes such as this, Brooks interrogated Bates with the goal of exposing inconsistencies or any other weaknesses in his testimony. Specifically, he attempted to explore the following possibilities: (1) that those Chinese males who were summarily executed by the Japanese troops were Chinese combatants in plain clothes; (2) that the atrocities were committed by individual Japanese soldiers, and not carried out as part of military policy; (3) that those individual soldiers who committed atrocities had already been court-martialed or had otherwise received proper disciplinary treatment from the Japanese military justice system; and (4) that most of the information Magee had was mere hearsay with no basis to support it. Brooks's intense questioning, however, could neither undermine the credibility of Magee's testimony nor elicit substantiation of any of the possibilities Brooks aimed to indicate. In fact, it did not take long for him to conclude that this witness was believable. Webb quickly recognized the change in the tone of Brooks's cross-examination. At one point, he interrupted and said, "I judge from your attitude that you are not really attacking the witness' credibility." Brooks, in response, said, "I think the witness has been very fair," thereby candidly affirming the correctness of Webb's observation. A while later, Webb interrupted again, saying, "Having admitted the credibility of this witness, the scope of your cross-examination has, of course, been very severely limited." He added, "The further the cross-examination goes the less favorable it becomes for the defense. You have to decide, Captain Brooks, whether you can profitably carry on this cross-examination." Brooks replied by saying, "I believe the witness is trying to be fair, your Honor," again affirming that he had little doubt about Magee's credibility. He wrapped up the cross-examination soon thereafter, following Webb's recommendation.[19] This episode attests to the difficulty—if not the impossibility—that defense counsel faced in its effort to rebut the prosecution's witnesses.

Defense counsel made no more than a perfunctory effort to challenge the prosecution's case when they were given full opportunity to tell their side of the story in court a year later. They initially professed to prove, among other things, that the stories of atrocities were in some cases exaggerated; that the alleged atrocities had been in fact committed by the Chinese; that the Chinese soldiers were mere "bandits, irregulars, or guerrillas," who were not entitled to legal protection as combatants under international law; and that the guilty ones had already been punished by courts-martial.[20] Having promised to prove these points, however, the defense produced little evidence to substantiate the claims. It introduced only eight poorly selected pieces of evidence (five of which were rejected). The number of witnesses, too, was limited to three. The paucity of evidence indicates that the defense effort at rebuttal was half-hearted at best. This came as a surprise to those Japanese spectators who had been following the trial proceedings from the court gallery. Kojima Noboru, then a high-school boy who later wrote a narrative history of the Tokyo trial, commented that "the defense 'counterattack' was surprisingly skimpy [*igaina hodo tanpaku*]" and wrote, further, that those in the courtroom were "dumb-founded [*akke ni torareta*]" by the abrupt conclusion of the defense presentation. Those who observed the trial—as many as 2,000 Japanese spectators on average visited the court each week in those days—understood that the Rape of Nanking was central to the prosecution's case on war crimes. However, all they saw in court was the defense lawyers' visible reluctance to confront the case, to the point of admitting Japanese guilt.[21]

The three main witnesses that defense counsel called to the stand were Hidaka Shinrokurō, the former Japanese consul in Shanghai; Col. Tsukamoto Kōji, the former chief of the Judicial Department of the Tenth Army; and Col. Nakayama Yasuto, a former staff member of the Central China Area Army. Generally speaking, the testimonies given by the three witnesses affirmed—though in varying manners—the prosecution's basic contention that the Japanese soldiers committed mass atrocities against Chinese civilians and prisoners of war in the aftermath of the fall of Nanking. Moreover, the three helped corroborate the responsibility of the accused Matsui, the commander-in-chief of the Central China Area Army. The following are the key facts that emerged from the three testimonial accounts: (1) that Matsui had been concerned about the general lack of discipline of his forces from the time of the conquest of Shanghai to the invasion of Nanking; (2) that he received information of atrocities committed by his troops soon after the capture of the city; (3) that he disapproved of the atrocities; (4) that he gave orders to his subordinates to observe strict discipline, both before and after the invasion; and (5) that despite his orders, the atrocities did not subside.[22] In all probability, the defense witnesses assumed that their accounts helped exonerate Matsui or at least served as mitigating factors, since they showed that Matsui personally disapproved of the atrocity. In reality, however, their testimony had just the opposite effect; it actually helped substantiate Matsui's guilt. The three witnesses essentially showed that the accused failed to exhaust all means available to him to stop the atrocities even though he knew, or had reason to know, that his subordinates were prone to commit, and did indeed commit, murder and rape of innocent people. In other words, the three key defense witnesses imputed knowledge to him and corroborated his dereliction of duty.

Right-wing nationalists and certain conservative politicians in Japan today contend that the Nanking atrocity never happened, or to draw upon their common parlance, that the Rape of Nanking was a "phantom" [*maboroshi*] created by the Tokyo trial.[23] The defense witnesses, the defense lawyers, and even the defendants themselves at Tokyo were far less daring, however, and would not concur with such claims. Consider, for instance, the opinion of a Japanese defense lawyer, Sugawara Yutaka. He had initially believed that the fleeing Chiang Kai-shek forces were responsible for the large-scale atrocities and that the Chinese prosecution team was making false allegations for propaganda purposes. However, he had to change his view when confronted with the prosecution's overwhelming evidence. He later described his coming-to-terms with the Japanese army's conduct in Nanking:

We, the Japanese defense lawyers, too, initially listened with a sneer, thinking that they [the prosecutors] were simply engaging in a malicious propaganda effort in order to shift the responsibility for the atrocities that had been routinely committed by the retreating Chinese army to the Japanese army. However, we had to somehow correct our thinking as the trial progressed. For sure, 80 to 90 percent of what they testified should be regarded as false and exaggerated. But we were compelled to suspect, to our regret, that 20 percent of it did actually take place. This was an admission of a sad fact—a fact sadder than the defeat of Japan—for the Japanese race, since nothing like this was ever heard of [*zendai mimon*] at the time of the Sino-Japanese War or the Russo-Japanese War.[24]

Though unwilling to accept the veracity of the prosecution's case in its entirety, Sugawara was resigned to admitting that the Japanese army committed violence on an unprecedented scale against innocent Chinese people in Nanking. He brooded that this would remain an indelible stain in the history of the Japanese race.

Another Japanese defense lawyer, Takigawa Masajirō, held a similar view. In the memoirs he published in 1953, he remarked that he "cannot bring [himself] to record the atrocities attested by these witnesses," since "while their testimony has some exaggeration, it is an indisputable fact [*ooi gataki jijitsu*] that the outrages the Japanese army committed against the citizens of Nanking after the capture of the city were dreadful [*sōtō hidoi monodatta*]." He went on to write that he personally visited Nanking, in the aftermath of the atrocities in 1938, to verify the rumors:

I lived in Peking in those days, but made a trip to Nanking by the Shinpo Line in the summer of 1938 because the rumors of the Nanking atrocity were very widespread. Finding that most houses were burned down in the urban area of Nanking, I presumed that they were burned due to the Japanese army's aerial bombardment. I was stunned by the power of the air raids. However, I learned from my close inquiries that all of these houses had actually been burned by the Japanese soldiers in the aftermath of the fall of Nanking. The sense of fear toward the Japanese had not dissipated among the citizens of Nanking yet, even though half a year had passed by then. When I gently talked to girls and women, they would run away and hide without responding. According to the account given to me by the chauffeur who drove me around, there was not a single woman who now lived within the city of Nanking and who had not been raped by the Japanese soldiers.[25]

From his personal observations, Takigawa concluded that the Japanese soldiers indeed committed rape and other cruelties on a vast scale against citizens of Nanking. His recollection also indicates that Japanese military violence in Nanking was widely acknowledged in Japanese expatriate communities. Such information might not have reached the people in Japan proper due to government and military censorship, but it apparently was carried far and wide through informal routes among Japanese people in China.

The defense lawyers were not the only ones who admitted the Japanese perpetration of atrocities in Nanking. Those defendants who testified on their own behalf, while downplaying the scale of atrocity, also admitted that Japanese soldiers had committed brutalities against the citizens of Nanking. The accused Mutō Akira was one such individual. He testified during the pretrial investigation that "[i]n the case of Nanking, two or three battalions were to enter the city. However, the whole army entered within the walls, *thereby resulting in the rape of Nanking [Nankin ryakudatsu bōkō jiken]*." When asked by the Allied interrogator, "Has it not troubled your conscience to find that so many innocent women and children were either killed or raped, either in China or the Philippines?" Mutō answered, "After the atrocities in Nanking and Manila, and being a member of the General Staff during both incidents, I felt that something was lacking in Japanese military education."[26] This reply shows not only Mutō's full awareness that the Japanese servicemen were habitually committing atrocities in different theaters of war, but also his view that military education may have been partly to blame for the Japanese soldiers' proclivity to violence. Once in court, Mutō offered consistent accounts as he testified: "After the formal entry at Nanking was held on 17 December, General MATSUI heard for the first time from Chief of Staff TSUKADA that most of the units had entered the city against the commander's order; that, following the entry of the units, *plunder and rape cases occurred there.*"[27] These accounts show that even the senior staff officer of Matsui's army did not dispute the fact that Japanese troops had committed violence against civilians in Nanking.

The Tokyo Precedents

The prosecution held three defendants directly answerable for the occurrence of atrocities in Nanking: Matsui Iwane, Mutō Akira, and Hirota Kōki. The prosecution's case against Matsui was based broadly on the theory of command responsibility in that the prosecutors accused him of failing to fulfill his duty to stop atrocities committed by his subordinates. He was not accused of giving orders or authorizations to commit war crimes. Since no one disputed the fact that Matsui had been the commander of the Japanese forces in Nanking, the prosecutorial effort centered on substantiating his knowledge of war crimes and his failure to take adequate measures to stop them. Matsui, for his part, took the witness stand himself in an effort to counter the prosecution's allegations. He denied knowledge of the atrocities and, at times, even his possession of the power and authority to stop them. However, he occasionally gave accounts that contradicted these denials. He contended that he, in fact, took actions in order to prevent atrocities and to punish perpetrators. Such contentions conversely substantiated his knowledge of atrocities as well as his power and duty to stop them. In the final analysis, Matsui became so caught up in the effort to deny all of prosecution's accusations that he failed to present credible testimony.

Let us analyze Matsui's defense in greater detail. With regard to his knowledge of the atrocities, his basic line of defense was to insist that he did not know, and could not have known, about the events in Nanking, because he was sick in bed in Soochow—140 miles away from Nanking—when his forces captured the city.[28] He admitted, however, that the two divisional commanders who were directly subordinate to him regularly reported to him on the progress of military operations. This part of his testimony indicated that Matsui knew, or had reason to know, that his troops were committing violence against innocent civilians and disarmed prisoners of war irrespective of his absence from Nanking.[29] Other evidentiary material affirmed that Matsui indeed learned about the atrocities, at the latest, when he made a triumphal entry into Nanking on December 17. Commanders and divisional commanders of his army, as well as Japanese diplomats in the area, informed him of the many outrages his troops had committed in preceding days.[30] He stayed in the city for about a week, during which atrocities continued to take place. Given these facts, it would have been hard for him to insist that he had no knowledge of war crimes. Furthermore, Matsui conceded that "in the busy and unsettled condition at the time of the capture of Nanking, it may have been some excited young officers and men who committed unpleasant outrages,"[31] thereby admitting in a roundabout way that his troops engaged in atrocities and that he knew about them. When asked what were the "unpleasant outrages," Matsui readily replied, "Rape, looting, forceful seizure of materials." He added that "murder," too, was one of the common outrages committed by his troops, about which he received reports from the Japanese military police.[32] These statements pointed to Matsui's awareness that his troops committed grave war crimes.

In yet another effort to deny his or other Japanese soldiers' responsibility for the mass atrocities, Matsui contended that the fleeing Chinese troops and outlaws were actually to blame. Hearing this, Myron Cramer—the American justice who was then serving as acting president of the tribunal—inquired on what basis Matsui made the allegation. Cramer asked, "You stated on the 14th of November that HAKAYAMA and HIDAKA reported atrocities committed by Chinese troops in Nanking. How many cases are reported to you?" Matsui then replied, "I did not hear any specific facts in regard to those. They only told me, conveyed to me of *general rumors* in regard to those cases."[33] By this response, Matsui conceded that his statement attributing guilt to the Chinese soldiers had no supporting objective evidence.

His testimony with regard to his duty as commander-in-chief of the occupying Japanese forces was equally evasive. On the one hand, Matsui contended that in his capacity as commander of the army, he ordered his troops to maintain discipline before entering the city. He also testified that he ordered the investigation of war crimes as soon as he learned about his troops' conduct after the triumphal entry. Having emphasized his fulfillment of these duties, however, Matsui made other statements that contradicted these accounts. On one occasion, he testified that he "did not have the authority directly to handle the discipline and morals" of his troops. He further told the Tribunal, "I had no authority except to express my desires as over-all Commander-in-Chief to the commander of the army under my command and the divisional commanders thereunder."[34] In other words, he claimed that he had no substantive power to take control of his forces even though he was the highest commanding officer of the army. Elaborating his point, Matsui remarked, "The authority that was vested in me was to command—was the overall operational command of the two armies under me. That was all. Hence it would be a very difficult matter to determine my legal responsibilities with regard to my—to the question of discipline and morals and I cannot make any statement, any definite statement, on that at the present time."[35] In this statement, Matsui declined to comment on the question of what constituted "my legal responsibilities," since it was "a very difficult matter to determine." He did not hesitate, however, to allude to the responsibility that his subordinate officers incurred.

An astute trial observer and a member of the defense counsel, Kainō Michitaka, took note of Matsui's evasive testimony. Recalling this portion of the witness account, Kainō later commented that, "Gen. Matsui, who was the Commander-in-Chief of the Army that committed these acts, knew the facts of the outrages, but simply watched blankly from the sidelines for the reason that he had no authority [*kengen ga naikara, pokanto shite bōkan shiteita to iu node aru*]." Matsui's allusion to the guilt of his subordinate officers also appeared very ironic to Kainō, since "the responsible army commander who had received instructions from Matsui was no one else but Lt. Gen. Prince Asaka, a member of the Imperial Family to whom all defendants used to express unanimous respect." Prince Asaka was the commander of the Shanghai Expeditionary Force, one of the two armies that fell under Matsui's direct control. While ordinarily revering the imperial family, Matsui was prepared to blame a member of it in order to escape the criminal accusation leveled against himself.[36]

The arguments Matsui advanced bear a striking resemblance to those advanced at a contemporaneous war crimes trial at Nuremberg: the Hostage Case (*U.S.* v. *Wilhelm List et al.*, 1947–48). This trial involved twelve senior officers of the German army who led the invasion and occupation of Greece and Yugoslavia. They were charged, among other things, with authorizing their forces to use the civilian population in the German-occupied territories as hostages and to execute them in disproportionate numbers in reprisal for the death or injury of German soldiers. The lead defendant, Field Marshal Wilhelm List, pleaded innocence by contending that he did not know about the killing of innocent civilians because he was—like General Matsui—away from the military headquarters in the occupied territories. He further argued that the Nazi Party security forces and the local police units were responsible for the executions, that these organizations fell outside of his army's tactical chain of command, and that therefore he could not be held personally accountable. The Nuremberg Tribunal rejected all these contentions, however. It ruled that "[a]bsence from headquarters cannot and does not relieve one from responsibility for acts committed in accordance with a policy he instituted or in which he acquiesced." Moreover, it held that List, "as commanding general of occupied territory," had the "duty and responsibility of maintaining order and safety, the protection of the lives and property of the population, and the punishment of crime." The judgment further read, "He cannot escape responsibility by a claim of a want of authority. *The authority is inherent in his position as commanding general of occupied territory.*"[37]

The final verdict of the Tokyo Tribunal fell in line with the judgment in the Hostage Case. It found that the evidence established Matsui's duty and power to take control of the Japanese occupation forces in Nanking as well as his knowledge of atrocities. Despite the possession of duty, knowledge, and power, Matsui did not take effective measures to stop his subordinates from committing war crimes. On these grounds, the judges pronounced him guilty under count 55.[38] It is worth recording in full the content of the verdict, since this is one of the earliest precedents for command responsibility in the history of international law:

At the heights of these dreadful happenings, on 17 December, MATSUI made a triumphal entry into the City and remained there from five to seven days. From his own observations and from the reports of his staff he must have been aware of what was happening. He admits he was told of some degree of misbehavior of his Army by the Kempeitai [military police] and by Consular Officials. Daily reports of these atrocities were made to Japanese diplomatic representatives in Nanking who, in turn, reported them to Tokyo. The Tribunal is satisfied that MATSUI knew what was happening. He did nothing, or nothing effective to abate these horrors. He did issue orders before the capture of the City enjoining propriety of conduct upon his troops and later he issued further orders to the same purport. These orders were of no effect as is now known, and as he must have known. It was pleaded in his behalf that at this time he was ill. His illness was not sufficient to prevent his conducting the military operations of his command nor to prevent his visiting the City for days while these atrocities were occurring. He was in command of the Army responsible for these happenings. He knew of them. He had the power, as he had the duty, to control his troops and to protect the unfortunate citizens of Nanking. He must be held criminally responsible for his failure to discharge this duty.[39]

This verdict is recognized as a valid precedent at international criminal courts today.[40]

The accused Mutō Akira was a staff officer in Matsui's army and was also charged with command responsibility. The prosecution's evidence established that Mutō, too, knew of the occurrence of atrocities but that he did not take any effective steps to stop them. Interestingly, however, the Tribunal acquitted him.[41] The judges apparently found that establishing Mutō's knowledge of Japanese atrocities was necessary but not sufficient to convict him, since his position as vice chief of staff did not confer on him the legal duty to take control of Matsui's troops. This acquittal is significant, since it shows that the Tokyo Tribunal carefully assessed all evidence against each accused instead of uncritically accepting the charges made by the prosecution. (That said, Mutō did not escape conviction in the end because the Tribunal found him guilty of other instances of large-scale atrocity.[42])

Turning to the case against Hirota Kōki, the prosecution departed from the theory of command responsibility and advanced instead the theory of cabinet responsibility to substantiate his guilt. The prosecution's major contentions were, first, that Hirota had been informed from the start of the atrocities committed by the Japanese forces in Nanking. Being the foreign minister, he was the first senior government official to receive reports from his diplomatic representatives and from other foreign sources in China on the Japanese army's violence. Second, when Hirota learned about the atrocities, he took the matter up with the war ministry and requested that proper actions be taken. He did so by personally seeing the then war minister, Gen. Sugiyama Hajime (who committed suicide after Japan's surrender in 1945), and by directing Hirota's immediate subordinate official, Ishii Itarō, to give repeated warnings to the officials concerned in the war ministry. Third, even though the war ministry gave him assurances that the matter would be handled properly, the situation remained the same. More reports of atrocities reached the foreign ministry. Fourth, Hirota realized that his warnings to the war ministry had had no effect in putting an end to the atrocities, but he took no other actions to influence the situation in Nanking.

On the basis of these findings, the prosecution argued that Hirota had the legal obligation to take further steps in order to end the Japanese military violence in Nanking. Specifically, as a top-ranking official of the government, he had the duty to ensure Japan's observance of the laws of war, such as by bringing the matter before the entire cabinet. Forwarding the incoming protests and making recommendations to the war ministry were surely part of his ministerial duty, but these tasks, in the prosecution's opinion, did not exhaust Hirota's duty as a minister of state. The facts that Hirota did no more than speak to war ministry officials, and that he chose to remain in the cabinet, could be regarded as proof that he tolerated the continuation of the atrocities in Nanking.

The defense, in response, gave a narrower interpretation of the duty that Hirota incurred than the prosecution did. The extent of Hirota's duty, as the defense saw it, was to forward incoming messages to the government bureaus and departments concerned, along with suggestions and recommendations when he deemed it necessary. Doing anything else would mean overstepping ministerial jurisdiction as had been determined by domestic constitutional practice. After all, it was a commonplace view among wartime Japanese leaders that all matters related to war including war crimes fell under the jurisdiction of the war ministry. The defense held that neither the foreign ministry nor the cabinet was thus in a position to meddle with matters in Nanking, which was essentially a military problem.

The different positions taken by the prosecution and the defense manifested themselves when the British lead prosecutor, Comyns-Carr, cross-examined Ishii Itarō.[43] Ishii was the former chief of the East Asiatic Affairs Bureau in the foreign ministry and was directly subordinate to Hirota at the time of the Rape of Nanking. Comyns-Carr interrogated Ishii in order to clarify how Hirota acted upon receiving information of atrocities. He was especially interested in making Ishii testify how Hirota responded after his realization that the war ministry was doing nothing effective to end the outrages. On one occasion, Comyns-Carr asked Ishii whether he ever urged Hirota to bring the matter before the cabinet. Ishii replied that they never discussed the possibility of taking such action, since he—and presumably Hirota, too—did not regard the cabinet as an appropriate body to deal with military matters. Comyns-Carr then changed the subject, asking Ishii a more general question on law. In this way, the British prosecutor aimed to elicit how Japanese government officials understood the obligation of state leaders concerning war crimes under international law. Following is the exchange between Comyns-Carr and Ishii Itarō in court. The relevant portion is somewhat long, but worth quoting in full:

Q: [Comyns-Carr] Did HIROTA ever discuss with you any further steps that should be taken to get these atrocities stopped?
A: [Ishii] I think we had several discussions.
Q: What did he suggest doing?
A: He told me quite frequently to lodge serious warning to the authorities concerned in the War Ministry.
Q: But we know that that had no effect. Didn't you suggest to him that he should bring it up in the cabinet?
A: We have never talked about bringing this question up before the cabinet. My reason for saying so is that I did not regard that the cabinet was a body to discuss such a question.
Q: Why not?
A: I think it so because the cabinet, as a cabinet, was not in any position to deal with questions which concerned the military in the field.
Q: Was it not necessary, in your position for you to know something about international law?
A: Yes, of course.
Q: And did you not know that the responsibility was on the government and not on the commanders in the field for the treatment of prisoners?
A: I can't quite comprehend the point in the question.[44]

In the last portion of the above exchange, Comyns-Carr referred to existing international conventions such as the Fourth Hague Convention of 1907, which placed squarely upon the government the primary responsibility for ensuring the proper treatment of prisoners of war and civilians under its control. Ishii seems perplexed, however, and unable to grasp the significance of Comyns-Carr's question. Apparently, he had never read the international conventions with the understanding that they stipulated the duty of civilian leaders of the government as well as that of the military.

With the arguments of the two parties in hand, the task presented to the Tribunal was to determine whether the prosecution's conception of duty had any validity, and to ask the same question with regard to the defense conception of ministerial duty. The Tribunal would then need to decide which one of the two duties was the overriding one for Hirota: the duty derived from the body of international law, or the one derived from Japanese constitutional practice. Depending on which way the Tribunal's ruling turned, Hirota's inaction vis-à-vis the cabinet could take on different meaning.

In the end, the Tokyo Tribunal upheld the prosecution's argument, finding that Hirota was "derelict in his duty." Hirota might have fulfilled his duty toward his own ministry, but failed to satisfy the higher duty he incurred vis-à-vis his government as a cabinet member. The pertinent part of Hirota's verdict reads as follows:

As Foreign Minister he received reports of these atrocities immediately after the entry of the Japanese forces into Nanking. According to the Defence evidence credence was given to these reports and the matter was taken up with the War Ministry. Assurances were accepted from the War Ministry that the atrocities would be stopped. After these assurances had been given reports of atrocities continued to come in for at least a month. The Tribunal is of opinion that HIROTA was derelict in his duty in not insisting before the cabinet that immediate action be taken to put an end to the atrocities, failing any other action open to him to bring about the same result. He was content to rely on assurances which he knew were not being implemented while hundreds of murders, violations of women, and other atrocities were being committed daily. His inaction amounted to criminal negligence.[45]

This verdict points to the following findings as constituting the basic grounds of Hirota's conviction: (1) he was fully aware that innocent civilians in Nanking were falling victim to killing, rape, looting, and other forms of violence day and night; (2) he eventually realized that the war ministry was not taking necessary measures to stop the atrocities immediately; (3) he did not explore if there were other means to stop the violence; (4) he knew that his government was failing to fulfill its international obligations; (5) he chose to remain in the government that, in effect, tolerated the continuation of mass atrocities. Given Hirota's knowledge of what was going on in the city, given his legal duty, and given his inaction, the Tribunal concluded that he was personally accountable for the continuation of the atrocities. Underscoring its legal position, the Tribunal further wrote, "A member of a Cabinet which collectively, as one of the principal organs of the Government, is responsible for the care of prisoners is not absolved from responsibility if, having knowledge of the commission of the crimes in the sense already discussed, and omitting or failing to secure the taking of measures to prevent the commission of such crimes in the future, he elects to continue as a member of the Cabinet."[46] This opinion generally conformed to the one expressed in the judgment of the international tribunal at Nuremberg, which read, "individuals have international duties which transcend the national obligations of obedience imposed by the individual State."[47]

Kainō Michitaka considered the Tokyo Tribunal's verdict a reasonable one. Recalling Ishii's testimony in later years, he remarked that the defense made a mistake in letting Ishii take the witness stand. He had testified, in essence, that Hirota agonized over the war ministry's inaction after learning about the continuation of Japanese military violence in Nanking. This kind of testimony might have been helpful under the wartime Japanese judicial system, where an accused was commonly presumed guilty from the outset and where the main defense task was to plead good actions and good character of the accused with the goal to secure a stay of execution or a lighter penalty. Kainō understood that legal practice at the Tokyo trial was, however, entirely different. The Tokyo Tribunal weighed evidence in order to determine the legal responsibility of the accused while adhering to the principle of the presumption of innocence. Under such court practice, pleading that the accused was a conscientious—yet ultimately ineffective—man, as made by Ishii on behalf of Hirota, would only substantiate Hirota's criminal inaction. Kainō regarded Ishii's mistake as one of many practical lessons on court techniques to be learned from the Tokyo trial.[48]

Hirota's conviction—and the death penalty that accompanied the conviction—was highly unpopular in Japan because many believed it to be too harsh if not a total miscarriage of justice. The fact that Hirota was a civilian with respectable professional backgrounds also made him a man of tragedy in the eyes of the Japanese public. The Hirota case, however, was by no means an anomaly by the standards of contemporaneous war crimes trials. Consider, for instance, the verdict and sentence meted out to Joachim von Ribbentrop, who was tried at the international court at Nuremberg. Like Hirota, he was foreign minister in a war cabinet. He was prosecuted on charges of conspiracy, crimes against peace, war crimes, and crimes against humanity. Again, like Hirota, he was found guilty of these charges and sent to the gallows.[49] The grounds of conviction in the two cases are not identical, but the Nuremberg Tribunal shared with the Tokyo Tribunal the readiness to mete out stern punishment to career bureaucrats when it established their individual responsibility for international crimes.

On this occasion, it is instructive to note that the judges at both tribunals reserved the death penalty for those individuals whom they found guilty of war crimes and/or crimes against humanity. They did not sentence to death any of those whom they convicted of crimes against peace alone. The common penalty for them was either life or a lesser term of imprisonment. The differential use of varied penalties suggests that the two tribunals regarded war crimes and crimes against humanity as graver offenses than crimes against peace. Alternatively, the judges might have hesitated to hand down capital punishment to those were convicted only of crimes against peace because this type of offense was seen as a novelty in those years. Webb at least thought so, which led him to recommend that no death penalty be meted out to those who were convicted of crimes against peace. The crime of aggression, he maintained, "was not usually regarded as a justiciable crime when they made war" and "[m]any international lawyers of standing still take the view that in this regard the Pact of Paris made no difference."[50]

The Hirota case has taken on special significance in international criminal justice in recent years, since it shows that a civilian could be held criminally accountable for mass atrocity even if he or she was not part of the military chain of command. This case became particularly relevant to the International Criminal Tribunal for Rwanda (ICTR), where, like Hirota, a number of civilians were prosecuted. Indeed, the murder of 800,000 Rwandans in a matter of three months could not have been achieved without the authorization, aiding, abetting, or complicity of prominent non-military leaders such as the cabinet members of the Rwandan government, other government officials at national and municipal levels, religious leaders, radio broadcasters, industrialists, and other men and women of influence in the Rwandan state and society.[51] In 1998, the ICTR handed down a historic judgment to a former Rwandan mayor, Jean-Paul Akayesu, finding him guilty of genocide, incitement to commit genocide, and crimes against humanity. When delivering the judgment, the Tribunal Chamber cited the Hirota case as a relevant historical precedent, writing, "It is, in fact, well-established, at least since the Tokyo trials, that civilians may be held responsible for violations of international humanitarian law. Hirota, the former Foreign Minister of Japan, was convicted at Tokyo for crimes committed during the rape of Nanking."[52]

The Burma-Siam Death Railway

The Burma-Siam Railway is a cross-border railroad that the Japanese government undertook to construct as a military supply line after the outbreak of the Pacific War. The railway, covering 258 miles between Kanchanaburi in Thailand and Thanbyuzayat in Burma, connected Bangkok with Rangoon. The construction started in mid-1942 and continued into late 1943. The railway and labor camps in the surrounding areas became major scenes of Japanese military violence as innumerable Allied prisoners of war and civilians were used for slave labor. This gave rise to the term "Death Railway."[53]

When presenting evidence concerning this case, the International Prosecution Section aimed to establish two separate but related war crimes. First, it charged that the wartime Japanese government authorized the use of Allied prisoners of war for work directly connected to military operation, which constituted a war crime. The use of prisoners of war for military purposes was explicitly prohibited under international law. Second, the Japanese government knew about the cruel working conditions to which the prisoners were subjected, but did nothing effective to ameliorate the situation. Matters known to the Japanese government included that the prisoners at the construction sites suffered severe deprivation of food, medical supplies, and proper shelter; that they were beaten and subjected to other forms of physical abuse; and that they were forced to work in a trying tropical climate for excessively long hours. The prosecution further showed that those prisoners who fell seriously ill were treated particularly harshly. They were either compelled to join the work units notwithstanding their illness, or were left to die in a state of starvation in filthy conditions and without medical attention. As a result of the horrendous living conditions, prisoners invariably became malnourished and suffered from diseases and exhaustion. Many died because of physical abuses that were inflicted by camp guards and overseers of the construction sites.

According to existing scholarship, 61,800 Allied prisoners of war were mobilized for the railway construction, of whom 12,300 died due to mistreatment, one in every five. Furthermore, a far larger number of the Asian civilian populations were brought from all over Southeast Asia. Approximately 200,000 Asians—more than triple the number of Allied prisoners of war—worked on the railway construction. Of these

200,000, between 42,000 and 74,000 died because of mistreatment, starvation, and disease, a mortality rate of Asian forced laborers of somewhere between 21 percent and 37 percent.[54]

The chief defendant for the Burma-Siam Railway was Gen. Tōjō Hideki, who was prime minister and concurrently war minister between 1941 and 1944. Substantiating his guilt was not complicated, since the accused frankly admitted in court that he authorized the use of prisoner-of-war labor. He did try to deny criminal responsibility, however, by testifying that he broke no laws of war because "[t]he railway route lay at a great distance behind the front lines and there [were] no military operations in progress in that area at that time." But he contradicted himself by also saying, "The object sought in plans for the construction of the Thailand-Burma Railway was to expedite supplies to the Japanese forces in Burma as well as to facilitate commerce and communications between the two countries." By admitting the military purpose of the railway construction, he affirmed the charge that he authorized the exploitation of prisoner-of-war labor in violation of international law.[55]

With respect to the allegations of the mistreatment of prisoners of war, Tōjō contended that there was no such widespread abuse. He testified, "Many Japanese soldiers, employed there side by side with the P.O.W.[s,] were treated equally with men of other and stronger nationalities, and there was not ever the faintest thought in our minds that this type of employment would ever be challenged as prohibitive under international standards." In other words, he claimed that if anything, prisoners of war were treated properly and in accordance with international standards. Having argued so, however, he conceded that the work conditions were trying and that there were some episodes of mistreatment. For example, he testified that in May 1943, he dispatched the chief of the prisoner-of-war administration bureau of the war ministry, along with many surgeons, as he learned of "deficiencies in the sanitary conditions and treatment of P.O.W.s." He also had one company commander court-martialed on grounds that he had "dealt unfairly with the prisoners" and one commanding general of the railway construction dismissed, apparently for the mistreatment of prisoner-of-war labor.[56]

On Tōjō's involvement in the Death Railway, the Tokyo Tribunal returned a guilty verdict, both on the use of prisoner-of-war labor for military-related construction and on the mistreatment of prisoners of war. In the judges' opinion, the accused knew about the widespread mistreatment of prisoners of war, had the power and duty to protect the prisoners of war, and yet did not take adequate actions to stop the atrocities. The relevant part of the Tribunal's ruling reads as follows:

[H]e advised that prisoners of war should be used in the construction of the Burma-Siam Railway, designed for strategic purposes. He made no proper arrangements for billeting and feeding the prisoners, or for caring for those who became sick in that trying climate. He learned of the poor condition of the prisoners employed on the project, and sent an officer to investigate. We know the dreadful conditions that investigator must have found in the many camps along the railway. The only step taken as a result of that investigation was the trial of one company commander for ill-treatment of prisoners. Nothing was done to improve conditions. Deficiency diseases and starvation continued to kill off the prisoners until the end of the project.[57]

As was the case with Matsui, Tōjō was convicted primarily on grounds of command responsibility.

Apart from the Death Railway, Tōjō was also charged with individual responsibility for the mistreatment of prisoners of war in other parts of the Pacific theater. For example, the prosecution provided the Tribunal with evidence that documented Tōjō's orders to use prisoner-of-war labor exhaustively. One such piece of evidence recorded the instructions he had delivered to the commander of the Zentsūji Division (responsible for the Zentsūji prisoner-of-war camp in Kagawa Prefecture on the island of Shikoku) regarding the treatment of prisoners of war during his visit of inspection on May 30, 1942. Tōjō had instructed, among other things, that "[i]t is necessary to take care not to be obsessed with a mistaken idea of humanitarianism or swayed by personal feelings towards these prisoners-of-war which may grow in the long time of their imprisonment," and that "[t]he present situation of affairs in this country does not permit anyone to lie idle doing nothing but eating freely."[58] In a separate document (dated June 25, 1942) that he issued to newly appointed chiefs of prisoner-of-war camps, he had similarly said, "In Japan, we have our own ideology concerning prisoners-of-war, which should naturally make their treatment more or less different from that in Europe and America." While instructing that "various regulations concerned" be observed, Tōjō told the camp chiefs that "you must place the prisoners under strict discipline and not allow them to lie idle doing nothing but eating freely for even a single day." Specifically, "[t]heir labor and technical skills should be fully utilized for the replenishment of production, and contribution rendered toward the prosecution of the Greater East Asiatic War, for which no effort ought to be spared," thereby sanctioning of the use of prisoner-of-war labor in the outright violation of laws and customs of war.[59]

The prosecution's evidence further showed that Tōjō had received reports on the results of his orders about the use of prisoner-of-war labor. One such report—introduced as evidence—was prepared by the headquarters of the Eastern District Army that had jurisdiction in the Tokyo and Yokohama areas. Dated October 21, 1942, the report informed the war ministry of the productive value of those Allied prisoners of war it had begun to use as stevedores since September 1942 in Kawasaki and Yokohama. The report read, "It is generally admitted by all the business proprietors alike that the use of P.W. labor has made the systematic operation of transportation possible for the first time, and has not only produced a great influence in the business circle[s], but will also contribute greatly to the expansion of production, including munitions of war, and the execution of industry."[60] Tōjō admitted that he was routinely briefed about the conditions of prisoner-of-war labor at biweekly meetings in the war ministry, where Allied protests concerning the Japanese mistreatment of prisoners of war were brought up for discussion.[61]

When confronted with documentary evidence that he had personally authorized the exhaustive use of prisoner-of-war labor, Tōjō argued that the duty to ensure the proper treatment of prisoners rested primarily with army commanders in the field and not with himself, and that he had naturally expected *them* to fulfill *their* responsibilities. During the Allied pretrial investigation (whose record was presented as evidence), he was asked to clarify how he could possibly continue trusting field commanders even when he learned from various sources that mistreatment of prisoners of war was widespread. Tōjō replied, "The matter of responsibility for humane considerations and the following of treaty provisions was the responsibility of the various army commanders. I believed that they were following them."[62] The Allied interrogator pressed on, asking whether that meant that Tōjō trusted the commanders in the field but could not believe numerous protests from the United States, Britain, and other governments. Tōjō explained in reply, "As I said before, when a protest would come in, I would forward it to the responsible army commander involved for action which I thought was taken. I could not tell whether the protest was appropriate or not, and I presumed that investigations were made, followed by courts-martial or other suitable action."[63] By providing these replies, Tōjō evaded the question of what authority, power, and duty he himself possessed as the chief of the war ministry and concurrently the head of the government. When it came to the duty of his own subordinate officers and field commanders, however, he was willing to point the finger at them. His evasiveness found its match in Matsui, who also declined to comment on his own responsibility, but readily put blame on his subordinate officers. In the end, the Tokyo Tribunal established that Tōjō was culpable for authorizing the widespread criminal use of prisoner-of-war labor. The verdict read, "He bears responsibility for the instruction that prisoners who did not work should not eat. We have no doubt that his repeated insistence on this instruction conduced in large measure to the sick and wounded being driven to work and to the suffering and deaths which resulted."[64]

Another key defendant who was implicated in connection with the Burma-Siam Railway—and the mistreatment of prisoners of war in general—was Shigemitsu Mamoru, who served as foreign minister between 1943 and 1945 (Fig. 6.2). His case was a mirror image of Hirota's in that the prosecution applied the theory of cabinet responsibility in establishing his guilt. In other words, it accused him of failing to fulfill his international obligation, as a minister of state, to ensure Japan's observance of laws and customs of war.

The prosecution produced two types of evidence when substantiating the case against this defendant. The first consisted of numerous protests that Foreign Minister Shigemitsu received from the Allied governments and protective powers abroad. With these diplomatic records, the prosecution showed that Shigemitsu was fully informed of the mistreatment of Allied prisoners of war across theaters of war. The same records also showed that the Japanese government was in the habit of denying all allegations of mistreatment and insisted instead on the Japanese fulfillment of its international obligation to treat prisoners of war humanely. Shigemitsu had taken charge of drawing up those replies that contained false information.

Fig. 6.2 Defendants in the dock, listening as Chief Justice Webb reads the judgment, November 9, 1948. Front row, left to right: Oka Takazumi; Araki Sadao; and Mutō Akira. Back row, left to right: Hiranuma Kiichirō; Tōgō Shigenori; Satō Kenryō; and Shigemitsu Mamoru. Courtesy National Archives, photo no. 238-FE.

Fig. 6.3 Suzuki Tadakatsu, the former chief of bureau in charge of Japanese nationals in enemy countries, foreign ministry, from December 1942 through July 1945. He is being sworn in by Capt. D. S. Van Meter, Marshal of the Court, January 17, 1947. Courtesy National Archives, photo no. 238-FE.

The second type of prosecution evidence was the testimony taken from Suzuki Tadakatsu (Fig. 6.3), who was the chief of the Bureau for the Affairs of Japanese Residents in Enemy Countries and Shigemitsu's immediate subordinate in the foreign ministry.[65] Suzuki's importance for the prosecution's case can be compared with that of Ishii Itarō, who testified on behalf of Hirota. The prosecution directed Suzuki's testimony in such a way as to have him clarify whether the foreign ministry transmitted the protests without fail to other government agencies concerned, and more importantly, what actions Shigemitsu personally took in order to address the mounting protests from the Allied powers about the Japanese mistreatment of war prisoners. According to Suzuki's account, Shigemitsu once decided on a plan "to have a Cabinet Committee set up" in order to discuss overseas broadcasts regarding the Japanese mistreatment of prisoners of war. He never got around to execute the plan, however, because "matters relating to prisoners of war were in the charge of and under the jurisdiction of the Army." Suzuki further testified, "Inasmuch as such matters were primarily and exclusively handled by the Army and departments other than the War Department—departments outside of the military could not on their own take up the matter."[66] As was the case with Hirota, Shigemitsu stopped short of taking action vis-à-vis the cabinet when he could not persuade War Minister Tōjō to take proper measures.

Suzuki continued to testify that on a separate occasion, Shigemitsu personally spoke to Tōjō about the requests from protecting powers for permission to inspect prisoner-of-war camps. When this action did not lead to the issuance of the requested permission, Shigemitsu did not press the matter any further. Suzuki gave the following explanation: "If permitted I should like to say, with regard to the question of whether or not this matter was brought up at the cabinet meeting, that according to Japanese practice and custom one cannot conceive of the question of the prisoners of war—anything relating to prisoners of war being taken up by the cabinet unless that matter were submitted by the War Minister."[67] Suzuki shared with Ishii Itarō the view that matters related to prisoners of war belonged exclusively to the war ministry. This view was unlikely to convince the judges, however, since it conflicted with their legal position that a minister of state had the international obligation to ensure his government's compliance with international law and that such obligation overrode whatever ministerial responsibilities he had under domestic law.

It is not surprising, then, that the Tribunal found Shigemitsu to share in the responsibility. Given the continuation of atrocities, the knowing inaction of the war ministry, and mounting foreign protests, Shigemitsu "should have pressed the matter, if necessary to the point of resigning, in order to quit himself of a responsibility which he suspected was not being discharged," the judgment read. In the Tribunal's opinion, his continuation in the cabinet while failing to take effective steps to stop the atrocity amounted to his supporting the government that he knew was neglecting its international obligation to ensure basic protection for prisoners of war.[68] Having convicted him, however, the Tokyo Tribunal handed down a surprisingly light sentence: a seven-year term of imprisonment. As mitigating circumstances, the judges noted that he was not party to the conspiracy to commit crimes against peace (they acquitted him of the conspiracy charge), and that the role he played in waging aggressive war was relatively minor. Shigemitsu did lend support to the execution of aggressive war, the judges found, but only after he became foreign minister in April 1943, "by which time his country was deeply involved in a war which would vitally affect its future." Furthermore, the judges concluded that given the military domination of major government agencies in those years, "it would have required great resolution for any Japanese to condemn them [military hard-liners]."[69] These factors led the Tribunal to give him an exceedingly light punishment.

Quite coincidentally, one of the twelve successive trials at Nuremberg handed down a strikingly similar verdict and sentence to a former German foreign ministry official. The trial in question was the Ministries Case, a joint trial involving 21 high-ranking German ministerial officials.[70] The lead defendant was Ernst von Weizsäcker, the vice foreign minister under von Ribbentrop between April 1938 and May 1943. Von Weizsäcker was, like Shigemitsu, a career diplomat, and again like Shigemitsu, he was "a personable and educated diplomat with numerous prominent friends in several European countries."[71] He was charged with crimes against peace, war crimes, and crimes against humanity. The Nuremberg Tribunal acquitted him on most charges related to crimes against peace, but did find him guilty of the invasion of Czechoslovakia.[72] It also established that von Weiszäcker had a share of responsibility for the deportation and mass murder of Jewish people in Poland. The accused, for his part, had pleaded his innocence, arguing that he remained in the German foreign ministry so as to assist the anti-Hitler underground movement and help the negotiation for peace. "We believe him," the judgment read, but concluded, "One cannot give consent to or implement the commission of murder because by so doing he hopes eventually to be able to rid society of the chief murderer. *The first is a crime of imminent actuality while the second is but a future hope.*"[73] Yet when it came to sentencing, the Nuremberg Tribunal handed down the same light penalty that Shigemitsu received from the Tokyo Tribunal: a seven-year term of imprisonment.

The similarity between the two cases might have been purely accidental (although the judgment in the Ministries Case was in fact delivered five months after that of Tokyo). Even so, the shared verdicts and sentences of the two foreign ministry cases indicate that the judgment of the Tokyo Tribunal conformed to the legal standards that emanated from Nuremberg, or vice versa.[74] This is not to say that the Nuremberg precedents should be regarded as the golden standard or, for that matter, that judgments at Nuremberg were always consistent. As David Cohen points out, the Nuremberg trials set out diverse—and at times contradictory—criteria of individual responsibility.[75] Nevertheless, together with the verdicts given to Hirota, Tōjō, von Ribbentrop, von Weiszäcker, and other German and Japanese government officials who were prosecuted at the Allied trials, one can regard the Shigemitsu case as an important precedent that began defining the notion of cabinet responsibility as a workable concept in international humanitarian law.

SEVEN

Documenting Japanese Atrocities

In making their case about Japanese war crimes, Allied prosecutors aimed at substantiating the recurrence of atrocities with common patterns throughout the Pacific theater and imputing such acts to the accused. The prosecutors had to rely heavily on this strategy because they had great difficulty securing conclusive evidence of the personal culpability of individual defendants. As discussed in Chapter 5, this difficulty stemmed largely from the Japanese government's coordinated effort in the last days of the war to destroy military records on a vast scale.

In pursuit of the strategy to establish commonalities among war crimes, each national team took charge of collecting evidentiary material for those cases that were closely related to the country or countries it represented. The individual teams had the discretion to decide which specific types of war crimes to substantiate for respective regions, as long as their presentation fell in line with the broader prosecutorial mission of establishing the widespread and recurrent character of the similarly patterned atrocities. Each team also had some latitude as to how to organize and present its evidence before the Tribunal. Differences in priorities and presentation methods were such that the prosecutorial goal to demonstrate commonalities ultimately had mixed results. This chapter explores the diversity of prosecutorial priorities and assesses the successes and failures in reaching this goal.

China

The Chinese presentation consisted of three parts: the mass atrocities in Nanking; war crimes committed in other combat zones in China; and the Japanese-sponsored opium and narcotics trade. The Chinese team presented the Rape of Nanking first (which, as discussed in the previous chapter, led to the convictions of Matsui and Hirota), then detailed atrocities in other Japanese-occupied territories. This segment of the Chinese case turned out to be brief. The adduced evidence contained a minimum of information about times, places, and types of crimes committed. A few witnesses were called to the stand, but they did no more than offer supplementary accounts on discrete instances of Japanese-perpetrated atrocities. The relatively poor quality of the evidence stood in sharp contrast to the detailed exhibits and witness accounts that were brought for the case of Nanking. This shortcoming immediately drew criticism from Webb, who remarked, "That is hardly evidence. There are no details. What court would act on evidence like that?"[1]

The prosecutorial strategy here appeared to focus on eliciting the recurrence of Japanese war crimes while avoiding redundancy. Put differently, the Chinese team, on the one hand, treated the Rape of Nanking as the representative case and took great care to document it in full. As for war crimes in other parts of China, it limited its task to briskly introducing a small selection to show how widespread the Japanese-perpetrated atrocities were. Webb soon understood the purport of the new method of presentation as he commented, "What they [the members of the Chinese prosecution team] are doing is using, I have no doubt, affidavits which were used before the United Nations War Crimes Commission to establish a mere prima facie case and which contained a minimum amount of facts, just enough of a very limited purpose."[2] This statement reflected Webb's critical opinion of the adduced evidence. He deemed that the Chinese team achieved no more than making a "prima facie case," that is, a case to initiate a prosecution, with respect to war crimes committed in places other than Nanking. His comment suggested that the Tribunal would not be prepared to convict unless the prosecution produced further proof of the offenses charged. As will be shown later, the sketchy documentation of Japanese war crimes had a material effect on the verdict and sentence given to Gen. Hata Shunroku, a key defendant in the Chinese phase.

The war crimes cases that the Chinese team attempted to substantiate nonetheless deserve some scrutiny in order to understand its prosecutorial priorities. One can find, for instance, that the Chinese team presented various exhibits concerning the Japanese commission of rape, organized sexual enslavement, other forms of sexual humiliation, and the use of rape, forced sexual intercourse, and sexual humiliation as means of torturing Chinese female prisoners.[3] This indicates that the prosecution attached importance to establishing the responsibility of wartime Japanese leaders for the sexual crimes committed habitually by Japanese troops, not only in Nanking but also in other parts of China.

One such court exhibit documented the Japanese army's use of Chinese women for sexual slavery in Kweilin in Kwangsi Province. According to the statement taken from the witnesses, Japanese occupation forces publicized employment opportunities for women during the last year of the war. When women gathered with the hope of finding work at the advertised new factories, the Japanese military authorities "sent them to the suburbs outside Li Shi Gate and forced them into prostitution with the Japanese troops."[4] Oral evidence on sexual violence was taken in court as well. A British journalist, John Goette, testified that he received reports of Japanese rapes from British and American missionaries when he was in Shansi between 1938 and 1940. He continued: "The formal demand by the Japanese Army on local Chinese officials to provide women for the use of the Japanese Army was a commonplace thing: it was commonly accepted by the Chinese officials and by the Japanese Army."[5] Having extracted this statement from Goette, however, the Chinese team stopped short of presenting further corroborative evidence concerning widespread rape in Shansi.

The use of civilians for slave labor also figured in the Chinese presentation. Ti Shu-tang, a 22-year-old native of Hopeh Province, was called to the stand to give testimony concerning one such episode. Ti attested that in 1944, Japanese forces apprehended him and four other youngsters from the same village, and made them join a large number of other captured Chinese. They then demanded that the captives either enlist in the Japanese army or become prisoners of war. Those who refused to join the army were deported to Akita Prefecture in northern Japan. Ti testified that the deported men were used as laborers for digging ditches and cutting rocks. According to his account, the labor force consisted of 981 Chinese (including himself), of which 418 died by the time the war ended. The place to which Ti Shu-tang was deported appears to be Hanaoka in Akita, where the Kashima Construction Company had used a large number of Chinese for mining operations and construction of a dam and waterways. Many died due to the severely cold climate, wholly inadequate clothing and shelter, excessive work hours, illness, starvation, and various forms of physical abuse. The "Hanaoka Incident"—as it became known—came to the attention of the legal section of the occupation authorities after the war, leading to the trial of seven officials from the Kashima Construction Company at the American military court in Yokohama.[6]

The third segment of the Chinese presentation followed, documenting the opium and narcotics trade sponsored by Japanese authorities from the time of the establishment of Manchukuo in 1932. The Chinese lead prosecutor, Hsiang Che-chun (Fig. 7.1), argued that Japan sponsored the drug trade in order to use the revenues to finance the Japanese military and to "undermine the will to resist on the part of the Chinese people."[7] In other words, he held that the Japanese actively promoted the popular use of opium and narcotics not only to make a profit but also to weaken the Chinese people physically and mentally. This act, Hsiang seemed to argue, constituted a crime against the Chinese people. Having made these allegations, however, his team fell short of substantiating them in full. Evidence did establish that the drug money helped finance further Japanese aggressive war in China, but it was not clearly demonstrated that the Japanese promoted the spread of opium and narcotics with the specific goal of destroying the Chinese race. The opium and narcotics case, in this respect, bore more on charges of aggressive war than on war crimes, and would have been better presented as such. The Tokyo Tribunal, for its part, gave no special ruling on Hsiang's claim that the alleged act constituted a war crime.

The Chinese decision to document Japanese sponsorship of the opium and narcotics trade is crucial, however, since it shows that the Chinese team projected country-specific concerns as well as adhering to the broader prosecutorial goal when preparing its case. The century-long fight against opium, perhaps, made the revival of large-scale drug consumption under Japanese rule a particularly poignant and unforgivable

Fig. 7.1 Hsiang Che-chun, Associate Prosecutor from China. Courtesy National Archives, photo no. 238-FE.

war experience. Whatever the motives, the opium and narcotics trade carried great weight in the Chinese presentation. As will be shown below, other Allied prosecutors, too, selected such cases that had become an important part of the war memory of the people or peoples they represented. This points to a fundamental but underappreciated characteristic of the Tokyo trial: the actual course of the prosecution case was shaped by the complex interplay of the various goals and priorities of the eleven national prosecution teams.

The Philippines and the United States

The Philippine prosecutor, Pedro Lopez (Fig. 7.2), divided his presentation into two parts. The first half concerned evidence of atrocities targeted at the civilian population. The highlight was the substantiation of the case known as the Rape of Manila. This refers to indiscriminate killing, torture, mass rape, sexual mutilation, arson, and other forms of brutality committed by the Japanese troops against residents of Manila before the American retaking of the city in early 1945. The victims were mostly Filipino men, women, and children, but there were also a number

Fig. 7.2   Pedro Lopez, Associate Prosecutor from the Philippines. Courtesy National Archives, photo no. 238-FE.

of foreign nationals. Prior to the Tokyo trial, Yamashita Tomoyuki, the commander-in-chief of the Fourteenth Area Army at the time of the Rape of Manila, was brought before the American military commission in Manila between October and December of 1945. He was tried and convicted on grounds of command responsibility.[8] Lopez presented the same case before the Tokyo Tribunal with the goal to hold, in particular, the defendant Mutō Akira—Yamashita's chief-of-staff—criminally accountable.

The second half of the Philippine presentation concerned atrocities targeted at Allied prisoners of war, the outstanding example being the Bataan Death March. This episode refers to the forced march of American and Filipino prisoners of war in the aftermath of their surrender at Bataan, which was the last American holdout in Luzon, on April 9, 1942. Approximately 85,000 exhausted, diseased, and injured soldiers fell under Japanese custody.[9] They were made to march without food or water under the scorching sun for nine consecutive days, during which many died. According to postwar American war crimes investigation, over 27,500 prisoners—1,500 Americans and 26,000 Filipinos—continued to die at the final destination, Camp O'Donnell, during their first eight to nine months of confinement. The major causes of death were lack of proper food and water, overcrowded and filthy shelters, beatings, and numerous other forms of mistreatment.[10] Homma Masaharu, who commanded the Fourteenth Army at the time of the Bataan Death March, was prosecuted at the American military commission in early 1946. Like Yamashita, he, too, was convicted. By bringing the same case before the Tokyo Tribunal, Lopez aimed at establishing the responsibility of Japanese leaders in the central government, such as the defendant Tōjō Hideki, who was prime minister and concurrently war minister at the time.

The Bataan Death March was one of the first instances of large-scale Japanese atrocity that Allied service personnel suffered in the Pacific theater. At the Tokyo trial, Lopez called to the witness stand three American servicemen, including a colonel, who had survived the Death March. Having three witnesses for a single episode was unusual by the standards of the Tokyo trial. (As discussed earlier, the prosecutors tended to limit the use of witnesses.) Lopez called to the witness stand two additional American army officers, who testified on mistreatment at other prisoner-of-war camps and at various military-related construction sites in the Philippines.[11] By calling a large number of American witnesses, Lopez took great care to represent the grievances of the United States as much as those of his own country when presenting evidence for the Philippine theater, where many American soldiers—as well as American civilians—fell victim to Japanese war crimes.

The organizational structure of the Philippine presentation resembled the Chinese one in that it treated a few instances of mass atrocity—the Rape of Manila and the Bataan Death March—as representative cases of Japanese war crimes. There was one notable difference, however. The evidentiary material Lopez prepared for the rest of the Japanese-occupied Philippines was far more detailed than what the Chinese team had prepared for the rest of China. At Lopez's disposal were 14,600 pages of war crimes investigation reports compiled by the U.S. Army after the retaking of the Philippines in 1945. He also had access to voluminous trial transcripts and court exhibits from the two preceding

American trials of Yamashita and Homma held in Manila. With these rich sources, Lopez documented the extent of Japanese atrocities much more thoroughly than the Chinese prosecution team had done.[12] Major patterns of atrocity that emerged from the Philippine presentation were: indiscriminate and systematic massacre, mass rape, murder, sexual mutilation, arson, and other forms of destruction and cruelty targeted at the civilian population. As for atrocities targeted at Allied prisoners of war, various forms of mistreatment in prisoner-of-war camps, cruel and illegal use of prisoner-of-war labor, and the inhumane ways that prisoners of war were transported on land and sea were substantiated as commonplace war crimes in the Philippine theater.

Other than these atrocities, Lopez also introduced some pieces of evidence that attested to the Japanese commission of certain war crimes that had not been widely recognized in the body of international law: cannibalism and medical experimentation. Three documents were presented with respect to cannibalism. One of them was a captured Japanese military record titled "Memorandum concerning the Training of All Officers and Men for the Prevention," dated November 18, 1944. This document gave instructions about dos and don'ts when eating human flesh, reading in part, "Although it is not prescribed in the criminal code, those who eat human flesh (except that of the enemy) knowing it to be so, shall be sentenced to death as the worst kind of criminal against mankind."[13] Another exhibit Lopez presented was a statement made by a Japanese private in the 9th Company of the 3rd Battalion, 239th Infantry Regiment, who was taken into Australian military custody. The private testified, "On 10 Dec 44 an order was issued from 18th Army Headquarters that troops were permitted to eat the flesh of Allied dead but must not eat their own dead." He continued, "At the time rumors were prevalent that troops were eating their own dead."[14] This account indicates that senior officers of the 18th Army were aware of widespread cannibalism, that they were concerned about the Japanese soldiers' feasting on their own kind, and that the army authorized the eating of the Allied dead in order to regulate the widespread practice of cannibalism.[15] In addition to these exhibits, Lopez introduced a war crimes report of the U.S. Army that recorded a specific episode of cannibalism. According to the report, six Japanese soldiers allegedly carried out a raid of a Filipino house in Cervantes,

Ilocos Sur (in Luzon), in early August of 1945. They killed all five occupants in the house including one child and stayed in the house for two days. They cooked and ate the flesh taken from three of the victims while occupying the house.[16]

These three pieces of evidence did not directly implicate any particular defendants tried at Tokyo, but they could be incriminating if other Allied prosecutors were to provide additional evidence. To reiterate, the prosecutorial strategy was to establish commonalities and substantiate that the presented cases were part of the war crimes that the Japanese forces widely committed throughout the Pacific theater. Under this prosecutorial strategy, documentation of cannibalism from other combat zones or Japanese-occupied territories could help establish either authorization or toleration of such atrocity by high-ranking government officials and military leaders in the central Japanese government.

As for medical experimentation, the evidence Lopez presented was of a fleeting kind. One might even say that its evidentiary value was very limited since it utterly lacked details about the circumstances of the crime. It is still worthwhile to take note of it on this occasion, since additional episodes of medical experimentation were introduced during the Australian presentation. The Philippine case in question was drawn from one of the U.S. Army war crimes investigations reports. It briefly stated that "[p]risoners were also forced to submit to medical experiments at the hands of Dr. NOGI" at the prisoner-of-war camp in Cabanatuan. Nogi appears to have been a Japanese medical officer at the camp.[17] There was no further explanation concerning the nature of the crime, but again, this piece of evidence might weigh with the judges when evaluated together with the Australian evidence.

Lopez's presentation covered many episodes of war crime involving American victims. This left the American assistant prosecutors—Charles Cole and James Robinson—with limited tasks in representing their countrymen. There are indications that the American staff was dissatisfied with its diminished role. Robinson had, in fact, openly contested the Philippine leadership and insisted on an equal share for the American team. In mid-August of 1946 (about four months before Lopez began his presentation), he questioned the "advisability of the facts relating to atrocities committed against U.S. personnel in the Philippines being presented by Mr. Lopez and not by an American." Lopez, for his part, had no desire to share the task that the chief prosecutor had already assigned to him. Seeing that the turf war between the Philippine and American prosecutors could not be resolved, Mansfield requested that Keenan step in because "work has been duplicated as both Mr. Lopez and U.S. counsel are preparing the same evidence for presentation to the Tribunal."[18] It is not clear whether the chief prosecutor intervened. The prosecution's record only shows that Lopez ultimately took charge while the American staff remained in the secondary position. This might be interpreted as an American willingness to allow the Philippines to enjoy prominence at the Tokyo trial in view of the latter's immense contributions to the American war effort. Alternatively, it may simply reflect the general policy of the United States to attach importance to the prosecution of Class A war crimes (crimes against peace), and not Class B or Class C offenses (war crimes or crimes against humanity).

That said, the American staff was not relegated completely to the background. One month after Lopez completed his presentation, Robinson took his turn and presented additional evidence regarding the massacre of Allied prisoners of war on Palawan Island in December 1944. In this episode of atrocity, the Japanese forced 141 Allied prisoners into air raid shelters by deception, burned them to death, and shot those who tried to escape. Lopez had already covered this case but Robinson reserved the right to take oral evidence in court from Sergeant Douglas Bogue of the U.S. Marine Corps, one of the few survivors of the atrocity.[19] Furthermore, the American team retained the right to introduce evidence of Japanese atrocities in connection with the central Pacific islands.

One of the cases introduced by the American team concerned an instance of cannibalism in the Bonin Islands. The exhibit presented in evidence was the record of the court proceedings of a U.S. Navy trial held in Guam, where a group of high-ranking Japanese army and navy officers were prosecuted.[20] According to a detailed testimonial account by co-defendant Major Matoba Sueo, he and his co-defendants as well as their subordinates committed cannibalism on more than a few occasions. He testified that since around February 1945, his superior and divisional commander General Tachibana Yoshio (co-defendant), began to discuss the eventual need to live on human flesh in order to sustain their war effort. At a conference he held at the divisional headquarters, for instance, Tachibana is said to have told all battalion commanders that "supplies would diminish and ammunition would run short," and that his men "would be forced even to eat their own comrades killed in combat" as well as "the flesh of the enemy." He said, moreover, that Allied prisoners of war would be executed and that "the flesh would be eaten." The accused Matoba also recalled a private conversation he had with Tachibana in which they discussed the Japanese troops on Bougainville and New Guinea who "had to eat human flesh" due to the lack of provisions and supplies.[21] This testimonial account is significant, since it shows that the Japanese army and navy officers in the Bonin Islands contemporaneously knew the dire military situations and widespread practice of cannibalism in the South Pacific notwithstanding the immense distance between the two theaters of war.[22] Matoba further testified that in late February, Tachibana ordered the flesh of a newly executed Allied airman to be cooked and served—along with *sake*—when the 308th Battalion under Tachibana's command held a private party in his and Matoba's honor. The general gave this order because (as Matoba claimed) he was dissatisfied with the host's failure to supply meat to go with the liquor. The accused testimony suggested, at the same time, that Tachibana decided to use this occasion to give his subordinates practical experience in the preparation and consumption of human flesh in anticipation of the future termination of supplies, as was the case in the South Pacific.[23]

The accused Matoba additionally testified that other than eating human flesh, they had engaged in the selective consumption of human livers as well. One admiral had once told him that "during the Chinese-Japanese war [1894–95] human flesh and liver was eaten as a medicine by the Japanese troops." Matoba also explained, "The medicine made from the liver was named Seirogan ["Conquer-Russia" Tablets]."[24] Seirogan is a powerful stomach medicine that had been developed at the time of the Sino-Japanese War and the Russo-Japanese War (1904–05). A medicine carrying the same brand name (although written with different ideographs) is commonly sold in Japanese drugstores to this day. It appears that the Japanese officers in the Bonin Islands attempted to free themselves from the burden of guilt by assuring to one another that their "medical knowledge" about the consumption of human liver had its roots in the heroic age of Japan's modern military history. These episodes of cannibalism show that the Japanese forces stationed in the region committed various forms of cannibalism for reasons other than the need to stave off starvation.

The British Commonwealth of Nations

Whereas Hsiang and Lopez organized their cases around representative episodes of mass atrocity, the team for the British Commonwealth did not single out any particular one as an example case. Rather, they introduced numerous episodes of war crimes from different theaters of war in order to stress the recurrence of Japanese military violence in the broad geographical area. The region they covered included Singapore, the Malay peninsula, Burma, Thailand, Hong Kong, the Andaman Islands, Hainan Island, Formosa, British North Borneo, Ambon (part of the Moluccas), New Guinea, New Britain (part of the Bismarck Archipelago), the Solomon Islands, Gilbert and Ellice Islands, Nauru, and Ocean Island. By covering many combat zones and occupied territories in the Pacific theater, the Commonwealth prosecutors contended that atrocities on such a vast scale could not have been committed without the awareness of leaders in the central Japanese government.

Another feature of the Commonwealth presentation was the prominence of Japanese war crimes targeted at Asian nationals, such as Indians, Chinese, Burmese, Malaysians, Andaman and Nicobar islanders, and other Pacific islanders. It would not be an exaggeration to say that half of its war crimes cases had to do with crimes against civilians and prisoners of war with non-Caucasian backgrounds. Critics of the Tokyo trial have recently argued that Japanese war crimes against Asian people were largely neglected because Allied prosecutors from the Western colonial powers were reluctant to grant colonial Asians the right to be represented on an equal footing.[25] This claim, however, is contradicted by the actual prosecutorial effort at the Tokyo trial and, more generally, the political circumstances of the colonial world in Southeast Asia in the immediate aftermath of the war. For the Western colonial powers in those months, it made little political sense to ignore Asian victims of war if they were to re-establish their leadership in the region. This was at least the understanding of the British government, whose moral, political, and military preeminence as a colonial master had been severely undermined by its ignominious defeat to the invading Japanese armies in British Malaya. The war crimes trials served as an important occasion for Britain to restore its moral authority by pursuing justice on behalf of its colonial subjects. Such political considerations were also reflected in the prosecutorial priorities of the British-run Class BC trials, as Hayashi Hirofumi's recent studies show.[26] With this understanding in mind, let us examine below a selection of substantiated cases by the Commonwealth team in order to see how multinational considerations were reflected in the actual prosecutorial effort.

One case that weighed greatly with the British team concerned a massacre that took place in the immediate aftermath of the fall of Singapore. The major victims were ethnic Chinese in the British colonies in Southeast Asia. Yamashita Tomoyuki led the invasion. With a relatively small number of troops, he succeeded in overwhelming the British forces and secured their surrender on February 15, 1942. According to the prosecution's evidence, he then ordered that a thorough "wiping out" of the Chinese male population be carried out because the Chinese were allegedly obstructing Japanese military movement and creating public disorder in the city. Pursuant to Yamashita's order, his subordinate troops swept the city to arrest ethnic Chinese, identified approximately 5,000 adult Chinese men as either former members of the Chinese Volunteer Corps or as anti-Japanese activists, and executed these men in a matter of days. To substantiate this case, the Commonwealth team made use primarily of the investigative report that had been produced by the First Demobilization Bureau (the former Japanese war ministry) in the immediate aftermath of war.[27]

The massacre of 5,000 Chinese in Singapore was one of the bitterest war memories for the British authorities in that it exposed the fragility of the largest British military base in the region. The British Empire not only failed to resist the Japanese invaders but also to protect its people in Singapore from Japanese military violence. As if to make up for their wartime incompetence, the British authorities held a separate war crimes trial in Singapore in March of 1947, which focused on this case. The Singapore trial is said to have attracted considerable public attention. Two senior officers and six army police officers (*kenpei*) were prosecuted. All were convicted, the former two receiving death sentences, and the remaining six, life imprisonment.[28] The prime suspect for this case, Yamashita, was not to be seen at this British trial, since he had already been convicted and executed in connection with the Rape of Manila in the previous year.

The Commonwealth team presented another episode of war crime that was connected to the fall of Singapore. The case in question is the massacre of Australian nurses on Banka Island east of Sumatra. A few days before Singapore fell, 65 members of the Australian Nursing Service accompanied approximately 200 civilians who tried to flee by sea. They soon came under Japanese air attack, resulting in many deaths. The survivors of the bombing sailed in life rafts and sought safe haven on Banka Island—however, they discovered that the island was already under Japanese military control. Realizing that they could not receive protection from the islanders, the refugees voluntarily surrendered to the Japanese forces so as to ensure their survival and safety. After accepting the surrender, the Japanese soldiers took all male captives to a nearby cliff and bayoneted them to death. Similarly, they ordered the 22 surviving female nurses to march into the sea, and machine-gunned them to death from behind.

The massacre on Banka Island may pale in terms of scale before the massacre of 5,000 Chinese in Singapore. But the killing of defenseless soldiers, civilians, and nurses in outright disregard of surrender is shocking. Mansfield, at least, believed so. Treating this case as a priority, he brought over Sister Vivien Bullwinkel (Fig. 7.3)—the only nurse who survived the massacre—all the way from Australia in order to take her oral evidence before the Tokyo Tribunal. Her testimony was concise and consistent, as was often the case with the witnesses the prosecution brought for war crimes phases. For her testimony, Bullwinkel received praise from Webb at the conclusion of the cross-examination.[29] She is remembered as a national war hero in Australia to this day because of her courage and service during World War II. Her portrait in the Australian War Memorial is a testament to national recognition of her heroism.

Another instance of atrocity that involved Australian victims figured prominently in the Commonwealth presentation. This case, known as the Sandakan Death Marches, took place in Borneo. This refers to a series of marches that Allied prisoners of war were forced to make in early 1945. The marches were intended partly for the relocation of useful prisoner-of-war labor to the northwestern front. They were also

Fig. 7.3 Sister Vivian Bullwinkel, Capt. Australian Army Nursing Service, testifying on the massacre on Banka Island. Courtesy National Archives, photo no. 238-FE.

undertaken to prevent the prisoners from being liberated by Allied forces, whose landing was believed imminent. About 1,300 prisoners of war were made to march in groups through a trying jungle environment with wholly inadequate food supplies. Many died of exhaustion, starvation, and disease on the way. The accompanying Japanese soldiers killed some of those who could not keep up with the march. Prisoners continued to die after they reached the prisoner-of-war camp at Ranau, located more than 100 miles away from their former camp in Sandakan. In the end, all but six prisoners perished in the Sandakan-Ranau area as a result of the Death Marches. The six survived only because they escaped from the Ranau camp, though at great risk, before they could suffer the fate of the other prisoners. Had they remained in the camp, they would probably have been dead before the war was over.[30] At the Tokyo trial, Mansfield prepared two survivors to testify in court. Preparing as many as two witnesses for a single war crimes case, again, was unusual by Tokyo standards, attesting to the great significance of the Sandakan Death Marches to the Australian prosecution team. One of the two witnesses failed to appear in court, however; the reason is not clear. (The prosecution submitted his affidavit to make up for it.) Another survivor, Warrant Officer William H. Sticpewich (Fig. 7.4), took the witness stand and testified about the circumstances of the Death Marches as well as the general camp conditions in Sandakan between 1942 and 1945.[31]

The Sandakan Death Marches are for Australians what the Bataan Death March is for Americans in terms of the place they occupy in Australian war memory. One notable difference is that the Sandakan Death Marches had a shockingly higher mortality rate: almost 100 percent. Understandably, the Sandakan Death Marches continue to be one of the unforgettable war experiences for Australians to this day. There is a permanent exhibition in honor of the victims of the Sandakan Death Marches at the Australian War Memorial in Canberra, where the photograph of every victim, when available, is exhibited. As a side note, Lt. Gen. Baba Masao, the highest-ranking officer who commanded the 37th Japanese Army in charge of the Sandakan prisoners of war, was tried at the Australian war crimes tribunal in Rabaul in June 1947. He was found guilty and sentenced to death by hanging.[32]

Of various Asian nationals, the Burmese occupied a prominent place in the Commonwealth presentation.[33] War crimes against them included the mistreatment of civilian laborers at the Burma-Siam Death Railway. The witness Wild stated that approximately 150,000 "Asiatic laborers" were mobilized. He identified Burmese as being in the work units; there were also Chinese, Malays, Tamils, and Thais.[34] Mansfield supplied additional documentary evidence, including a detailed affidavit taken from Thakin Sa, a Burmese and a former labor superintendant. According to his account, the Japanese army initially recruited Burmese for the railway project with the false promise of good work and good rewards, and later by forceful arrest when recruitment by deception no longer worked. The work environment was extremely cruel, he said, and in fact, "Labourers were treated as slaves." This statement was by no means a figure of speech, as he added, "Whips and sticks were freely used on the labourers." Thakin Sa also testified that many Burmese came with family members, friends, and relatives, whose age ranged "between 12 and 60." He further recounted that a "fair proportion of the labourers were women," who "suffered a good deal of molestation from the Japanese

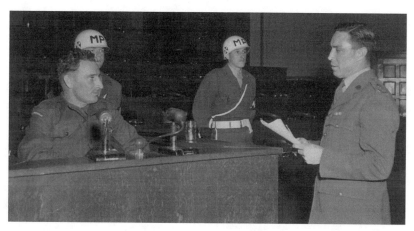

Fig. 7.4 Assistant Prosecutor Col. Thomas F. E. Mornane (Australia) examining Warrant Officer 1st Class William Hector Sticpewich, Australian Army, on the Sandakan Death Marches. Courtesy National Archives, photo no. 238-FE.

Army Personnel" until after July 1943 "when the Army authorities imported about 300 prostitutes to serve the Army personnel engaged on the project."[35] This last piece of information indicates that Burmese women became the target not only of the Japanese slave labor program but also of sexual violence, and that the latter type of violence subsided only by the introduction of what appears to be comfort women.

Mansfield provided other exhibits further showing that Asian civilian laborers died by the thousands in a few months at railway construction sites, due to excessive work, daily beatings, lack of proper food and medical supplies, and other forms of cruel treatment. The prosecution's evidence, moreover, showed that Japanese medical officers used "medical" means to kill the seriously ill, such as overdosing them with morphine, giving other types of poisonous injections, or feeding them poisoned food.[36] Together with Wild's testimony, the Commonwealth team showed that the victims at the Death Railway were not only Allied prisoners of war but also a very large number of the Asian male and female civilian populations.

Mansfield introduced other cases of Burmese-targeted mass atrocities. One case concerned Kalagon, a village located near Moulmein (in southeastern Burma), in early July of 1945. The Japanese soldiers and the *kenpeitai* (army police) visited the village one afternoon. They detained men, women, and children of the village in mosques and adjacent buildings by claiming that they had collaborated with guerrilla forces. They then interrogated and tortured the villagers for the rest of the day. The following day, the Japanese took the captives out of confinement in small groups, bayoneted them to death, and disposed of the bodies in the well. Six hundred villagers were killed in this manner, leaving about 400 to survive.[37] The Kalagon massacre was the very first case to be brought before the British war crimes tribunal in Rangoon, attesting to its importance in the eyes of both the British authorities and the Burmese people. Eight Japanese army officers in the ranks of major, captain, and lieutenant, as well as six members of the *kenpeitai*, were prosecuted for the crimes of unlawful killing, beating, and torture. Ten were found guilty and four received the death sentence. The Commonwealth team used the record from this British trial as evidence at Tokyo.[38]

Turning southward to British Borneo, the Commonwealth team introduced evidence of large-scale and systematic massacres that Japanese forces committed against an island tribe known as the Suluks. The mass atrocity in question was triggered by a Chinese-led revolt in October 1943 at Jesselton (present-day Kota Kinabalu) in northern Borneo. Forty Japanese were killed as a result of the revolt. The Japanese military authorities immediately retaliated, launching a counteroffensive against the Chinese rebels in reprisal. According to the prosecution's evidence, the Japanese armed forces arrested, tortured, and executed at least 179 ethnic Chinese men and women. An additional 500 to 600 Chinese were estimated to have died as a result of torture, hunger, or disease while in custody. Japanese authorities subsequently found out that the Suluks, a fishing tribe who lived on small islands near Jesselton, had assisted the Chinese rebels. Four months later, they began raiding the Suluk villages, arrested boys and men, and executed them all after torturing and forcing them to confess their complicity in the rebellion. Those Suluk women and children who were left behind were either killed or deported elsewhere to work as slave labor. Many of them died due to starvation and disease.[39]

A member of the British war crimes investigation team, Capt. M. J. Dickson, wrote a report on the Japanese actions against the Suluks, which was introduced as evidence at Tokyo. In Dickson's assessment, the Japanese retaliated so thoroughly that the Suluk community was brought to the point of extinction. He observed that there were no Suluk males to transmit the cultural heritage to their children, nor for that matter were there any adult males to produce Suluk descendants; the male population was virtually wiped out in the mass execution. The health of the Suluk women, too, had deteriorated and their reproductive capacity was in peril. Having made these observations, Dickson made the following remark:

> I do not think the evidence justifies an accusation against the Japanese authorities of deliberately planning the extermination of this race. They treated the Suluks in the same way that they treated other peoples in this area whom they suspected of disaffection, for example, the Chinese; yet it would not be held that they tried to exterminate the Chinese in North Borneo. . . . The treatment of the women and children deported from Sulug to Bangawan . . . was in keeping with the Japanese attitude to other native peoples. . . . The treatment of the Suluk men and boys in jail, the tortures and the executions, were similar to, or only a little worse than, the treatment of the Chinese.[40]

In Dickson's opinion, Japanese treatment of the Suluks was standard in that Chinese and any other peoples who were deemed anti-Japanese were treated in the same manner. In other words, it was common practice for the Japanese armed forces to carry out systematic killing of civilian populations on grounds of ethnicity or for political reasons.

From the Andaman Islands in the Indian Ocean came another example of massacre of a civilian population. Mohamed Hussain, whose affidavit was presented as evidence at Tokyo, was the sole survivor of this atrocity. According to his account, the Japanese military authorities one day announced to the islanders that "as from August [1945] onwards no rations would be supplied to the public" and that the islanders were to be sent to "a new place to cultivate the land." With this explanation, boats carrying about 700 men, women, and children set off on the evening of August 3, 1945. When they reached about 400 yards offshore, the Japanese forced everyone to go overboard by using "sticks and bayonets." About 200 managed to swim back to shore, but all of them except the affiant died in the following six weeks due to lack of food.[41] The Andaman case indicates that the Japanese military authorities planned and carried out the massacre for reasons other than the elimination of anti-Japanese elements. In this case, they apparently decided to drown the entire island population in order to secure the food supply for themselves.

Evidence of the Japanese commission of a similar massacre was presented in connection with Ocean Island as well. The one who offered testimony was a man by the name of Kabunare, a native of Nikunau Island and a survivor of the atrocity. According to his account, the Japanese military authorities on the island shot and killed the entire island population—100 of them—even though the war was already over. "The hands of the natives of KABUNARE's section were tied," the account goes, and they were "lined up on the edge of a cliff and the Japs opened fire." When the affiant recovered consciousness, he found himself floating in the sea alongside many dead bodies. He hid himself in a cave until December 2, 1945, when he learned that the war had been over and that the island was now under Allied control.[42] The justification for the massacre is not known. It might have had to do with food shortages, or there might have been another explanation. Whatever the motives may have been, the important fact is that the Japanese occupation forces committed a massacre of innocent civilians even after hostilities had ceased.

The Commonwealth team introduced evidence of cannibalism and medical experimentation as well, thereby further substantiating the charges that were separately made by the Philippine and American teams. One court exhibit contained information about an episode of cannibalism in New Britain, an island off New Guinea, in late 1944. It documented that the Japanese conducted what appears to have been ritual consumption of human flesh. According to an eyewitness account, an American fighter pilot about 19 years old made a forced landing one afternoon. He was decapitated half an hour later, whereupon his flesh was cut into pieces, fried, and served for a gathering of Japanese army personnel stationed in the area that evening. The witness, Havildar Chandgi Ram of the Indian Army, recounted the circumstances of the gathering as follows: "About 1800 hours a Japanese high official (a Major-General) addressed about 150 Japanese, mostly officers. At the conclusion of the speech a piece of the fried flesh was given to all present, who ate it on the spot."[43] This episode of cannibalism bears a striking resemblance to the case related at the U.S. Navy trial in Guam, pointing to the possibility that the Japanese forces in New Britain, too, practiced the eating of human flesh for the eventuality of supply termination as experienced on the neighboring island of New Guinea.

Fig. 7.5 Lt. John Charles Van Nooten, a member of the Australian Infantry Battalion, testifying on the Japanese mistreatment of Allied prisoners of war at Ambon, Molucca Islands. Courtesy National Archives, photo no. 238-FE.

Regarding medical experiments, one court exhibit made a passing reference to the routine Japanese practice of medical experimentation on captives in New Guinea. One of the entries in a unit diary recorded the unsuccessful interrogation of some local people:

28 April—Although we today re-examined them [captives] at the Mountain Gun Unit sentry group, they did not confess. Perhaps MAHI and the other natives took separate roads to come here, so the latter did not see them. However, *considering the future, one person was handed over to the Chief Medical Officer of No. 4 Air Medical Unit for medical experiments,* and the other five persons were stabbed to death.[44]

This court exhibit offered no further details about the actual medical experiments. Yet it is still an important piece of evidence that shows the Japanese practice of medical experimentation in the South Pacific area.

The Commonwealth team introduced additional evidence of medical experimentation in an account taken from Lt. John C. Van Nooten (Fig. 7.5) of the Australian Imperial Forces. He was brought to Tokyo so that he could testify on the circumstances at the Tan Toey Barracks in Ambon. He had been held prisoner at the Tan Toey camp along with 800 Australian and 300 Dutch prisoners of war since February 1942.

During the examination-in-chief, the Australian assistant prosecutor, Thomas Mornane, drew from Van Nooten the testimony that the Japanese had conducted a series of medical experiments on selected prisoners of war in April 1945. Mornane asked him to elaborate on what had taken place. In response, Van Nooten related the following incident:

Nine groups, each consisting of ten men, and each group consisting of men of similar condition, that is, one group would consist solely of men who were hospital patients and suffering from beri-beri; another group would consist of patients who were not in hospital but who suffered from beri-beri; another group consisted of men who were a little stronger; or another group would be reasonably fit men. A Japanese medical officer then took a blood test of each men of all—of each of these groups. They then gave a course of injections, injections that were supposed to be vitamin B-1 and casein. After two or three days a further injection was given, this time of T.A.B., and the course of injections continued over a period of one month. During this period certain groups received a slightly increased ration. The additional ration consisted of 150 grams of sweet potato and about 200 grams of sage. If a man was still alive at the end of the one month's period a further blood test was taken.[45]

He testified that 50 prisoners of war died as a result.

The testimony above is the most extensive piece of evidence concerning Japanese medical experimentation that the prosecution introduced at the Tokyo trial. The very detailed nature of the evidence itself deserves attention. Moreover, the Australian team actively sought this particular account before the Tribunal, indicating its intention to treat this type of offense as a widespread war crime. Such effort on the part of Australia shows that the exemption allowed to Unit 731 did not apply to all cases of Japanese medical experimentation. The Australian members, after all, were under no obligation to tailor their prosecutorial priorities according to the political considerations of the United States or of any other countries. Their primary task was to substantiate what they themselves considered to be the prosecutorial priorities of the country they represented.

In addition to these instances of medical experimentation, the Commonwealth team introduced two cases of vivisection. One of them took place in the Ocean Island sector. The Japanese were reported to have conducted vivisection on a "healthy, unwounded" prisoner of

Fig. 7.6 Assistant Prosecutor Lt. Col. J. S. Damste (Netherlands) examining Maj. Michael C. G. Ringer, British Indian Army, concerning the treatment of Allied prisoners of war held in Sumatra. Courtesy National Archives, photo no. 238-FE.

war at Khandok. The other case introduced in court took place during the early phase of the Pacific War, at Kokumbona in Guadalcanal in September 1942. According to the diary of a Japanese officer (his military unit is not known), a medical officer dissected alive two recaptured escapees. The officer who observed the vivisection commented that "for the first time I saw the internal organs of a human being" and that "[i]t was very informative."[46] In both instances, the Japanese servicemen conducted vivisection apparently as "practical anatomy lessons" for medical students and officers.

The Dutch East Indies

Of all presentations concerning Japanese war crimes, the one by Sinninghe Damste (Fig. 7.6), the Dutch representative, was the most decentralized in terms of its structure. He handled all cases as if they were of equal importance, clustered them according to various "types" of offenses, and introduced the evidence in such a way as to underscore the recurrence of the atrocities with common patterns across the Japanese-occupied Dutch East Indies. The other prosecutors did the same, except that they did not devise any special method of presentation that would elicit common patterns of atrocity as systematically as Damste did. The Dutch presentation, in this respect, followed the general prosecutorial strategy most faithfully. It showed in a lucid manner that the Japanese armed forces committed the same kinds of war crimes repeatedly in various theaters of war.

Under his scheme of presentation, Damste broadly divided the Dutch evidence first by region (as did most of the other Allied prosecutors). The primary regions he covered were Dutch Borneo, Java, Sumatra, Timor and the Lesser Sunda Islands, and the Celebes and surrounding islands. Then materials for each region were further divided according to the types of victims involved: prisoners of war, civilian internees, and non-interned civilians. The evidence of war crimes against prisoners of war was subdivided into the following four categories: murder, mistreatment at prisoner-of-war camps, illegal and criminal executions, and mistreatment during the transfer of prisoners. There were two common patterns of war crime with regard to civilian internees: mistreatment at internment camps and murder. Finally, atrocities targeted at non-interned civilians fell under the following five categories: use of the native population as *rōmusha* (coolies); atrocities perpetrated by the *kenpeitai*; cruelties committed against civilian prisoners; the use of women for forced prostitution; and atrocities perpetrated by the *tokkeitai* (navy special police).

One type of war crime that stood out in the Dutch presentation was the Japanese mistreatment of Dutch civilians in internment camps. Evidence showed that the Japanese authorities not only neglected their responsibility to attend to the internees' basic needs for survival, such as providing minimum food, shelter, and medicine, but they also tolerated widespread violence against the internees. The treatment meted out to the internees was so horrific that it resulted in a high death rate. By illustration, one court exhibit recorded the death of 1,500 people at the internment camps at Tjimahi in Java, caused by "malnutrition, stomach complaints and the lack of medicine."[47] Another affidavit related that 300 civilian internees died in two years due to dysentery and malnutrition at the Pematang Sianter Jail in northeast Sumatra. The gravely sick usually received no proper medical treatment. On the contrary, "the dying was speeded up by putting the patient outside the cell in the tropical sun."[48] Other Dutch documents similarly attested to a high death rate and chronic physical abuse, such as beating, torture, deprivation of food and medical supplies, and other forms of cruelty including summary execution.[49]

The extremity of Japanese cruelty against internees was such that it became a major diplomatic problem between the Dutch and Japanese governments after the war. By the time the Tokyo trial was over (November 1948), many Allied governments were warming to the idea of normalizing diplomatic relations with Japan and rehabilitating Japan into the international community. Amid the ameliorating international relations, the Dutch government continued to hold a hard position because of the horrendous Japanese treatment of Dutch citizens in the internment camps. When the time came to negotiate the San Francisco Peace Treaty in September 1951, the Dutch government pressed for, and secured, a special letter that recognized Dutch entitlement to demand reparations on behalf of Dutch civilian victims. This letter is known as the "Stikker-Yoshida letter," named after the then Dutch foreign minister, D. U. Stikker, and the Japanese prime minister, Yoshida Shigeru. The note did not require the Japanese government to take any formal responsibility to compensate the Dutch victims; it stated only the understanding that Japan had the moral duty to do so. The lack of legal effect notwithstanding, this letter enabled the Dutch government to negotiate reparations in subsequent years.[50]

At the Tokyo trial in December 1946, Damste documented Japanese mistreatment of Dutch internees by introducing a large number of evidentiary records from all five regions (Dutch Borneo, Java, Sumatra, Timor, and the Celebes). Two of the only three witnesses he called for the Dutch phase specifically testified on Japanese atrocities against civilian internees. One of the two witnesses was Lt. Col. Nicholas Read-Collins, the chief of the British Legal Section for the occupation authorities at Tokyo, and the other, Maj. Cornelius Leenheer, was a former civilian internee who joined Read-Collins's war crimes investigation team after being freed from Japanese military rule. Read-Collins testified mostly on his visits to former internees in Java immediately after the war. He gave testimony about their abnormal mental and physical condition. Leenheer centered his testimony on his personal experiences as an internee in the Japanese-controlled Dutch East Indies.[51]

In addition to oral and documentary evidence, Damste also screened a film, *Nippon Presents*, as an additional court exhibit concerning the Japanese mistreatment of civilian internees. This documentary film provided a commentary on a Japanese wartime propaganda film, *Australia Calling*. For the production of *Australia Calling*, the Japanese had forced several English, Australian, and Dutch prisoners of war and female internees in Java into acting, so as to give viewers a false impression of camp conditions. The purpose of the Japanese film had been to incite antiwar sentiment in Australia by showing that internees were treated humanely. The postwar production, *Nippon Presents*, incorporated segments of *Australia Calling* next to visual images of the same camps, which the Allied forces had filmed after the liberation. The postwar footage was designed to contrast the Japanese propaganda film with the actual conditions of the internment camps as they were found at the end of the war. In producing *Nippon Presents*, the Dutch East Indies cooperated with Australia in assembling those male and female prisoners who had been forced to act in *Australia Calling*. Recorded testimonial accounts taken from survivors accompanied the film.[52]

The Japanese use of women for sexual slavery figured in the Dutch presentation as another common type of war crime. The Chinese team had made passing reference to such offenses. Damste took a step further, specifying it as one of the recurrent patterns of war crime for which the Japanese leaders at the highest level should be held accountable. The episodes of sexual slavery—or "forced prostitution" as he termed it—that he introduced were the following. First, the Japanese naval forces stationed in Pontianak in Dutch Borneo set up nine or ten new brothels for navy and civilian personnel in 1943. Three of them were meant for navy personnel, five or six for civilians, and one exclusively for higher-ranking officials of the naval civil administration. The *tokkeitai* formally took charge of hunting for local women on the streets, having them medically examined, and putting them into the brothels. Second, certain Dutch girls and women in internment camps in Java were put into a brothel in early 1944. They were forced to engage in sexual intercourse with Japanese officers and soldiers under threats and physical compulsion; this lasted for three weeks. Third, the Japanese occupation forces in Portuguese Timor compelled local chiefs to provide women for Japanese military brothels. The Japanese authorities threatened the chiefs, saying that if they failed to provide women, their own female relatives would be detained for sexual enslavement. Finally, a Japanese expeditionary force that invaded Moa Island off Timor committed a similar offense. The army attacked the island population in retaliation for the killing of some Japanese military police. After executing approximately 100 rebels, the army detained six women and used them as sex slaves for 25 Japanese men over the course of eight months.[53]

The cases of military sexual slavery in the Dutch phase were limited to these four. The small number notwithstanding, Damste's presentation fulfilled the common prosecutorial strategy in two important respects. First, the cases he selected covered a broad region in and around the Dutch East Indies, thereby indicating the widespread and recurrent character of this type of offense. Second, the victims of sexual enslavement were women of various racial and ethnic backgrounds, thereby further underscoring that Japanese servicemen systematically committed this type of offense against the female population that came under their military control. Since three of the four introduced cases involved non-Caucasian women, one might say that Damste attached importance to documenting Japanese sexual violence against Asian women. Alternatively, this might simply reflect his finding that Asian women had been the principal victims of Japanese military sexual slavery.

Together with the cases introduced during the Chinese phase, these four episodes from the Dutch presentation constitute the first oral and documentary evidence of organized military sexual slavery that the Japanese public was made to confront in the aftermath of war. However, if the Dutch evidence had any educational effect, it was probably minimal. Damste was one of those prosecutors who made extensive use of the synopsis method in view of the need to expedite the trial. (See Chapter 5 for related discussion.) He would give no more than a brief summary of each evidentiary document when introducing it in court. As a result, the spectators in the court gallery could learn very little about the circumstances of the sexual crimes the Dutch prosecutor substantiated.

To see how the use of synopses was reflected in the court proceedings, one may consider the way in which Damste introduced a Dutch intelligence report concerning the navy brothels in Pontianak. He read the summary of the report only, which went as follows: "The terrible measures regarding enforced prostitution are described in the report of the investigator Captain J. F. HEYBROEK."[54] No additional explanation was given beyond this. The judges and the defendants could find out about the details of the crime later on, since they were provided with the full text of the court exhibit. Those in the court gallery, however, were left with virtually no information as to what exactly were the "terrible measures regarding enforced prostitution" with which the highest-ranking Japanese political and military leaders were charged. Yet it was in such unread court exhibits that some of the most important pieces of information about Japanese wartime atrocity were included. This Dutch intelligence report, in particular, offered an unusually detailed account of the Japanese system of sexual slavery. Titled "Report on Enforced Prostitution in Western Borneo, N.E.I. during Japanese Naval Occupation," it explained when the garrisoned navy established the brothels, who took charge of the operation, who procured women, and how the brothels were actually run. With respect to the procurement of women for the brothels, the report also included the following account about Japanese treatment of local women:

In their search for women the Tokei Tai [navy special police] ordered the entire female staffs of the Minseibu [civil administration bureau] and the Japanese firms to report to the Tokei Tai Office, undressed some of them entirely and accused them of maintaining relations with Japanese. The ensuing medical examination revealed that several were virgins. It is not known with certainty how many of these unfortunates were forced into brothels. Women did not dare escape from the brothels as members of their family were then immediately arrested and severely maltreated by the Tokei Tai. In one case it is known that this caused the death of the mother of the girl concerned.[55]

The above excerpt shows how much detail an unread court exhibit could contain about the nature of the crimes committed.

Due largely to the Allied prosecutors' reliance on the synopsis method, the content of many court exhibits escaped the attention not only of contemporary trial observers but also of researchers in subsequent years. Various misconceptions about the prosecutorial effort became widespread as a result. For instance, it was said that no charges concerning Japanese military sexual slavery were made at Tokyo, or that because of racial bias Allied prosecutors purposely dropped cases involving Asian women. Yuki Tanaka's publication, *Japan's Comfort Women: Sexual Slavery and Prostitution during World War II and the U.S.*

Occupation (2002), is one example that advances these interpretations. Tanaka argues that Allied prosecutors knowingly withheld evidence of organized military sexual slavery, especially when the victims involved were Asian women, because they had gender and racial biases. He also contends that Allied investigators did not press charges of sexual slavery because they were aware of Allied soldiers being equally guilty of committing comparable sexual crimes against women in occupied Japan after the war. Making reference to postwar Dutch war crimes trials in Java, Tanaka further holds that Allied investigators were prepared to prosecute Japanese military sexual slavery only when the victims concerned were Caucasian women. Tanaka's book, in this manner, portrays the Allied war crimes program as tainted by the sexism and racism of the predominantly white male war crimes trials.[56] The accusation that the Allied prosecutorial effort suffered gender and racial imbalances may hold true with respect to some of the war crimes trials, but such characterization does not apply to the Tokyo trial. Actual trial records unambiguously show that the Allied prosecutors—and in particular, the Dutch member—substantiated the Japanese commission of various forms of sexual violence including sexual slavery, targeted in principal at the Asian female population.

Misunderstandings about the Allied prosecutorial effort are being revised in Japan in recent years. Hayashi Hirofumi's research on the British war crimes trials is a case in point, in which he shows that Japanese military sexual violence against Asian women was, in fact, an important part of the prosecutorial priorities.[57] Similarly, Utsumi Aiko analyzed a portion of the record of the Tokyo trial in preparation for the Women's International War Crimes Tribunal, a non-binding people's court organized by national and international NGOs, held in Tokyo in December 2000. Her research showed that evidence of sexual violence including sexual slavery was actually presented during the Tokyo proceedings notwithstanding the general belief to the contrary.[58] In April 2007, the Center for Research and Documentation on Japan's War Responsibility (Nihon no Sensō Sekinin Shiryō Sentā) took a step further, compiling and releasing to the international as well as national media the documentary evidence of Japanese military sexual slavery as substantiated as the Tokyo trial.[59] Jurists and human rights scholars outside Japan, in the meantime, have come to recognize the Tokyo trial as a historic proceeding that established the criminality of wartime sexual violence under international humanitarian law.[60]

The Dutch presentation also had as its crucial component the Japanese use of the Indonesian civilian population for slave labor. This part of the Dutch case deserves special attention here, since it could serve as cumulative evidence for the overall prosecution's case on the Japanese perpetuation of slave-labor programs that had relied not only on Allied prisoners of war but also on civilian populations throughout the Asia-Pacific region. In the Dutch East Indies, this practice was so commonplace that the Japanese term for coolies, *rōmusha*, had gained wide currency during the war. Damste, too, used this loan word when substantiating slave labor cases before the Tokyo Tribunal.

He introduced the slave-labor cases by first claiming that *rōmusha* were those who were subjected to involuntary servitude, as he said, "The conscription of Romusha was carried out by a series of round-ups through the medium of the village chiefs." He elaborated further, saying that *rōmusha* were forced to do things such as "digging trenches, constructing air raid shelters and other military works, making roads and railways, working in oilfields, coal mines," among other activities. Moreover, "Javanese youths in particular" were the major victims of slave labor, and were sent "all over South East Asia: Sumatra, Borneo, Celebes, Ambon, and even as far as Malaya, Burma, Siam and the Philippines."[61]

After making these introductory remarks, Damste presented evidence that substantiated the Japanese mistreatment of Asian civilian laborers. Most cases he introduced had taken place in Singapore, through which many Javanese civilians were routed before being sent off to various work destinations. One of the exhibits was an affidavit taken from a Javanese by the name of Achmad Bin Ketajoeda. It attested to the high death rate of Javanese civilians who were deported to Singapore. According to the summary of the affidavit, he was made to work at a place called Kampong Barow, where "only 1,000 among 2,000 coolies were physically able to work" and "4 or 6 died everyday."[62] Similarly, a former *rōmusha* by the name of Rebo attested to the cruelties meted out to civilian laborers at Tandjong Pinang. The summary of the court exhibit stated that "[i]n 9 months 400 out of 750 coolies died," or in other words, that more than half of the deportees perished.[63]

Another affidavit—taken from a man by the name of Goedel, a native of Rapiah near Solo (Java)—was introduced, further substantiating the cruel treatment the Japanese camp guards meted out to the Javanese deportees in Singapore. According to the affidavit, Goedel was told by his village headman to work for the Japanese at Klatan, only to find that he was actually bound for a camp at Henderson Road in Singapore. Damste apparently regarded this affidavit as singularly important, since he chose to read out a long excerpt from it instead of limiting to his usual practice of reading the synopsis only. Describing the condition of the deportees' camp, the affiant stated, among other things, that "[t]here were very many sick, above all with dysentery, beriberi and tropical ulcers; there was also a great deal of malaria. There was no quinine or any other medicines. . . . Very many people died here; everyday certainly 15 to 20 people died. I do not know how many died in toto, but certainly estimate the number at about 2000." Goedel himself was subjected to brutal treatment on the allegation that he stole a blanket. The camp guards bound and suspended him from the ceiling, thrashed him with leather straps and leather shoes, forced his face into a basin of water to simulate drowning, and repeated these and other forms of torture for a week. The damage done to his body was so serious that Goedel could not move for about a month.[64] These accounts from the Dutch team show that the Japanese military authorities recruited civilian populations for slave labor not only from China and mainland Southeast Asia but also from maritime Southeast Asia, and perpetrated unspeakable violence against them on a vast scale.

French Indochina

The French presentation was significantly shorter than those made by other Allied prosecutors; about 44 pieces of evidence were presented. Many cases concerned atrocities committed by the *kenpeitai*, such as arrest, torture, and murder of civilians and prisoners of war in Japanese-occupied French Indochina. These types of atrocity were commonly committed in the name of quashing espionage and anti-Japanese activism. Rape was one another common pattern of Japanese military violence that figured prominently in the French presentation. Most victims were French women, but at least one document pointed to the Japanese detention of Vietnamese women for sexual enslavement. According to an affidavit taken from one Vietnamese woman, Japanese military authorities accused her and other women of having sexual liaisons with French soldiers. They then ordered them to serve at a Japanese military brothel in Tie Yen. The affiant escaped before being forced into the brothel, but other women apparently did not.[65] Their fate is unclear, since the affiant stopped short of providing further information. Nevertheless, this affidavit can be treated as another crucial piece of evidence that the Japanese armed forces used women for organized military sexual slavery in Japanese-occupied French Indochina as well.

The Defense Response

When confronted with overwhelming evidence of the Japanese commission of mass atrocities from across the Pacific theater, what did the defense do? The answer is fairly straightforward. As was the case with the prosecution's evidence concerning Nanking, the defense team did little to contest it, thereby allowing the facts established by the prosecution to stand. The defense lawyers did challenge, however, the allegations that their clients were individually responsible for the widespread atrocities. While admitting that the Japanese forces committed acts of brutality virtually everywhere, they argued that there were no discernible patterns of atrocities emerging from the wealth of documents produced by the prosecution. It was therefore impossible, so the defense argument went, to assume that these crimes were committed with the knowledge, or on the orders, of the central government.

In the effort to exculpate the accused, Takayanagi Kenzō (Fig. 7.7)—a lead Japanese defense lawyer—set forth an additional argument during the summation. He contended that the Japanese troops might have committed similar patterns of atrocity, but that the commonality of the Japanese military violence could have resulted from a Japanese cultural proclivity, not from the alleged orders from the central government. He explained:

Even if the alleged atrocities or other contraventions assume a similar singular pattern of acts it cannot justify such an assumption [that there were orders from superiors]. Such a matter may have been a sheer reflection of national or racial traits [*kokuminsei moshiku wa minzokusei no han'ei*]. Crimes no less than masterpieces of art may express certain characteristics reflecting the *mores* of

Fig. 7.7 Takayanagi Kenzō, one of the Japanese defense lawyers, at the lectern. Courtesy National Archives, photo no. 238-FE.

a race. Similarities in the geographic, economic, or strategic state of affairs may in part account for the "similar pattern" assumed.[66]

By this explanation, Takayanagi seemed to be making a last-ditch effort to rebut the charges of leadership responsibility for war crimes. In substance, however, his argument only helped affirm the prosecution's central contentions: that the Japanese armed forces habitually committed war crimes in various theaters of war and that the Japanese leaders *knew, or had reason to know*, that the Japanese soldiers would commit atrocities.[67] Deploying soldiers whom government leaders knew to have violent behavioral problems was tantamount to giving them authorization to commit war crimes.

The Findings of the Tokyo Tribunal

After hearing all oral and documentary evidence from the two parties, The Tokyo Tribunal gave the following ruling:

The evidence relating to atrocities and other Conventional War Crimes presented before the Tribunal establishes that from the opening of the war in China until the surrender of Japan in August 1945 torture, murder, rape and other cruelties of the most inhumane and barbarous character were freely practised by the Japanese Army and Navy. During a period of several months the Tribunal heard evidence, orally or by affidavit, from witnesses who testified in detail to atrocities committed in all theaters of war on a scale so vast, yet following so common a pattern in all theatres, that only one conclusion is possible that atrocities were either secretly ordered or willfully permitted by the Japanese Government or individual members thereof and by the leaders of the armed forces.[68]

By this ruling, the Tribunal upheld the prosecution's contention that atrocities so widespread and following common patterns could not have been committed at the whim of individual military officers or their subordinates alone. Rather, they must have been committed with the understanding of the central government that it was the general policy of the Japanese conduct of war and military occupation. The phrase "secretly ordered" here is interesting, since it points to the Tribunal's implicit recognition that the prosecution fell short of providing conclusive evidence of criminal orders.[69] As discussed earlier, this shortcoming was conditioned by the Japanese government's empire-wide effort to destroy incriminating evidence *en masse* for at least two full weeks at the end of the war.

The above ruling was followed by the discussion of the major patterns of atrocities for which the Tribunal considered the Japanese government at the highest level should be considered answerable. Just under 20 particular patterns of atrocities were listed.[70] They included: the complete disregard of prisoner-of-war status for Chinese soldiers by calling them "bandits"; massacre, rape, looting, and other cruelties and destruction in Nanking; excessive and unlawful punishments of prisoners of war, especially captured Allied aviators; massacres of prisoners of war, civilian internees, the sick and wounded, medical personnel, and civilian populations with no military justification; death marches; illegal and cruel use of prisoner-of-war labor, in particular at the Burma-Siam Death Railway; illegal warfare and killing on the high seas; failure to provide prisoners of war with proper food, clothing, medical supplies, and shelter; forced signing of non-escape oaths at prisoner-of-war camps; public humiliation of prisoners of war; and obstruction of the protecting powers from inspecting prisoner-of-war camps. The commonly patterned war crimes that the Tribunal identified fell largely in line with those that had been listed in the Bill of Indictment. Furthermore, the Tribunal recognized other types of atrocities that had not been explicitly identified in the indictment. One of them was torture perpetrated by the *kenpeitai* and camp guards. The Tribunal found that torture was inflicted on prisoners of war and civilian internees "at practically all places occupied by Japanese troops, both in the occupied territories and in Japan" throughout the entire period of war in the Pacific.[71] Vivisection, cannibalism, and mutilation were also established as widespread war crimes. The Tribunal noted in passing that the Japanese at times committed cannibalism "from choice and not of necessity."[72]

Some other types of atrocity did not receive any special ruling from the Tribunal as commonly patterned war crimes. For instance, medical experimentation was not included in the Tribunal's list. This is not surprising, given the paucity of evidence in support of the charge. The only evidence the prosecution presented was a passing reference to the practice of medical experimentation in a prisoner-of-war camp in the Philippines, another passing reference in one court exhibit concerning New Guinea, and oral evidence taken from Charles Van Nooten concerning medical experimentation at the Tan Toey camp in Ambon. The Tribunal might have faced criticism for an arbitrary ruling if it had established the responsibility of the central government on the basis of such poor documentation.

Similarly, the Tribunal did not specifically identify Japanese military sexual slavery as another commonly patterned war crime. At first, in documenting one such episode the judges seemed prepared to recognize that this type of atrocity constituted a war crime. The relevant part in the judgment read: "During the period of Japanese occupation of Kweilin, they [the Japanese forces] committed all kinds of atrocities such as rape and plunder. They recruited women labour on the pretext of establishing factories. They forced the women thus recruited into prostitution with Japanese troops."[73] Having made this point, however, the Tribunal stopped short of giving an unequivocal ruling that the leaders of the central government were answerable for the perpetration of military sexual slavery. One plausible explanation for the judges' seeming hesitation is that, like medical experimentation, they found the prosecution's evidence insufficient to establish high-level governmental involvement. The prosecutors representing China, the Netherlands, and France did document the Japanese commission of military sexual slavery. Nevertheless, the cases they introduced were not many. Their court exhibits did not contain much information about the circumstances of the crimes either, except a few presented for the Dutch phase. In all probability, the Tribunal concluded that the prosecution did not meet the burden of proof for establishing the responsibility of the central government. The prosecution, in other words, failed to convince the judges that Japanese state leaders had either ordered or tolerated in the commission of this offense as a matter of policy.

After delivering general rulings on Japanese war crimes, the Tribunal handed down guilty verdicts to ten defendants while acquitting others. The convicted included Kimura Heitarō, the vice minister of war between 1941 and 1943, and the commander of the Burma Area Army between 1944 and 1945. He was found guilty of the criminal use of prisoner-of-war labor during his years in the war ministry, and of the failure to take adequate measures to stop his subordinates from committing atrocities against the Burmese population during his military assignment in southeast Asia. His responsibility extended to the massacre in Kalagon, which was only a few miles away from his army headquarters in Moulmein.[74] The accused Dohihara Kenji and Itagaki Seishirō were convicted of deliberately withholding food and medical supplies from prisoners of war while serving as commanders of the Seventh Area Army successively between April 1944 and September 1945. The Seventh Area Army had jurisdiction over Japanese-occupied Malaya, the Andaman and Nicobar Islands, Sumatra, Java, and Borneo.[75] Mutō Akira was similarly held criminally responsible for the gross mistreatment of prisoners while serving as commander of the Second Imperial Guards Division in Sumatra between April 1942 and October 1944. He was also found guilty of the Rape of Manila, during the occurrence of which he served as chief of staff of Yamashita's army.[76] Tōjō Hideki was found guilty of multiple instances of mass atrocity. It was established that while he was prime minister and concurrently war minister, he authorized the policy not to accord prisoner-of-war status to captives in the Chinese theater; approved the criminal use of prisoner-of-war labor (as exemplified in the Burma-Siam Death Railway case); promoted the exhaustive use of prisoner-of-war labor; failed to put an end to the cruel treatment of prisoners of war; and failed to discipline those responsible for the Bataan Death March.[77]

Another defendant, Koiso Kuniaki, received a similar verdict. He had served as prime minister for six months in 1944, during which the Japanese armed forces continued to commit atrocities against prisoners of war and the civilian population in various theaters of war. The Tribunal ruled that atrocities "had become so notorious that it is improbable that a man in KOISO's position would not have been well-informed either by reason of their notoriety or from interdepartmental communications." Koiso admitted his knowledge of widespread atrocities.[78] The verdicts given to the three other convicted defendants—Hirota, Shigemitsu, and Matsui—have already been discussed in the previous chapter.

One guilty verdict, given to the accused Hata Shunroku, deserves special attention here, since it allows insight into the complex ways in which the judges weighed evidence when determining the final verdicts and sentences. Hata was the successor to Matsui as commander-in-chief of the Central China Area Army in 1938, and was later appointed supreme commander for all Japanese armies in China in 1941. The Tribunal found that he was derelict in his duty to ensure the proper conduct of his forces. Hata's verdict read as follows:

In 1938 and again from 1941 to 1944 when HATA was in command of expeditionary forces in China atrocities were committed on a large scale by the troops under his command and were spread over a long period of time. Either HATA knew of these things and took no steps to prevent their occurrence, or he was indifferent and made no provision for learning whether orders for the humane treatment of prisoners of war and civilians were obeyed.[79]

This verdict is interesting, since the Tribunal took an ambiguous position concerning the nature of Hata's knowledge about the atrocities committed by his troops. The passage above states that Hata either knew, or he simply did not (care to) know due to sheer indifference. The penalty the Tribunal gave him was equally ambivalent. Hata escaped capital punishment even though he was found individually responsible for innumerable instances of grave war crimes committed by the forces under his command in China over the course of four years; he received life imprisonment instead.

The reason for the ambivalence in the verdict and sentence might have to do with the testimony given by defense witnesses on behalf of Hata. The defense team called as many as seventeen former staff officers of Hata's army to the witness box. They appeared in the courtroom one after another, uniformly denying the commission of atrocities under Hata's command, and uniformly attesting to their commander's strictness on matters regarding military discipline. One defense witness went so far as to say that "the three principles 'don't burn, don't violate, don't loot,' which the Commander [Hata] always advocated, were printed and distributed among the entire army" at the time of the attack on Hankow in 1938.[80]

There is considerable irony that testimony of this kind was introduced in court, since the Japanese armed forces had adopted just the opposite policy when fighting the communist Chinese. From August to October of 1940, the Eighth Route Army—the Chinese Red Army—under the command of Chu Te mobilized all of its regiments, consisting of 400,000 troops, to launch highly coordinated attacks on the garrisoned Japanese army in Hopeh and Shansi Provinces. This proved to be hugely successful, resulting in immense loss and damages on the Japanese side. Gravely humiliated by the defeat and awakened by the enormous military strength of the communist forces, the North China Area Army (commanded by Gen. Okamura Yasuji) developed a "Three-Year Liquidation and Construction Plan" in the summer of 1941. Aimed at decimating anti-Japanese forces in the region, his armed forces encircled villages that were suspected of serving as operational bases for the Eighth Route Army, and massacred those men, women, and children who came within such areas. Recent research has revealed that the Japanese forces also made use of poison gas in order to ensure the success of their scorched-earth policy. Because of the thoroughness of the Japanese destruction effort, the Chinese people came to refer to it as "Three-All Policy," meaning "burn all, kill all, and loot all."[81] This genocidal killing, which was openly carried out by the Japanese armed forces, however, was not prosecuted at the Tokyo trial. It was because the Chinese prosecution team represented the interests of the Nationalist government and not necessarily those who fell under communist leadership—even though, in principle, it represented all China. Chiang Kai-shek and Mao Tse-tung were hardly on good terms at the end of the war. They had, in fact, resumed civil war as soon as Japan surrendered in the summer of 1945. This situation led to the serious under-representation of Japanese war crimes targeted at the communist Chinese at the Tokyo trial.

To get back to Hata's case: the number of witnesses brought on behalf of Hata was certainly impressive, but it is doubtful that their testimony contributed to an effective defense. In essence, most defense witnesses did nothing other than to deny the charge that Hata's forces committed atrocities while simultaneously insisting on the impeccable moral integrity of their commander. It conversely meant that none of them squarely rebutted concrete pieces of evidence that the prosecution had introduced. The credibility of these defense witnesses was inherently suspect in any event, because they were Hata's subordinates. Any tribunal would have treated their testimony with skepticism. The explanation for the ambivalence of the Tribunal's ruling, then, needs to be sought elsewhere.

The Tribunal's difficulty, it appears, was that the prosecution did not provide sufficient evidence to establish Hata's knowledge of war crimes. Furthermore, the nature of the evidence was such that it did not justify capital punishment. The prosecutorial strategy, one may recall again, was to demonstrate how commonly and widely the Japanese army committed similarly patterned war crimes in many theaters of war and to show that these crimes could not have been committed without orders from, or the tacit approval of, the highest-ranking political and military leaders. The Chinese prosecution team applied this strategy, but the kind of evidence it produced only served to establish a *prima facie* case, falling far short of supplying sufficient evidence to allow the judges to infer Hata's knowledge. Given this shortcoming in the prosecution's presentation, the Tribunal most likely could not take too definitive a position when reaching its judgment on Hata's case. The final decision of the Tribunal was, therefore, a guilty verdict but without capital punishment.[82]

EIGHT

The First Trial Analysts

The first in-depth studies of the Tokyo trial began to appear in Japan soon after the court proceedings commenced in May 1946. The first generation of trial analysts—as one might call them—consisted mainly of jurists, historians, and political scientists who had been teaching at the leading research universities in Japan such as the University of Tokyo. These scholars were interested in finding out, above all, how this trial would reveal the truth about Japan's path to war. They were particularly eager to know the details of the decision-making processes of wartime leaders in order to determine who was responsible for the disastrous consequences of the war. They followed the trial proceedings closely as they also attempted to find out how the Tokyo Tribunal would resolve various complicated legal questions that arose in the prosecutorial effort, such as the question of whether charges of crimes against peace were justified under international law (Fig. 8.1).

Dandō Shigemitsu, then an up-and-coming professor of criminal law at the University of Tokyo and later a Supreme Court judge (1974–83) and a noted opponent of the death penalty, was the first to write an extensive commentary on the Tokyo trial. His article, "Sensō hanzai no rironteki kaibō" (The Theoretical Anatomy of War Crimes), was completed soon after the trial began, in June 1946. In this article, Dandō made a preliminary assessment of the applicable law and the purpose of the Tokyo trial. He was especially interested in determining whether it was valid to charge a group of wartime Japanese leaders with launching

Fig. 8.1 The defense box, seen from the Japanese spectators' seats in the balcony. At the far back
VIP guests are seated. Courtesy National Archives, photo no. 238-FE.

aggressive war. Although the Tokyo Tribunal had yet to give its legal
opinion (since the trial had just started), Dandō undertook to answer
this question himself in light of his expertise in law.

Dandō first discussed certain underappreciated yet crucial features of
international law governing war, which, he observed, were concerned

primarily with defining the rights and duties of individuals in the context of armed conflict, whereas the purpose of international law in general was to regulate the behavior of states. For individuals to fall under the direct jurisdiction of the international justice system was not the norm in existing international law. Only in special circumstances—such as piracy, counterfeiting, and the trafficking of women and children—did individuals become subject to international criminal prosecution as well as protection. He also pointed out that international law governing war did, nonetheless, fall under traditional international legal discourse in one important respect: this law took effect when *international* conflict broke out. In light of these two basic features, Dandō held that law governing war should be considered as standing at the intersection of "global citizenship law" (*sekai shimin hō*) and conventional, state-centric international law.[1]

He continued considering the different ways in which law had historically developed in domestic and international contexts. Referring to the opinions of contemporary legal authorities, and especially that of Lord Wright of the United Nations War Crimes Commission, he made the point that while a country usually had a central legislative body that created law at the national level, no equivalent organization existed in the international community. What had existed historically in the latter, instead, was the general understanding that principles of justice and the humanitarian ideal were the common heritage of the civilized world, and that they constituted the fundamental norms of international law. In Dandō's understanding, the international community began codifying laws in the last century or so to give concrete expression to principles that had already been universally accepted.[2]

With these theoretical preliminaries, he turned to the central question of his article: whether the concept of crimes against peace was applicable at the Tokyo trial. At first, Dandō readily agreed that the provisions on crimes against peace as well as crimes against humanity in the Charter of the Tokyo Tribunal were "statutory-laws-in-the-making" (*seiseichū no jitteihō*) and that they were susceptible to the criticism of ex post facto law,[3] but he took the position that such criticism was unwarranted. Even though the law applied at the present trial might not have been explicitly codified in legal documents, he thought that the notion of aggressive war as a crime had long been recognized as a basic principle in the field of international law. Moreover, he considered that the criticism of ex post facto could not be made in light of the civic tradition from which this legal principle came. In his understanding, the law prohibiting the retroactive application of new law originated in legal thinking concerning the rights of the individual, that is, each and every citizen was entitled to legal protection from state authorities' arbitrary exercise of power. It would defeat the purpose of the ex post facto principle if one were to use it in order to protect those who abused the state's power. Dandō emphasized that the fundamental purpose of international law governing war was precisely to protect such individual rights, as he wrote:

In domestic law, the principle of non-retroactive application of law guarantees individuals' freedom from state power. Now, when it comes to international law, and in particular, the law pertaining to war crimes, this law by itself is designed to restrict the unjust exercise of state power. One might also argue that where its relationship with state power is concerned, this law shares with domestic law the philosophical foundation of the principle of non-retroactive application of law. And of course, individual liberty must be equally respected here as much as possible.[4]

In light of this understanding, Dandō thought that the international judicial system could and should apply law in such a way as to fulfill its foundational ideals.

He further held that one could not afford *not* to apply new law concerning aggressive war. The world in the wake of World War II, as he saw it, faced an unprecedented situation that called for the urgent development of the international system for deterring future aggression and maintaining peace. The Tokyo trial, in his opinion, had a crucial role in institutionalizing such a system. Dandō was certainly not so naïve as to believe that the Tokyo trial alone could have a deterrent effect. He was rather of the opinion that future aggressors would not be dissuaded from waging war by the examples of Nuremberg or Tokyo. They would launch a war anyway on the assumption that they could escape war crimes trials by winning it. They would probably act the same way even if they should find themselves on the losing side, since they would not want to confront war crimes prosecution that a peace accord might entail. In this respect, Nuremberg and Tokyo were unlikely to make any impression on those who might contemplate waging aggressive war in the future. Yet Dandō still thought that the Tokyo trial could contribute to peace-building in the world today. Specifically, he believed that this trial would help develop public confidence in the role of the judiciary in instituting peace. Once set in motion, the dissemination of the rule of law would nurture a world community that would make a greater commitment to maintaining peace and stability. In Dandō's own words, "On reflection, the essence of trial and punishment is not simply to achieve these kinds of goals [punishment and deterrence] as propounded in goal-centric criminal theory [*mokuteki keiron*]. When one considers the significance of trial and punishment to humanity, one realizes that its significance rests with the effort to realize justice."[5] The punishment of specific wrongdoers was surely an important task, but he believed that the purpose of war crimes trials went beyond the immediate goal of retributive justice. Its ultimate purpose, in his opinion, was to spread the common understanding of justice and strengthen faith in the rule of law.

Seen in this light, it was not entirely unreasonable for him to attribute deterrent and peace-building possibilities to the Tokyo trial. Indeed, he found that the Tokyo trial had already begun to have an impact on this front. The Japanese public was now witnessing the practical form that the rule of law could take at an actual international court of justice. The defendants' right to a defense was a case in point. There was once a time when the most educated in Japan could not agree on whether an accused on trial was entitled to a defense. Disregard of defense rights, however, "has become the talk of a time now past" (*ima dewa kore mo mukashi gatari*).[6] The trial at Tokyo demonstrated that judges had the responsibility to allow both the prosecution *and* the defense to make their cases on an equal footing. They would reach their final judgment only after the two parties had been given the opportunity to present their respective cases and arguments. Acknowledgment of these basic rights, in Dandō's view, was an important step toward developing public trust in the justice system and, by extension, a significant step toward building the mechanism for peace.

Dandō took special note of the concrete way in which defense rights were protected at Tokyo. The United States supplied a group of American lawyers to represent the 28 Japanese defendants jointly with Japanese defense counsel. "[T]he passionate defense led by the American defense lawyers is sufficient to make a deep impression on us," Dandō wrote.

The commitment of the American defense lawyers was such that it led him to recall the biblical adage, "He that is without sin among you, let him first cast a stone at her." In the willingness of the United States to have its own nationals assist the leaders of a former enemy country, Dandō found the genuine spirit of a fair trial, a spirit that had rarely been seen under Japan's old regime. "One can interpret this phrase in various ways," he commented on the adage, "but is it not possible to read this as to sanctify the trial, and even demand such sanctification, rather than deny the authority of the trial?"[7] How the Tokyo trial would live up to the principle of a fair trial was yet to be seen, but Dandō had high hopes for the contribution that this trial would make to the general progress of justice in Japan and beyond.

Sensō hanzai ron (A Treatise on War Crimes), published in 1947, conveyed a similarly favorable assessment of the Tokyo trial. Its author, Yokota Kisaburō, was a senior professor at the University of Tokyo and an authority on international law in Japan (and also the chief justice of the Supreme Court, 1960–66). He had been a leading critic of the Japanese invasion of China for many years, openly questioning the legality of the Japanese military action from the time of the Mukden Incident in 1931.[8] Because of his credentials, in 1948 he was commissioned to translate the judgment of the Tokyo Tribunal from English into Japanese. Yokota's *Sensō hanzai ron* can best be described as an up-to-date guide to basic legal theories on war crimes. It offers a brief history of the law pertaining to war crimes leading up to World War II and an in-depth discussion of the three principal categories of offense that came under the jurisdiction of the Nuremberg and Tokyo Tribunals: crimes against peace, war crimes, and crimes against humanity. This book also contains the summary of the Nuremberg judgment. The summary of the Tokyo Tribunal would be included in the expanded edition, which was published after the conclusion of the Tokyo trial.

Yokota wrote *Sensō hanzai ron* on the premise that international law was undergoing a transitional period. He took this situation into account when assessing the historical significance of the Tokyo trial. In his view, the current transition was so radical in the field of international law that it could be understood as "a revolution in international law."[9] The clearest evidence of the revolutionary change was the fact that the term "war crimes" was no longer restricted to the violation of rules and customs of war; it also came to include the planning and waging of aggressive war. In other words, war itself as well as the conduct of war fell under the scrutiny of the international criminal justice system. This indicated that the basic tenet of international law on war, and the very international community that was governed by the law, was undergoing a major reconceptualization.

Yokota was favorably disposed toward the revolutionary transformation he was witnessing, but not all of his contemporaries shared his sentiments. In the preface to the book, he noted especially that the legal questions surrounding the crime of aggression had given rise to heated debates in Japan. Crimes against peace drew criticism not just because the notion underlying them was very radical but, as Yokota observed, also because the defendants charged with them consisted of influential political and military leaders. Those who opposed the charges of aggressive war generally based their opposition on the "newness" of this type of crime. "They argue," Yokota wrote, "that these crimes have not been defined as war crimes previously in any clear terms, and that no individual has been punished for these crimes." He found this line of criticism one-sided and unconvincing, since it merely attacked technical deficiencies of the law while failing to determine whether the act of aggression constituted a crime in substance: "The question is whether the act under consideration possesses a criminal character in substance, and whether there is any legitimate ground for the act to be punished. If there are sufficient substantive reasons, one should not insist on pointing out minor defects in form, let alone cite the defects and ignore the substance purely on technical grounds."[10] On these grounds, he contested the validity of the criticism of ex post facto law.

Yokota further held that in light of the evidence produced before the Tokyo Tribunal thus far (up to late 1946), the charge that Japan had committed aggression was by no means a theoretical proposition but an indisputable fact. On these grounds, too, he thought that legal technicalities should not hamper the prosecution of aggressors at the Tokyo trial. "Under the leadership of the military and bureaucrats," Yokota wrote, "Japan waged blatantly aggressive war [*kyokutan na shinryaku senso*] for an extended period of fifteen years, dating back to the Manchurian [Mukden] Incident. She committed imperialistic aggression by eating up the weak one after another. She ignored treaties, flouted justice."

Japanese aggression, in other words, was a plain fact. "That these were wrongful acts is now clear to everyone," he wrote.[11] Given the undeniability of the Japanese commission of aggressive war, Yokota found no good reason why one should object to establishing the criminality of aggressive war and punishing the culprits at the present trial. Besides, he could not accept the objection raised by the critics "even if it is a pure argument for argument's sake." Such an objection served only to obfuscate the question of where the responsibility lay.[12]

Kainō Michitaka, another member of the law faculty at the University of Tokyo, discussed the relevance of the legal principle of aggressive war in his article, "Sensō saiban no hōritsu riron" (Legal Theory of a War Trial). This article was carried in the history journal *Rekishi hyōron* in April 1948. Kainō was one of the assistant defense lawyers at the Tokyo trial. The article came out just as the prosecution and the defense had completed their respective cases and the Tribunal went into recess in order to write its judgment. The timing of the publication suggests that this article was Kainō's attempt to give his personal opinions on various legal questions that had been raised during the trial while waiting for the judges to offer theirs.

Quite significantly, Kainō shared Yokota's view that there was no controversy regarding the fact of Japanese aggression. The war Japan had waged was "a clear case of aggressive war," one "for which there really is no other adequate definition but aggressive."[13] As for the matter of law, he observed that there were disputes over whether aggressive war was a crime under international law and whether individuals could be held criminally responsible for the act. He further maintained that, from a strict legal point of view, no existing codified law stipulated the definition of aggressive war or made it a punishable crime in international law.[14] This did not lead him to conclude, however, that the criticism of retroactive legislation was valid. In his understanding, the idea of criminalizing aggressive war was not entirely new in international law; it had already been articulated in the Pact of Paris of 1928. In light of the Pact, Kainō considered that the law applied at Tokyo could be regarded as a concretized form of an already existing legal principle.[15]

Furthermore, he held that the principle of non-retroactive application of law could not be invoked because doing so would contradict the general principle of justice. Echoing the discussion in Dandō's article,

he pointed out that the notion of non-retroactivity of new law originated in the democratic ideal of ensuring freedom of thought and political action to those who may be subject to oppressive rulers' abuse
of power, not to protect the oppressors themselves. It would be a logical contradiction if one were to invoke the prohibition of ex post facto
law to give legal protection to those who violated basic human rights.
Kainō recalled the Nuremberg judgment in this connection, which he
found to have rejected the criticism of ex post facto legislation precisely
on this ground.[16] The Nuremberg Tribunal had ruled in its judgment
that those who knowingly committed a wrong in defiance of the international community should be punished even if international law
fell short of supplying codified rules. Letting them go unpunished, the
Nuremberg Tribunal had held, would be contrary to the principle of
justice. Kainō fully concurred with this legal opinion.

On this occasion, he did not forget to mention that the old Japanese
ruling class had no appreciation of the democratic tradition from which
the principle of non-retroactivity of law had arisen. This principle was
"neither respected nor understood," to put it plainly. In light of the
authoritarian tendency of the old regime, he found it ironic that Shidehara Kijūrō—a career diplomat and politician who briefly served as
prime minister in the early months of the Allied occupation—criticized
the aggressive war charges on grounds of retroactive legislation. Shidehara used to belong to the liberal wing of the prewar and wartime Japanese government, and was known for pursuing a policy of cooperation
with the Anglo-American powers and non-interference in the Chinese
revolution when he served as foreign minister between 1924 and 1931.
His liberal outlook notwithstanding, he by no means represented the
most democratic-minded of wartime Japan's public figures. Shidehara's
comment on retroactive legislation appeared to Kainō only as telling
proof of "how pervasive and incorrigible the influence of those who
are responsible for war remains" in Japan today, even in the wake of
defeat.[17] These thoughts led Kainō to the view that the criticism concerning ex post facto law was immaterial to the case at Tokyo.

Gushima Kanesaburō, a professor of international politics at Kyūshū University, expressed similar views. In his article, "Tōkyō saiban
no rekishiteki igi" (The Historical Significance of the Tokyo Trial), Gushima attempted, as Kainō had, to give his own assessment of the evi-

dence produced during the trial while waiting for the Tokyo Tribunal to give its judgment. This article appeared in the same April 1948 issue of *Rekishi hyōron*. First, Gushima, too, found that the fact of Japanese aggression had been established beyond doubt. The defense had argued, he recalled, that Japan was forced into war because the Western powers imposed economic embargoes and had choked the Japanese economy. The defense had also contended that the dramatic increase in the population and the lack of natural resources in Japan necessitated her outward military expansion. Gushima dismissed these contentions, remarking that, "I was made to listen [to these same arguments] so much that my ears got callused" (*mimi ni tako ga dekiru kurai kikasareta*). The defense argument was nothing other than the repetition of the "explanation that the Japanese militarists contrived in order to justify their acts of aggression."[18] The truth was that Japanese political, economic, and military leaders were responsible for exacerbating social stratification and creating economic misery for the underclass population. In Gushima's opinion, these leaders ought to have reviewed their own mistaken policies when confronted with mounting domestic crises. However, they chose instead to invade, exploit, and destroy the lives of people in neighboring countries so as to find quick and profitable solutions to domestic problems. "What else could we term this but aggression?" Gushima asked.[19]

These were poignant remarks coming from someone like Gushima, who had been a target of political persecution during war. A law graduate of Kyūshū University, he emerged as a leading scholar of fascism in the late 1920s. After his brief assistant professorship at Dōshisha University in Kyoto, he and many of his colleagues were forced to give up their posts in the face of governmental efforts to expel leftist and liberal intellectuals from major universities throughout the country. He eventually landed a job as a politico-military analyst for the Research Division of the Southern Manchurian Railway Company—the top-ranking wartime Japanese think-tank—in Japanese-controlled Talien (now Dalian; Dairen in Japanese) in 1937. In the freer intellectual environment in Talien, Gushima could continue his research and writing on world affairs. Soon after Japan plunged into war against the United States in December 1941, however, he was arrested as a "thought criminal" (*shisōhan*). The arrest, Gushima suspected, was connected with reports he had written in which he predicted the fragility of the Axis alliance and the resiliency of Chinese military strength. He was detained under inhumane conditions and shut off from the outside world for three years. The subsequent course of war only proved that Gushima had correctly evaluated the course of the war in Europe and the Far East.[20]

As for the question of the legality of aggressive war charges, Gushima took the view, as Kainō had, that existing international agreements, conventions, and treaties constituted sufficient grounds for such charges to be made without provoking the criticism of ex post facto legislation. In addition, he thought that the validity of crimes against peace should be determined in terms of the fundamental purpose of law, since "[i]t is not that our lives exist for the benefit of law, but that law exists for the benefit of our lives." He continued: "There are those who permit the perpetration of violence that leads to the destruction of the world, arguing that there is no precedent [for criminalizing aggressive war]. These are precisely the kind of people who do not understand for what purpose law exists."[21] Gushima rejected the critics' opposition to charges of crimes against peace from both the legal and the ethical points of view.

The same issue of *Rekishi hyōron* carried yet another article that approved the prosecutorial effort at Tokyo. "Hō no ronri to rekishi no ronri" (Logic of Law and Logic of History) was written by Inoue Kiyoshi, a graduate of the University of Tokyo and a rising scholar of modern Japanese history. As a historian, Inoue was interested mainly in analyzing documents that were presented before the Tokyo Tribunal and in determining whether charges of aggressive war were justified as a matter of substance.[22]

The central contention of the prosecution, as Inoue recalled, had been that the successive political and military leaders of the wartime Japanese government had waged a war of aggression beginning with the Mukden Incident of 1931. The defense had contended, in response, that Japan had never pursued any consistent policy of aggressive war as had been alleged. The military attacks Japan initiated were nothing more than acts of self-defense, their sole purpose being to respond to various anti-Japanese measures taken by neighboring countries in the Pacific region. The defense had also challenged the prosecution's contention that Japanese political and military leaders had cooperated in pursuit of aggressive war, arguing that the civilian leaders in the government were actually pacifists at heart and that there was no collaborative relationship between them and the military.

Assessing the arguments advanced by the two parties, Inoue found that the prosecution had made a compelling case while the defense had utterly failed to refute it. For one thing, Inoue found no supporting evidence for the defense claim that Japan had waged war only to defend herself in the face of Allied provocation. The historical truth, as he found from evidence presented at the Tokyo trial, was just the opposite. The Allied powers took economic measures against Japan so as to stop the latter's pursuit of aggressive war in China—starting with the Mukden Incident—and beyond. Put differently, it was Japan's refusal to comply with repeated warnings to observe its international obligations, such as the obligation to respect the independence and integrity of China, that led to the Allies' decision to impose economic sanctions. There was a logical contradiction, Inoue held, in overlooking these basic facts and in portraying Japan as a victim of hostile neighbors.[23]

He found it equally unconvincing when the defense argued that civilian leaders had had only peaceful intentions and that they should not be found guilty of crimes against peace. These individuals may have opposed military hard-liners on certain occasions, but *that* alone, in his opinion, did not tell the whole story of the policy-making process of the wartime Japanese government. Facts established at the Tokyo trial rather showed that these civilian leaders at times had given support to military leaders in a positive way, assisting the planning and execution of aggressive war. Underscoring such civilian-military collaboration, he wrote:

> But what did they [the government leaders] do on behalf of the people of Japan, or the people in China and in the world? Not even once did they appeal to their so-called peaceful intentions for the Japanese people. While opposing each other, the government, the military, and the political parties in the ruling class were always united against the general populace and carried out despotic rule as they pleased.[24]

As far as Inoue was concerned, what the defense claimed as opposition within leadership circles was nothing but "a mere quarrel among those in power" (*kenryokusha naibu no uchiwa mome ni suginakatta*).[25] By the same token, he found that the argument advanced on behalf of military leaders was unconvincing. He wrote, "As for those defendants with military backgrounds, they tried to escape responsibility by arguing either that they only stamped their seal mechanically when serving as the supreme commander, or that they only acted according to the orders of the superior on other occasions." Inoue was not prepared to take either argument seriously. Rather he said that, "such puerile arguments only served to disclose their shameless and base character."[26]

He found that the defense argument fell apart in the last weeks of the trial. During the summation, the defense reiterated that Japanese wartime leaders had only peaceful intentions at heart. Having little else to say, it went on to make "a surprisingly wild argument" (*odorokubeki bōron*) that war was an inevitable consequence of human biological instinct and that therefore no one should be punished for the occurrence of this phenomenon.[27] Inoue was not at all prepared to accept this line of argument.

After assessing the cases made by the prosecution and the defense, Inoue moved on to consider certain issues that the prosecution had left unaddressed. They were (1) the responsibility of the "Emperor System" (*tennōsei*); (2) the responsibility of Emperor Hirohito himself; and (3) the responsibility of the economic elite such as Japanese capitalists and landlords. Interestingly, Inoue did not fault the Allied prosecutors for these omissions. He understood that the task of the International Prosecution Section was limited to establishing the responsibility of selected individuals. "Law completes its mission when it determines their [the defendants'] crimes and metes out punishment," as Inoue put it. The task of investigating the unresolved problems was left to "those Japanese who were now determined never to entrust power to militarists ever again."[28] With this understanding, he spent the remainder of his article on analyzing the trial records and resolving these outstanding questions.

Of the three questions Inoue tackled, the one regarding Hirohito's culpability deserves special attention here because Inoue was among the first Japanese scholars to produce a detailed analysis on this subject in the wake of the war. In his article, Inoue primarily made use of the diary kept by Kido Kōichi, the Lord Keeper of the Privy Seal and the personal adviser to Hirohito during the Pacific War. This highly sensitive document had been introduced as evidence by the prosecution and was thus available to Inoue for scrutiny.[29] As he found, the Kido diary's entries leading up to the Pearl Harbor attack unequivocally showed that the Emperor was active in the decision-making process. It documented that Hirohito had personally sought information from his subordinates about the wisdom of initiating war against the United States since at least July 1941; that he had deliberated the possibility of war by weighing various factors; that he had discussed the matter with his advisers and had made the decision to go to war; that he had then personally ordered his subordinates to prepare for the execution of the war plan. In light of these records, Inoue concluded, "This was a man who, with all power in his hands, made the decision after taking into consideration all opinions and ascertaining all information with great care. It was not at all a decision made by a person whose freedom was deprived mentally or physically, or who had lost the ability to think. Nor was the decision a rash judgment."[30] In other words, Inoue found that Hirohito was a man in full command of himself as well as of his subordinate ministers.

Inoue moved on to determine the legal implications of the above finding in light of the theory of responsibility that the International Prosecution Section had set out in court. He recalled the summation given by Frank Tavenner, the deputy chief prosecutor, concerning the responsibility of the accused Class A war criminals. He quoted the pertinent part of Tavenner's summation in full:

[*Tavenner:*] These defendants were not mere automatons; they were not replaceable cogs in a machine; they were not playthings of fate caught in a maelstrom of destiny from which there was no extrication. These men were the brains of an empire; they were the leaders of a nation's destiny. . . . These men were supposed to be the elite of the nation, the honest and trusted leaders to whom the fate of the nation had been confidently entrusted. Some of them were men who were held in high respect and esteem as men of peace and good will by the leaders and representatives of other nations. These men knew the difference between good and evil. They knew the obligations to which they had solemnly pledged their nation.[31]

"From the viewpoint of us Japanese," Inoue wrote, "exactly the same applies to the Emperor with even greater aptness." The Emperor, too, was not a cog in a machine, or a plaything at the mercy of fate. He was the leader of Japan. He had the intelligence, power, and duty to make responsible decisions on behalf of his people regarding the future of Japan. With all the power and responsibility vested in him, however, he chose to approve the continuation of the war in China, to appoint a known war advocate, Gen. Tōjō, as prime minister on the eve of the Pearl Harbor attack, and personally to sanction the initiation of war against the United States and other Western powers in the Pacific region. In light of the prosecution's concept of individual liability, Inoue concluded that Hirohito was individually responsible for starting the war as much as were the accused at Tokyo.[32]

This article served Inoue as preliminary research on Hirohito's culpability, as he provided an in-depth analysis of the same historical problem in the book he published in 1975. It appeared under the title *Tennō no sensō sekinin* (The Emperor's Responsibility for War). He subsequently revised it and republished it in 1989 with a new title, *Shōwa tennō no sensō sekinin* (Emperor Shōwa's Responsibility for War). By adding "Shōwa" to the title, Inoue emphasized that his book was not about the responsibility of the imperial institution in general, but the individual responsibility of Emperor Hirohito, the person, for starting the war in the Asia-Pacific region. Inoue's book became the foundational text on Hirohito's culpability in Japanese academia thereafter, and is regarded and read as such to this day.[33]

Inoue's conclusion, incidentally, resonated with the opinions that were separately expressed by two justices of the Tokyo Tribunal at the end of the trial. One is Henri Bernard, the French member. "It cannot be denied," he wrote in his dissenting opinion, that "it [the Tokyo trial] had a principal author who escaped all prosecution."[34] Like Inoue, Bernard pointed to the inculpatory evidence documented in the Kido diary. He quoted the relevant part at length in order to let the evidence speak for itself:

I visited the Emperor at 3.30 PM in response to his request. He said that Prince Takamatsu had told him that the Navy's hands were full and it appeared that he wished to avoid war, but did not know what to do. I advised the Emperor to ask the opinions of the Navy Minister, the Chief of the Naval General Staff, and the premier, for the situation was really grave. We could not be too prudent in the matter. At 6.35 PM I again visited the Emperor in response to his request. He said that he had ordered the Premier to act according to the program on account of the affirmative answers of the Navy Minister and the Chief of the Navy General Staff concerning the question as to the success of war.[35]

In Bernard's opinion, there was no good reason why Hirohito should be exempt from prosecution when evidence clearly indicated that he had personally given authorization to start the war.

The other judge who independently reached a similar conclusion was Webb. While he was party to the majority opinion, he disagreed with it on certain issues, including the Emperor's culpability. Webb held that Hirohito's share of responsibility for starting the war was established as he wrote, "The Emperor's authority was required for war," and, "If he did not want war he should have withheld his authority." He rejected the characterization of Hirohito as a mere figurehead even though both the prosecution and the defense portrayed him as such during the trial. Webb reasoned: "The suggestion that the Emperor was bound to act on advice is contrary to the evidence. If he acted on advice it was because he saw fit to do so. That did not limit his responsibility. But in any event even a Constitutional Monarch would not be excused for committing a crime at International Law on the advice of his Ministers." While stressing that he was "not suggest[ing that] the Emperor should have been prosecuted," he held that Hirohito's special exemption should be taken into account when determining penalties for the convicted. He wrote, "This immunity of the Emperor, as contrasted with the part he played in launching the war in the Pacific, is I think a matter which this Tribunal should take into consideration in imposing sentences."[36]

It should be noted on this occasion that Webb had attempted to have his opinion above reflected in the majority judgment in preceding months. In a memorandum dated September 15, 1948, he had told the American justice Cramer—the chairman of the drafting committee of the majority opinion—that "I notice the complete absence of any reference to the part played by the Emperor in starting and ending the war. I think that if the judgment plays down his part to this extent it will lead to devastating criticism."[37] The majority judges did not heed Webb's recommendation, however, making virtually no reference to Hirohito's responsibility in the judgment. (But as discussed in Chapter 6, the Tribunal did refrain from imposing capital punishment on those whom they convicted of crimes against peace only.)

While awaiting the judgment of the Tokyo Tribunal, Uchida Rikizō, another law professor at the University of Tokyo, contributed an article to the journal *Chōryū*, titled "Kyokutō saiban no hōrironteki igi: shu to shite eibei hōgaku no tachiba kara" (Significance of the Far Eastern Trial to Legal Theory: Primarily from the Viewpoint of the Field of Anglo-American Law). Uchida wrote this article when he belatedly realized, in 1948, that scholars who specialized in Anglo-American law had yet to analyze the Tokyo trial from the viewpoint of judicial reform. This was a sad revelation for him, since he believed that the Tokyo trial was a landmark event in the ongoing effort by the occupation authorities to introduce Anglo-American legal practices and to overhaul the Japanese justice system. The Tokyo trial, as he saw it, served as "practical teaching" (*jitsubutsu kyōiku*) of Anglo-American criminal procedure.[38] His article was an attempt to highlight this underappreciated aspect of the Tokyo trial.

In Uchida's opinion, the most important practical lessons were, first, that the Tokyo trial taught that the judges acted as "fair umpires" whose main task was to ensure the observance of court rules by the two adversarial parties and to ensure a fair trial. This aspect of the criminal proceedings may have been nothing new in the Anglo-American legal tradition, but it was novel in the context of Japanese legal practice under the old regime. Second, both the prosecution and the defense had an equal right to present their cases. This was, again, new to the Japanese people, who were "used to seeing a confrontation between the prosecution, which represented the government and police authorities, and the accused, which had little power," Uchida remarked.[39] Third, the Tokyo trial demonstrated that the prosecution had to assume the burden of proof while the accused enjoyed the presumption of innocence. This, too, was novel in the Japanese justice system, as Uchida wrote:

A principle like this is diametrically opposed to the general practice of the Japanese people, who are used to treating those arrested by the government and police authorities as criminals from the start. This legal principle [of the presumption of innocence] is primarily derived from the principle of the protection of human rights. All the burden of proof is placed upon the prosecution because of this legal principle. Here rests the pride of Anglo-American law that, if one were to put it in extreme terms, is prepared to save ninety-nine guilty ones in order to save one innocent man.[40]

Fourth, the Tokyo trial demonstrated that trial proceedings must be open to the public. The transparency of trials was not always respected under the old Japanese judicial system. Fifth and finally, both the prosecution and the defense had the right to cross-examine. Uchida noted that this was in accordance with Anglo-American legal tradition, where testimony that could not be subjected to cross-examination had little probative value.

Other than discussing the relevance of the Tokyo trial to domestic legal practice, Uchida also considered the controversies surrounding the notions of ex post facto law and individual responsibility. With respect to controversy over the law pertaining to crimes against peace, Uchida made the point that mainstream legal thinking in the Anglo-American tradition permitted the applicability of ex post facto law on certain occasions. Citing various case law, including judicial opinions of the U.S. Supreme Court from as early as 1798, Uchida argued that the central question in Anglo-American law had been to determine whether there was criminal *substance* in the alleged criminal act rather than rigidly adhering to the principle of the non-retroactive application of new law.[41] As for the controversy over the principle of individual responsibility, Uchida maintained that it would be necessary to envision a "criminal law governing global civil society" (*sekai shimin shakai ni okeru keihō*) in order to address this question. By going beyond the conventional notion of the state as the supreme juristic person under international law, and by incorporating the global-citizenship perspective in the interpretation of law, it would become theoretically possible to declare that individuals could be held responsible for crimes committed in violation of international law.[42] Uchida's legal position resonated with what Dandō had expressed earlier in his 1946 article.

In sum, the arguments advanced by contemporary trial analysts converge on the following three points. First, they all thought that the sheer fact of Japanese aggression justified or even necessitated the application of the legal doctrine of crimes against peace at Tokyo. They saw no good reason why those who planned, prepared, and executed aggressive war should escape punishment. Second, they held that making the charge of aggressive war was legitimate also on legal grounds. In their opinion, existing international treaties, agreements, and conventions formed a sound basis for concluding that the principle of prohibiting aggressive war existed prior to World War II. Moreover, they all took the position that the fundamental principle of justice did not permit the dismissal of aggressive war charges. Letting the aggressors go unpunished by rigidly interpreting the law might have the appearance of "legality," but doing so did not serve the cause of justice. The purpose of law was not to uphold minor legal technicalities; the law should be interpreted in such a way as to allow the court to dispense justice in substance. Such was the basic purpose of law, in their opinion, that it was out of the question to let the aggressors escape prosecution on grounds of retroactive legislation. Third, certain of the trial observers held that the Tokyo trial had a positive impact on the Japanese domestic justice system as well. Dandō and Uchida highlighted this aspect of the trial. Both thought that the criminal procedure followed at Tokyo was superior to the one followed in the wartime Japanese justice system. In particular, the principle of a fair trial, the protection of defense rights, and the presumption of innocence were important lessons for improving legal practice in Japan.

Assessing the Tokyo Trial in Its Aftermath

As the Tokyo Tribunal handed down its judgment in November 1948, these trial analysts began writing additional commentaries in which they assessed its significance. Among the first to respond to the Tokyo judgment was Yokota Kisaburō, the author of *Sensō hanzai ron* (A Treatise on War Crimes). He contributed a short article to the *Mainichi* newspaper on November 13, 1948, the day after the Tokyo Tribunal handed down sentences to the individual defendants.[43] In the piece, he discussed the findings of the Tokyo Tribunal and explained their relevance, especially with respect to the Tribunal's opinion concerning crimes against peace.

First, he pointed out that the Tokyo Tribunal followed the Nuremberg precedent when it gave its ruling on the charges of aggressive war. The Nuremberg Tribunal had concluded, Yokota recalled, that aggressive war constituted a crime under international law and that those who committed this type of offense must take individual responsibility. Four nations that directly participated in the Nuremberg trial, and nineteen others that endorsed the Nuremberg Charter, supported this ruling, thereby elevating the Nuremberg ruling to the status of an internationally recognized legal principle. *This* judicial opinion, Yokota stressed, was the very one the Tokyo Tribunal adopted when making its findings on the Japanese case. This meant that the Tokyo judgment came to take on the character of the "Verdict of the World" (*sekai no shinpan*), as he put it, and not victors' justice, as critics might like to call it. Second, the Tokyo Tribunal disclosed the truth about the war in full public view. As Yokota recalled, the fact of aggression was "not necessarily a new thing" to the Japanese people, but they could not verify information due to policing and propaganda by the wartime government. The Tokyo Tribunal dispelled all uncertainties by firmly establishing the fact of aggression. Third, the Tribunal rejected the Japanese government's long-standing contention that Japan had waged war in self-defense. "This argument was repeatedly made at the time of the Manchurian [Mukden] Incident, and on other occasions later as well, as if one could justify any action as long as one called it 'defensive.'" But the Tribunal rejected this line of argument in its entirety. Finally, and in connection to the third point, the Tribunal ruled that the ultimate power to determine the legal character of war did not rest with the country that waged the war. The war-waging country may claim that it had acted in self-defense, but the validity of such a contention must be tested by other objective criteria. The Tribunal, in other words, rejected any arbitrary interpretation of the state's right of self-defense. Yokota apparently attached great importance to this part of the judgment, as he subsequently wrote a separate article to explore it in greater detail.[44]

Meanwhile, Kainō Michitaka and certain of his colleagues at the University of Tokyo held a roundtable discussion in order to assess the significance of the Tokyo judgment. The participants included four legal scholars: Takano Yūichi, Tsuji Kiyoaki, Ukai Nobushige, and Kainō himself. Maruyama Masao, a leading political thinker in postwar Japan, took part in the discussion as well. A record of the discussion was published in the law journal *Hōritsu jihō* the following year.[45] The five scholars freely exchanged opinions on a broad range of legal and factual questions stemming from the trial. The major topics were: the principle of individual responsibility for war crimes; the principle of non-retroactive application of law; the doctrine of defensive war; the significance of having American defense lawyers; the significance of having separate opinions; the relationship between the Japanese superiority complex and the occurrence of atrocities; and facts established by the Tribunal concerning the responsibility of the army, the navy, the Emperor, his wartime advisers, right-wing nationalists, business circles, and the Japanese people themselves.

What most concerned them was the Tribunal's opinion on the criminality of aggressive war. They were particularly interested in determining the long-term implications of this part of the Tokyo judgment on the development of international law. Prompted by Kainō, Takano presented his opinion on the matter. He observed, to start with, that the law pertaining to crimes against peace was still controversial and that legal disputes persisted, but he assessed the significance of the Tokyo judgment generally in a positive light. He held that international institutions such as the United Nations and the International Court of Justice would continue debates on the legal status of crimes against peace, such as what criteria should be applied to determine the legal character of war and whether there should be individual responsibility. He cautioned that one should not expect the international community to resolve these complex legal questions overnight. "However," he continued, "it is clear that things must move in that direction and we can discern such a trend in history as well." By this he indicated his understanding that the world trend was indeed toward outlawing aggressive war. He went on to say, "As we contemplate on peace mechanisms for the future, I think it is important to develop international organizations and an international justice system, such as the United Nations and the International Court, for the deterrence of war."[46] While holding certain reservations about the immediate legal effect of the Tokyo judgment, Takano concluded that the Tokyo trial was a step forward in the development of peace mechanisms in the international community.[47]

Tabata Shigejirō, an international law professor at Kyoto University, offered his analysis of the Tokyo judgment in the article "Tōkyō saiban no hōri" (Legal Theory of the Tokyo Trial), published in the journal *Sekai* in June 1949. Tabata, too, was interested in assessing the significance of the two central legal opinions given by the Tokyo Tribunal concerning aggressive war charges. One of them was the ruling that the Tribunal had jurisdiction over crimes against peace on grounds that the Pact of Paris made aggressive war a crime under international law. The other was that there was individual responsibility for the crime of aggression.

Tabata generally concurred with the former ruling, but he thought that the Tokyo Tribunal could have given a far bolder interpretation of law. International law in eighteenth-century Europe, as he understood it, used to cherish the principle of state sovereignty so as to ensure legal protection to emerging nation-states. He believed that the same principle could no longer serve as the basic tenet of international law in the twentieth-century world, where imperial powers invoked the right of sovereignty to justify their expansionist wars. The trend of international law today, in his opinion, was now moving toward preventing such abuse of power. *This*, in his opinion, should have been the legal ground on which the criminality of aggressive war ought to have been established.[48]

He fully concurred with the validity of the Tribunal's second ruling, that is, the rejection of the act-of-state doctrine. He considered that, after all, it was individual human beings who could make decisions and commit war crimes, not an abstract entity called "the state." The responsibility for the breach of international law must, therefore, be ultimately attributed to individual actors. Furthermore, he thought that the act-of-state doctrine should be deemed inapplicable when the case at issue involved an absolutist state such as the one in wartime Japan. The decision-making power in the old regime, in his understanding, had been concentrated in a handful of political and military leaders at the top of the government. The loci of responsibility were thus very clear and hardly controversial. For this reason, he considered it appropriate to attribute responsibility for crimes against peace squarely to these individual power holders.[49]

Not all leading jurists in those years endorsed the judgment of the Tokyo Tribunal. Takayanagi Kenzō was one such legal scholar. A law professor at the University of Tokyo, he had long been regarded as an authority on Anglo-American law and had also served as a defense lawyer at the Tokyo trial. He had taken charge, among other things, of presenting the defense summation on points of law. The summation was later published in book form under the title, *The Tokio Trials and International Law: Answer to the Prosecution's Arguments on International Law Delivered at the International Military Tribunal for the Far East on 3 & 4 March 1948.* He published this as the counterpoint to Yokota's *Sensō hanzai ron*, which he described as "the prosecution's legal position."[50]

Takayanagi published two articles after the trial ended in the law journal *Hōritsu taimuzu* in 1949. In both articles, he questioned the validity of the judgments given by both the Nuremberg and Tokyo Tribunals. Rather, he thought that the two tribunals merely set out precedents for future victor nations to create new laws and to arbitrarily try the leaders of the vanquished nation under the pretense of legality. The world today, Takayanagi also held, continued to operate on the premise of the supremacy of state sovereignty. In other words, he believed that the state-centric view had been, and would remain, at the heart of international law. In light of this understanding, he feared that the Nuremberg and Tokyo Tribunals did nothing but set dangerous precedents that tolerated the imposition of victors' justice. He was also of the opinion that the two trials would have little effect to deter future aggressive wars.[51]

Takayanagi further disputed the validity of Tabata's view concerning the principle of individual responsibility. The state, he believed, continued to be the indivisible juristic person under international law. He argued that this principle should be scrupulously respected so that the basic human rights of the accused at Tokyo—who, in his opinion, had acted only to fulfill their duty as state officials—would be protected. Moreover, he considered it logically contradictory for the international community to apply the principle of "individual" responsibility on matters related to war crimes, while continuing to adhere to the principle of "state" (or "collective") responsibility on other international controversies such as war-related compensation. On this ground, too, he held that the concept of individual responsibility should be deemed inapplicable under international law.[52]

The Japanese debates on the Tokyo trial in the years immediately afterward centered on charges of crimes against peace. However, there were also a limited number of commentaries concerning war crimes. Yokota was one such jurist who discussed the Tokyo Tribunal's findings on war crimes when he published the expanded edition of *Sensō hanzai ron* in 1949. In the new edition, Yokota took special note of the principle of cabinet liability. According to the Tokyo judgment, the members of the cabinet had "the responsibility to set up a system of protection for prisoners of war, and more important, to ensure the continuous and effective functioning of the system" in their capacity as the representatives of the central government. Moreover, "they are to be held responsible when they knew that atrocities were committed and did not take any measures, or if they did not learn about the atrocities due to their negligence of duty."[53] Although Yokota did not discuss in detail the historical significance of this ruling, he expressed his support by listing it in his *Sensō hanzai ron* as a legal opinion worthy of attention.

Irie Keishirō, a law graduate of Waseda University and later a journalist for the Jiji Tsūshin wire service, similarly took note of the ruling on cabinet responsibility in the summary of the Tokyo judgment that he contributed to the law journal *Hōritsu jihō*.[54] This article embraced the significance of cabinet responsibility more clearly than Yokota's book had done. Irie wrote that the Tokyo Tribunal "developed extremely important legal theory [*kiwamete jūyō na hōri*]" concerning leadership responsibility for war crimes. As he put it, this theory "did not limit the responsibility of the proper treatment of prisoners of war to administrative organs or their staff that were directly in charge, but also extended the responsibility to cabinet members." He further pointed out the significance of guilty verdicts given to the former prime minister, Koiso Kuniaki, and the former foreign minister, Shigemitsu Mamoru. The Tokyo Tribunal convicted the two on grounds that they were derelict in their duty to end the mistreatment of prisoners of war. Irie found that these two cases were "extremely important" since they "expanded the boundary of human responsibility" (*sekinin no jinteki genkai o hirogeta*). He also added that the guilty verdict given to another former foreign minister, Hirota Kōki, for the Nanking atrocities was also significant. Hirota's case showed that a cabinet member could be held responsible—on grounds of both direct and superior responsibility—not only for the mistreatment of prisoners of war but also for various other widespread war crimes.[55] Irie's commentary is perceptive, since what he wrote in 1949 is the position generally accepted by international jurists today.

Kainō's Vision

By the time Kainō published his last article-length commentary on the Tokyo trial in 1953, Japan had regained sovereignty from the Allied occupiers and had become a key cold-war ally of the United States. Titled "Kyokutō saiban: sono go" (The Tokyo Trial: Afterwards), this article was an attempt to assess the popular perception of the trial in the changing political conditions in Japan in the post-occupation era.

He began by reexamining the charge of ex post facto legislation that had been leveled repeatedly against the Tokyo trial. He affirmed—as he had done before—that no international or domestic law had previously stipulated the criminality of aggressive war in clear codified form and that, in this respect, the law pertaining to crimes against peace was indeed ex post facto law. Yet as before, he held that the application of this new law was justifiable. His reasoning in support of this position, however, was slightly different from what he had advanced in his earlier writings. This time, he argued that the Tokyo trial was essentially a "revolutionary trial" (*kakumei saiban*) in which the application of ex post facto law was legitimate or even imperative. He continued his explanation as follows:

A revolutionary trial always applies ex post facto law, and it always rejects the norm or the principle that no punishment can be meted out without pre-existing law. It is because the revolutionaries who had been pursued and hunted down as criminals by the ruling class naturally try to suppress those rebellions that are organized by their former foes once they achieve revolution and attain legality. It is a sheer logical contradiction if one were to demand that revolutionaries strictly observe the principle of the non-retroactive application of law. . . . This kind of switchover in political ethics may appear to be loathsome confusion for those who love orderliness. However, the matter at issue is that no revolution can ever take place if revolutionaries do not possess the right to punish those who suppress revolution. . . . In this respect, revolution does not know law.[56]

In earlier years, Yokota Kisaburō had spoken of the Tokyo trial in terms of revolution, but he had done so in consideration of the trial's contribution to the development of international law. As for Kainō in 1953, the Tokyo trial appeared revolutionary not so much in the field of law as in the history of modern Japan. He found that, in the Japanese context, the trial served as a marker of the end of the old regime and the beginning of a new political order. Kainō reasoned that it was thus a matter of course for new law to be applied at this historic trial.

With this understanding in mind, Kainō considered how the Japanese people now understood the legacy of the Tokyo trial. He personally thought that the trial was "an achievement in its own right," but the people on the street talked critically of the punishment meted out to the convicted as if to suggest that injustice had been done.[57] Kainō sought the explanation for the pervasive negative sentiments in the growing influence of reactionary forces in the Japanese state and society. One indication that pointed to the rise of reactionary trends, Kainō found, was Shigemitsu Mamoru's ascendancy on the political scene. Even though he had been convicted, the Japanese government released him from Sugamo in November 1951, before completing his sentence. He soon assumed the presidency of Kaishintō, then the second largest political party in the Diet. This made Shigemitsu a viable candidate for the next prime minister of Japan. Noting Shigemitsu's early release, Kainō asked, "Doesn't this act deny the validity of the Tokyo trial in its entirety?" He was troubled also by the fact that the American occupation authorities, which had hosted the revolutionary trial, did nothing to stop this development. Such inaction on the part of the United States—the early release of convicted war criminals required MacArthur's approval—appeared to Kainō to provide tacit approval of Shigemitsu's resumption of political leadership in the new Japan. This effectively gave the Tokyo trial "the appearance of an unnecessary proceeding."[58] Incidentally, the former chief prosecutor at the Tokyo trial, Joseph Keenan, approached Shigemitsu's former American defense lawyer in those months, informing the latter that he had been personally opposed to indicting Shigemitsu and that he regretted Shigemitsu's conviction. Keenan's confessional letter was read out at the party convention of Kaishintō on June 13, 1952, thereby absolving Shigemitsu of guilt in full public view. Kainō did not mention this particular episode, but he must have been aware of this publicized event when writing his article.[59]

Putting things into proper historical perspective, Kainō found that Shigemitsu's political comeback was not the first reactionary symptom to occur. He recalled that a graver event had taken place much earlier, and, again, by American initiative. On June 18, 1946, Keenan made a public statement that Emperor Hirohito would not be prosecuted. "[T]he Tokyo trial changed its character completely" from the moment this statement was made, and the reason, Kainō explained, was the following:

If the Emperor—who was ultimately responsible for starting war, who approved all the military actions, and who let his name be used in order to mobilize the people—can escape prosecution on grounds that he was a "pacifist," those capitalists who sold war supplies for high prices and those landed aristocrats who denounced many liberals, or paid to have them denounced, will naturally find themselves in the same position. That is, they, too, should fall out of the prosecutorial effort because they did not take direct part in starting war and were "pacifists" deep at heart.[60]

The Emperor's immunity as announced by Keenan provided a convenient exculpatory argument for those wartime political and economic leaders who had supported the war effort. They could claim exemption from criminal prosecution, too, by insisting that they were civilians and that they had never really wanted war. Since the time of the chief prosecutor's announcement, "the Tokyo trial lost its revolutionary character" and "more damagingly still, it took on the appearance of a victors' trial for the sake of taking revenge against the two dozen accused."[61]

The symbolic meaning of the Tokyo trial as a revolutionary trial was further compromised when the Japanese people came to learn about the Allied governments' anti-democratic, militaristic activities in the world outside Japan. Kainō noted, for example, the fact that the United States government became involved in the civil war in China by giving military support to Chiang Kai-shek. It also began to remilitarize Japan in order to fight the Korean War. The Netherlands used force to quell the Indonesian independence movement in the Dutch East Indies. France similarly began countering the Vietnamese resistance movement by using its military power in French Indochina. McCarthyism in the United States in the 1950s, above all, reminded the Japanese of their own repressive regime in the recent past and made them wonder if the American revolution-maker and the old Japanese ruling class might actually have something in common. Although these events were not directly related to the Tokyo trial, they were sufficient to tarnish the moral authority of the Allied occupiers in the eyes of the Japanese people.[62]

The cumulative effect of these events in and outside Japan was that the Tokyo trial ceased to be the beacon of a new, democratic Japan. It instead turned into a symbol of political conservatism. "If things had to get this far," Kainō wrote, "one could not have rejected the view that it would have been more logical if the Tokyo judgment had been 'more' faithful to existing international law, and if it ruled that while war was unpleasant and condemnable, there was no law to punish war."[63] In other words, the Tokyo Tribunal might have been better off if it had insisted on maintaining the appearance of "legality" by rejecting the ap-

plication of ex post facto law. This would have meant no trial or punishment of Japanese wartime leaders on charges of crimes against peace.
(But it would not have affected the charges of war crimes.) What the
victor nations decided to do instead was to take the bold step of applying new law, and then later chose not to pursue it to its logical end. As
a result of the victors' seeming change of heart, the Tokyo trial came to
symbolize a "failure" in the victors' effort to transform Japan.[64]

Having made the above observation, Kainō nonetheless believed
that the failure to follow through on the revolutionary trial did not necessarily nullify its substantive achievements. At least "those who have
labored in order to enjoy the taste of democracy," he wrote, should be
able to appreciate the trial's positive legacies, since they were the ones
who could "put the trial back in the proper perspective and attempt to
discern its core issues with open-mindedness." Kainō continued, "only
truly democratic-minded people can understand the democratic revolutionary trial" (*minshuteki kakumei saiban o rikai shiuru mono wa, honrai min-
shushugisha no hoka ni nai*). It was true that the United States—which
Kainō identified as the revolution-maker in charge of the Tokyo trial—
chose to preserve rather than destroy the conservative elements of Japan's old regime. It was also true that the Americans began providing
political and economic assistance to the remaining wartime Japanese
political leaders in order to bring them back to power and make Japan
the bulwark of the cold war in the Pacific region. Japanese conservative
leaders, in turn, began to defy the Tokyo judgment with the knowledge
that the United States counted on their political survival to maintain
American leadership. Despite these trends, however, Kainō continued
to have faith in Japan's democratic future. He concluded his article on
a tone of optimism, trusting in the Japanese people's good judgment
to determine whether the Tokyo trial should indeed be remembered as
a travesty of justice.[65]

Kainō was probably right to have confidence in the democratic future
of Japan, but what he might not have fully appreciated was the resiliency
of the reactionary forces and the popular mistrust of American leadership in the postwar world order. As will be shown in the next chapter,
these two trends came to shape the way in which the Japanese people
came to assess the historical significance of the Tokyo trial in subsequent
decades, clouding the trial's democratic and humanitarian legacies.

NINE

Pal's Dissent and Its Repercussions

As the Allied occupation ended in 1952, those who had been sympathetic
to the defendants at the Tokyo trial began to spread the view that the
victor nations had wrongfully punished the Japanese leaders for crimes
they had never committed. In this advocacy, critics commonly cited
the dissenting opinion written by Justice Radhabinod Pal, the Indian
member of the Tokyo Tribunal, as an authoritative legal opinion in
support of their advocacy. While there were three dissenting judges at
Tokyo, Pal was unique in that he disagreed with virtually all of the findings made by the majority judges. His final verdict was the acquittal of
each and every defendant on all charges. This highly unusual opinion
caught the public's attention, and it was soon catapulted to center stage
in Japanese postwar debates on the trial. Pal, for his part, visited Japan
in 1952, 1953, and 1966, galvanizing the rightist campaign to discredit the
Tokyo trial.

The greatest disagreement Pal had with the majority opinion was the
application of the law pertaining to crimes against peace. He thought
that no war had become punishable under international law before or
during World War II and that, therefore, all charges concerning aggressive war fell outside the jurisdiction of the Tokyo Tribunal. Similarly, he held that criminal conspiracy had never been a recognized
category of offense in the body of international law. For this reason, no
charge of conspiracy could come under the consideration of the Tokyo
Tribunal, either. To allow the inclusion of aggressive war and conspiracy as chargeable offenses, in his opinion, violated the principle of non-

retroactive application of new law and was tantamount to the victors' arbitrary exercise of power.[1]

Second, even if one were to hypothesize that aggressive war and conspiracy had become punishable crimes under international law, Pal held that the evidence did not establish the Japanese commission of these offenses. As a matter of principle, he considered that no war could be regarded as aggressive or conspiratorial as long as there were reasonable grounds to believe that the war-waging country had "*bona fide* belief" that its national security was being threatened by menacing circumstances. In the case of the war waged by Japan, he found that evidence pointed to the existence of such genuine belief on the part of the Japanese leaders. For this reason, he concluded that the Japanese war did not merit being labeled as an international offense. Interestingly, the threats he identified as valid justifications for waging war were principally economic, political, and ideological, not necessarily military. He cited, for example, the rise of communism in China, Chiang Kai-shek's support of popular boycott movements against Japanese commercial activities, Western powers' breach of neutrality by siding with Chiang after the Marco Polo Bridge Incident in July of 1937, and Western economic embargoes of Japan. Pal did not establish that Japan had come under actual military attack or that it had been threatened by imminent invasion.[2] The basic legal principle he set out, then, was that Japan, or any other country for that matter, was free to initiate war when confronted with an inhospitable international environment. In other words, the state had the right to use force proactively against unfriendly neighbors in the name of self-defense, even if the latter posed no threat of immediate military attacks.

As for war crimes, Pal again disagreed with the majority judges by holding that the Fourth Hague Convention of 1907 was not legally binding upon Japan. He pointed out that not all signatory nations ratified it despite the requirement indicated in the general participation clause. He held, moreover, that the Prisoner of War Convention of 1929 did not apply to Japan either, even though the Japanese government did agree to observe it by transmitting assurances to the Allied powers after the outbreak of the Pacific War. Concurring with the defense contention, Pal contended that the Japanese government gave these assurances only out of good will and without incurring legal obligations. "This, of course, does not mean that the fate of the prisoners of war was absolutely at the mercy of the Japanese," Pal wrote.[3] But he did not clarify what were, then, Japan's international responsibilities with respect to the treatment of prisoners of war and the civilian populations under its military control. He was also silent about the effect of customary law, even though it was the central component of the majority opinion as well as the judgments at Nuremberg.

With regard to the factual findings about Japanese military violence, he established that Japanese forces committed "devilish and fiendish" acts in certain theaters of war,[4] but concluded that there was no ground to convict any of the individuals on trial at Tokyo. The ones responsible for war crimes were soldiers and officers at the lower levels, he maintained, many of whom had already been prosecuted, convicted, and punished at Class BC war crimes trials. "It should be remembered that in the majority of cases 'stern justice' has already been meted out by the several victor nations to the persons charged with having actually perpetrated these atrocious acts along with their immediate superiors," he wrote. "These actual perpetrators are not before us." Therefore, he deemed it pointless to press charges of war crimes against the 28 accused.[5] In sum, Pal took the position that the International Prosecution Section made the wrong charges against the wrong individuals, on the basis of inapplicable laws and inadequate evidence.

Other than these four major points of dissent, Pal had another level of criticism to the majority opinion. He disagreed with it not only on technical points of law but also on the philosophical foundation in which modern international law originated. Throughout his dissenting opinion, he repeatedly questioned the assumption that the purpose of modern international law was to protect international peace and the well-being of mankind. Such noble principles had been enunciated in the body of international law, he readily admitted. But he doubted that the world had reached such a stage where one could entrust international courts to dispense justice in the name of world peace. Reality, as he understood it, was that the great powers—or "pure opportunist 'Have and Holders'" in his words—had concerned themselves with developing such law that would protect their expansionist claims and gains at the expense of the weak.[6] Deeming that the fundamental purpose of international law was to sustain the existing egocentric and competitive Darwinian world system, Pal could not bring himself to accede to its validity.

Some of Pal's criticisms concerning the law pertaining to crimes against peace merit consideration, since as discussed earlier, how to interpret the Kellogg-Briand Pact was highly controversial in those years. However, his opinions on other issues are problematic when read against case law literature. Take, for example, his view on the state's right to wage defensive war. The kind of expansive interpretation of "threat" that he provided was rejected by the judgment of the Einsatzgruppen Case at Nuremberg (*U.S.* v. *Otto Ohlendorf et al.*, 1947–48). A group of 24 individuals who represented the leadership corps of the special killing units, the Einsatzgruppen, was prosecuted on grounds that they had participated in the mass killing of Poles, Jews, and other unarmed civilian populations during the invasion and occupation in the eastern front. To justify the killing, the accused argued, among other things, that they had to respond to the bolshevism that threatened the security of their homeland. This argument was essentially the same as the one presented at Tokyo, where the defense justified the Japanese invasion and atrocities targeted at the Chinese people by citing the spread of communism. The judges of the Einsatzgruppen Case squarely rejected this line of argument, writing that "[t]he mere adherence to the political doctrine of bolshevism did not of itself constitute an aggression or potential aggression against Germany."[7]

Pal's treatment of laws pertaining to war crimes also runs counter to the current of international humanitarian law. His opinion on the general participation clause in the Fourth Hague Convention of 1907 is a case in point. The Nuremberg Tribunal (IMT) ruled that it was "not necessary" to determine whether all signatories had ratified the convention, since by the time World War II had broken out, "these rules laid down in the Convention were recognized by all civilized nations, and were regarded as being declaratory of the laws and customs of war which were referred to in . . . the Charter."[8] In other words, what was articulated in the 1907 Hague Convention had become part of customary law. The general participation clause, in this regard, was a non-issue and could not constitute a defense. The judgments of the successive trials at Nuremberg as well as the Tokyo judgment upheld the same legal opinion, which then became the foundation of the subsequent development of international humanitarian law.

Pal's treatment of the legal principles concerning individual responsibility is also open to critical assessment. Take, for instance, his opinion on the theory of cabinet responsibility. He wrote that this theory "may be an ideal one for the golden age of an international community" but that "[a]t present no government in the world functions in that way, and I would not expect any extraordinary standard of conduct of the present accused."[9] In other words, he rejected the validity of cabinet responsibility by deeming that it was an unrealistic legal concept and that it might be workable only in a utopian world. As for the theory of command responsibility, Pal held that "a commander-in-chief is entitled to rely on the efficient functioning of the machinery supplied for the purpose of enforcing discipline in the army" and that he "[does] not believe that it is the function or duty of a commander-in-chief to proceed to prosecute such offenders."[10] On these grounds he acquitted Matsui and all other military officers who were on trial at Tokyo. Yet these very legal principles Pal rejected were applied widely at contemporaneous war crimes trials, and are now accepted as basic rules in international humanitarian law.

Throughout the postwar period, the Japanese people were both fascinated and puzzled by the Indian judge's dissenting opinion: despite its seemingly contradictory legal findings, it conveyed some deeply philosophical meanings. Certain researchers conducted preliminary investigations on Pal's biography soon after the trial, and significant research progress has been made, especially in recent years.[11] There remain, however, some issues that require further in-depth analysis in order to explain fully the idiosyncratic nature of the dissenting opinion.

To begin with, it is known from existing historical literature that Pal was trained as a scholar of ancient Hindu law in his formative years, and that he taught this subject as well as law in general at Calcutta University in the 1920s and 1930s. His two major publications focused on his area of expertise. One of them, his doctoral dissertation, was *The Hindu Philosophy of Law*. The other was *The History of Hindu Law in the Vedic Age and the Post-Vedic Times Down to the Institutes of Manu* (1953).[12] His thorough immersion in ancient Indian legal philosophy might explain his deep skepticism toward modern international law that had its roots in the Western legal tradition. Ashis Nandy has explored this possibility in his thought-provoking article, "The Other Within: The Strange Case of Radhabinod Pal's Judgment on Culpability" (1992).

One should not hastily conclude, however, that Pal had no confidence in law that originated in the West. He received modern education in British India and—like numerous Bengali lawyers of his time—was well versed in Anglo-American law. Moreover, he served as a judge for the Calcutta High Court for two years prior to joining the Tokyo Tribunal. This points to his credentials in law of both Eastern and Western origins. Quite apart from his qualifications, it is also interesting to note that, of some 60 cases he heard during his high court years, *not even once did he write a dissenting opinion*. This suggests that Pal served as, and was generally perceived as, a centrist judge from whom neither the colonial government nor his fellow judges anticipated any controversial rulings.[13] While the exact circumstances of his nomination to the Tokyo Tribunal requires further investigation, it would be fair to assume that the Indian government nominated him for what he was: a respectable Bengali jurist with no apparent inclination for radicalism.[14] In this connection, it is also worthwhile to note that the first prime minister of India, Jawaharlal Nehru (1947–64), expressed his great displeasure when he learned about Pal's dissenting opinion. Deeming that it reflected nothing for which his government stood, he immediately contacted the countries concerned and informed them that the government of India did not wish to be associated with it.[15]

In exploring Pal's legacy, it would also be necessary to place him in the context of the larger nationalist movement in twentieth-century India. He was a native of Bengal, a hotbed of anti-British imperialism and of the pro-independence movement. There is no conclusive evidence of Pal's political activism. It is possible, however, that the contemporaneous nationalist movement inspired him later, leading him to use the Tokyo trial as a platform to voice the grievances of fellow Asians over the centuries-long subjugation to Western colonial powers. Quite coincidentally, Bengali jurists at the Calcutta Bar in Pal's time included Sarat Chandra Bose, a barrister and the elder brother of Subhas Chandra Bose. During the war, Sarat Bose led the regional branch of the Indian National Congress in Bengal, while Subhas Bose assumed leadership of the Indian National Army (INA)—the anti-British armed forces established in Singapore—which joined forces with Japan and participated in the Burma campaign. While Pal's surviving sons doubt that their father had been closely associated with the Bose brothers or with any other leaders of the independence movement,[16] the heroism of the Boses and other flamboyant Bengali nationalists could have possibly shaped Pal's intellectual outlook.

Pal in Japan

Those who had supported the accused at Tokyo welcomed Pal's dissent wholeheartedly as soon as they learned of its contents. One of its greatest appeals was the sweeping verdict of not guilty. This verdict was interpreted as a vindication of the convicted and more broadly of Japan, which—critics believed—had been branded a criminal nation by the victors' arbitrary justice. Pal's dissenting opinion also appealed to the supporters of the accused because the Indian judge rejected with an air of judiciousness every finding made by the majority judges. The extraordinary length of the dissenting opinion might have added an appearance of thoroughness to the refutation: it took up 1,235 pages of the trial transcript (as opposed to 1,444 pages of the majority opinion).

Pal's dissenting opinion particularly fascinated one Tanaka Masaaki, a former civilian secretary of the accused Matsui Iwane between 1932 and 1942 and a member of a nationalist group, the Greater Asia Society (Dai Ajia Kyōkai), founded by Matsui in 1933. He became acquainted with the content of Pal's dissenting opinion when he attended Matsui's private funeral. Deeply impressed by the bold legal opinion, Tanaka borrowed copies of the Japanese translation from former defense lawyers and put together a selection of excerpts. He published it nationwide on April 28, 1952, the day Japan formally regained sovereignty from the Allied powers. Titled *Pāru hakase jutsu, shinri no sabaki, Nihon muzai ron* (The Truthful Judgment as Told by Dr. Pal: The Japan-Is-Not-Guilty View), it became an instant bestseller and, "thanks to this work," Tanaka recalled, "the name of Dr. Pal became widely known among the Japanese people."[17]

The book's favorable reception inspired Tanaka's mentor, Shimonaka Yasaburō, who began to consider inviting Pal to Japan in order to spread the judge's words among the Japanese people. For this purpose, he formed a "Welcome Dr. Pal Committee" (*Pāru hakase kangei iinkai*) and developed a concrete plan for Pal's visit.[18] In his youth, Shimonaka had been a progressive social activist and a co-founder of Keimeikai, the first teachers' association in Japan. But his activism took a turn as he was drawn to the idea of Greater Asianism. During the war, he played a leading role in various nationalist associations including the Imperial Rule Assistance Association (Taisei Yokusankai), the nationwide political party that Prime Minister Konoe created in 1940 in order to eliminate opposition parties. Shimonaka's role in promoting government policy made him a target of purge by occupation authorities in 1948. The purge was lifted in 1951, however, allowing him to resume his work as the head of the Heibonsha publishing company.[19] He took part in the Tokyo trial briefly as a defense witness, where he testified concerning Matsui's role in the Greater Asia Society. Shimonaka had once served as its chief secretary.[20]

Pal's visit materialized quickly. The judge arrived on October 26, 1952, and spent about a month traveling across Japan, giving speeches on the Tokyo trial and on a variety of other issues concerning war, peace, and justice. According to Tanaka's recollection, Pal delivered speeches at Hōsei, Meiji, and Waseda Universities in Tokyo, Kyūshū University, meetings of regional bar associations, and various other special conferences and gatherings in Fukushima, Hiroshima, Kobe, Kyoto, Osaka, and Tokyo. (He may have visited other cities as well.) [21]

Of all the speeches that Pal delivered, the one given at the Hiroshima High Court Welcome Reception is particularly interesting, as it brings to light some of the central ideas that ran through his dissenting opinion as well as his attitude toward the Tokyo trial itself.[22] One major message in the speech was his condemnation of the Tokyo judgment. Pal charged that the majority opinion failed to provide supporting evidence or arguments in full, and went so far as to characterize it as an opinion written "on an emotional impulse." He continued to argue that by contrast, "I explained reasons and evidence of the ruling in great detail." Moreover, "I gathered various material from diverse fields and investigated them" in order to establish facts. This points to his unusual behavior as a judge. He apparently went about collecting evidentiary documents himself when his sole task was to determine what the facts were on the basis strictly of the evidence presented by the prosecution and the defense. According to recent research findings, Pal even stopped attending the court proceedings on a regular basis, and instead confined himself in the Imperial Hotel—where he was lodged—in order to read through the documents he had assembled and finish writing the lengthy dissenting opinion. The rate of his absence was indeed record-breaking: he missed as many as 109 court days out of the total of 466.[23] These repeated absences must have made it increasingly difficult for him to have full grasp of developments in court as the trial approached its end.

There was no hint of regret in Pal's words, however. In the same speech in Hiroshima, he went on to air his concerns about the negative repercussions that the majority's opinion would have upon the Japanese people. "The time has come to reveal history," he said, and exhorted the Japanese people to read his dissenting opinion rather than the majority opinion. He explained his position as follows:

It should become clear by reading my judgment that the Western powers were the very ones that committed the detestable invasion of Asia. Nevertheless, many Japanese intellectuals have hardly read my judgment, and they teach their children, "Japan committed international crimes," or, "Japan dared to commit reckless aggression." I beg you to investigate thoroughly the truthful history from the Manchurian [Mukden] Incident through the outbreak of the Greater East Asia War by reading my judgment. I cannot let it pass when Japanese children are being burdened by a perverted sense of guilt and go down the road of servility and decadence. Wipe out the deception of their [Allied] wartime propaganda. Mistaken history must be rewritten.[24]

In the above statement, Pal attributed the responsibility for the Japanese launching of war—quite oddly—to the Western powers. It is possible that he was referring obliquely to the general infiltration of Western colonial powers in Asia in recent centuries, although there appears to be no mix-up in his mind because he did clearly indicate that he was talking about the "history from the Manchurian Incident through the outbreak of the Greater East Asia War."

Pal's criticism went beyond the Tokyo trial. When he paid personal visits to convicted Class BC war criminals and their families in Fukuoka, he was quoted as saying, "They [the convicted] are called war criminals, but they are not criminals at all. They are all innocent. They committed no crime. You need not feel ashamed. People in other parts of the world, too, are beginning to understand that war crimes trials were mistaken. . . . I deeply regret my powerlessness. . . . Please forgive me."[25] This remark is significant, since it shows that Pal lacked confidence not only in the Tokyo trial but also in the Allied war crimes trials as a whole. Equally remarkably, he seemed genuinely to believe that Japanese soldiers did not commit war crimes, notwithstanding the overwhelming evidence to the contrary as presented at the Tokyo trial. Such belief, if it was indeed his, conflicts with the position he had taken earlier in the dissenting opinion. As discussed earlier, he had dismissed all charges of war crimes on grounds that the guilty ones had already been punished at Class BC war crimes trials. His statement during the Fukuoka visit, however, suggests that he had had no faith in the legitimacy of Class BC trials, and that the position he had taken in the dissenting opinion actually did not reflect his view. Admittedly, Pal's words and deeds above could have suffered misrepresentation when translated and recorded by Japanese interpreters. Yet these recorded words cannot be easily dismissed on grounds of such suspicion; their underlying message does resonate with the deep-seated misgivings Pal had expressed in his dissenting opinion about the purpose of modern international law.

He reiterated his criticism of the Allied war crimes trials when visiting some 130 convicts who were serving their sentences at the Sugamo Prison. They included those who had received prison terms from the Tokyo Tribunal. Pal spoke to the Sugamo inmates and said, "None of you bore any guilt. The Peace Treaty is now concluded. Once the Peace Treaty is over, it is certain that you will all be released. It is only a matter of procedure now. That is what international law stipulates. Please do take good care of yourself until then."[26] In addition to conveying these messages to Sugamo inmates, Pal met in person with the bereaved families of the seven war criminals who had been sentenced to death by the Tokyo Tribunal, and with the widow of Tōgō Shigenori, who had died before completing his prison term.

As his tour in Japan progressed, Pal began to fashion himself as an opinion leader on matters of law, justice, and peace. As if to monumentalize his new sense of mission, he swore brotherhood with his new friend in Japan, Shimonaka Yasaburō. They pledged that they would strive for an "everlasting peace built on Greater Asianism [*dai Ajia shugi*] and the World Federation [*sekai renpō*]."[27] In making this pledge, Pal appeared oblivious to the question of how millions of Asians who had fallen victim to Japanese brutality in Burma, China, the Philippines, and other Japanese-occupied islands in the Indian and Pacific Oceans figured into this picture of Greater Asianism. The evidence of Japanese atrocities, as presented at Tokyo, included Japanese mistreatment of numerous Indian civilians and prisoners of war. Such evidence apparently made little impression on Pal. He instead dreamed about pan-Asian solidarity, an ideal that—as he must have known—had resulted in complete failure under Japanese leadership by the end of World War II.

In pursuit of his vision of Greater Asianism, Pal urged that the full translation of his dissenting opinion be published. Shimonaka concurred. Preparation began immediately, enabling Pal to see a fresh copy of the translation before traveling back to his home in Calcutta. "It goes without saying that Dr. Pal was extremely delighted to have it in his hands," Tanaka recalled. Meanwhile, Shimonaka set up a special group within Heibonsha, which was named the "'Japan-Is-Not-Guilty View' Dissemination Committee" ("Nippon Muzairon" Fukyūkai). This committee was to continue spreading the word of Pal's dissenting opinion nationwide.[28]

Pal visited Japan twice more after his initial trip, in 1953 and 1966. By the third visit, Shimonaka had died, and Pal himself was quite old (age 80) and had been suffering from chronic illness. Notwithstanding his health problems, he continued to make a huge impression on the Japanese public. The highlight of his third—and last—visit was the speech he was to deliver at the Ozaki Memorial Hall. He planned to speak on "World Peace and International Law: How to Understand the Pacific War" (*Sekai heiwa to kokusaihō: Taiheiyō sensō no kangaekata*). Due to his deteriorating physical condition, however, all he could do on the day of the event was to bring his frail body to the podium, bow deeply, pray in silence in front of the large audience for a moment, and leave. This "voiceless lecture" (*mugon no kōen*) provoked such tremendous emotion among those present that the auditorium was filled with the sound of sobbing, reported the *Yomiuri* newspaper.[29] This episode is indicative of the personal commitment Pal continued to display in spreading among the Japanese people his vision of international peace and justice.

By this time, the Japanese government had officially recognized Pal's activism. For instance, Emperor Hirohito decorated him with the First Order of Merit for his "contribution" to world peace and justice in 1966; Shimonaka received the same honor posthumously.[30] Similarly, a high-level Japanese government representative was sent to pay homage to Pal soon after his death in 1967. A memorial service was held at the Tsukiji Honganji temple in Tokyo, about which the *Mainichi* newspaper reported as follows:

Approximately 300 people attended, including Tōjō Katsuko (widow of Tōjō Hideki) from Shiragiku Izokukai, the association for the bereaved families of the convicted war criminals. Vice-Foreign Minister Tanaka gave a memorial address on behalf of Foreign Minister Miki, which read, "The Precepts of Truth [*shinri no oshie*] that Dr. Pal has taught mankind will never be weakened by his death."[31]

This official homage to Pal suggests that the leaders of the Japanese government then in power had little regard for the judgment of the Tokyo Tribunal—with which they knew Pal had dissented—despite the pledge made in the San Francisco Peace Treaty (1951) that "Japan accepts the judgments of the International Military Tribunal for the Far East and of other Allied War Crimes Courts both within and outside Japan" (Article 11).[32] Moreover, they seemed to take an ambivalent position about Japan's commitment to international justice by subscribing to Pal's idea of justice that seems at odds with the central tenets of international humanitarian law.

Veneration of Pal culminated in the opening of a "Pal-Shimonaka Memorial" in Hakone in 1975. Established by the Heibonsha publishing company, this memorial was designed to perpetuate the memory of the two men by preserving their belongings and mementos. It still stands in Hakone and is open to the public.[33] In recent years the Yasukuni Shrine, too, has come to play a part in the remembrance of Pal. Formerly the center of state Shintoism, and commonly regarded as the symbol of Japanese militarism today, the Yasukuni Shrine memorializes 2.5 million war dead, which includes a large number of convicted Japanese war criminals. In the late 1970s, the shrine authorities decided to accept the enshrinement of 14 of the 25 convicted Class A war criminals at the Tokyo trial, thereby implicitly taking a defiant position vis-à-vis the Tokyo judgment. Then in June 2005, the shrine authorities erected a memorial to Pal nearby. This amounted to the celebration of Pal's dissenting opinion in a very public manner. This latest episode attests to how deeply Pal's dissenting opinion has today become entrenched at the heart of Japanese nationalist debates on the Tokyo trial.[34]

Assessing Pal's Dissenting Opinion

New books and articles on the Tokyo trial appeared in Japanese book-stores as Pal and his supporters began shaping Japanese debates about the trial. Unlike the works produced by the first generation of trial analysts during the occupation era, the authors of new publications rarely showed any interest in investigating the judgment of the Tokyo Tribunal. Instead, they focused either on reiterating the arguments made by the defense at the Tokyo trial or on promoting Pal's dissenting opinion—the substance of which, in any event, was essentially the same as the defense contention.

Among the first book-length denunciations of the trial to be published was the memoir by Takigawa Masajirō, a former assistant defense lawyer. Titled *Tōkyō saiban o sabaku* (Judging the Tokyo Trial, 1953), the two-volume memoir charged that the primary purpose of the Tokyo trial had been to quench the thirst of the victor nations for vengeance. While he acknowledged the victors' attempt to give legitimacy to the trial by claiming their leadership of the civilized world, the reality of the Tokyo trial as he had witnessed it had little to do with civilization. The trial rather served as a tool for the victors to inculcate a defeatist mentality in Japanese minds. A trial with such an effect did not deserve to be considered a judicial event, but a sheer "extreme vice" (*mōaku*), Takigawa declared.[35] (He did not contest, however, the charge that the Japanese army had committed mass atrocity in Nanking, as discussed in Chapter 6.)

Another former defense lawyer and a member of the Welcome Dr. Pal Committee, Sugawara Yutaka, also denounced the Tokyo trial in the memoir he published in 1961 entitled *Tōkyō saiban no shōtai* (The True Character of the Tokyo Trial). He, too, regarded the Tokyo trial as nothing but a barbaric revenge trial. This was a "blasphemy against civilization" (*bunmei no bōtoku*), as he put it.[36] One proof of the blasphemous nature of the trial, in his view, was the death sentence given to seven defendants. He believed that the true reason for meting out capital punishment had little to do with their individual guilt. It was rather to please the bloodthirsty Allied powers, offering them one "head" for each war-related event about which they had borne a grudge. The heads that rolled were those of Matsui Iwane for the Nanking atrocity, Kimura Heitarō for the Burma-Siam Death Railway, Itagaki Seishirō for the Chinese massacre in Singapore, Mutō Akira for the Bataan Death March, Tōjō Hideki for the Pearl Harbor attack, Dohihara Kenji for various army plots in China, and Hirota Kōki for civilian leaders' mismanagement of China-related affairs, Russian policy, support of the military domination of the government, and the Nanking atrocities.[37] By making these accusations, however, Sugawara only made public his poor comprehension of sentencing practice as well as of the basic factual findings of the Tokyo Tribunal. (But he, too, admitted Japanese responsibility for the Rape of Nanking, as discussed in Chapter 6.)

Another memoir, written by Kiyose Ichirō, reiterated the views advocated by the above two former defense lawyers. Kiyose published his book, titled *Hiroku: Tōkyō saiban* (A Secret Record about the Tokyo Trial), in 1966. As was the case with Takigawa and Sugawara, he declared that "the principal purpose of the Tokyo trial was revenge," and that the victors applied wholly new laws to fulfill their vengeful goals. He also believed, as Sugawara did, that the charges of war crimes had no valid grounds. In his opinion, the actual purpose of including these charges was to give the victors a means to justify severe punishment of the accused.[38] While Kiyose's memoir related a number of interesting episodes about the trial, it shed no new light on the way in which Japanese defense counsel perceived the Tokyo trial.

This is not to say that all former defense lawyers rejected the Tokyo trial. Kainō Michitaka, for instance, regarded it as a valid proceeding. While acknowledging certain shortcomings, he thought that the Tokyo trial was an important judicial event in the development of the international criminal justice system as well as in Japan's transition to democracy. (Chapter 8 explored Kainō's viewpoint in detail.) Similarly, another former defense lawyer, Shimanouchi Tatsuoki, thought that criticism of victors' vengeance did not hold true when assessed against the reality of the trial. He was rather of the opinion that the judgment of the Tokyo Tribunal made sound legal and factual findings.[39] Moreover, he was reluctant to subscribe to the criticism of victors' justice since it "sounded like a shriek of the weak" (*jakusha no himei no yō na hibiki o motsu*). Referring to the warrior ethos of traditional Japan, he remarked, "The samurai warriors of old, who held high esteem for themselves, would never let out such comments [of victors' justice] in the face of their enemies, or for that matter, come up with such thoughts in the first place."[40] In other words, those who criticized the Tokyo trial as being victors' justice only exposed their inability to accept defeat with grace and honor. *This* appeared to Shimanouchi as a manifestation of a defeatist mentality, which he found quite unpalatable.

The dissenting voices of Kainō and Shimanouchi were in the minority, however. A growing number of publications beginning in the early 1960s joined in the repudiation of the Tokyo trial. For instance, Tanaka Masaaki published a book-length commentary on Pal's dissenting opinion in 1963. It was titled *Pāru hakase no Nihon muzai ron* (Japan Is Not Guilty: The View Propounded by Dr. Pal). The purpose of this book was to show to general readers how flawed the Tokyo trial was by quoting and paraphrasing pertinent passages from Pal's dissenting opinion. This book went through a number of printings thereafter, achieving its twenty-seventh by 1998. This shows that *Pāru hakase no Nihon muzai ron* was a success in terms of popularizing Pal's dissenting opinion across generations. (Reprints of the memoirs by Sugawara and Kiyose, too, were published as recently as 2002.)

In 1966, a group of researchers named Tōkyō Saiban Kenkyūkai (Tokyo Trial Research Group) published *Kyōdō kenkyū: Paru hanketsusho* (Collaborative Research on Pal's Judgment). Two war crimes investigators from the Japanese Ministry of Justice,[41] one former assistant defense lawyer, and two legal scholars led this group. Their publication provided an unabridged version of the dissenting opinion in Japanese translation and five articles that discussed the context, content, and significance of the text in question. They chose Pal's dissenting opinion as the subject of research in view of the controversy it continued to provoke in ongoing debates about the Tokyo trial. The purpose of this book was to familiarize general readers with the original text, and help them make a balanced assessment of its historical significance by providing background information. It is open to question, however, if this publication accomplished its stated purpose. *Kyōdō kenkyū* did offer a subtler interpretation of the dissenting opinion than Tanaka's book did. Nevertheless, it, too, treated Pal's dissenting opinion as offering an authoritative legal opinion while relegating the majority judgment to the realm of insignificance. In other words, by singularly focusing on the dissenting opinion, it fed into the ever-growing popular sentiment that Pal's dissenting opinion should be regarded as *the* judgment of the Tokyo Tribunal. It is probably no coincidence that the term "Pal's Judgment" (*Pāru hanketsusho*), as opposed to Pal's dissenting opinion, had by then become the standard way to refer to this text in Japan.[42]

The enthusiasm for Pal's dissenting opinion continued into the second quarter-century of the postwar period. Nakamura Akira, a professor at Dokkyō University, published the two-volume English reader *In Defense of Japan's Case* for college use in 1976. This publication contained passages from Pal's dissenting opinion in its original language (English) with Japanese-language annotations. Nakamura also had a Japanese publishing company, Kokusho kankōkai, print the entire text of Pal's dissenting judgment in English in 1999. The purpose of this new publication was to have the text "read widely by people and researchers of many different nationalities, thereby furnishing them an excellent opportunity to question and reexamine the 'time-honoured' conclusion of the Tokyo Tribunal."[43] It was actually unnecessary to take such trouble, since Pal's dissenting opinion in its entirety had been available to the English-speaking world for more than two decades by then. The former Dutch member of the Tribunal, Justice Röling, compiled and published the majority judgment and all separate opinions in 1977. These texts are also included in the transcripts of court proceedings that were compiled, edited, and published by R. John Pritchard and Sonia Magbanua Zaide in 1981.

Beyond the general goal of making the dissenting opinion available outside Japan, however, Nakamura had another purpose. He hoped to use it as a tool to refute the charge that Japanese armed forces had committed mass atrocity in Nanking. As far as he was concerned, this episode of atrocity was wholly fabricated. He feared, however, that many people in the Western world had been misinformed and did not know the truth. The blame for this, he believed, in part could be laid on Iris Chang's *The Rape of Nanking: The Forgotten Holocaust of World War II*. This book was an instant bestseller when it came out in the United States in 1997. It, in turn, became the target of rightist Japanese attacks. Nakamura thought that Pal's dissenting opinion could effectively counter Chang's work and correct misunderstandings.

The preface to the reprint of Pal's dissenting opinion speaks eloquently of Nakamura's position regarding the ongoing debate on the Rape of Nanking. Citing Pal's dissenting opinion, he wrote:

As jealous lover of truth, Justice Pal had nothing but truth to guide him in trying the accused at the Tribunal, and yet the spirit of the court as a whole was not generous enough to listen to the reason and justice of the defeated. Seeing how much is made of, say, Iris Chang's *The Rape of Nanking* in some parts of the world today, I cannot but question how far the world has progressed over the last half century in the search for truth as well as knowledge and reason.[44]

He continued that "despite the world-famous tale of the holocaust of hundreds of thousands of Chinese or of knee-deep pools of blood in the city of Nanking, not a single panoramic photograph of heaps of corpses in Nanking is known to us nor is there even a single person who witnessed the scene of the holocaust." Simply put, the Nanking massacre was "one of the biggest lies ever told in history," to use Nakamura's exact words. Nevertheless, the Tokyo Tribunal established the prosecution's allegation, and this finding was accepted as the historical truth outside Japan thereafter. Nakamura lamented this situation as he wrote, "The same shameless lies that once deceived the military court at Tokyo and elsewhere, thereby sending a number of innocent Japanese to the scaffold, are still being blatantly repeated, producing a perverted sense of pleasure in some corners of the world."[45] Remarks such as these by Nakamura are important, since they show the use to which Pal's dissenting opinion is being put in Japan today.

In fairness, Nakamura was not completely mistaken to believe that the dissenting opinion rejected the Japanese responsibility for the mass atrocity in Nanking. Pal did admit that Japanese troops committed brutalities in Nanking, but he also went to great lengths to challenge the credibility of the prosecution's evidence and to play down the scale of the atrocity. For example, he argued that many reports introduced as evidence could not be accepted at face value, because they were most likely products of wartime propaganda spread by the enemies of Japan. For this reason, "even the published accounts of Nanking 'rape' could not be accepted by the world without some suspicion of exaggeration." Pal also questioned the credibility of the prosecution's key witnesses even though the defense had admitted their credibility. He contended that the witness testimony, including that of John Magee—whom the American defense lawyer, Alfred Brooks, had found entirely credible— were generally "accounts of events witnessed only by excited or prejudiced observers."[46] He continued:

If we proceed to weigh the evidence carefully we shall find that in many cases the opportunity for observing the happening must have been of the most fleeting kind; yet the positiveness of the witnesses is sometimes in the inverse ratio to their opportunity for knowledge. In many cases, their conviction was induced only by excitability which perhaps served to arouse credulity in them and acted as a persuasive interpreter of probabilities and possibilities. All the irrelevancies of rumours and canny guesses became hidden under a predisposition to believe the worst, created perhaps by the emotions normal to the victims of injury.[47]

Here, Pal held the factor of trauma against the witnesses and argued that the testimony given by them could not be trusted. Given the kind of hostile attitude he had held toward the witnesses, and given his effort to rebut the prosecution's witnesses when the defense counsel had already admitted their credibility, it is not surprising that the deniers of the Rape of Nanking found Pal to be their natural ally.

Amid Pal's growing popularity in Japan, a new monograph examining the Tokyo trial arrived from the United States. Richard Minear's *Victors' Justice: The Tokyo War Crimes Trial* was originally published in the United States in 1971, and the Japanese translation of it appeared as early as 1972. Significantly, the argument it advanced bore a striking resemblance to the one advocated by the critics of the Tokyo trial in the preceding two decades. Minear, too, argued that the Tokyo trial was ritualized vengeance orchestrated by the victor nations. Moreover, he treated Pal's dissenting opinion as the only authoritative judgment while charging that the majority judgment was a mere "repetition of Allied propaganda issued during the war."[48]

There are, however, a few important differences between Minear's work and the advocacy of Japanese guilt deniers. First, Minear's *Victors' Justice* based its argument on the analysis of a much broader selection of primary documents related to the Tokyo and Nuremberg trials. The sources he used included the records of the London Conference of 1945 (where the Nuremberg Charter was drawn up); Justice Jackson's reports to President Truman concerning the planning for the Nuremberg trial; various legal documents and scholarly tracts on international law; and the trial transcripts, the judgment, and the separate opinions of the Tokyo trial itself. The deniers of Japanese guilt as established at the Tokyo trial, by contrast, had shown no interest in analyzing any trial records except Pal's dissenting opinion. Second, Minear traced the flaws of the Tokyo trial to its predecessor, the Nuremberg trial, and denounced *both* trials as victors' justice. In other words, Minear's book was premised upon the understanding that the problems he identified in the Tokyo trial had their origins in Nuremberg. Those Japanese critics who repudiated the Tokyo trial, for their part, appear to have had no interest in assessing the significance of the two trials side by side. Nuremberg was perhaps someone else's problem for them, and they might have even thought that Nazi leaders deserved the punishment they received anyway.

Minear's monograph was, and continues to be, singularly influential in the study of Far Eastern war crimes trials in Western academia.[49] For this reason, its main contentions merit critical summary on this occasion. *Victors' Justice* assesses the Tokyo trial from three different angles: legal, procedural, and historical. With respect to the legal dimension, Minear considers that the laws applied at Tokyo—which were essentially the same as the ones applied at Nuremberg—were flawed. The most problematic of all were the doctrine of criminal conspiracy, the law criminalizing aggressive war, the principle of individual liability (as opposed to the act-of-state doctrine), and the principle of command responsibility (or "negative criminality" in his words). After examining various legal tracts as well as Pal's dissenting opinion, Minear concludes that none of these principles was applicable under international law before, during, or even after World War II. Neither Nuremberg nor Tokyo, therefore, had had any valid legal foundation to carry out trials as far as these laws were concerned.[50]

As for procedural problems, Minear finds that both Nuremberg and Tokyo were heavily biased against the accused. At the two trials, only citizens of the Axis powers were indicted while those of the victor nations enjoyed blanket immunity. The fact that key war crimes suspects escaped prosecution—and in particular Emperor Hirohito—appears to Minear to be evidence of the politicized nature of the trial. He further makes the point that all judges appointed for the Tokyo Tribunal were "citizens of the victor nations," as had been the case at Nuremberg. He holds that some judges at Tokyo were not qualified to sit on the judge panel at all because they "had prior involvement in the issues to come before the tribunal" or had never served as judges in any court. That said, he believes Pal to be an exception. The Indian justice, in his opinion, was the only person who "had any background in international law." The only piece of information he provides to support this assertion, however, is the mere fact that Pal had been a member of an International Law Association prior to coming to Tokyo.[51] He is also silent about credentials of Webb, Bernard, and Cramer, who had worked as war crimes experts before joining the Tokyo Tribunal. Other than problems associated with the selection of defendants and judges, Minear finds that the Tokyo Tribunal applied rules of trial procedure and evidence in such a way as to prevent the defense from fully exercising its right to a fair trial. He considers that this, too, showed the highly biased character of the Tokyo trial.

With respect to the historical dimension, Minear thinks that the Tokyo Tribunal made a grave mistake when it upheld the charge of conspiracy. In his opinion, it was probably justified for the Nuremberg Tribunal to do so, since the existence of Nazi Germany's "dark plot against civilization" was a fact. He contends that the same verdict, however, ought not to have been given to the accused at Tokyo. "Japan was not Germany; Tojo was not Hitler; the Pacific War was not identical with the European war," Minear argued. "Yet," he continues, "in spite of these crucial differences the legal trappings set up to punish the Nazis were applied in precisely the same manner to the Japanese leaders."[52] What, then, were the "crucial differences"? From the legal viewpoint, there may not have been many. According to the Nuremberg judgment, the proof of the existence of concrete plans to wage aggressive war was sufficient to establish criminal conspiracy. Nazi leaders at Nuremberg were convicted of conspiracy on these grounds, not on the basis of the finding that the accused engaged in a "dark plot against civilization." If one follows the legal opinion of the Nuremberg Tribunal, it is possible to establish the conspiracy count with little controversy at the Tokyo trial as well.

Victors' Justice came under criticism in Japan soon after its publication.[53] In a book review he published in 1973, Okuhara Toshio—an international law professor at Kokushikan University—acknowledges the significance of Minear's research, noting that it was the first extensive English-language monograph on the Tokyo trial. But he finds that the argument advanced in *Victors' Justice* was already "thoroughly known in our country," because the Japanese people had been acquainted with the opinions of dissenting justices from early on.[54] In this respect, this work had nothing particularly new to offer as far as scholars in Japan were concerned. He further doubts that Minear made valid arguments, especially where they concerned points of law.

One major shortcoming he finds is the author's apparent unfamiliarity with the history of international law from the time of Nuremberg and Tokyo to the present. For instance, *Victors' Justice* fails to take into consideration how legal principles established by the two tribunals— such as the rejection of the act-of-state doctrine and the application of command responsibility—had become the basic principles of international law today. Because of Minear's silence on the matter, "readers are left with the impression that this type of criticism [as provided in *Victors' Justice*] can be considered valid even today."[55] Similarly, Minear makes no mention of the fact that the substance of the law governing crimes against humanity had also gained statutory expression in the body of international law thereafter. Okuhara specifically makes the point that the United Nations had adopted the Genocide Convention in 1948 and the Convention on the Non-Applicability of Statutory Limitations to War Crimes and Crimes against Humanity in 1970. There was suspicion, Okuhara also notes in passing, that Minear was "not fully aware of the conceptual difference between this crime [crimes against humanity] and conventional war crimes."[56]

While pointing out these problems in *Victors' Justice*, Okuhara contemplated what might be the adequate way to approach the Tokyo trial as a subject of legal as well as historical inquiry. "If one fails to discuss the validity of the Tokyo trial today in consideration of the above understanding of international law," he wrote, "one may give the impression of using the Tokyo trial as a means to air one's own past grievances" (*kako no uramigoto o mushikaesu tame ni Tōkyō saiban o dōgu to shite mochiiteiru*). He continued, "Unless this is the primary research goal, it is important to comprehend the circumstances of the subsequent development of international law, and either criticize, or give positive assessments to, the Tokyo trial from that standpoint."[57]

Okuhara's criticisms were apt, but they seemed to have no impact on Minear's scholarship. The 2001 reprint of *Victors' Justice* not only includes no revision but also continues the assertion that anyone interested in the Tokyo trial would need to come to terms with Pal, because he was the only level-headed justice with the ability to give a dispassionate judgment in the Tokyo trial.[58] By firmly rejecting the validity of the Tokyo trial and lending support to Pal's dissenting opinion, then, Minear assumes the same rhetorical stance as the Japanese guilt deniers. He is aware of the appearance of this position, as he writes that the "denunciation of the trial may play into the hands of reactionary elements in Japanese politics."[59] But he so strongly repudiated the validity of the Tokyo trial that he chose to take the risk.

At a deeper level, Minear believes that this trial was a historical precedent of misguided foreign policy culminating in U.S. involvement in Vietnam. This understanding, as he frankly admits, was the major motive for writing *Victors' Justice*. He writes, for instance, that "Vietnam turned my scholarship in a political direction," and that it "led me to reexamine the recent history of America's relations with Japan."[60] In the conclusion of his book, he reiterates that he was "concerned about the whole course of postwar American foreign policy, particularly in Asia and most obviously in Vietnam," and "I think that many of the ideals and preconceptions that lay behind the Tokyo trial have played a contributing role in the more recent mistakes that the United States had made and continues to make in Asia."[61] These remarks reveal that his book is essentially about Vietnam although, on the surface, its topic is the Tokyo trial. One can also learn that the underlying message of *Victors' Justice* is leftist, resonating with the anti-war and anti-establishment sentiments of American youth in the 1960s and early 1970s. Yet the same book took on an entirely different meaning in the Japanese context; it found a receptive, if unlikely, audience among the Japanese right, whose ideological inclination was just the opposite of Minear's.

Ienaga's Legacy

Some years before the publication of *Victors' Justice*, an alternative assessment of Pal's dissenting opinion appeared in the journal *Misuzu*, an article by Ienaga Saburō, professor of history at the former Tokyo University of Education. He was an emerging public figure in those years as a result of the first of the so-called "Textbook Trials" he initiated. He filed a lawsuit against the Ministry of Education in 1965, charging that it had violated his freedom to teach by instituting a high-school textbook screening process. Deeming it virtual censorship,

Ienaga fought a total of three lawsuits up to the Supreme Court until 1997. These lawsuits marked a watershed in the development of civil society in postwar Japan, since they set precedents for Japanese citizens to use the courts to resist state authorities' abuse of power, and more specifically, to challenge government monopoly of the historical memory of the war. Ienaga lost the first two cases, but won a partial victory in the third with an award of damages.[62] Just a few years after he began the first lawsuit, he published an article-length commentary on Pal's dissenting opinion ("Jūgonen sensō to Pāru hanketsusho" [The Fifteen-Year War and Pal's Judgment]).

Ienaga was motivated to write this article because he became deeply concerned about the ways in which conservative forces had come to use Pal's dissenting opinion in their effort to deny the fact of Japan's aggression and to glorify militarism. In Ienaga's own words, "my impression is that Pal's Judgment has been used as a perfect tool to strengthen the mood in favor of the 'Affirmation-of-the-Greater-East-Asia-War View' [*Daitōa sensō kōteiron*], which has become increasingly dominant due to the effort of those in power and other corresponding non-governmental forces these days."[63] By the Affirmation-of-the-Greater-East-Asia-War view, Ienaga was referring to a particular conception of war that had been advanced by a novelist, Hayashi Fusao. In a series of articles carried in *Chūō kōron* in 1963, Hayashi argued that the Pacific War that broke out in 1941 was the "denouement" (*shūkyoku*) of a hundred-year war Japan had waged against the West since the late Tokugawa period (1603–1868).[64] Pal's dissenting opinion lent support to the Greater-East-Asia-War perspective, since it upheld the contention that Japan had waged defensive war against the Western imperial powers on behalf of Asia.

Noticing the link between Pal's dissenting opinion and the Affirmation-of-Greater-East-Asia-War view in recent years, Ienaga worried that few people had actually read the dissenting opinion in question, let alone analyzed its content. Many, in fact, had "a very vague, or an awfully inaccurate knowledge" of the text. Due to the lack of concrete understanding, many Japanese became susceptible to the popularized view of "Japan Is Not Guilty," the piecemeal and inaccurate information about Pal's dissenting opinion as carried in newspapers, and the image of "Pal" as a symbol of impartiality simply because he came from India, the leader of the Third World.[65] Ienaga himself was not prepared to accept Pal's dissenting opinion because he found some glaring misjudgments in this controversial text.

Ienaga had the following two points of disagreement in particular. First, he found that Pal's interpretation of the right of self-defense was too broad to be regarded as valid. According to the dissenting opinion, no war should be deemed aggressive or conspiratorial as long as there was *bona fide* belief among the leaders of the war-waging state that they faced menacing circumstances. Ienaga did not think that this legal opinion was sound, since it "permit[ed] an expansive interpretation [*kakudai kaishaku*] of the concept of self-defense and the state's arbitrary use of the concept."[66] Ienaga noted that he was not the only person to think so. Taoka Ryōichi, a legal scholar and one of the contributors to *Kyōdō kenkyū* (1966), had also expressed his reservations about the validity of Pal's interpretation. While generally regarding the dissenting opinion as an authoritative judgment, Taoka argued that "[the exercise of] the right of self-defense cannot be entirely the state's discretion" and that "it has to be left with society to determine whether the right of self-defense, when exercised, went beyond the boundaries of justifiability."[67]

Second, Ienaga found that Pal made a grave factual mistake by establishing that the Japanese army had acted in self-defense at the time of the Mukden Incident in 1931. Pal had held in his dissenting opinion that the Chinese might have had a premeditated plan to initiate military attacks on the Japanese army and that unless this possibility was disproved, he could not establish the charge of conspiracy as alleged in the indictment. He had also held that, after all, "there existed sufficient OBJECTIVE CONDITION so as to entitle Japan to plead that she *bona fide* decided upon this measure as necessitated by self-defense," referring to the threat of communism, Chinese boycott movements, and the spread of anti-Japanese feelings in China. As for the Kwantung Army's military actions at Mukden, Pal had described them in a favorable light, writing, "Remembering the tense situation and high feeling preceding the incident, and keeping in view the relative military strength of the parties in the locality, this preparedness on the part of Japan is nothing unusual and may indicate nothing beyond efficient farsightedness and vigilance on the part of the army authorities."[68]

Responding to Pal's findings, Ienaga pointed out that none of them had stood the test of history. Specifically, former ringleaders of the

Mukden Incident had published testimonial accounts beginning in 1955, confirming that the Kwangtung Army did indeed have a premeditated plan to instigate an "incident" at Mukden, mobilize its forces, and establish Japanese control of Manchuria. Such a confession had left "no room for the kind of argument Pal made to stand."[69] Pal, of course, did not have access to these postwar accounts, which led Ienaga to wonder if his misjudgment had to do with the prosecution's failure to provide sufficient evidence to establish the facts. But he ruled out this possibility, since he knew that the Tokyo Tribunal did receive from the prosecution compelling evidence such as the investigative report produced by the Lytton Commission of the League of Nations.

The central problem of Pal's misjudgment, as Ienaga identified it, lay in his uncritical acceptance of the defense contention that the Chinese side was to blame for plotting an attack on the garrisoned Japanese army. Even though the defense had failed to provide supporting evidence for such contention in court, Pal upheld it anyway and dismissed the charges of crimes against peace on that ground. As a way to explain away this seemingly illogical ruling, Ienaga speculated that Pal had a personal bias against Chinese communism. Such prejudice, Ienaga considered, might have prevented Pal from making an impartial assessment of evidence. As if to attest to his possession of anti-Chinese sentiments, Pal had, in fact, argued that the spread of communism ought to be taken into consideration when determining the validity of the conspiracy charge. He wrote, for instance, "When the whole world is reverberating with expressions of terror of communistic development, and when from every quarter we are having reports of extensive and immediate preparations, economic and military, against the apprehended menace of communistic spread, it is, I believe needless to remind that, justifiable or not, Japan's fear of this supposed menace and its consequent preparations and actions were at least explicable without the aid of the theory of any enormous conspiracy as alleged in Counts 1 to 5."[70] A statement such as this convinced Ienaga that Pal's anti-communist stance impeded his sound judgment about the circumstances of the Mukden Incident.

Having considered Pal's possible ideological biases, however, Ienaga was not totally comfortable with this interpretation. He could not explain why Pal should have ill feelings toward Chinese communism in the first place. As far as his knowledge of modern Indian history went, many of Pal's countrymen were actually *not* anti-communist during the war. The Indian National Congress led by Gandhi had given open support to the Chinese communists' fight against Imperial Japan.[71] Nonetheless, Ienaga could not find any other feasible explanation to make sense of Pal's puzzling misjudgments. Important for him, in any event, was that Pal failed to weigh adduced evidence judiciously when the task presented to him was relatively uncomplicated. This single failure was sufficient for Ienaga to call for a reassessment of Pal's dissenting opinion.

Ienaga's criticism elicited no immediate response from scholarly circles, but eventually his argument was rebutted by Minear. He published a response article titled, "In Defense of Radha Binod Pal," in the journal *Misuzu* (November 1975).[72] Disagreeing with Ienaga, Minear argued that it was Ienaga who misread Pal's dissenting opinion, not that Pal misinterpreted the evidence adduced before the Tokyo Tribunal. Minear wrote that Pal was "simply say[ing] that anticommunism is entirely credible as an explanation of Japanese actions," by which he meant that the war waged by Japan could be considered as falling within the realm of legality as long as Japanese leaders could prove their *"bona fide* belief" that the communist Chinese were a menace to Japan.[73] He added that in any case, the legal character of the Mukden Incident was "still wide open among historians today," which was "perhaps telling evidence that Pal's skeptical stance was well taken."[74]

Minear's article prompted Ienaga to respond immediately, with the article "Futatabi Pāru hanketsu ni tsuite: Mainia kyōju ni kotaeru" (On Pal's Judgment for the Second Time: My Response to Professor Minear) that appeared in *Misuzu* in December of the same year.[75] Ienaga was not at all convinced by Minear's rebuttal, as he wrote, "I feel it is a little peculiar to make two totally contradictory sets of claims related to the Mukden Incident, presumably only one of which can be true, and to relegate both fact and fiction to the status of hypothesis."[76] By this remark, Ienaga made the point that Pal treated cases by both the prosecution and the defense as mere hypotheses without fully engaging in the evaluation of the adduced evidence. He continued, "Even though he [Pal] claims that whichever hypothesis is adopted has little impact on the final legal judgment, his very strong intent to prove the 'rationality' of the hypothesis that imputes malicious intent to the Chinese supports my own initial contention."[77] In other words, having treated the cases advanced by the two parties as mere hypotheses, Pal upheld the defendants' unfounded claim that the Chinese plotted to initiate a surprise attack. Ienaga could not see anything legally or factually sound in this kind of ruling.

Furthermore, Ienaga disagreed with Minear's assertion that the legal character of the Mukden Incident remained controversial among historians to this day. He wrote, "Professor Minear observed that 'the fact that these issues are still wide open among historians today is perhaps telling evidence that Pal's skeptical stance was well taken'; however, given research findings to date, I doubt there are any Japanese scholars, other than those who support the Greater East Asia war, who would agree with Professor Minear's statement."[78] In other words, only those who believed that Japan waged war against the West on behalf of "Greater Asia" would concur with Minear's conclusion. The consensus of Japanese historians was rather that the Mukden Incident was a clear-cut case of aggressive war. This sur-rebuttal from Ienaga put an end to the trans-Pacific debate over the interpretation of Pal's dissenting opinion.

The postwar controversy that culminated in the Ienaga-Minear debate is significant, since it brings to light an underappreciated yet crucial legacy of the Tokyo trial. It shows that one of the Tribunal's central findings concerning aggressive war charges survived the test of time and has become an important part of the Japanese conception of World War II. Consider, again, Ienaga's response in the article cited above. It indicates that Japanese historians reached the same conclusion as the Tokyo Tribunal when they, too, came to identify the Mukden Incident as an act of aggression that marked the beginning of the war in the Pacific theater. Ienaga, for one, was convinced of the correctness of such a conclusion, and tirelessly advocated the concept of the Fifteen-Year War—as it came to be known—on the basis of this understanding. The 1967 article was one example of his advocacy. The Textbook Trials were another. He did the same in his other central publications on World War II, such as *Taiheiyō sensō* (The Pacific War, 1967), "Kyokutō saiban ni tsuite no shiron" (A Tentative Essay on the Far Eastern Trial, 1968), and *Sensō sekinin* (Responsibility for War, 1985).

By the mid-1980s, Eguchi Keiichi, a leading historian of Japanese imperialism and World War II, commented that the concept of the Fifteen-Year War "has come into wide use both in academic circles and among the general public these days." Conflicting interpretations continued to exist as to how to conceptualize the war among certain people, but Eguchi thought that the Fifteen-Year War had more or less "won citizenship" (*shiminken o eta*).[79] His own publication on the Japanese war, titled *Jūgonen sensō shōshi* (A Concise History of the Fifteen-Year War, 1986), is regarded as a standard university text today. Similarly, Yoshida Yutaka, another leading historian of modern Japan at Hitotsubashi University, commented in the 2002 reprint of Ienaga's *Taiheiyō sensō* that it had won the place of a "classic" (*koten*) in the field of modern Japanese history.[80] Comments such as these show that while those who had repudiated the Tokyo trial succeeded in disseminating Pal's dissenting opinion far and wide in Japanese society, its counterarguments had also gained firm ground, providing the basic conceptual framework for the study of World War II in Japan today.

CONCLUSION

Beyond Victors' Justice

Research on the Tokyo trial began to take a new turn in the early 1980s, when a large number of trial-related records around the world became declassified and were made available to researchers. The new sources gave the younger generation of historians an opportunity to consider afresh the trial's historical significance. These historians—who often identify themselves as the "postwar generation" (*sengo sedai*), since many of them were born after or toward the end of the war—challenged the first generation of trial analysts, who regarded the Tokyo trial generally as a success, and the trial critics, who characterized it as a pseudo-legal event. Historians in the 1980s did not subscribe to either position, since both views appeared to them too crude to be an accurate portrayal of the trial's historical reality. With new primary sources at hand, they hoped to break away from the binary interpretation and to develop a more nuanced understanding.[1] This concluding chapter traces the trajectory of recent Japanese scholarship, elucidates the difficulties and challenges that historians confront today, and considers the future direction of studies of the Tokyo trial.

Another Victors' Justice Perspective

Awaya Kentarō, a historian of modern Japan at Rikkyō University, breathed new life into the Japanese scholarly community by introducing a wealth of trial-related records from abroad, in particular, records that had been declassified at the American national archives in College Park, Maryland. The documents he unearthed were mostly pretrial records of the International Prosecution Section, but also included some records of the occupation authorities, documents of the U.S. State Department, and diplomatic records of the Allied governments. The sources from the International Prosecution Section consisted of voluminous interrogation records, American prosecutors' records of correspondence, minutes of staff meetings, and a wide variety of internal memos that had been circulated among the lead prosecutors. As a way to raise Japanese awareness about these untapped sources, Awaya and his associates compiled, annotated—at times translated—and then published several selections.[2]

Awaya himself published a number of articles in which he reported his findings from the new sources. Among the first was an article carried in the journal *Chūō kōron* in 1984, titled "Tōkyō saiban no hikoku wa kōshite erabareta" (This Was How the Defendants for the Tokyo Trial Were Selected). This article brought to light for the first time the minutes of the Allied prosecutors' pretrial meetings that recorded when and how they selected the defendants for the Tokyo trial. In 1984 and 1985, Awaya published far more extensive reports on his findings in a serialized article in *Asahi Journal*, titled "Tōkyō saiban e no michi" (The Road to the Tokyo Trial). In the series, he discussed the documents he unearthed from the American archives regarding pretrial planning and preparation. Some other articles that he published piecemeal in the 1970s and 1980s later appeared in book form as *Tōkyō saiban ron* (A Treatise on the Tokyo Trial, 1989). He also assisted NHK (the Japanese public broadcasting corporation) in making documentaries on the Tokyo trial, which enabled him to disseminate his research findings among a popular audience nationwide.

By the time Awaya's *Tōkyō saiban ron* came out, a large number of memoirs, journalistic accounts, and other commentaries on the Tokyo trial were in wide circulation in Japan.[3] Amid the abundance of historical literature on the Tokyo trial, Awaya's research stands out because of his extensive use of new archival records. Eventually, his research came to define the scope and direction of research on the Tokyo trial in Japan—and to some extent, in the United States as well—for the next two decades.

A new understanding of the Tokyo trial emerged from these records as Awaya accumulated research results. He found that this trial was neither a revenge trial nor a just trial, but one that fell somewhere in between. He shared the view of the first trial analysts that the Tokyo trial was important for disclosing facts about the war. But he also distanced himself from them because he found that the Allied powers pursued their fact-finding mission only half-heartedly. He lodged this criticism especially against the United States, which, according to his findings, withheld evidence of a number of politically sensitive war crimes. This, in his opinion, resulted in compromising the Tokyo trial's function of revealing the truth about the Japanese war.[4]

Awaya identified the major acts of American obstructionism. First, the fate of Unit 731—the notorious military unit of the Kwantung Army that experimented with bacteriological weapons on live humans—was omitted from the indictment due to the intervention of the United States. In making this point, Awaya was not claiming that he was the first to disclose this fact. The activities of Unit 731 had been widely known to the Japanese public since Morimura Seiichi published *Akuma no bōshoku: "Kantōgun saikinsen butai"* (Devil's Insatiability: The "Bacteriological Unit of the Kwantung Army") in 1981. Contemporaneously, an American researcher, John Powell, published his research findings concerning the role the United States played in protecting Unit 731 from prosecution. They appeared as "Japan's Germ Warfare: The U.S. Cover-Up of a War Crime" (1980) and "Hidden Chapter in History" (1981). Sheldon Harris's publication, *Factories of Death: Japanese Biological Warfare 1932–45 and the American Cover-up* (1994), documented in greater detail the process by which the American authorities shielded Unit 731 from war crimes trials. Building on earlier research by other scholars, Awaya provided additional documents to show that the American prosecution team at the Tokyo trial had acquired information about Unit 731, but withheld it in light of the policy of high-ranking officials in the United States government.[5]

Second, the failure to prosecute the Japanese for using poisonous gas in China was another problem that, in Awaya's opinion, undercut the integrity of the trial. The internal record of the International Prosecution Section, again, indicated that the American prosecution staff had secured evidence of Japan's chemical warfare in China but never presented it in court. Awaya did not have a conclusive explanation for why the American staff decided not to introduce the evidence. He did, however, offer some speculation:

They [the American authorities] avoided it because, should they pursue the case concerning the Japanese army's poison gas warfare, it was highly probable that the defense would confute it by citing the American use of atomic bombs. In addition, the United States intended to conduct chemical warfare in later years, and was afraid of having its hands tied by setting a legal precedent against chemical warfare under international law at the Tokyo trial. The United States abandoned the prosecution for this reason.[6]

Awaya did not point to any particular episodes to substantiate this contention, although he seemed to be making an oblique reference to the Vietnam War, where American forces used defoliation tactics and deployed napalm bombs. The recent study by Yoshimi Yoshiaki confirms U.S. intervention in withholding evidence of Japanese poisonous gas warfare.[7]

Third, Awaya found that the United States and other Allied governments allowed themselves immunity from prosecution while putting Tōjō and 27 other Japanese war criminals on trial. This, in Awaya's opinion, also tarnished the moral integrity of the Allied proceedings before the Tokyo Tribunal. He acknowledged that the same principle of exemption applied at Nuremberg. But he considered that the blanket immunity that victor nations gave themselves at Tokyo was more problematic than at Nuremberg because it meant that the United States protected itself from prosecution with respect to its deployment of atomic bombs on Hiroshima and Nagasaki. "The exemption of the dropping of the atomic bombs from prosecution symbolizes," Awaya wrote, "the unilateral character of the Tokyo trial as 'victors' justice.'"[8] By making this statement, Awaya took the position that the use of atomic bombs constituted a special class of war crime. The failure to prosecute those who authorized the use of this weapon, he seems to suggest, is inexcusable for this reason.

Fourth, blanket immunity was extended further to various wrongdoings committed by Western colonial powers against their own colonial subjects in Southeast Asia. This could explain, Awaya maintained, why the Allied prosecutors fell short of substantiating Japanese crimes against Koreans and Taiwanese, who were Japanese colonial subjects. In his opinion, the Allied governments turned a blind eye to the Japanese mistreatment of Koreans and Taiwanese because they feared that they might become subject to similar accusations by virtue of being colonial powers themselves.[9] This criticism points to Awaya's assumption that the Tokyo trial had a historical mandate not only to disclose facts about the Japanese war and war crimes but also other wrongs Japan had committed in connection with colonialism.

Finally, the fate of Emperor Hirohito and many other wartime business and political leaders, too, was decided outside the court. From the time of the Tokyo trial, the Japanese public commonly understood that the American authorities protected Hirohito and certain Japanese political and economic leaders from prosecution in order to use them as tools for entrenching American politico-military domination over postwar Japan. Awaya affirmed the validity of this view by providing additional information he garnered from archival records. For instance, his sources suggested that the decision not to prosecute Hirohito reflected the desire of MacArthur and his personal secretary, Bonner F. Fellers, who had been chief of psychological warfare operations in the South Pacific. Awaya's research also indicated that occupation authorities decided for political reasons to release Class A war crimes suspects instead of putting them on trial.[10]

When confronted with a list of these cases of special exemption, Awaya had to conclude that the Tokyo trial dispensed justice only to the extent that it conformed to political expediency for the victor nations. The Tokyo trial, in this respect, became "an obstruction to 'overcoming the past'" (*"kako no kokufuku" no sogai yōin*) for the Japanese people rather than the facilitator of the process.[11] The alternative "victors' justice" perspective that emerged from Awaya's scholarship stands in sharp contrast to the one advanced by the earlier trial critics. The former found the Tokyo trial problematic because it *did not do enough* to disclose Japanese war crimes or to punish responsible individuals. The latter, on the other hand, criticized the same trial because they believed that the victor nations went *too far* in criminalizing the leaders of vanquished Japan.

Awaya is quite correct to find that the Allied prosecutorial effort was selective. Should this fact, however, necessitate the characterization of the Tokyo trial as an obstacle to Japanese coming to terms with the past? As preceding chapters have shown, the accusation that victor nations concealed evidence of important war crimes cases captures only one segment of a much broader story of the prosecutorial effort at

Tokyo. While it is true that evidence of Unit 731 was withheld due to American intervention, Allied prosecutors substantiated many other war crimes cases including certain types of medical experimentation and military sexual violence. The International Prosecution Section also introduced voluminous evidence of Japanese war crimes targeted at the peoples of colonial Southeast Asia. As Awaya correctly pointed out, no cases of wartime atrocity targeted at Taiwanese or Koreans were brought before the Tokyo Tribunal. It is difficult to argue, however, that the Western powers and Japan joined hands to silence the voice of Asian colonial subjects, when Allied prosecutors extensively documented Japanese crimes against such people.

With respect to criticisms concerning the immunity from prosecution tacitly granted to Allied war criminals, it is an indisputable fact that the postwar Allied war crimes programs—in both the European and Pacific theaters—suffered this type of glaring prosecutorial imbalance. The judges for the Justice Case at Nuremberg (*U.S.* v. *Josef Altstoetter et al.*, 1947) recognized this shortcoming, too, as they wrote, "It must be admitted that Germans were not the only ones who were guilty of committing war crimes; other violators of international law could, no doubt, be tried and punished by the state of which they were nationals, by the offended state if it can secure jurisdiction of the person, or by an international tribunal if of competent authorized jurisdiction." Regrettably, however, the "enforcement of international law has been traditionally subject to practical limitations." The judges regarded this kind of prosecutorial one-sidedness as hardly desirable, and concluded that it was "[o]nly by giving consideration to the extraordinary and temporary situation in Germany" in the wake of World War II were the Allied powers justified to focus on the trial of German war criminals.[12]

As for Awaya's criticism specifically concerning the use of atomic weapons, one could argue that the failure to establish accountability on this issue does not nullify the historical significance of the Tokyo trial. However, the destruction that the bombs had wrought on Hiroshima and Nagasaki went far beyond the horizon of human imagination, thus defying any easy dismissal of the weighty charge that the United States committed an unprecedented form of mass destruction with impunity. Since the Tokyo Tribunal did not discuss this issue in the judgment, it is instructive, again, to turn to the Nuremberg trials, where certain jurists touched on the controversy surrounding the deployment of atomic weapons.

One relevant opinion is advanced by Telford Taylor, the chief prosecutor of the twelve successive trials at Nuremberg. In his final report to the War Department (submitted in 1949), Taylor discussed how he understood the legal status of aerial bombardment when explaining his decision not to press any charges against German war criminals concerning German air attacks on Allied cities. In essence, he held that it would have been difficult to establish this type of military action as constituting a war crime, since notwithstanding codified prohibitions, both the Allied and Axis powers shared the understanding that customary law made aerial bombardment a legitimate means of warfare. Taylor wrote, "If the first badly bombed cities—Warsaw, Rotterdam, Belgrade, and London—suffered at the hands of the Germans and not the Allies, nonetheless the ruins of German and Japanese cities were the results not of reprisal but of deliberate policy, and *bore eloquent witness that aerial bombardment of cities and factories has become a recognized part of modern warfare as carried on by all nations.*"[13]

The judgment in the Einsatzgruppen Case expands on this point, treating the deployment of atomic weapons as falling under the rubric of aerial bombardment. The relevant section in the judgment reads:

There is no doubt that the invention of the atomic bomb, when used, was not aimed at non-combatants. Like any other aerial bomb employed during the war, it was dropped to overcome military resistance. Thus, as grave a military action as is an air bombardment, *whether with the usual bombs or by atomic bomb*, the one and only purpose of the bombing is to effect the surrender of the bombed nation. The people of that nation, through their representatives, may surrender and, with the surrender, the bombing ceases, the killing is ended. Furthermore, a city is assured of not being bombed by the law-abiding belligerent if it is declared an open city.[14]

In the above ruling, the judges recognized that atomic weapons possessed an unusual power to destroy, but maintained that the purpose of their deployment was essentially military as much as that of any other forms of aerial bombardment. These opinions stemming from Nuremberg point to difficulties—at least during and in the immediate aftermath of World War II—of treating the use of atomic weapons as a chargeable offense under the customary law on aerial warfare.

As Awaya's scholarship became known to the Japanese public through his many publications and various other educational outreach efforts, it gained firm support from those who had separately reached similar conclusions in their own historical investigations. One such researcher was Ōnuma Yasuaki, a law professor at the University of Tokyo, who had earlier produced an in-depth monograph on crimes against peace.[15] In his argumentative book *Tōkyō saiban kara sengo sekinin no shisō e* (From the Tokyo Trial to the Concept of Postwar Responsibility) on the postwar Japanese confrontation with war guilt, Ōnuma wrote that the Tokyo trial was undoubtedly "victors' justice" (*shōsha no sabaki*) in the sense that the victor nations knowingly overlooked the issue of Emperor Hirohito's culpability, Japanese atrocities against Asian people, and Allied war crimes against Japanese people.[16] Utsumi Aiko, the author of the path-breaking work on Korean Class BC war criminals, *Chōsenjin BC-kyū senpan no kiroku* (The Records of the Korean Class BC War Criminals), held the same view. She considered it problematic that the Tokyo trial did not probe into the Emperor's culpability, medical experimentation, the Japanese use of poisonous gas, and the American use of atomic weapons, among other things. She also faulted the Tokyo trial for sidelining Japanese atrocities against Asian victims, especially those targeted at Koreans and Taiwanese.[17]

The new victors' justice perspective faced its major test in the mid-1990s when Kajii Sumihiro—then a graduate student at Ritsumeikan University—examined a section of the trial transcripts and questioned the validity of the prevailing interpretations concerning Japanese crimes against Asian peoples. He published his findings in an article titled "Tōkyō saiban ni okeru 'BC-kyū hanzai' tsuikyū" (The Charge of "Class BC Crimes" at the Tokyo Trial) in 1996. This piece provided statistical data on the prosecution's evidentiary material concerning war crimes, such as the number of court exhibits, the list of witnesses, and the theaters of war covered by the prosecution's case, along with a short description of adduced evidence. Kajii showed that, contrary to what was commonly believed, Allied prosecutors actually introduced a significant number of evidentiary documents and witnesses to substantiate Japanese crimes against Asian peoples. He also mentioned in passing that the Allied prosecutors introduced documentary evidence of military sexual slavery as well.

Kajii's article was important since it showed that the record of the trial itself undercut the claim that the Tokyo trial stopped far short of fulfilling its fact-finding mission. The impact of his article is difficult to gauge, however. Leading scholars continued to give mixed assessments of the Tokyo trial in the ensuing years. Consider, for instance, a recent roundtable discussion held for the journal *Sekai*. (The record of the discussion was published in the January 2003 issue.) During the discussion, one of the participants, Utsumi, was asked about her opinion concerning the place "Asia" occupied in the Tokyo trial. She acknowledged, in response, that Asia was not entirely "absent" since the prosecutors did bring evidence of Japanese crimes against people in the Philippines, China, and some parts of Southeast Asia. Having said that, she made the point that "the colonial question was completely omitted" from the Tokyo prosecution and that "[t]he Japanese lack of self-awareness [*mujikaku*] about the colonial problem was enhanced because of its non-prosecution at Tokyo."[18] Ōnuma—another participant in the discussion—joined Utsumi. He agreed that the claim of Asia's absence was valid because the Japanese people were never compelled to confront their colonial past at the Tokyo trial.[19] The criticisms advanced by these two scholars show how closely the Japanese assessment of the Tokyo trial is tied with Japan's colonial past.

Awaya, too, was open to revising his earlier assessment, but with some reservations. In an article published in 1995, he acknowledged that the prosecutors at Tokyo actually substantiated Japanese crimes against Asians. He particularly noted that Japanese violence against the Chinese people was covered extensively, such as Japanese military and economic aggression, the Rape of Nanking, and the narcotics and opium trades. He also pointed out that a Burmese prosecutor helped collect evidence of Japanese atrocities, and that evidence of the notorious massacre of 5,000 Chinese males in Singapore, too, was presented before the Tokyo Tribunal.[20] Having recognized the breadth of the prosecutorial effort concerning Asian-targeted atrocities, however, he reached a seemingly contradictory conclusion. He went back to the lack of prosecutorial effort concerning colonial Korea and Taiwan, and wrote, "there is undeniably an overall feature of the 'slighting of Asia' [*Ajia no keishi*]" at the Tokyo trial.[21] While avoiding the term "absence," Awaya confirmed the general view that the Asian victims of war were not fully represented at the Tokyo trial in the sense that Korea and Taiwan were not included.

Quite apart from criticisms that the Tokyo trial failed to address issues related to Japanese colonialism, the staying power of the "absence of Asia" seems to rest also with the ways in which the Japanese people had confronted war guilt in preceding decades. Historical literature indicates that the Japanese people used to be preoccupied with the portrayal of themselves as "victims" of war in its immediate aftermath. The victim narrative found a very broad, receptive audience because many Japanese believed that their wartime leaders had deceived and misled them into the disastrous war. There was also widespread sentiment that millions of innocent Japanese men, women, and children had fallen victim to indiscriminate Allied aerial bombings, the most extreme of which was the dropping of the atomic bombs on Hiroshima and Nagasaki. This kind of victim rhetoric, however, lost its initial efficacy in the early 1970s when Japan had grown into a regional power partly by benefiting from the Vietnam War and partly from its aggressive economic expansionism in Southeast Asia. While enjoying the fruits of success, the Japanese people were awakened to the image of themselves as "victimizers" who had exploited their Asian neighbors. The notion of "neglected Asia" emerged in this context as collective self-criticism in Japanese society. Burdened by belated consciousness of guilt, Japanese historians, journalists, and other researchers thereafter began investigating the violence that Japan had inflicted upon fellow Asians in the past as well as in the present.[22]

The very same kind of criticism—the absence or slighting of Asia— was raised against the Tokyo trial in this intellectual atmosphere. It is not entirely clear who first made this accusation. Whatever its origin, the notion that the Tokyo trial was complicit in silencing Asian voices quickly gained currency.[23] The logic seems to be that the Allied powers must have failed to make Asian-targeted atrocities a prominent part of the trial and that *that* was why until recently the Japanese people allowed themselves to suffer from collective amnesia. This kind of thinking—if it was indeed the thinking of the Japanese people in the early postwar period—subsequently received endorsement from Justice B. V. A. Röling, a Dutch member of the Tokyo Tribunal. Röling visited Japan in 1983, having been invited to participate in an international symposium on the Tokyo trial. During his visit, he remarked that Asia was indeed underrepresented in the war crimes phase at Tokyo and that it was probably because the trial participants had racial biases. The record of the trial itself does not support Röling's remark, but few Japanese had reason to doubt the veracity of comments coming from a judge who had personally heard and read the entire trial record.[24]

Beyond the Victors' Justice Debate

As these different notions of victors' justice gained firm ground, some scholars attempted to offer still other interpretations. In a book published in 1992, Yoshida Yutaka suggested that a more apt characterization of the Tokyo trial might be American-Japanese collaboration rather than victors vs. vanquished. In setting forth this concept, he pointed out that Japanese political leaders and American war crimes investigators worked closely in gathering information and developing the prosecution's case during the pretrial investigation phase. The Japanese informants had such a marked impact on the content of American prosecutors' thinking that the Japanese and the Americans were, in Yoshida's opinion, more like collaborators than adversaries. The Tokyo trial, in *this* particular respect, might better be termed an "international trial," he wrote. This interpretation was introduced to American academia thereafter and is incorporated in some recent English-language studies of the Tokyo trial.[25]

Yoshida's argument is significant in that it brought to light yet another underappreciated dimension of the pretrial investigation work. However, the validity of the collaboration thesis is open to debate. His interpretation is premised upon the understanding that the Tokyo trial was an American trial, when in fact it was not. Ten other countries took part, and moreover, the prosecution's case developed through the complex interplay of diverse prosecutorial priorities that the representatives of eleven countries brought with them. One may also recall on this occasion the New Zealand prosecutor's assessment of the American pretrial war crimes investigation. As discussed in Chapter 1, he had found that the oral evidence that the American team gathered from Japanese informants proved to be largely useless. Such an observation, if accurate, would undercut Yoshida's claim of U.S.-Japan pretrial collaboration. The collaboration thesis, one might add, is no more than a variation on the victors' justice theme. The idea of victors vs. vanquished is still there, the only new element being that Japanese collaborators were now included in the class of victors.

Another scholar who presented an alternative conception of the Tokyo trial was Higurashi Yoshinobu, a professor at Kagoshima University. In his latest publication, *Tōkyō saiban no kokusai kankei: kokusai seiji ni okeru kenryoku to kihan* (International Relations of the Tokyo Trial: Power and Norms in International Politics, 2002), he made use of a large corpus of archival documents gathered from the United States, Britain, Australia, and Japan, and voluminous secondary literature. The result was the most comprehensive account of Allied diplomacy surrounding the Tokyo trial as well as the internal workings of the trial itself ever to be published in Japan or elsewhere.[26] Higurashi's central contention is that the Tokyo trial was neither a revenge trial in the guise of law, as the trial critics in early years had charged, nor a successful war crimes trial, as the first generation of trial analysts had contended. It was rather *a place of diplomacy*, where the world powers attempted a delicate balancing of power in order to develop a new normative framework for international relations in the Pacific region in the postwar era.[27] This interpretation was highly original in that it enabled Higurashi to depart completely from the victors' justice paradigm. Yet one must ask how valid it is to frame the Tokyo trial as a diplomatic event and to determine the trial's significance on that basis. The Tokyo trial was a *war crimes trial* after all, not an international diplomatic forum. This is not to say that the Tokyo trial had no significance in the realm of international politics, but one cannot entirely bypass the question—as Higurashi seems to do—of what relevance this trial has in the area of international justice.

While historians continued to struggle in the confines of the victors' justice discourse, an entirely different assessment was set forth from the Japanese legal community. In 1989, Fujita Hisakazu published "Tōkyō saiban no konnichiteki imi" (The Relevance of the Tokyo Trial Today) in the law journal *Hōritsu jihō*. A professor of international law at Kansai University, he framed the Tokyo trial strictly as a legal problem and considered its significance within this framework. In this article, he pointed out that the Tokyo Tribunal inherited various legal principles from the Nuremberg Tribunal and that in subsequent decades they became fully incorporated into the body of international law. He made the same point in *Sensō hanzai to wa nanika* (What Is a War Crime?), published in 1995. This book gave a more detailed discussion of how the Tokyo trial, along with the Nuremberg trial, contributed to codifying new legal principles and developing the international criminal justice system. In both publications, he emphasized that the two World War II tribunals provided the foundation for international humanitarian law as it exists today.

Fujita's 1989 article had no immediate impact in the field of history, but there are indications that historians have begun to accommodate the Fujita-type treatment of the Tokyo trial in recent years. Yoshida Yutaka is one such scholar. In a 1997 article, he reiterated the view that the Tokyo trial had "historical limitations" (*rekishiteki genkai*)[28] as manifested in the non-prosecution of Emperor Hirohito, the release of major war crimes suspects without charge, and the slighting of the Asian voice. But he also wrote, "the Tokyo trial, along with the Nuremberg trial that judged the case against the leaders of Nazi Germany, had great significance as the first international trial that prosecuted those individuals who occupied leadership positions in the state for their criminal responsibility for starting aggressive war." One of the most important legacies of the Tokyo trial, he continued, was that it "addressed deficiencies in existing international law and contributed to its development." To support this claim, Yoshida further pointed out that the two World War II international trials prompted the United Nations to codify and universalize various new legal principles concerning war crimes, crimes against humanity, genocide, and the crime of aggression.[29] Yoshida did not detail the concrete contributions the Tokyo trial made to develop new legal principles, but his readiness to draw upon the body of international law indicates that he found in the interdisciplinary approach a way to break away from the existing binary debate on the Tokyo trial.

More recent writings by Yoshida show a higher level of integration between historical and legal methods of research. For instance, he cited international legal codes extensively when rebutting in his article "Nankin jiken ronsō to kokusaihō" (The Debate on the Nanking Incident and International Law, 2006) those Japanese rightist critics who continue to deny Japanese responsibility for the Nanking atrocities. This article points to his growing conviction that one can develop a constructive research framework on Japanese war crimes by bridging the gap between the fields of law and history.

Considered in the broader context of Japanese society today, Yoshida is actually not alone in adopting legal approaches. He is one of many Japanese historians, lawyers, and other researchers—professional and non-professional—who have come to use similar methods in their investigations of war crimes.[30] The growing interest in law may have to do with the end of the cold war and the recent proliferation of international criminal tribunals. Reparations lawsuits—which have been on the rise domestically in the last decades—may be another contributing factor.[31] Whatever the reasons behind it, a dynamic intellectual community in pursuit of law and justice is taking shape in Japan today, making it conceptually possible as well as acceptable for Japanese scholars to go beyond the limits of the victors' justice perspective. If this correctly assesses the current state of Japanese war crimes studies, the study of the Tokyo trial may also enter a new research phase in the not too distant future.

Where to Now?

The Japanese people have assessed the historical significance of the Tokyo trial in contradictory ways for the past six decades. The greatest paradox perhaps is that some of the most perceptive assessments appeared in abundance at the very time the trial was taking place. The first generation of trial analysts did not enjoy the historical vantage point of later researchers. Despite such a historical handicap, they determined, with the limited trial records accessible to them, what might be the long-term significance of this trial in furthering the cause of justice and the rule of law. They reached the common conclusion that the Tokyo trial monumentalized the historical trend toward the prohibition of aggressive war, that it upheld democratic ideals and humanitarian principles as the foundation of international law, and that it set in motion Japanese coming to terms with the past. History proves that while they might have been overly optimistic about the future progress in outlawing aggressive war, they correctly assessed the contribution of the Tokyo trial to the general development of the international criminal justice system.

To recapitulate, international law governing war today prohibits aggressive war and does not condone such action in international relations, at least in principle. As has been pointed out in Chapter 4, however, the question of whether the international community can prosecute individuals for this type of offense remains highly contested. The fact that this principle has been applied only selectively in history has probably done disservice to its development as well. To understand the complexity of the problem, consider, for instance, the response of the international community when it faced the Iraqi invasion of Kuwait in 1991. While there was little dispute over the legal character of Iraq's military action (that is, aggression),[32] debates immediately followed as to what actions to take against the Iraqi aggressors. The United Nations decided to take punitive action by the use of force but not by holding trials à la Nuremberg or Tokyo against those who planned and initiated aggression. This episode shows that the idea of outlawing aggressive war survived Nuremberg and Tokyo as a valid legal principle, but that the world has hardly reached consensus on whether a judicial proceeding should follow when aggression does take place. The international community today continues to face this hard question, and will in the future as well.

It is also an established principle today that there must be individual responsibility for atrocities committed against prisoners of war and the civilian population during armed conflict. This principle applies to the leaders of the government and the military as much as to actual perpetrators of atrocities. The Tokyo Tribunal specifically ruled that government leaders incurred the highest duty, under international law, to ensure protection for those civilians who fell under their general control. The failure to fulfill this duty could have grave consequences, as exemplified in the convictions and sentences meted out to Hirota and other high-ranking Japanese and German wartime government officials at Nuremberg and Tokyo. The significance of the precedents established by the two tribunals may not have been readily appreciated when the judgments were delivered, but international tribunals today affirm the principle that civilian leaders incur the legal duty to stop genocide, war crimes, and crimes against humanity committed by the armed forces under their control. The challenge for jurists and world leaders today is to make this legal principle more universally enforceable. So far, its application has been limited to a handful of cases because political will—without which no international prosecutorial effort can take place—is often in short supply. If the notion of leadership responsibility is to win credence, existing imbalances in international prosecutorial efforts will have to be alleviated in one way or another.

While the commentaries of the first trial analysts have generally stood up to the test of time, they have found virtually no place in popular remembrance of the Tokyo trial. Instead, notions of victors' justice have shaped Japanese postwar debates. This constitutes another major paradox of the Tokyo trial. What compounds this paradox is that the victors' justice perspective has received support from both reactionary and progressive forces in Japan. The former made a concerted effort to reject everything about the Tokyo trial in order to resist the humiliation of being branded a criminal nation. They invited the dissenting Indian judge to Japan and had him play a leading role in the denial campaigns. Rallying around Pal turned out to be effective in shaping public opinion, since the Japanese people—who came to doubt the true intention of Allied occupation with the onset of the cold war—were receptive to the deniers' contentions. Progressive historians, for their part, attempted to challenge the guilt deniers' rhetoric, but their effort did not quite succeed because they themselves held certain misconceptions about the trial: some approached the Tokyo trial with the assumption that it was a tool of the United States to establish hegemony in cold-war Asia, others approached it assuming that it was a remnant of Western racism and colonialism, and so on. The alternative assessments they produced, in the end, illuminated the historical reality of the Tokyo trial only in part. There were, however, those who went beyond the victors' justice debate by adopting legal perspectives. If this trend continues, it will significantly broaden the horizon of World War II war crimes studies, and help bring back the Tokyo trial to the ongoing process of Japan coming to terms with its wartime past.

This exploration of one topic of modern Japanese history as reflected in the records of the Tokyo trial shows how much there is still to learn from these too often neglected historical sources. The fact that the basic trial records of the major war crimes trial have yet to be thoroughly analyzed is one stark reminder of the decades of relative scholarly neglect. There is a bright side to this, however. Still in its early stage, the study of the Tokyo trial has enormous research potential for expanding our understanding of the Japanese war, war crimes, and war guilt as well as concepts of law, justice, and individual responsibility. Moreover, beyond the records of the Tokyo trial, a vast corpus of historical documents remains largely untapped: the records of national war crimes trials that individual Allied governments held in the Pacific region after the war. There were more than 2,200 trials against some 5,600 war crimes suspects at 51 locations in Australia, Burma, China, Hong Kong, Indonesia, Japan, Malaysia, the Philippines, Singapore, and on other Pacific islands. Reports on a small selection of these trials were published contemporaneously through the efforts of the United Nations War Crimes Commission, and some of the trial records have been analyzed in recent years.[33] However, the bulk of these records remains buried in the archives of the former Allied countries, awaiting full scholarly scrutiny. The research potential of these records cannot be stressed enough, since the voluminous trial transcripts, court exhibits, judgments, and reports of war crimes investigations from these trials constitute an extremely rich body of oral and documentary history of World War II in the Asia-Pacific region. One can find in them a wide array of firsthand accounts of the Japanese war as experienced by victims, bystanders, and perpetrators.[34] The task of assimilating the records of the Tokyo trial and other still larger bodies of evidence will be a major challenge for future researchers.

Reference Matter

Notes

Introduction

1. Minear, *Victors' Justice.*

2. Awaya has published a number of works on the Tokyo trial, the central one being *Tōkyō saiban ron.*

3. The transcripts of the court proceedings and the judgment of the Tokyo Tribunal are also available in Japanese: *Kyokutō kokusai gunji saiban sokkiroku* and *Tōkyō saiban hanketsu.*

4. A comprehensive finding aid of the NARA records related to Japanese war crimes is available at the website of the Nazi War Crimes and Japanese Imperial Government Records Interagency Working Group (IWG) at the following URL: http://www.archives.gov/iwg/japanese-war-crimes. Accessed October 31, 2007. The same finding aid is also available in Bradsher, *Researching Japanese War Crimes Records.*

5. For an overview of the Allied war crimes trials, see Piccigallo, *Japanese on Trial;* Hayashi Hirofumi, *BC-kyū senpan saiban.*

6. *Tokyo Judgment,* vol. 1, 23.

7. A Japanese contractor later recalled a photographic image of the Nuremberg court, which was presented to him as the model he should follow. Kojima, *Tōkyō saiban,* vol. 1, 111–12.

8. The selection of the city of Nuremberg for the trial of the Nazi leaders had a comparable symbolic effect. It was the city where the Nazi Party used to hold its annual mass demonstrations and where it issued in 1935 the "Nuremberg Laws" that sanctioned anti-Semitism as a matter of law. Taylor, *Anatomy of the Nuremberg Trials,* 61.

9. Shimanouchi, *Tōkyō saiban,* 21–56.

10. To get a general sense of public interest in the Tokyo trial, see *Shinbun shiryō ni miru Tōkyō saiban*; Asahi shinbun hōtei kishadan, ed., *Tōkyō saiban*; Ikeda, ed., *Hiroku*.

11. Defense counsel at Nuremberg did not enjoy this type of international cooperation. German lawyers and defendants carried out the defense themselves.

12. The Potsdam Declaration was issued jointly by Britain, China, and the United States. The Soviet Union signed on to it later.

13. At Nuremberg, the Russian judge submitted a partial dissent while remaining party to the final judgment.

14. Ikō Toshiya uses the term "victims' trial" when characterizing Chinese participation in the Tokyo trial. Ikō, "Chūgoku kokumin seifu," 115.

15. Very little is known about the activities of the Burmese and Javanese members of the International Prosecution Section. One Burmese prosecutor arrived in early June of 1946 and assisted the British prosecutor. *DNZ*, 1596. The Indonesian (Javanese) member joined the Dutch team to translate Japanese newspapers and propaganda movies in the Netherlands East Indies. Van Poelgeest, *Tōkyō saiban to Oranda*, 53–54.

16. Ch'ing China ceded Taiwan to Japan when it concluded the Treaty of Shimonoseki that ended the Sino-Japanese War (1894–95). Japan forcefully annexed Korea in 1910, ending the 518-year rule of the peninsula by the Chosŏn dynasty.

17. The full texts of the Cairo Declaration, the Potsdam Declaration, and the San Francisco Peace Treaty can be found at the website of "The World and Japan" Database Project. http://www.ioc.u-tokyo.ac.jp/~worldjpn/documents/indices/docs/index-ENG.html. Accessed April 25, 2007.

18. According to a study by Ronald Takaki, the wartime United States government classified Koreans as "enemy aliens" and even "Japanese" on certain occasions. Takaki, *Strangers from a Different Shore*, 365–66. For a study of trials involving Korean war criminals, see Utsumi, *Chōsenjin BC-kyū senpan no kiroku*. For an example of Korean soldiers' war experience, see Cook and Cook, *Japan at War*, 113–20.

19. The concept of crimes against humanity will be discussed in Chapter 5.

20. See, for instance, "The Report on Comfort Women by International Commission of Jurists" (1994) by Ustinia Dolgopol and Snehal Paranjape, International Commission of Jurists, Geneva, Switzerland; "Coomaraswamy Report to United Nations" (1996) by Radhika Coomaraswamy, Special Rapporteur, the Economic and Social Council, the United Nations; "McDougall Report to UN Commission on Human Rights" (August 1998) by Gay J. McDougall, Special Rapporteur, the Economic and Social Council, the United Nations. Major

international investigative reports on comfort women are available at the website Digital Museum: The Comfort Women Issue and the Asian Women's Fund at http://www.awf.or.jp/e4/un-00.html. Accessed on December 20, 2007. See also Totsuka, *Nihon ga shiranai sensō sekinin*; VAWW-Net Japan, ed., *Nihongun seidoreisei o sabaku.*

21. "War Crimes Investigation in Australia," in A1838/1, 1550/1, *NAA*.

22. For the defense challenge of Webb's right to serve as a member of the Tribunal, see *Transcripts*, vol. 1, 92–98. On Webb's attitude toward his appointment, see "Webb to the Secretary of the Department of External Affairs" (December 13, 1945), A1066/4, H45/590/3, *NAA*; "Webb to Mansfield" (January 6, 1946), A6238/2, 3, *NAA*.

23. Robertson, *Crimes against Humanity*; "Sierra Leone Judge Bias Claims" (March 10, 2004), BBC News: World Edition. Accessed March 20, 2004; "Special Court for Sierra Leone: Justice Geoffrey Robertson to Remain on Appeals Chamber But Won't Hear RUF Cases" (March 13, 2004), Sierra Leone Live News. Accessed March 20, 2004; "War Crimes Tribunal Bars Its Judge," Global Policy Forum, http://www.globalpolicy.org/intljustice/tribunals/sierra/2004/0315bars.htm. Accessed January 10, 2007. Schabas, *UN International Criminal Tribunal*, 417.

24. Much more severe assessments of Webb's judgeship are given in Harries, *Sheathing the Sword*, 166–72; Pritchard, "An Overview," 17–20; Stanton, "Canada and War Crimes," 392–93; Trotter, "New Zealanders," 148–51; Higurashi, *Tōkyō saiban no kokusai kankei*, 411–34.

25. *Tokyo Judgment*, vol. 1, 497–515.

26. For narrative accounts of the state of international law and its enforcement prior to World War II, see, for instance, Taylor, *Anatomy of the Nuremberg Trials*, 3–20; Bass, *Stay the Hand of Vengeance*, 37–146; United Nations War Crimes Commission, ed., *History*, 1–86.

27. According to the statistical information compiled by the International Prosecution Section, the total number of prosecution staff was 509 (277 Allied staff including 72 attorneys, and 232 Japanese staff) and that of the defense section, 404 (46 Allied staff including 25 American attorneys, and 358 Japanese staff including 79 Japanese attorneys). *TKK*, vol. 5, 322.

28. "The Acting Secretary of State to the Chargé in the Soviet Union (Kennan)," *FRUS*, 1946, vol. 8, 391.

Chapter One

1. Taylor, *Anatomy of the Nuremberg Trials*, 21–42.
2. Ibid., 37–38.
3. Ibid., 43–77.

4. "Establishment of the State-War-Navy Coordinating Committee" (November 29, 1944), in *FRUS*, 1944, vol. 1, 1466–70; "State-War-Navy Coordinating Subcommittee for the Far East, The Apprehension and Punishment of War Criminals" (March 5 and August 9, 1945), T1205 (microfilm), Reel #1/ RG 353, *NARA*.

5. "Report by the State-War-Navy Coordinating Subcommittee for the Far East" (September 12, 1945), in *FRUS*, 1945, vol. 6, 926–36.

6. Ibid., 929.

7. Ibid., 933–34.

8. Ibid., 932.

9. Kojima, *Tōkyō saiban*, vol. 1, 131.

10. "Report by the State-War-Navy Coordinating Subcommittee for the Far East" (September 12, 1945), in *FRUS*, 1945, vol. 6, 932–33; Tōkyō saiban handobukku henshū iinkai, ed., *Tōkyō saiban handobukku*, 84.

11. "Report by the State-War-Navy Coordinating Subcommittee for the Far East" (September 12, 1945), in *FRUS*, 1945, vol. 6, 930–36.

12. "President Truman to General of the Army Douglas MacArthur" (August 14, 1945), in *FRUS*, 1945, vol. 6, 647–48.

13. Taylor, *Anatomy of the Nuremberg Trials*, 56–77.

14. "The Assistant Secretary of War (McCloy) to the Acting Secretary of State (Acheson)" (September 7, 1945), in *FRUS*, 1945, vol. 6, 922.

15. "The Under Secretary of State (Acheson) to the Director of the Office of Far Eastern Affairs (Ballantine)" (September 6, 1945), in *FRUS*, 1945, vol. 6, 921.

16. Ibid.

17. "Report by the State-War-Navy Coordinating Subcommittee for the Far East" (September 12, 1945), in *FRUS*, 1945, vol. 6, 934.

18. "Commander in Chief Army Forces Pacific Advance, Tokyo, Japan [MacArthur], to the War Department" (October 7 and November 12, 1945), File: ASW 000.5/ Box 2/ Entry 180/ RG 107, *NARA*.

19. "Advanced Echelon, General Headquarters, Army Forces Pacific, Tokyo, Japan (MacArthur), to the War Department" (October 31, 1945), File: ASW 000.5/ Box 2/ Entry 180/ RG 107, *NARA*.

20. "John J. McCloy to MacArthur" (November 19, 1945), File: ASW 000.5/ Box 2/ Entry 180/ RG 107, *NARA*.

21. "The British Embassy to the Department of State" (December 12, 1945), in *FRUS*, 1945, vol. 6, 982.

22. For the French reply, see "The French Embassy to the Department of State" (December 6, 1945), in *FRUS*, 1945, vol. 6, 981. For the Soviet replies, see a series of letters between the Chargé in Moscow, the U.S. State Depart-

ment, and the occupation authorities in Tokyo in the first months of 1946. *FRUS*, 1946, vol. 8, 388–92, 397–99, 401–5, 409–10, 417–18.

23. William Webb was second on the Australian list of nominees. The first was Lord Wright of Durley, the Australian representative and chairman of the United Nations War Crimes Commission. "The Australian Legation, Washington, to the Department of External Affairs" (November 29, 1945), A1066/4, H45/590/3, *NAA*.

24. "The Department of External Affairs to the Australian Legation, Washington" (December 4, 1945), A1066/4, H45/590/3, *NAA*.

25. "General Orders, No. 7: Appointment of Members of the International Military Tribunal for the Far East" (February 15, 1946), *TSM*, vol. 3, 64. "The New Zealand Member, International Military Tribunal for the Far East, to the Acting Prime Minister" (February 7, 1946), in *DNZ*, 1520. For the appointment of the New Zealand judge, see Trotter, "New Zealanders," 142–43.

26. "The British Embassy to the Department of State" (December 12, 1945), in *FRUS*, 1945, vol. 6, 983.

27. "The Secretary General of the Far Eastern Commission (Johnson) to the Secretary of State" (April 4, 1946), in *FRUS*, 1946, vol. 8, 423–28.

28. "The Acting Secretary of State to Certain American Diplomatic and Consular Officers" (April 26, 1946), in *FRUS*, 1946, vol. 8, 430.

29. "The Charter of the International Military Tribunal for the Far East," in *Transcripts*, vol. 1. This document is also available at the Avalon Project website. American lawyers led by Joseph Keenan drew up the Charter in their capacity as legal advisors to the Supreme Commander for the Allied Powers.

30. There was no provision for appeals, following the Nuremberg example.

31. "The Charter of the International Military Tribunal," in Taylor, *Anatomy of the Nuremberg Trials*, 645–53. This document is also available at the Avalon Project website.

32. The Charter originally stipulated that the panel should have between five and nine judges. With the subsequent Allied decision to include representatives from India and the Philippines, the numbers were changed to between six and eleven.

33. According to Kojima Noboru's account, Courtney Whitney and George Atcheson, Jr.—the chief of the Government Section of the occupation administration and the political advisor to MacArthur respectively—recommended the appointment of Webb as president of the tribunal. Kojima, *Tōkyō saiban*, vol. 1, 109.

34. "The Secretary General of the Far Eastern Commission (Johnson) to the Secretary of State" (April 4, 1946), in *FRUS*, 1946, vol. 8, 425.

35. "The New Zealand Member, International Military Tribunal for the Far East to the Prime Minister" (March 11, 1946), in *DNZ*, 1532, footnote 3.

36. Ibid.

37. "Webb to Evatt" (March 5, 1946), in *DA*, vol. 9, 166.

38. "The New Zealand Member, International Military Tribunal for the Far East to the Prime Minister" (March 11, 1946), in *DNZ*, 1531.

39. "The New Zealand Associate Prosecutor, International Military Tribunal for the Far East, to the Deputy Secretary of External Affairs" (March 11, 1946), in *DNZ*, 1533; Trotter, "New Zealanders," 147.

40. Ibid. (March 11, 1946), in *DNZ*, 1533.

41. "The New Zealand Associate Prosecutor, International Military Tribunal for the Far East, to the Secretary of External Affairs" (June 17, 1946), in *DNZ*, 1599.

42. Ibid., 1600.

43. Frustration among associate prosecutors about Keenan's absence and his lack of communication are constantly articulated in the prosecution team's pretrial internal memoranda. See, for instance, "The New Zealand Associate Prosecutor, International Military Tribunal for the Far East, to the Deputy Secretary of External Affairs" (March 26 and April 4, 1946), in *DNZ*, 1544, 1551; "Memorandum for Mr. Keenan" (March 25, 1946), in *TSM*, vol. 4, 64–69.

44. "The New Zealand Associate Prosecutor, International Military Tribunal for the Far East, to the Secretary of External Affairs" (June 17, 1946), in *DNZ*, 1598–99.

45. Ibid. (June 25, 1946), in *DNZ*, 1603.

46. Ibid. (July 15, 1946), in *DNZ*, 1622.

47. Ibid. (June 25, 1946), in *DNZ*, 1603.

48. "The New Zealand Associate Prosecutor, International Military Tribunal for the Far East, to the Deputy Secretary of External Affairs" (March 25, 1947), in *DNZ*, 1665.

49. Ibid. (May 9, 1947), in *DNZ*, 1670.

50. Ibid. (July 2, 1947), in *DNZ*, 1684.

51. Ibid. (October 31, 1947), in *DNZ*, 1698.

52. *Transcripts*, vol. 15, 36533–35.

53. "Keenan to Maurice Fay, United States District Attorney, Washington" (August 18, 1947), in *TKK*, vol. 4, 95.

54. "Moto kyokutō kokusai gunji saiban bengonin, Shiobara Tokisaburō-shi kara no chōshusho, daiikkai" (The Record of the Interview with Shiobara Tokisaburō, Former Defense Lawyer at the International Military Tribunal for the Far East, no. 1), Inoue Tadao shiryō, Senkō bunko, Yasukuni Shrine.

55. "The New Zealand Associate Prosecutor, International Military Tribunal for the Far East, to the Secretary of External Affairs" (January 9, 1948), in *DNZ*, 1701, footnote 3.

56. Ibid., 1700–1701.

57. The copy of Tōjō's affidavit was published immediately after his cross-examination ended. Tōkyō saiban kenkyūkai, ed., *Tōjō Hideki sensei kyōjutsusho.* For the changing Japanese perception of Tōjō, see Yoshida Yutaka, *Nihonjin no sensōkan*, 38–42. Major national dailies such as *Mainichi* and *Asahi* were critical of Tōjō's testimony. Jōhō, *Tōkyō saiban to Tōjō Hideki*, 61–62. The recent film on the Tokyo trial, *Puraido: unmei no toki* (Pride: The Fateful Moment), dramatizes the confrontation between Tōjō and Keenan. Tōjō is shown as a patriot who successfully rebuts Keenan.

58. *Transcripts*, vol. 13, 31331.

59. "The New Zealand Associate Prosecutor, International Military Tribunal for the Far East, to the Deputy Secretary of External Affairs" (October 31, 1947), in *DNZ*, 1698.

60. On Truman's appointment of Biddle and Parker for the Nuremberg Tribunal, see Taylor, *Anatomy of the Nuremberg Trials*, 94–95.

61. "The New Zealand Associate Prosecutor, International Military Tribunal for the Far East, to the Secretary of External Affairs" (July 9, 1946), in *DNZ*, 1618. A different explanation for Higgins's resignation is given in Brackman, *Other Nuremberg*, 117.

62. For information concerning the third Australian war crimes commission, see File: "Australian War Crimes Commission: 1. Trial Regulations; 2. National Security (Inquiry) Regulations; 3. Board of Enquiry Constitution," A6238/2, 6, *NAA*; File: "War Crimes Australian Account of Investigations for the Commission," A1838, 1550/1, *NAA*; File: "Australian War Crimes Commission—Mr. Justice Mansfield," A6238, 3, *NAA*.

63. "Alan J. Mansfield to Sir William Webb" (December 14, 1945), A 6238/2, 3, *NAA*; File: "War Crimes Exhibition London," A1067, UN46/WC/2, *NAA*. The proposed exhibition of Japanese war crimes did not take place, as Mansfield left for Japan to join the International Prosecution Section.

Chapter Two

1. In the 1970s Takeda Kiyoko published a path-breaking monograph on Allied diplomacy centering on the treatment of Hirohito as a war criminal. Her interpretation, however, differs from the one presented in this chapter. Takeda, *Tennō kan no sōkoku.* The English translation of this book is available as *The Dual-Image of the Japanese Emperor.*

2. "The Potsdam Proclamation" (July 26, 1945), in *DNZ*, 11–13.

3. "The Minister in Sweden (Johnson) to the Secretary of State" (August 10, 1945), in *FRUS*, 1945, vol. 6, 625.

4. "Memorandum by Mr. Benjamin V. Cohen, Special Assistant to the Secretary of State" (August 10, 1945), in *FRUS*, 1945, vol. 6, 625.

5. Truman, *Memoirs*, vol. 1, 428.

6. Ibid.

7. "The Secretary of State to the Ambassador in the United Kingdom (Winant)" (August 10, 1945), in *FRUS*, 1945, vol. 6, 626.

8. Ibid.

9. "The Ambassador in the United Kingdom (Winant) to the Secretary of State" (August 11, 1945), in *FRUS*, 1945, vol. 6, 628–29.

10. "The Secretary of State to the Swiss Chargé (Grässi)" (August 11, 1945), in *FRUS*, 1945, vol. 6, 632. Italics added.

11. For the account of the Australian military contribution in the South Pacific, see Bergerud, *Touched with Fire*.

12. Diplomatic records indicate in unambiguous terms the Australian discontent about the attitude of the British government. See, for instance, *DA*, vol. 8, 258, 267–70, 280, 283–86, 289, 291–96, 299–301, 303–5, 308–9, 312–16, 319, 329–32, 334–36.

13. "Commonwealth Government to Addison" (August 11, 1945), in *DA*, vol. 8, 323.

14. Ibid., 322.

15. "Attlee to Chifley" (August 12, 1945), in *DA*, vol. 8, 329–30.

16. "Commonwealth Government to Addison" (August 12, 1945), in *DA*, vol. 8, 330.

17. "Addison to Commonwealth Government" (August 17, 1945), in *DA*, vol. 8, 350.

18. Ibid.

19. "The Swiss Chargé (Grässi) to the Secretary of State" (August 4, 1945), in *FRUS*, 1945, vol. 6, 662–63.

20. "Report by the State-War-Navy Coordinating Subcommittee for the Far East" (September 12, 1945), in *FRUS*, 1945, vol. 6, 936.

21. "State-War-Navy Coordinating Subcommittee for the Far East, Minutes of Meeting" (August 21, 1945), T1198 (microfilm)/ RG 353, *NARA*.

22. "State-War-Navy Coordinating Committee: Treatment of the Person of Hirohito, Emperor of Japan" (October 26, 1945), T1205 (microfilm), Reel #6/ RG 353, *NARA*.

23. Ibid.

24. The nine governments-in-exile were Belgium, Czechoslovakia, France, Greece, Luxembourg, the Netherlands, Norway, Poland, and Yugoslavia. The six additional countries were Australia, Britain, Canada, China, India, and the United States. For information regarding the origin and activities of the United Nations War Crimes Commission, see United Nations War Crimes Commission, ed., *History*.

25. For the Australian advocacy to name Hirohito as a major war criminal at the United Nations War Crimes Commission, see *FRUS*, 1945, vol. 6, 907–9, 924–26; *FRUS*, 1946, vol. 8, 384, 386–87, 392, 400–401, 411–12, 415, 421.

26. "The Ambassador in the United Kingdom (Winant) to the Secretary of State" (January 10, 1046), *FRUS*, 1946, vol. 8, 386–87; "Memorandum Prepared by Australian National Office in Support of Charges Made in Australian List No. 1, Particularly the Charges against Hirohito," in *TSM*, vol. 2, 402–31.

27. "Memorandum Prepared by Australian National Office in Support of Charges Made in Australian List No. 1, Particularly the Charges against Hirohito," in *TSM*, vol. 2, 408–25; "Alan J. Mansfield to Sir William Webb" (January 4, 1946), A6238/2, 3, *NAA*.

28. The Allied Council for Japan consisted of representatives from Australia (sitting on behalf of the British Commonwealth), China, the Soviet Union, and the Supreme Commander for the Allied Powers (i.e., Gen. MacArthur) or his deputy.

29. "Joint Chiefs of Staff. Australian First List of Major Japanese War Criminals" (April 30, 1946), LM54 (microfilm), Reel # 7/ RG 353, *NARA*.

30. "Transcript of Seventh Meeting of the Far Eastern Commission" (April 3, 1946), File: "F.E.C. Verbatim Transcript of Meetings 1–10"/ Box 1/ Entry 1067/ RG 43, *NARA*.

31. Ibid.

32. Takemae, "Shōchō tennōsei e no kiseki"; Takeda, *Tennō kan no sōkoku*, 297–301; Awaya, *Tōkyō saiban ron*, 197–203; Awaya and NHK Reporters, *NHK supesharu*, 127–43; Higurashi, *Tōkyō saiban no kokusai kankei*, 173–80; Nakamura, *Sengoshi to shōchō tennō*, 110. Nakamura's book is available in English translation: Nakamura, *Japanese Monarchy*.

33. "The New Zealand Associate Prosecutor, International Military Tribunal for the Far East, to the Deputy Secretary of External Affairs" (April 9, 1946), in *DNZ*, 1554.

34. "Joint Chiefs of Staff. Australian First List of Major War Criminals" (April 30, 1946), LM 54 (microfilm), Reel # 7/ RG 353, *NARA*.

35. MacArthur, *Reminiscences*, 288.

36. "General of the Army Douglas MacArthur to the Chief of Staff, United States Army (Eisenhower)" (January 25, 1946), in *FRUS*, 1946, vol. 8, 395–97.

37. "Joint Chiefs of Staff. Australian First List of Major Japanese War Criminals. Report by the Joint Civil Affairs Committee" (June 4, 1946), File: "740.00116PW/5-146—6-3046"/ Box 3642/ Entry 205H/ RG 59, *NARA*.

38. "State-War-Navy Coordinating Committee. Corrigendum to SWNCC 57/15. Australian First List of Major Japanese War Criminals" (October 11, 1946), File: "740.00116 PW/5-146—6-3046"/ Box 3642/ Entry 205H/ RG 59, *NARA*; "State-War-Navy Coordinating Committee. Decision Amending SWNCC 57/13. Australian First List of Major Japanese War Criminals" (October 22, 1946), T1205 (microfilm), Reel # 1/ RG 353, *NARA*.

39. "The Counsellor, New Zealand Legation, Washington, to the Secretary of External Affairs" (July 29, 1948), in *DNZ*, 1719–21.

40. "Far Eastern Commission. Trial of Japanese War Criminals. Policy Decision No. 55" (February 25, 1949), File: "War Crimes—FEC-314" (Folder 1 of 2)/ Box 21/ Entry 1378/ RG 59, *NARA*.

41. "Far Eastern Commission. Trial of Japanese War Criminals. Policy Decision No. 57" (April 7, 1949), File: "War Crimes—FEC-314" (Folder 1 of 2)/ Box 21/ Entry 1378/ RG 59, *NARA*.

42. "USSR Overseas & Far East Service. 'Japs Indicted on Germ Warfare Charges'" (December 27, 1949), File: "War Crimes—Emperor (Japanese)"/ Box 23/ Entry 1371/ RG 59, *NARA*. For the records of the trial, see *Materials on the Trial of Former Servicemen of the Japanese Army Charged with Manufacturing and Employing Bacteriological Weapons.*

43. "London (Holmes) to the Secretary of State" (February 10, 1950), File: "War Crimes—Emperor (Japanese)"/ Box 23/ Entry 1371/ RG 59, *NARA*.

44. "No Trial Likely for Hirohito" (February 3, 1950), a clipping from an unidentified Australian newspaper; "U.S. Rejects Proposal to Try Hirohito: Emphatic 'No' to Russians" (February 3, 1950), *Daily Telegraph*, A1838/280, 3103/1/3/1, Part 1, *NAA*.

45. Harris, *Factories of Death*; Powell, "Hidden Chapter in History"; Powell, "Japan's Germ Warfare: The U.S. Cover-Up of A War Crime"; Tsuneishi, trans. and ed., *Hyōteki Ishii*.

46. "The Australian Embassy (Washington) to the Department of External Affairs" (February 3, 1950), A1838/280, 3103/1/3/1, Part 1, *NAA*.

47. "Soviet Note Requesting New War Crimes Trials" (February 8, 1950), File: "War Criminals (International Military Tribunal)"/ Box 20/ Entry 1084/ RG 43, *NARA*. Emphasis in the original.

48. Takeda, *Tennō kan no sōkoku*, 319.

Chapter Three

1. For correspondence between Washington and Tokyo regarding the arrest of Class A war crimes suspects, see *FRUS*, 1945, vol. 6, 941–42, 944, 952–53, 961–74, 976–78, 985–86. The names of the individuals listed for arrest can be found in Tōkyō saiban handobukku henshū iinkai, ed., *Tōkyō saiban handobukku*, 200–203.

2. "Report by Mr. Robert A. Fearey, of the Office of the Political Adviser in Japan" (November 26, 1945), in *FRUS*, 1945, vol. 6, 974.

3. Awaya, "Tōkyō saiban no hikoku wa kōshite erabareta," 95.

4. Horwitz, "The Tokyo Trial," 496.

5. Ibid.

6. "The Indictment," in *Transcripts*, vol. 1.

7. "Comyns-Carr to Keenan" (February 25, 1946), in *TSM*, vol. 3, 160–63.

8. Ibid., 161–62.

9. "Notes Taken at Conference on Subject of Objectives of Trial, etc." (February 26, 1946), in *TSM*, vol. 3, 169.

10. "Confidential Memorandum to Mr. Keenan from Mr. Higgins re General Policy" (February 27, 1946), in *TSM*, vol. 3, 173–74.

11. "Notes of the Meeting of All Staff" (March 2, 1946), in *TSM*, vol. 4, 139.

12. Ibid., 141.

13. Ibid., 140–41.

14. A comprehensive account of the successive proceedings at Nuremberg can be found in Taylor, *Final Report*.

15. Awaya, "Tōkyō saiban e no michi," *Asahi Journal* 27, no. 15.

16. "Report by the Former New Zealand Associate Prosecutor on the Proceedings of the International Military Tribunal for the Far East" (January 29, 1948); "The New Zealand Associate Prosecutor, International Military Tribunal for the Far East, to the Deputy Secretary of External Affairs" (June 25, 1947), in *DNZ*, 1706 and 1678.

17. "SCAP (MacArthur) to Joint Chiefs of Staff" (May 12, 1947), File: 010.2/Box 1416/ Entry 1289/ RG 331, *NARA*.

18. Ibid.

19. Ibid.

20. "The War Department to Commander-in-Chief Far East (MacArthur)" (June 19, 1947), File: 010.2/Box 1416/ Entry 1289/ RG 331, *NARA*.

21. "The War Department (Keenan) to Commander-in-Chief Far East (for Frank Tavenner, IPS)" (June 19, 1947), File: 010.2/Box 1416/ Entry 1289/ RG 331, *NARA*.

22. "The New Zealand Associate Prosecutor, International Military Tribunal for the Far East, to the Deputy Secretary of External Affairs" (June 25, 1947), in *DNZ*, 1678.

23. Ibid., 1679.

24. "Class 'A' Suspects to be Tried Soon, Keenan Declares" (August 13, 1947), *The Nippon Times*, File 010.2/Box 1416/ Entry 1289/ RG 331, *NARA*.

25. "The British Commonwealth Sub-Area, Tokyo, to the Minister of External Affairs" (August 14, 1947), in *DNZ*, 1687.

26. "SCAP (MacArthur) to the War Department (pass to Draper)" (October 28, 1947), File: 010.2/Box 1416/ Entry 1289/ RG 331, *NARA*.

27. "Commander-in-Chief Far East (MacArthur) to the Department of the Army" (January 1948), File: 010.2/Box 1416/ Entry 1289/ RG 331.

28. "Alva C. Carpenter, Chief, Legal Section, to the Supreme Commander for the Allied Powers (MacArthur). Trial of Class A Suspects on B and C Charges" (September 25, 1948), File: 010.2/Box 1416/Entry 1289/RG 331, *NARA*.

29. "The Legal Section to SCAP (MacArthur). Interim Report and Recommendations concerning 19 former Class A War Crimes Suspects," (April 16, 1948), File: "Class A Japanese War Crimes at Sugamo"/ Box 1414/ Entry 1294/ RG 331, *NARA*.

30. "Alva C. Carpenter, Chief, Legal Section, to the Supreme Commander for the Allied Powers. Trial of Class A Suspects on B and C Charges" (September 25, 1948), File: 010.2/ Box 1416/ Entry 1289/ RG 331, *NARA*.

31. "The Secretary of the Army (Royall) to MacArthur" (September 17, 1948), File: "War Crimes—Far East (Minor)"/ Box 23/ Entry 1371/ RG 59, *NARA*.

32. "Alva C. Carpenter, Chief, Legal Section, to the Supreme Commander for the Allied Powers. Trial of Class A Suspects on B and C Charges" (September 25, 1948), File: 010.2/ Box 1416/ Entry 1289/ RG 331, *NARA*.

33. "The Legal Section to the Diplomatic Section. Appointment of Judges for War Crimes Trials" (October 23, 1948), File: 010.2A/ Box 1416/ Entry 1289/ RG 331, *NARA*.

34. "The Legal Section to the Chief of Staff. Invitation to Recommend War Crimes Judges" (October 27, 1948), File: 010.2A/ Box 1416/ Entry 1289/ RG 331, *NARA*.

35. "The Diplomatic Section to the Legal Section. UK Participation in War Crimes Trials" (November 4, 1948), File: 010.2A/ Box 1416/ Entry 1289/ RG 331, *NARA*.

36. "The Legal Section to the Diplomatic Section. Participation in Trial of Adm. Toyoda and Lt. Gen. Tamura" (January 12, 1949), File 010.2A/ Box 1416/Entry 1289/ RG 331, *NARA*.

37. "SCAP Tokyo, Japan (MacArthur), to the Department of the Army" (December 4, 1948), File: "War Crimes—Far East (Minor)"/ Box 23/ Entry 1371/ RG 59, *NARA*.

Chapter Four

1. Gutman and Rieff, eds., *Crimes of War*, 109.

2. Electronic texts of these legal documents can be obtained at the United Nations website.

3. Lee, ed., *International Criminal Court*, 81–85; Cassese, Gaeta, and Jones, eds., *Rome Statute*, vol. 1, 427–41; Schabas, *An Introduction to the International Criminal Court*, 31–34.

4. The Kellogg-Briand Pact is named after the American and French representatives, Frank B. Kellogg and Aristide Briand, who initiated it. For the history of the Pact, see Oppenheim, *International Law*, 177–97.

5. For the texts of the Hague Conventions of 1899 and the Pact of Paris, see *Law of War*, vol. 1, 204–50, 469–71. Also see the Avalon Project website.

6. "The Charter of the International Military Tribunal," the Avalon Project website.

7. Cassese, Gaeta, and Jones, eds., *Rome Statute*, vol. 1, 428–29.

8. "The Charter of the International Military Tribunal for the Far East," the Avalon Project website. Italics added.

9. Court Exhibit 255: "Allied Post-War Interrogation of Mutō Akira," in *Transcripts*, vol. 2, 3436–39.

10. "The Indictment," in *Transcripts*, vol. 1.

11. Ibid.

12. See, for instance, Takigawa, *Tōkyō saiban o sabaku*, vol. 1, 144; Kiyose, *Hiroku*, 86–89; and Kojima, *Tōkyō saiban*, 130–31.

13. Okuhara, "Tōkyō saiban ni okeru kyōdō bōgi riron."

14. Hosoya et al., eds., *Tokyo War Crimes Trial*, 108.

15. *Tokyo Judgment*, vol. 1, 31–32.

16. The full record of the defense summation on points of law can be found in *Transcripts*, vol. 17, 42111–284. For its reprint, see Takayanagi, *Tokio Trials and International Law*.

17. *Tokyo Judgment*, vol. 1, 28.

18. *Nuremberg Judgment*, 38.

19. Ibid., 39.

20. Ibid.

21. Ibid.

22. Ibid., 40.

23. The corresponding stipulation is given in Article 6 of the Charter of the Tokyo Tribunal, which reads as follows: "Responsibility of Accused. Neither the official position, at any time, of an accused, nor the fact that an accused acted pursuant to order of his government or of a superior shall, of itself, be sufficient to free such accused from responsibility for any crime with which he is charged, but such circumstances may be considered in mitigation of punishment if the Tribunal determines that justice so requires." The Avalon Project website.

24. *Nuremberg Judgment*, 41.

25. A fuller legal argument in support of the Nuremberg ruling on crimes against peace can be found in the judgment of the Ministries Case (*U.S.* v. *Ernst von Weizsäcker et al.*): *TWC*, vol. 14, 317–23.

26. *Tokyo Judgment*, vol. 1, 439.

27. Hosoya et al., eds., *Tokyo War Crimes Trial*, 76.

28. Tōkyō saiban kenkyūkai, ed., *Kyōdō kenkyū*, vol. 1, 202.

29. Minear, *Victors' Justice*, 129, 130.

30. Okuhara, "Tōkyō saiban ni okeru kyōdō bōgi riron (3)," 190–91; Hosoya et al., *Tokyo War Crimes Trial*, 109.

31. *Nuremberg Judgment*, 43.

32. *Tokyo Judgment*, vol. 1, 195.

33. Ibid., 441.

34. Ibid., 207–8.

35. Ibid., 208

36. Ibid., 209.

37. Ibid., 319–20.

38. Ibid., 322–24.

39. Ibid., 324.

40. The preamble to Article 6 of the Nuremberg Charter reads as follows: "The Tribunal established by the Agreement referred to in Article 1 hereof for the trial and punishment of the major war criminals of the *European Axis countries* shall have the power to try and punish persons who, acting in the interests of the *European Axis countries*, whether as individuals or as members of organizations, committed any of the following crimes." Similarly, the preamble to Article 5 of the Tokyo Charter reads as follows: "The Tribunal shall have the power to try and punish *Far Eastern war criminals* who as individuals or as members of organizations are charged with offenses which include Crimes against Peace." Italics added.

41. The defense also attempted to dismiss the charges of war crimes related to French Indochina on grounds that France and Japan did not engage in war. For the defense argument on this matter, see "Testimony by Captain Fernand

Gabrillagues, French Army Delegate for War Crimes in Indo-China," in *Transcripts*, vol. 6, 15424–72.

42. *Tokyo Judgment*, vol. 1, 341.

43. *Nuremberg Judgment*, 13. Italics added. Taylor, *Anatomy of the Nuremberg Trials*, 575–77.

44. *TWC*, vol. 14, 333; Taylor, *Final Report*, 222–23.

45. The two counts that the Tribunal did not establish concerned Thailand and the Philippines. With respect to the one on Thailand, the Tribunal concluded the Thai government acted in "complicity" with the Japanese government, effectively supporting the Japanese pursuit of the occupation of French Indochina. As for the count concerning the Philippines, the Tribunal did find that Japan waged aggressive war against the Philippines. However, in light of the fact that the Philippines was a subject nation of the United States during war, the judges concluded that this count should be considered as being subsumed under the count on the war against the United States. *Tokyo Judgment*, vol. 1, 383–84.

46. *Tokyo Judgment*, vol. 1, 379–80. The shortcomings of the 1907 Hague Convention concerning the opening of hostilities is discussed in Oppenheim, *International Law*, 290–95.

47. Strictly speaking, the note the Japanese government handed to the United States government was not a formal warning or declaration of war. It was an "ultimatum" stating Japan's intention to terminate the negotiations it had held with the United States government in preceding months.

48. Higurashi, *Tōkyō saiban no kokusai kankei*, 457.

49. *Tokyo Judgment*, vol. 1, 381.

50. Eguchi, *Jūgonen sensō shōshi*, 4; Ajia ni taisuru Nihon no sensō sekinin o tou minshū hōtei junbikai, ed., *Toinaosu Tōkyō saiban*, 6; Okabe, *Jūgonen sensōshi ron*, 14–35, 60–61.

Chapter Five

1. *Tokyo Judgment*, vol. 1, 31–33.

2. The full text of the Fourth Hague Convention of 1907 and the Prisoner of War Convention can be found at the Avalon Project website.

3. "Testimony by Matsumoto Shun'ichi," in *Transcripts*, vol. 11, 27136.

4. "Testimony by Togo Shigenori," in *Transcripts*, vol. 15, 35770.

5. *Tokyo Judgment*, vol. 1, 424–25.

6. For the Nuremberg interpretation of the Fourth Hague Convention (1907) concerning laws and customs of war on land, see *Nuremberg Judgment*, 64–65. The ruling given by the IMT was affirmed at the twelve successive trials. See, for instance, the Krupp Case (*U.S. v. Alfried Krupp von Bohlen und Halbach*),

TWC, vol. 9, part II, 1340–41; the High Command Case (*U.S.* v. *Wilhelm von Leeb et al.*), *TWC*, vol. 11, 532–42.

7. On the development of the concept of crimes against humanity, see United Nations War Crimes Commission, ed., *History*, 188–220.

8. Gutman and Rieff, eds., *Crimes of War*, 107–8.

9. *Nuremberg Judgment*, 64–65. Lawrence Douglas discusses the narrow construction of the law pertaining to crimes against humanity at Nuremberg and its long-term impact on Holocaust historiography. Douglas, *Memory of Judgment*.

10. Taylor, *Anatomy of the Nuremberg Trials*, 21–77.

11. The Tokyo Tribunal briefly considered the applicability of crimes against humanity in connection with the Japanese mistreatment of the people of French Indochina. *Transcripts*, vol. 7, 15424–472.

12. The question of how to interpret "permission" was very controversial at the American trial of Gen. Yamashita Tomoyuki in Manila (Oct.–Dec. 1945). Some of the best analyses of the Yamashita case can be found in: United Nations War Crimes Commission, ed., *Law Reports of Trials of War Criminals*, vol. 4, 1–96; Reel, *Case of General Yamashita*; Lael, *Yamashita Precedent*; Cohen, "Beyond Nuremberg." B. V. A. Röling, the Dutch justice at Tokyo, discussed the use of the term "permission" in his separate dissenting opinion. *Tokyo Judgment*, vol. 2, 1063–64.

13. "The Indictment," in *Transcripts*, vol. 1. Italics added.

14. *Transcripts*, vol. 16, 40111.

15. Ibid., 40112.

16. Jurisprudence of command responsibility is very complex; I lack the expertise to provide an in-depth discussion of it. For the opinions of international jurists today, one may refer to the judgments of the International Criminal Tribunals for Rwanda and the former Yugoslavia. The texts are available at the websites of the International Criminal Tribunal for the Former Yugoslavia and the International Criminal Tribunal for Rwanda at the United Nations.

17. *Transcripts*, vol. 16, 40112–113.

18. Yoshida Yutaka, "Haisen zengo ni okeru kōbunsho no shōkyaku to intoku." Bradsher, *Researching Japanese War Crimes Records*, 9. For Bradsher's detailed study on the Japanese destruction of wartime records, see *World War II Japanese Records* (forthcoming).

19. Court Exhibit 2000: "Certificate by Miyama Yōzō, Chief of Correspondence Section, First Demobilization Bureau, August 5, 1946," in *Transcripts*, vol. 6, 14699–700.

20. Court Exhibit 2011: "Message from Chief, Prisoner of War Camps, Tokyo, to Maj. Gen. Higuchi Keishichirō, Taiwan Army Chief of Staff, Repeated to Korean Army, Kwantung Army, North China Area Army and Hong Kong;

re. Korea, Taiwan, Mukden, Borneo, North China, Hong Kong, Thailand, Malaya, Java; Each Prisoner-of-War Commanding Officer, August 20, 1945," in *Transcripts*, vol. 6, 14718–719. The Tokyo Tribunal quoted this exhibit in its final judgment. *Tokyo Judgment*, vol. 1, 409.

21. Yoshimi, *Jūgun ianfu*, 5. The English translation of this book is available as Yoshimi, *Comfort Women*. Yoshimi assembled additional documents that attested to the government sponsorship of comfort women. Yoshimi, ed., *Jūgun ianfu shiryōshū*. See also Yoshimi and Hayashi, eds., *Kyōdō kenkyū*; VAWW-Net Japan, ed., *Nihongun seidoreisei o sabaku*.

22. Sugihara, *Chūgokujin kyōsei renkō*, 45–53.

23. Alan Mansfield, "Opening Statement concerning Phase XIV: Japanese Violations of the Laws and Customs of War," in *Transcripts*, vol. 6, 12861.

24. "The Indictment," in *Transcripts*, vol. 1.

25. According to recent research, the United States government had a part in deciding against the prosecution of Japanese use of poison gas in wartime. Awaya, "Tōkyō saiban e no michi," *Asahi Journal* 26, nos. 43–45; Awaya, *Miketsu no sensō sekinin*, 44–45; Yoshimi, *Dokugasusen to Nihongun*.

26. Court Exhibit 1355: "Lists of 317 Reports by the Judge Advocate General's Office of the United States Army," in *Transcripts*, vol. 5, 12378–379.

27. Court Exhibit 2036: "Record of Proceedings of a U.S. Military Commission Convened at the U.S. Naval Air Base, Kwajalein Island, Marshall Islands, December 21, 1945," in *Transcripts*, vol. 6, 14972–983; Court Exhibit 2056: "Record of Proceedings of a United States Military Commission Convened at Guam by United States Pacific Fleet, Commander Marianas Area, August 15, 1946, in the case of Lt. Gen. Tachibana, Vice-Adm. Mori, Capt. Yoshii, Maj. Matoba *et al.*," in *Transcripts*, vol. 7, 15032–42; Court Exhibit 1540: "Affidavit by Lt. Col. E. L. St. J. Couch, Enclosing the Charge Sheet and Abstract of Evidence Produced for the British Minor War Crimes Trial Concerning the Kalagon Massacre," and Court Exhibit 1541: "Report by Lt. Col. A. M. Sturrock, British Army, President of No. 4 War Crimes Court, Rangoon," in *Transcripts*, vol. 6, 12968–971; Court Exhibit 2141: "Memoranda & Record of Judgment by Permanent Military Tribunal, Saigon, Sent by the French Embassy in Tokyo to SCAP," in *Transcripts*, vol. 7, 15360–363.

28. Van Poelgeest, *Tōkyō saiban to Oranda*, 43–45.

29. "Testimony by Colonel Cyril Hew Dalrymple Wild, British Army, War Crimes Liaison Officer with Allied Land Forces in South-East Asia (ALFEA)," in *Transcripts*, vol. 3, 5350–497, 5504–846.

30. "Testimony by Nicholas D. J. Read-Collins, Royal Artillery, Chief of SCAP (British Section) Legal Division," *Transcripts*, vol. 6, 13528–553; "Testimony by C. G. Ringer, British Indian Army," in *Transcripts*, vol. 6, 13554–604;

"Testimony by Cornelius Leenheer, British Army," in *Transcripts*, vol. 6, 13733–780; "Testimony by Fernand Gabrillagues, French Army Delegate for War Crimes in Indo-China," in *Transcripts*, vol. 7, 15424–472.

31. "Letter from W. W. Webb to Judge Alan J. Mansfield" (October 20, 1945), A6238/2, 3, *NAA*; "Testimony by Lt. Col. Albert Ernest Coates, Australian Army Medical Corps," *Transcripts*, vol. 5, 11403–526. See also Daws, *Prisoners of the Japanese*, 198–201.

32. "Letter from Alan J. Mansfield to W. W. Webb" (September 27, 1945), A 6238/2, 3, *NAA*; "Testimony by Lt. John Charles Van Nooten, Australian Imperial Forces," *Transcripts*, vol. 6, 13943–14051.

33. "Letter from Alan J. Mansfield to Sir William Webb" (October 22, 1945), A6238/2, 3, *NAA*; "Testimony by Warrant Officer (First Class) William Hector Sticpewich, Australian Imperial Forces," in *Transcripts*, vol. 6, 13344–403.

34. Prisoners were transported across the Pacific in filthy, crowded, heated holds without adequate supplies of food, water, or sanitary systems for days. Many died of starvation, suffocation, dehydration, or diseases, and some lost their sanity. Daws, *Prisoners of the Japanese*, 273–300.

35. "Introduction to Volume III," in *The Tokyo War Crimes Trial: Index and Guide*, vol. 3, i.

36. "The New Zealand Associate Prosecutor, International Military Tribunal for the Far East, to the Deputy Secretary of External Affairs" (December 2, 1946), in *DNZ*, 1650.

37. "Memorandum from Justice Mansfield to Chief of Counsel (Keenan). (B) and (C) Offences" (November 5, 1946), A1067/1, UN46/WC/15, *NAA*.

38. "Memorandum from Chief of Counsel (Keenan) to Justice Mansfield. (B) and (C) Offences" (November 6, 1946), and, "Memorandum from Justice Mansfield to Chief of Counsel (Keenan). Class B and C Offences" (November 7, 1946), A1067, UN46/WC/15, *NAA*.

39. "The New Zealand Associate Prosecutor, International Military Tribunal for the Far East, to the Deputy Secretary of External Affairs" (December 2, 1946), in *DNZ*, 1650.

40. Van Poelgeest, *Tōkyō saiban to Oranda*, 65–66.

41. For the discussion between President Webb and Mansfield regarding the prosecution's request to use synopses, see *Transcripts*, vol. 5, 11417–424, 11457–458, 11528.

Chapter Six

1. Chiang Kai-shek moved the capital of the Nationalist government to the inland city of Chungking in Szechuan Province, from where he continued to command his armed forces in the war against Japan.

2. Honda, *Nanjing Massacre*.

3. *Dai roppō zensho*, 116, 126.

4. Kasahara, "Chūgoku sensen ni okeru Nihongun no seihanzai," 9–10. According to Japanese military records, the Japanese army court-martialed 523 soldiers for committing sexual violence in the Chinese theater between 1937 and 1941, and 548 soldiers in the Pacific theater (excluding China) between 1941 and 1944. These trials apparently did little to deter widespread rape. *Jūgonen sensō gokuhi shiryōshū*, vol. 5, 8–39; VAWW-Net Japan, ed., *Nihongun seidoreisei o sabaku*, vol. 1, 62–65, 97–98.

5. Kasahara, "Chūgoku sensen ni okeru Nihongun no seihanzai," 9–10; Kasahara, *Nankin jiken*, 191–200; Honda, *Nanjing Massacre*; Eguchi, *Jūgonen sensō shōshi*, 117.

6. Many witness reports on the atrocities in Nanking have been translated and published in Japan. Some of the major publications are Hora, ed., *Nicchū sensō Nankin daizangyaku jiken shiryōshū*; Nankin jiken chōsa kenkyūkai, ed., *Nankin jiken shiryōshū*; Rabe, *Nankin no shinjitsu*; Vautrin, *Nankin jiken no hibi*; Ishida and Kasahara, eds., *Shiryō*; Zhang, ed., *Eyewitnesses to Massacre*.

7. Court Exhibit 329: "Dispatches from Oscar Trautmann, German Ambassador to China, Hankow, to the German Foreign Ministry, January 1938," in *Transcripts*, vol. 2, 4594.

8. The major part of the prosecution's presentation on Nanking can be found in the following sections of the trial transcripts: *Transcripts*, vol. 2, 2527–615, 2624–75, 3367–89, 3435–39, 3453–65, 3505–13, 3893–944, and 4451–604.

9. Yamamoto Masahiro offers a different assessment of the cases made by the prosecution and the defense regarding the Rape of Nanking. See Yamamoto, *Nanking*, 199–210.

10. "Testimony by Shang Teh-yi," in *Transcripts*, vol. 2, 2599–602.

11. "Testimony by Wu Chang-teh," in *Transcripts*, vol. 2, 2603-7. Wu Chang-teh offered a fuller account of the massacre he had experienced in his interview with Honda Katsuichi, a leading Japanese investigative journalist. Honda, *Nanjing Massacre*, 213–19, 284–85.

12. "Testimony by Dr. Miner Searle Bates," in *Transcripts*, vol. 2, 2624–75.

13. Ibid., 2661.

14. Prewar Japanese criminal proceedings followed the inquisitorial system.

15. *Transcripts*, vol. 2, 2595.

16. Ibid., 2597.

17. Ibid., 3918–19.

18. For research findings on Japanese sexual violence in the Chinese theater, see, for example, Kasahara, "Chūgoku sensen ni okeru Nihongun no seihanzai"; Kasahara, "Nihongun no zangyaku kōi to seihanzai."

19. *Transcripts*, vol. 2, 3935, 3940–43.

20. "Opening Statement for Division III of the Defense Case (China)—Sub-Division (iv) Occupation of Nanking and Japanese Attempt to Bring about Peace," in *Transcripts*, vol. 9, 20499–500. The successive trials at Nuremberg considered the rights of guerrilla forces under international law. See, for instance, the Hostage Case in *TWC*, vol. 11, 1243–47, and the High Command Case in *TWC*, vol. 11, 529–32.

21. Kojima, *Tōkyō saiban*, vol. 2, 81, 84.

22. The main defense evidence and witnesses concerning the atrocities in Nanking can be found in the following sections of the trial transcripts: *Transcripts*, vol. 9, 21431–474, 21559–581, 21885–948.

23. For the postwar debates on the Rape of Nanking, see Suzuki, "Nankin daigyakusatsu o meguru dōkō to kadai"; Yang, "The Malleable and the Contested"; Takashi Yoshida, *Making of the "Rape of Nanking."* For the specific views of those who deny the Nanking massacre, see Takemoto and Ohara, *Alleged "Nanking Massacre."*

24. Sugawara, *Tōkyō saiban no shōtai*, 143–44.

25. Takigawa, *Tōkyō saiban o sabaku*, vol. 2, 114.

26. Court Exhibit 2242: "Allied Post-War Interrogation of Mutō Akira," in *Transcripts*, vol. 7, 16130–132; *Kyokutō kokusai gunji saiban sokkiroku*, vol. 4, 264. Italics added.

27. "Testimony by Mutō Akira," in *Transcripts*, vol. 14, 33089. Italics added.

28. "Testimony by Matsui Iwane," in *Transcripts*, vol. 14, 33822.

29. Ibid., 33850.

30. Court Exhibit 257: "Allied Post-War Interrogation of Matsui Iwane, March 8, 1946," in *Transcripts*, vol. 2, 3453–54; "Testimony by a Maj. Gen. Nakayama Yasuto," in *Transcripts*, vol. 9, 21925.

31. "Testimony by Matsui Iwane," in *Transcripts*, vol. 14, 33821–822.

32. Ibid., 33849.

33. Ibid., 33822, 33917–918. Italics added.

34. Ibid., 33873–875.

35. Ibid., 33876. Matsui's testimony is somewhat fractured here, due to difficulties arising from the simultaneous translation. For the original statement in Japanese, see *Kyokutō kokusai gunji saiban sokkiroku*, vol. 7, 616.

36. Kainō, "Kyokutō saiban," 393. Matsui's testimony has come under intense scholarly scrutiny in the postwar period: Maruyama, *Gendai seiji no shisō to kōdō*, 84–134; Ushimura, *"Bunmei no sabaki" o koete*, 42–70. Both publications are available in English translation: Maruyama, *Thought and Behaviour in Modern Japanese Politics*; Ushimura, *Beyond the "Judgment of Civilization."* See also Yamamoto, *Nanking*, 210–217.

37. *TWC*, vol. II, 1271–72. Italics added. The High Command Case also considered the legal duty of a commanding officer in occupied territories. See *TWC*, vol. II, especially 542–49.

38. For the standards of command responsibility set out by the Tokyo Tribunal, see *Tokyo Judgment*, vol. 1, 29–31. The Dutch justice, Röling, discussed the criteria of command responsibility differently in his dissenting opinion: *Tokyo Judgment*, vol. 2, 1063–64.

39. *Tokyo Judgment*, vol. 1, 454.

40. For example, the Matsui case is discussed in "III. Applicable Law: G. Individual Criminal Responsibility Under Article 7 (3)," in *Mucic et al. (IT-96-21) "Celebici" Judgment* (November 16, 1998). This judgment is available at the United Nations website for the International Criminal Tribunal for the Former Yugoslavia.

41. *Tokyo Judgment*, vol. 1, 455.

42. Ibid.

43. "Testimony by Ishii Itarō," in *Transcripts*, vol. 12, 29969–997. Hirota and several other defendants chose not to testify in court.

44. Ibid., 29992–993.

45. *Tokyo Judgment*, vol. 1, 447–48. Justice Röling dissented from the majority verdict. *Tokyo Judgment*, vol. 2, 1125–27.

46. *Tokyo Judgment*, vol. 1, 30.

47. *Nuremberg Judgment*, 42.

48. Kainō, "Hōtei gijutsu," especially 21.

49. *Nuremberg Judgment*, 88–90, 130.

50. *Tokyo Judgment*, vol. 1, 477–78. Röling also pointed out that the Nuremberg Tribunal did not give capital punishment to those who were convicted of crimes against peace alone. *Tokyo Judgment*, vol. 2, 1060.

51. There are a number of excellent books on the Rwandan genocide. Some of the path-breaking titles are: Des Forges, *Leave None to Tell the Story*; Dallaire, *Shake Hands with the Devil*; Neuffer, *Key to My Neighbor's House*; Gourevitch, *We Wish to Inform You That Tomorrow We Will Be Killed with Our Families*.

52. "6. Law: 6.5. Violations of Common Article 3 and Additional Protocol II (Article 4 of the Statute)," in *Prosecutor versus Jean-Paul Akayesu, Case No. ICTR-96-4-T: Judgment* (September 2, 1998). The Akayesu judgment is available at the United Nations website for the International Criminal Tribunal for Rwanda. Timothy Brook is critical of the Hirota and Matsui precedents, writing that these guilty verdicts "would be unlikely to stand up in a war crimes tribunal today." Brook, "The Tokyo Judgment and the Rape of Nanking," 696.

53. Daws, *Prisoners of the Japanese*, 183–251.

54. Hayashi Hirofumi, *Sabakareta sensō hanzai*, 154.

55. "Testimony by Tojo Hideki," in *Transcripts*, vol. 15, 36421.

56. Ibid., 36421–422.

57. *Tokyo Judgment*, vol. 1, 462–63.

58. Court Exhibit 1960: "Instructions concerning the Treatment of Prisoners of War, Issued by War Minister Tojo Hideki to the Commander of the Zentsūji Division during his Inspection Visit on May 30, 1942," in *Transcripts*, vol. 6, 14424.

59. Court Exhibit 1962: "Text of Address Delivered by Tojo at the War Ministry to Newly-Appointed Commanders of Prisoner of War Camps from Korea, Manchukuo, Formosa and Japan Proper, June 25, 1942," in *Transcripts*, vol. 6, 14427.

60. Court Exhibit 1969: "Transmittal from Headquarters, Eastern District Army, to the War Ministry, October 21, 1942, Enclosing Report on Prisoner of War Labor Conditions by Kondo Jotaro," in *Transcripts*, vol. 6, 14494.

61. Court Exhibit 1980-D: "Excerpts from the Allied Post-War Interrogation of Tojo Hideki, March 25, 1946," in *Transcripts*, vol. 6, 14565.

62. Court Exhibit 1981-B: "Excerpts from the Allied Post-War Interrogation of Tojo Hideki, March 26, 1946," in *Transcripts*, vol. 6, 14580.

63. Ibid.

64. *Tokyo Judgment*, vol. 1, 463.

65. Shigemitsu did not testify in court.

66. "Testimony by Suzuki Tadakatsu," in *Transcripts*, vol. 16, 38908–909.

67. Ibid., 38913.

68. *Tokyo Judgment*, vol. 1, 458. Röling dissented from Shigemitsu's conviction. *Tokyo Judgment*, vol. 2, 1137–38. Lord Hankey—a member of the House of Lords—also questioned the validity of Shigemitsu's conviction. Hankey, *Politics, Trials and Errors*. He had made friends with Shigemitsu during the latter's service as Japanese ambassador to Britain between 1938 and 1941.

69. *Tokyo Judgment*, vol. 1, 458.

70. The charges against the accused were crimes against peace, war crimes, and crimes against humanity.

71. Taylor, *Final Report*, 214.

72. *TWC*, vol. 14, 354.

73. Cohen, "Bureaucracy, Justice, and Collective Responsibility," 329; *TWC*, vol. 14, 497–98. Italics added.

74. Generally speaking, with the passage of time the Allied trials seemed to become increasingly lenient in sentencing in both Europe and the Pacific region. Commenting on the successive trials at Nuremberg, Telford Taylor remarked that "the sentences became progressively lighter as time went on." Taylor, *Final Report*, 92.

75. Cohen, "Beyond Nuremberg"; Cohen, "Bureaucracy, Justice, and Collective Responsibility."

Chapter Seven

1. *Transcripts*, vol. 2, 4609.

2. Ibid., 4610.

3. Some relevant—though fragmentary—documentation of sexual violence can be found in ibid., 2622, 4612–13, 4615, 4638, 4642, 4647.

4. Court Exhibit 353: "Statement by Nine Kweilin Citizens," in *Transcripts*, vol. 2, 4653.

5. "Testimony by John Goette," in *Transcripts*, vol. 2, 3774–75.

6. "Testimony by Ti Shu-tang," in *Transcripts*, vol. 2, 4618–29. There is a large body of literature on the Hanaoka Incident in Japan. For instance, Nozoe Kenji published *Hanaoka jiken to Chūgokujin*; *Hanaoka jiken no hitotachi*; and *Kiki aruki Hanaoka jiken*. For an English-language account, see Buruma, *Wages of Guilt*, 275–91.

7. *Transcripts*, vol. 2, 3892.

8. For the summary of the Yamashita trial, see United Nations War Crimes Commission, ed., *Law Reports of Trials of War Criminals*, vol. 4, 1–96.

9. Tōkyō saiban handobukku henshū iinkai, ed., *Tōkyō saiban handobukku*, 107.

10. Court Exhibit 1450: "Summary of JAG Report, no. 75," in *Transcripts*, vol. 6, 12597–599. Daws, *Prisoners of the Japanese*, 60–90.

11. "Testimony by Staff Sergeant Samuel B. Moody, U.S. Army"; "Testimony by Donald F. Ingle"; "Testimony by Lieutenant-Colonel Franklin N. Fliniau, U.S. Army"; "Testimony by Lieutenant-Colonel Austin J. Montgomery, U.S. Army"; "Testimony by Col. Guy H. Stubbs, U.S. Army," in *Transcripts*, vol. 6, 12578–591, 12610–667, 12672–724, 12738–775.

12. Nagai Hitoshi is critical of Lopez's presentation, contending that Lopez did not present conclusive evidence to link Mutō with Japanese atrocities in the Philippines. Nagai, "Firipin to Tōkyō saiban," 58.

13. Court Exhibit 1446: "Captured Japanese Memorandum, Dated November 18, 1944," in *Transcripts*, vol. 6, 12576. The parentheses appear in the original.

14. Court Exhibit 1447: "Statement by Pte. Yanagisawa Eiji," in *Transcripts*, vol. 6, 12577.

15. Cannibalism in the Philippine theater is portrayed in *Nobi* (Fires on the Plain), a 1959 film based on Ōoka Shōhei's novel and directed by Ichikawa Kon.

16. Court Exhibit 1387: "Summary of JAG Report 137," in *Transcripts*, vol. 6, 12468–469.

17. Court Exhibit 1459: "Summary of JAG Report 99," in *Transcripts*, vol. 6, 12736.

18. "Memorandum from Mansfield to Keenan, Class B and C Offences" (October 2, 1946), in *TKK*, vol. 3, 168.

19. "Testimony by Sergeant Douglas Bogue, United States Marine Corps," in *Transcripts*, vol. 7, 15204–279.

20. Court Exhibit 2056: "Record of Proceedings of a United States Military Commission Convened at Guam by United States Pacific Fleet, Commander Marianas Area, August 15, 1946, in the Case of Lt. Gen. Tachibana, Vice-Adm. Mori, Capt. Yoshii, Maj. Matoba *et al.*," in *Transcripts*, vol. 7, 15033–42.

21. Ibid., 15033–35.

22. Hara Kazuo produced a documentary film on cannibalism in New Guinea in collaboration with a war veteran, Okuzaki Kenzō: *The Emperor's Naked Army Marches On* (1987),

23. *Transcripts*, vol. 7, 16033–34.

24. Ibid., 15040.

25. On the alleged Allied failure to represent the Asian voice at the Tokyo trial, see Ōnuma, *Tōkyō saiban kara sengo sekinin no shisō e*, 9, 19, 29–31.

26. Hayashi Hirofumi, *Sabakareta sensō hanzai*, 111–12, 293; Hayashi Hirofumi, *BC-kyū senpan saiban*, 76–82. The Australian war crimes program, too, prosecuted war crimes targeted at Asian people. According to statistics compiled by David Sissons, 128 out of 294 Australian national trials concerned Japanese atrocities against South Pacific islanders, Chinese, Indonesians, and Indians. Sissons, "Ōsutoraria ni yoru sensō hanzai chōsa to saiban," 293.

27. Court Exhibit 476: "Investigation of Cruel Acts Committed during the Malaya (Singapore) Campaign," in *Transcripts*, vol. 3, 5610–81. For details of the massacre in Singapore, see Hayashi Hirofumi, *Shingapōru kakyō shukusei*.

28. Hayashi Hirofumi, *Sabakareta sensō hanzai*, 209–27.

29. "Testimony by Sister Vivien Bullwinkel, Capt. Australian Nursing Service," in *Transcripts*, vol. 6, 13454–476.

30. Daws, *Prisoners of the Japanese*, 326–27; Yuki Tanaka, *Hidden Horrors*, 45–74.

31. "Testimony by Warrant Officer (First Class) William Hector Sticpewich, Australian Imperial Forces," *Transcripts*, vol. 6, 13344–403; Court Exhibit 1668: "Affidavit by Pte. Keith Botterill, Australian Imperial Forces," in *Transcripts*, vol. 6, 13420–425.

32. "Trial of Lt.-Gen. Baba Masao," in United Nations War Crimes Commission, ed., *Law Reports of Trials of War Criminals*, vol. 5, 56–61.

33. This may have to do with the brief participation of the Burmese war crimes investigator on the British team. He assisted in the collection of evidence related to Burma.

34. *Transcripts*, vol. 3, 5442–45. The Tribunal referred to a segment of Wild's extensive court testimony in the final judgment: *Tokyo Judgment*, vol. 1, 405.

35. Court Exhibit 1577: "Affidavit of Thakin Sa," in *Transcripts*, vol. 6, 13090–93. Some of the quoted passages do not appear in the trial transcripts. For the full text of the court exhibit, I made use of a copy obtained from the Australian War Memorial Library. File: "International Military Tribunal for the Far East, Documents Presented in Evidence," *AWM 83* Series.

36. Court Exhibits 1576: "Affidavit by R. E. Peterson," in *Transcripts*, vol. 6, 13090; *AWM 83* Series.

37. Court Exhibit 1540: "Affidavit by Lt. Col. E. L. St. J. Couch," and Court Exhibit 1541: "Report by Lt. Col. A. M. Sturrock, British Army, President of No. 4 War Crimes Court, Rangoon," in *Transcripts*, vol. 6, 12968–971; *AWM 83* Series.

38. For a detailed study of the Rangoon trial on the Kalagon massacre, see Hayashi Hirofumi, *Sabakareta sensō hanzai*, 253–62.

39. Court Exhibits 1659 through 1665 in *Transcripts*, vol. 6, 13332–343.

40. Court Exhibit 1659: "Report by Captain M. J. Dickson (British Army)," in *Transcripts*, 13322–331; The quoted passage is taken from a copy of the court exhibit, *AWM 83* Series.

41. Court Exhibit 1614: "Excerpts from the Declaration by Mohamed Hussain," in *Transcripts*, vol. 6, 13189–190; *AWM 83* Series.

42. Court Exhibit 1884-A: "Excerpts Received from the Record of Interrogation of Kabunare," in *Transcripts*, vol. 6, 14150–151.

43. Court Exhibit 1873: "Affidavit by Havildar Chandgi Ram, Indian Army," in *Transcripts*, vol. 6, 14130.

44. Court Exhibit 1850: "Daily Record of Investigation of Prisoners, March 8–May 14, 1942, ATIS Bulletin," in *Transcripts*, vol. 6, 14102. Italics added.

45. "Testimony by John Charles Van Nooten, Australian Imperial Forces," in *Transcripts*, vol. 6, 13961–962.

46. Court Exhibit 1850-A: "Excerpts from the ATIS Bulletin," in *Transcripts*, vol. 6, 14139–140.

47. Court Exhibit 1721: "Affidavit by Gergardus de Langu, Police Officer," in *Transcripts*, vol. 6, 13646.

48. Court Exhibit 1778: "Affidavit by F. R. Kramer, Head Manager of the Deli Tobacco Company," in *Transcripts*, vol. 6, 13820.

49. The Dutch evidence concerning atrocities against civilian internees can be found in *Transcripts*, vol. 6, 13512–513, 13528–553, 13643–653, 13704–780, 13795–808, 13833–835, 13920–923.

50. Van Poelgeest, *Tōkyō saiban to Oranda*, 155–99.

51. "Testimony by Lieutenant-Colonel Nicholas D. J. Read-Collins, Royal Artillery, Chief of SCAP (British Section) Legal Division," in *Transcripts*, vol. 6,

13528–553; "Testimony by Major Cornelius C. Leenheer, British Army," in *Transcripts*, vol. 6, 13733–780.

52. For the transcripts of *Nippon Presents*, see *Transcripts*, vol. 6, 13706–732.

53. Court Exhibit 1701: "Statement by S. Hayashi"; Court Exhibit 1702: "Report by Capt. J. F. Heybroek, Royal Netherlands Indies Army"; Court Exhibit 1725A: "Excerpts from the Affidavit by Mrs. J. Beelman"; Court Exhibit 1792-A: "Excerpts from the Affidavit by Luis Antonio Nunes Rodreigues"; Court Exhibit 1794: "Statement by Lt. S. Ohara, Japanese Army," in *Transcripts*, vol. 6, 13526–528, 13651–652, 13841–842, and 13843. For the full text of the Dutch evidence on sexual slavery, I used the copies kept in the *AWM* 83 Series.

54. *Transcripts*, vol. 6, 13527.

55. *AWM* 83 Series.

56. Yuki Tanaka, *Japan's Comfort Women*.

57. Hayashi Hirofumi, "BC-kyū saiban."

58. Utsumi, "Senji seibōryoku to Tōkyō saiban." For information about the Women's Tribunal, see VAWW-NET Japan, ed., *Nihongun seidoreisei o sabaku*.

59. Nihon no sensō shiryō sentā kenkyū jimukyoku, ed., "Tōkyō saiban de sabakareta Nihongun 'ianfu' seido"; "Reference Materials of the Press Conference on Japanese Military Sexual Slavery ("Comfort Women"), 17 April 2007 at the Foreign Correspondents' Club of Japan," the Center for Research and Documentation on Japan's War Responsibility website; Totani, "Tōkyō saiban ni okeru sensō hanzai sotsui to hanketsu."

60. Gutman and Rieff, eds., *Crimes of War*, 323–24; Neier, *War Crimes*, 181–82.

61. *Transcripts*, vol. 6, 13654–655.

62. Court Exhibit 1733: "Affidavit by Achmad Bin Ketajoeda," in *Transcripts*, vol. 6, 13663.

63. Court Exhibit 1736: "Affidavit by Rebo," ibid., 13668.

64. Court Exhibit 1734: "Affidavit by Goedel," ibid., 13663–667.

65. Court Exhibit 2120: "Affidavit by Nguyen-thi Thong," in *Transcripts*, 15315–316.

66. Takayanagi, *Tokio Trials and International Law*. This book contains both the English and Japanese versions of the defense summation. The quoted passage appears on 57 in the English text, and 71 in the Japanese text.

67. The standard of responsibility applied at the Allied war crimes trials (including the Tokyo trial) appeared more commonly to be that of "knew, or should have known," than "knew, or had reason to know." For the opinion of the Tokyo Tribunal on this issue, see *Tokyo Judgment*, vol. 1, 30–31.

68. *Tokyo Judgment*, vol. 1, 385.

69. David Cohen points out the influence of the Yamashita precedent in this part of the Tokyo Judgment: "This language repeats almost verbatim the

military commission's finding against Yamashita." Cohen, "Beyond Nuremberg," 76.

70. *Tokyo Judgment*, vol. 1, 385–421.

71. Ibid., 406.

72. Ibid., 410.

73. Ibid., 392–93.

74. Ibid., 452.

75. Ibid., 444, 449–50.

76. Ibid., 455.

77. Ibid., 462–63.

78. Ibid., 453.

79. Ibid., 446.

80. "Testimony by Major-General Amano Masakuzu," in *Transcripts*, vol. 9, 21750.

81. On the Three-All Policy, see Kasahara, *Nankin jiken to sankō sakusen*; Ishida et al., eds., *Chūgoku Kahokushō ni okeru sankō sakusen*; Fujiwara, "'Sankō sakusen' to kitashina hōmen gun"; Fujiwara, "Kainantō ni okeru Nihon kaigun no 'sankō sakusen.'" For a firsthand account of the Three-All Policy by the Japanese perpetrators themselves, see Chūgoku kikansha renrakukai, ed., *Sankō*. This book is available in various editions. One of the latest editions is published under the title *Shinryaku*.

82. Röling dissented from Hata's conviction on the grounds that Hata's knowledge had not been established. *Tokyo Judgment*, vol. 2, 1120.

Chapter Eight

1. Dandō, "Sensō hanzai no rironteki kaibō," 165–66.

2. Ibid., 169–72.

3. Ibid., 172.

4. Ibid., 173.

5. Ibid., 180–81.

6. Ibid., 183.

7. Ibid., 183–84.

8. Asahi shinbunsha, ed., *Gendai Nihon Asahi jinbutsu jiten*, 1731–32; Ienaga, *Taiheiyō sensō*, 187.

9. Yokota, *Sensō hanzai ron*, 3.

10. Ibid., 4–5.

11. Ibid., 6.

12. Ibid.

13. Kainō, "Sensō saiban no hōritsu riron," 18.

14. Ibid., 14.
15. Ibid., 21.
16. Ibid., 23–24.
17. Ibid., 21.
18. Gushima, "Tōkyō saiban no rekishiteki igi," 27.
19. Ibid., 28.
20. Gushima, *Honryū.*
21. Gushima, "Tōkyō saiban no rekishiteki igi," 31.
22. Inoue, "Hō no ronri to rekishi no ronri."
23. Ibid., 3–4.
24. Ibid., 5.
25. Ibid.
26. Ibid., 6–7.
27. Ibid., 7.
28. Ibid.
29. Kido, *Kido Kōichi nikki.*
30. Inoue, "Hō no ronri to rekishi no ronri," 9.
31. Ibid.; *Transcripts,* vol. 19, 48410–411.
32. Inoue, "Hō no ronri to rekishi no ronri," 9.
33. Inoue, *Shōwa tennō no sensō sekinin.* There is a very large number of books on Hirohito's culpability in Japan today. The most thorough research on this topic to date is Yamada, *Shōwa tennō no gunji shisō to senryaku.*
34. *Tokyo Judgment,* vol. 1, 496.
35. Ibid.; Court Exhibit: "Kido Diary entry for 30 November 1941," in *Transcripts,* vol. 5, 10468.
36 *Tokyo Judgment,* vol. 1, 478. On the historical significance of the two separate opinions on Hirohito's culpability, see Okabe, *Jūgonen sensōshi ron,* 220.
37. "W. F. Webb to Major General Myron C. Cramer: Your Draft of the Pacific War" (September 15, 1948), M1417/1, 26, *NAA.*
38. Uchida, "Kyokutō saiban no hōrironteki igi," 24. On postwar judicial reform, see Sawanobori, Sawanobori, and Niwayama, *Keiji sosho hō shi.*
39. Uchida, "Kyokutō saiban no hōrironteki igi," 29.
40. Ibid., 30.
41. Ibid., 27–29.
42. Ibid., 29.
43. Yokota, "Sekai no shinpan."
44. Yokota, "Tōkyō hanketsu to jiei ron."
45. Kainō et al., "Zadankai."
46. Ibid., 28.

47. For an account of the development of international peace and justice mechanisms since the late-nineteenth century through the end of World War II, see Jones, *Toward a Just World.*

48. Tabata, "Tōkyō saiban no hōri," 13–18.

49. Ibid., 19–20.

50. Takayanagi, "Kyokutō hanketsu no hōritsuron," 1.

51. Ibid., 10–11.

52. Takayanagi, "Tōkyō hanketsu no hamon," 51.

53. Yokota, *Sensō hanzai ron*, 297–98.

54. Irie, "Tōkyō hanketsu no yōryō to sono shōkai."

55. Ibid., 39–40.

56. Kainō, "Kyokutō saiban," 276.

57. Ibid., 278.

58. Ibid.

59. Kiyose, *Hiroku*, 183–87; Furness, "Tōkyō saiban no butaiura," 50–52. Commenting on Keenan's letter, Shigemitsu wrote, "I take off my hat to Mr. Keenan's sense of justice. Everyone makes mistakes. But it is only those people with a strong sense of justice who admit the mistakes and try to correct them." Shigemitsu, "Hikokuseki no kaisō," 61.

60. Kainō, "Kyokutō saiban," 280

61. Ibid.

62. Ibid., 280–81.

63. Ibid., 282.

64. Ibid., 283.

65. Ibid., 284.

Chapter Nine

1. *Pal's Opinion*, 35–73.

2. Ibid., 123–31.

3. Ibid., 649.

4. Ibid., 609.

5. Ibid., 609, 658.

6. Ibid., 117.

7. *TWC*, vol. 4, 464.

8. *Nuremberg Judgment*, 65.

9. *Pal's Opinion*, 659.

10. Ibid., 634.

11. Asahi shinbun shuzaihan, ed., *Sensō to tsuitō*, 87–118; Nakajima, *Pāru hanji*; NHK supesharu shuzai chīmu, dir., *Pāru hanji wa nani o toikaketanoka*; Tōkyō saiban kenkyūkai, ed., *Kyōdō kenkyū*; Higurashi, "Kyokutō kokusai gunji saiban-

sho kōseikoku no jōken"; Higurashi, "Paru hanketsu saikō"; Ushimura, *"Bunmei no sabaki" o koete*, 181–207; Ushimura, *"Senso sekinin" ron no shinjitsu*, 135–81. Pal's dissenting opinion also came under scrutiny in English-language academia. See, for instance, Brook, "The Tokyo Judgment and the Rape of Nanking"; Dower, *Embracing Defeat* (Chapter 15); Kopelman, "Ideology and International Law"; Minear, *Victors' Justice*; Nandy, "The Other Within."

12. Pal also published *Crimes in International Relations* in 1955, which gives an abridged version of his dissenting opinion at the Tokyo trial.

13. *All India Reporter: Calcutta Section* (1941–43); *Calcutta Weekly Notes* (1941–43).

14. For information regarding the appointment of an Indian member to the Tokyo Tribunal, see External Affairs Department File No. 27W/46: "Correspondence between War Department and the Chief Justice of India and Chief Justices of High Court in Madras, Bombay, Calcutta, and Lahore. Nomination by Government of India," and External Affairs File No. 306 FEA/46: "Continuance of Mr. Pal to Serve as a Judge on the International Military Tribunal in Japan," National Archives of India.

15. Naitō Masao, "M. K. Gāndī to Nihonjin," 127–28; Nakajima, *Pāru hanji*, 187.

16. I gathered this piece of information when I met with Pal's surviving sons and daughters in Calcutta in the summer of 2001. For background information concerning Bengali nationalism, see, for instance, Gordon, *Bengal*; Chatterji, *Bengal Divided*; Broomfield, *Elite Conflict in a Plural Society*; Nakajima, *Nakamuraya no Bōsu*; Bose and Jalal, *Modern South Asia*.

17. Tanaka Masaaki, ed., *Pāru hakase no kotoba*, 17; Tanaka Masaaki, ed., *Pāru hakase jutsu*.

18. The Welcome Dr. Pal Committee had 48 members. They included former Class A suspects and defense lawyers at the Tokyo trial. Tanaka Masaaki, ed., *Pāru hakase no kotoba*, 21.

19. Asahi shinbunsha, ed., *Gendai Nihon Asahi jinbutsu jiten*, 824.

20. For Shimonaka's testimony, see *Transcripts*, vol. 13, 32689–698.

21. Speeches made by Pal during his visit in Japan are recorded in various publications. See, for instance, Pal, *Heiwa no sengen*, "Ajia minzokushugi no shisōteki kiso"; "Paru hanji ooi ni kataru!"

22. Sugawara, *Tōkyō saiban no shōtai*, 158–60; Tanaka Masaaki, ed., *Pāru hakase no kotoba*, 31–32. The text discussed here is my English rendering of the Japanese translation of the original speech.

23. Ushimura, *"Senso sekinin" ron no shinjitsu*, 145; Nakajima, *Pāru hanji*, 84; Harries, *Sheathing the Sword*, 149. The one who had the best attendance record was the Dutch judge, B. V. A. Röling, whose absences totaled 14 days.

24. Tanaka Masaaki, ed., *Pāru hakase no kotoba*, 32.

25. Ibid., 33–34.
26. Ibid., 34–35.
27. Ibid., 18.
28. Ibid., 41–42; Pal, *Zen'yaku*.
29. Nakajima, *Pāru hanji*, 283–85. A photographic copy of the news clipping appears in Tanaka Masaaki's *Pāru hakase no Nihon muzai ron*.
30. Pāru-Shimonaka kinenkan kensetsu iinkai, ed., "Pal-Shimonaka Memorial Hall."
31. This report, made in the *Mainichi* newspaper on February 11, 1967, is quoted in Ienaga, "Jūgonen sensō to Pāru hanketsusho," 23.
32. "The World and Japan" Database Project website.
33. Pāru-Shimonaka kinenkan kensetsu iinkai, ed., "Pal-Shimonaka Memorial Hall"; Nakajima, *Pāru hanji*, 10. According to Nakajima's fieldwork, the memorial is so badly maintained today that it hardly receives any visitors.
34. To understand the political valence of Pal in Japan today, see, for instance, Nakane, *Kike! Nihon muzai no sakebi*, 128–33; Kikuchi, *Nihon o suibō e michibiku "Tōkyō saiban shikan,"* 29.
35. Takigawa, *Tōkyō saiban o sabaku*, vol. 1, 4 (preface).
36. Sugawara, *Tōkyō saiban no shōtai*, 34.
37. Ibid., 173–74.
38. Kiyose, *Hiroku*, 42.
39. Shimanouchi, *Tōkyō saiban*, 279–96. Chapters of this book originally appeared in Shimanouchi's earlier publication, *Tōkyō saiban bengo zatsuroku*. Shimanouchi subsequently joined the defense team for the trial of Toyoda Soemu, one of the two successive trials held at Tokyo (1948–49). He also served as a defense lawyer at the Australian war crimes tribunal on Manus Island between 1950 and 1951.
40. Ibid., 284.
41. The Ministry of Justice began compiling the records of World War II war crimes trials in 1955 and produced a report of, and an index to, the collected trial records in 1973: *Sensō saiban kiroku kankei shiryō mokuroku* and *Sensō hanzai saiban gaishiyō*, respectively. These sources have not been published, but the ministry has published compilations of the laws applied at the Allied war crimes trials: *Sensō hanzai saiban kankei hōreishū*.
42. The two-volume *Kyōdō kenkyū* was later reprinted as pocket-size books in 1984 and went through several printings, reaching its fifteenth by 1997.
43. *Pal's Opinion*, iii–iv.
44. Ibid., vi.
45. Ibid., vi–vii.
46. Ibid., 606, 608.

47. Ibid., 608–9.

48. Minear, *Victors' Justice*, 148.

49. Some other major English-language books and articles that discuss the Tokyo trial are: Hankey, *Politics, Trials and Errors*; Horwitz, "The Tokyo Trial"; Piccigallo, *Japanese on Trial*; Harries, *Sheathing the Sword*; Pritchard, "An Overview"; Brackman, *Other Nuremberg*; Trotter, "New Zealanders"; Kopelman, "Ideology and International Law"; Van Poelgeest, "The Netherlands and the Tokyo Tribunal"; Röling and Cassese, *Tokyo Trial and Beyond*; Cohen, "Beyond Nuremberg"; Dower, *Embracing Defeat*; Bix, *Hirohito*; Stanton, "Canada and War Crimes"; Brook, "The Tokyo Judgment and the Rape of Nanking"; Maga, *Judgment at Tokyo*; Buruma, *Wages of Guilt*. For a fuller list of English-language publications, see *Bibliography on the International Military Tribunal for the Far East*; *Uncertain Judgment*; *The Tokyo Trial: A Bibliographic Guide to English-Language Sources*.

50. Minear, *Victors' Justice*, 34–73.

51. Ibid., 86.

52. Ibid., 134.

53. Okuhara, "Shōkai."

54. Ibid., 362.

55. Ibid., 363.

56. Ibid.

57. Ibid., 361–62.

58. Minear, *Victors' Justice*, x–xi.

59. Ibid., 177.

60. Ibid., xxi.

61. Ibid., 177–78.

62. There are a number of publications on Ienaga's textbook trials. For a general overview of the trials, see Ienaga kyōkasho soshō bengodan, ed., *Ienaga kyōkasho saiban*; Kyōkasho kentei soshō o shien suru zenkoku renrakukai, ed., *Ienaga kyōkasho saiban no subete*; Ienaga and Takashima, *Kyōkasho saiban wa tsuzuku*. For Ienaga's autobiography leading up to the first history textbook lawsuit, see Ienaga, *Ichi rekishi gakusha no ayumi*. The English translation of the autobiography is available as *Japan's Past, Japan's Future*.

63. Ienaga, "Jūgonen sensō to Pāru hanketsusho," 24.

64. Hayashi Fusao, *Daitōa sensō kōteiron*. For a concise account of the historiography of World War II in Japan, see Duus, "Remembering the Empire."

65. Ienaga, "Jūgonen sensō to Pāru hanketsusho," 24.

66. Ibid., 29–30.

67. Tōkyō saiban kenkyūkai, ed., *Kyōdō kenkyū*, vol. 1, 31–32.

68. *Pal's Opinion*, 248, 230. Capitalized words in the original.

69. Ienaga, "Jūgonen sensō to Pāru hanketsusho," 33–34.

70. *Pal's Opinion*, 218.

71. Ienaga, "Kyokutō saiban o dō kangaeru bekika," 112. Naitō Masao confirms the aptness of Ienaga's observation: Naitō, "M. K. Gāndī to Nihonjin."

72. This article was also published in *Japan Interpreter* 11 (Winter 1977).

73. Minear, "In Defense of Radha Binod Pal," 269.

74. Ibid., 267.

75. Ienaga, "Futatabi Pāru hanketsu ni tsuite." The English translation appears as, "Bias in the Guise of Objectivity."

76. This quotation is taken from the English translation of Ienaga's article ("Bias in the Guise of Objectivity"), 274.

77. Ibid., 275.

78. Ibid. Okabe Makio confirms that the controversy surrounding the Mukden Incident is already a settled issue among historians today. Okabe, *Jūgonen Sensōshi ron*, 36–38, 41.

79. Eguchi, *Jūgonen sensō shōshi*, 4.

80. Ienaga, *Taiheiyō sensō*, 457; *The Pacific War* (English translation, 1978).

Conclusion

1. Hosoya et al., *Tokyo War Crimes Trial*, 123–24; Awaya, "Tōkyō saiban e no michi," *Asahi Journal* 26, no. 42, 36.

2. The major publications that resulted from this research were: *Tōkyō saiban shiryō: Kido Kōichi jinmon chōsho* (Sources of the Tokyo Trial: The Records of Kido Kōichi's Interrogation), 1987; *Tōkyō saiban shiryō: Tanaka Ryūkichi jinmon chōsho* (Sources of the Tokyo Trial: The Records of Tanaka Ryūkichi's Interrogation), 1994; *Kokusai kensatsu kyoku (IPS) jinmon chōsho* (The Records of Interrogations by the International Prosecution Section), 52 vols., 1993; *Tōkyō saiban e no michi: kokusai kensatsu kyoku, seisaku kettei kankei bunsho* (The Road to the Tokyo Trial: The Records Related to the International Prosecution Section's Policy-Making), 5 vols., 1999; and *Tōkyō saiban to kokusai kensatsu kyoku: kaitei kara hanketsu made* (The Tokyo Trial and the International Prosecution Section: From the Opening of the Court to the Judgment), 5 vols., 2000.

3. To name just a few, there are *Asahi* newspaper reporters' *Tōkyō saiban* (The Tokyo Trial), 3 vols., 1946–49, revised and reprinted in 1962; Kojima Noboru's *Tōkyō saiban* (The Tokyo Trial), 2 vols., 1971; and Fuji Nobuo's *Watakushi no mita Tōkyō saiban* (The Tokyo Trial I Witnessed), 2 vols., 1988. Some other major publications have already been discussed in the preceding chapters.

4. Awaya, "Tōkyō saiban," 90.

5. Awaya, "Tōkyō saiban e no michi," *Asahi Journal* 26, no. 43.

6. Awaya and NHK Reporters, *NHK supesharu*, 215; Awaya, "Tōkyō saiban e no michi," *Asahi Journal* 26, nos. 44–45.

7. Yoshimi, *Dokugasusen to Nihongun*, 261–72.

8. Awaya and NHK Reporters, *NHK supesharu*, 216.

9. Ibid., 215; Awaya, *Tōkyō saiban ron*, 157–58.

10. Awaya and NHK Reporters, *NHK supesharu*; Awaya, *Tōkyō saiban ron*, 197–203; Awaya, "Tōkyō saiban"; Higashino, ed., *Shōwa tennō futatsu no "dokuhaku."*

11. Awaya and NHK Reporters, *NHK supesharu*, 212.

12. *TWC*, vol. 3, 970–71.

13. Taylor, *Final Report*, 65. Italics added.

14. *TWC*, Vol. 4, 467. Italics added.

15. Ōnuma, *Sensō sekinin josetsu*.

16. Ōnuma, *Tōkyō saiban kara sengo sekinin no shisō e*, 8.

17. Ajia ni taisuru Nihon no sensō sekinin o tou minshū hōtei junbikai, ed., *Jikō naki sensō sekinin*, 42–43, 49; and *Toinaosu Tōkyō saiban*, 13.

18. Ōnuma et al., "Renzoku tōron," 282.

19. Ibid., 283.

20. Awaya, "Senryō, hi-senryō," 196–99. See also Awaya and Utsumi, "Tōkyō saiban."

21. Awaya, "Senryō, hi-senryō," 199.

22. Ara, "Tōkyō saiban, sensō sekinin ron no genryū"; Sumitani, "Sensō hanzai saiban ron, sensō sekinin ron no dōkō"; Ōnuma, "Tōkyō saiban, sensō sekinin, sengo sekinin"; Awaya, "Sensō hanzai saiban to gendaishi kenkyū."

23. Awaya, "Sensō hanzai saiban to gendaishi kenkyū," 18.

24. Röling, "Tōkyō saiban no gendaishiteki igi," 192. Röling's remark on racial biases is discussed in Ubukata Naokichi's assessment of the Tokyo trial. Ubukata, "Tōkyō saiban o meguru shoronten," 104.

25. Yoshida Yutaka, *Shōwa tennō no shūsenshi*, 173–74. Yoshida's interpretation is partly reflected, for instance, in Dower's *Embracing Defeat* and Bix's *Hirohito and the Making of Modern Japan*.

26. This work caps existing research that explored the diplomatic dimension of the Tokyo trial. Some preceding publications include: Nagai, "Firipin to Tōkyō saiban"; Trotter, "New Zealanders"; Higurashi, "Kyokutō kokusai gunji saibansho kōseikoku no jōken"; Higurashi, "Paru hanketsu saikō"; Van Poelgeest, *Tōkyō saiban to Oranda*; Stanton, "Canada and War Crimes"; Song, "Shūsen zengo ni okeru Chūgoku no tainichi seisaku"; Yamagiwa, "Kenkyū nōto."

27. Higurashi, *Tōkyō saiban no kokusai kankei*, 12, 26, 626–32.

28. Yoshida Yutaka, "Kyokutō kokusai gunji saiban," 147–48.

29. Ibid., 144–45.

30. To get some sense of changing research trends in Japan, see *Sensō sekinin kenkyū* (Report on Japan's War Responsibility). This journal, first published in the fall of 1993, is the leading scholarly journal on war crimes studies in Japan.

Also visit the website of the Center for Research and Documentation on Japan's War Responsibility.

31. Mizushima, *Mirai sōzō to shite no "sengo hoshō"*; Chūgokujin sensō higai baishō seikyū jiken bengodan, ed., *Sajō no shōheki*; Onodera, "Sensō sekinin to sengo hoshō."

32. Cassese, Gaeta, and Jones, eds., *Rome Statute*, vol. 1, 427–28; Taylor, *Anatomy of the Nuremberg Trials*, 637.

33. United Nations War Crimes Commission, ed., *Law Reports of Trials of War Criminals*. For examples of recent research on Class BC trials, see, for instance, Hayashi Hirofumi, *Sabakareta sensō hanzai*; Hayashi Hirofumi, *BC-kyū senpan saiban*; Hayashi Hirofumi, "BC-kyū saiban."

34. The War Crimes Studies Center at the University of California, Berkeley, collects the records of World War II war crimes trials from both Europe and the Pacific region. This huge undertaking makes the Center the leading research institute on World War II war crimes trials.

Works Cited

Archival Sources

Australian War Memorial, Canberra, Australia.
   International Military Tribunal for the Far East, Documents Presented in Evidence, AWM 83 Series.
National Archives of Australia, Canberra, Australia.
   Correspondence Files of the Department of External Affairs, A1066, A1067, and A1838 Series.
   General Correspondence Files of the Second Australian War Crimes Commission, A6238 Series.
   Cuppaidge Papers, M1417 Series.
National Archives of India, New Delhi, India.
   External Affairs Department Files.
National Archives and Records Administration (NARA), College Park, MD, United States.
   Records of International Conferences, Commissions, and Expositions, RG 43.
   Records of the United States Department of State, RG 59.
   Records of the Office of the Secretary of War, RG 107.
   Records of the Allied Operation and Occupation Headquarters, World War II, RG 331.
   Records of Interdepartmental and Intradepartmental Committees (State Department), RG 353.

Senkō bunko, Yasukuni Shrine, Tokyo, Japan.
Inoue Tadao shiryō, kyokutō kokusai gunji saiban kankei chōshu shiryō (Sources gathered by Inoue Tadao: Records of the interviews relative to the International Military Tribunal for the Far East), 1961.

Other Primary Sources

All India Reporter: Calcutta Section. 34 vols. Nagpur, 1914–47.
Calcutta Weekly Notes. 69 vols. Calcutta: Eastern Book Company, 1896–1965.
Dai roppō zensho (The Compendium of Laws). Tokyo: Hōbunsha, 1940.
Documents on Australian Foreign Policy, 1937–1949. 16 vols. Canberra: Australian Government Publishing Service, 1975–2001.
Documents on New Zealand External Relations, Vol. II: *The Surrender and Occupation of Japan.* New Zealand: P. D. Hasselberg, Government Printer, 1982.
Foreign Relations of the United States. U.S. Department of State. Washington, DC: U.S. Government Printing Office.
International Military Tribunal for the Far East: Dissentient Judgment of Justice Pal. Tokyo: Kokusho kankōkai, 1999.
Jūgonen sensō gokuhi shiryōshū, 5: *Tōkyō saiban Ōyama Ayao kankei shiryō* (Secret Documents of the Fifteen-Year War, Vol. 5: The Tokyo Trial. Documents Related to Ōyama Ayao). Tokyo: Fuji shuppan, 1987.
Kokusai kensatsu kyoku (IPS) jinmon chōsho (The Records of Interrogations by the International Prosecution Section). 52 vols., ed. Awaya Kentarō and Yoshida Yutaka. Tokyo: Nihon tosho sentā, 1993.
Kyokutō kokusai gunji saiban sokkiroku. 10 vols. Yūshōdō, 1968.
The Law of War: A Documentary History. 2 vols., ed. Leon Friedman with a Foreword by Telford Taylor. New York: Random House, 1972.
Materials on the Trial of Former Servicemen of the Japanese Army Charged with Manufacturing and Employing Bacteriological Weapons. Moscow: Foreign Language Publishing House, 1950.
Sensō hanzai saiban kankei hōreishū (Legal Documents on War Crimes Trials). 3 vols., ed. Hōmudaijin kanbō shihō hōsei chōsabu (The Judiciary and Legislation Investigation Division, Secretariat of the Ministry of Justice). Tokyo, 1963–67.
Sensō saiban kiroku kankei shiryō mokuroku (Index to the Sources Related to the Records of War Trials), ed. Hōmudaijin kanbō shihō hōsei chōsabu (The Judiciary and Legislation Investigation Division, Secretariat of the Ministry of Justice). Tokyo, July 1973.
Sensō hanzai saiban gaishiyō (A Concise Historical Survey of War Crimes Trials), ed. Hōmudaijin kanbō shihō hōsei chōsabu (The Judiciary and Legislation

Investigation Division, Secretariat of the Ministry of Justice). Tokyo, July 1973.

Shinbun shiryō ni miru Tōkyō saiban, BC-kyū saiban, 1: *Tōkyō saiban* (The Tokyo Trial and Class BC Trials Seen in Newspaper Sources, Vol. 1: The Tokyo Trial), ed. Nagai Hitoshi and Utsumi Aiko. Tokyo: Gendai shiryō shuppan, 2000.

The Tokyo Judgment: The International Military Tribunal for the Far East (I.M.T.F.E), 29 April 1946–12 November 1948. 2 vols., ed. B. V. A. Röling and C. F. Ruter. Amsterdam: APA-University Press, 1977.

Tōkyō saiban e no michi: kokusai kensatsu kyoku, seisaku kettei kankei bunsho (The Road to the Tokyo Trial: Records Relative to the International Prosecution Section's Policy Making). 5 vols., ed. Awaya Kentarō, Nagai Hitoshi, and Toyoda Masayuki. Tokyo: Gendai shiryō shuppan, 1999.

Tōkyō saiban hanketsu: kyokutō kokusai gunji saibansho hanketsubun (The Judgment of the Tokyo Tribunal: The Judgment of the International Military Tribunal for the Far East). Tokyo: Mainichi shinbunsha, 1949.

Tōkyō saiban shiryō: Kido Kōichi jinmon chōsho (Sources of the Tokyo Trial: The Records of Kido Kōichi's Interrogation), ed. Awaya Kentarō, Adachi Hiroaki, and Kobayashi Motohiro, trans. Okada Nobuhiro. Tokyo: Ōtsuki shoten, 1987.

Tōkyō saiban shiryō: Tanaka Ryūkichi jinmon chōsho (Sources of the Tokyo Trial: The Records of Tanaka Ryūkichi's Interrogation), ed. Awaya Kentarō, Ika Toshiya, Okada Nobuhiro, and Otabe Yūji, trans. Okada Ryōnosuke. Tokyo: Ōtsuki shoten, 1994.

Tōkyō saiban to kokusai kensatsu kyoku: kaitei kara hanketsu made (The Tokyo Trial and the International Prosecution Section: From the Opening of the Court to the Judgment). 5 vols., ed. Awaya Kentarō, Herbert P. Bix, and Toyoda Masayuki. Tokyo: Gendai shiryō shuppan, 2000.

The Trial of German Major War Criminals, by the International Military Tribunal Sitting at Nuremberg, Germany (Commencing 20th November, 1945). Buffalo, NY: William S. Hein & Co. Inc., 2001.

Trials of War Criminals before the Nuernberg Military Tribunals under Control Council Law No. 10. 15 vols. Buffalo, NY: William S. Hein & Co., Inc., 1997.

The Tokyo War Crimes Trial, 22 vols. annot., comp., and ed. R. John Pritchard and Sonia Magbanua Zaide. New York and London: Garland, 1981.

The Tokyo War Crimes Trial: Index and Guide, 5 vols. annot., comp., and ed. R. John Pritchard, Sonia Magbanua Zaide, and Donald Cameron Watt. New York and London: Garland, 1981–87.

304 — Works Cited

Electronic Sources

BBC News, World Edition.
http://news.bbc.co.uk

Center for Research and Documentation on Japan's War Responsibility.
http://space.geocities.jp/japanwarres/center/english/index-english.htm

Digital Museum: The Comfort Women Issue and the Asian Women's Fund.
http://www.awf.or.jp/e4/un-00.html

The Avalon Project at Yale Law School: Documents in Law, History and Diplomacy.
http://www.yale.edu/lawweb/avalon/avalon.htm

Global Policy Forum.
http://www.globalpolicy.org

Nazi War Crimes and Japanese Imperial Government Records Interagency Working Group (IWG), National Archives and Records Administration.
http://www.archives.gov/iwg/japanese-war-crimes

Sierra Leone Live News.
http://www.sierraleonelive.com

The United Nations, International Law.
http://www.un.org/law/

The United Nations, International Criminal Tribunal for the Former Yugoslavia.
http://www.un.org/icty

The United Nations, International Criminal Tribunal for Rwanda.
http://www.un.org/ictr

U.C. Berkeley War Crimes Studies Center.
http://socrates.berkeley.edu/~warcrime

"The World and Japan" Database Project.
http://www.ioc.u-tokyo.ac.jp/~worldjpn/front-ENG.shtml

Secondary Sources

Ara Takashi. "Tōkyō saiban, sensō sekinin ron no genryū: Tōkyō saiban to senryō ka no yoron" (The Origin of the Debate on the Tokyo Trial and Responsibility for War). *Rekishi hyōron* 408 (April 1984): 2–22.

Asahi shinbun hōtei kishadan (Asahi newspaper court reporters), ed. *Tōkyō saiban* (The Tokyo Trial). 3 vols. Tokyo: Tōkyō saiban kankōkai, 1963.

Asahi shinbunsha, ed. *Gendai Nihon Asahi jinbutsu jiten* (Modern Japan: Asahi's Who's Who). Tokyo: Asahi shinbunsha, 1990.

Asahi shinbun shuzaihan (Asahi newspaper reporters), ed. *Sensō to tsuitō: rekishi to mukau* (War and Mourning: Confrontation with the Past). Tokyo: Asahi shinbunsha, 2006.

Ajia ni taisuru Nihon no sensō sekinin o tou minshū hōtei junbikai (Preparatory committee for the establishment of the people's tribunal to clarify Japan's responsibility for waging war against Asia), ed. *Jikō naki sensō sekinin: sabakareru tennō to Nihon (zōhoban)* (Responsibility for War without the Statute of Limitations: The Emperor and Japan on Trial. Expanded edition). Tokyo: Ryokufū shuppan, 1998.

———, ed. *Toinaosu Tōkyō saiban* (Questioning the Tokyo Trial Afresh). Tokyo: Ryokufū shuppan, 1995.

Awaya Kentarō. *Miketsu no sensō sekinin* (Unresolved Responsibilities for War). Tokyo: Kashiwa shobō, 1994.

———. "Senryō, hi-senryō: Tōkyō saiban o jirei ni" (The Occupying and Occupied: Through the Lens of the Tokyo Trial). In *Iwanami kōza Nihon tsūshi: kindai* 4 (Iwanami Lecture Series: Modern Era 4), vol. 19, ed. Asao Naohiro et al. Tokyo: Iwanami shoten, 1995, 171–208.

———. "Sensō hanzai saiban to gendaishi kenkyū" (War Crimes Trials and the Study of Modern History). *Rekishigaku kenkyū*, no. 453 (February, 1978): 17–27.

———. "Tōkyō saiban e no michi" (The Road to the Tokyo Trial). 26 installments. *Asahi Journal*, vol. 26, no. 42–vol. 27, no. 15 (October 1984–April 1985).

———. "Tōkyō saiban no hikoku wa kōshite erabareta" (This Was How the Defendants for the Tokyo Trial Were Selected). *Chūō kōron* (February 1984): 80–96.

———. *Tōkyō saiban ron* (A Treatise on the Tokyo Trial). Tokyo: Ōtsuki shoten, 1989.

———. "Tōkyō saiban: sotsui to menseki" (The Tokyo Trial: Prosecution and Exoneration). In *Jūgonen sensōshi, 4: senryō to kōwa* (The History of the Fifteen-Year War, Vol. 4: Occupation and the Peace Treaty), ed. Fujii Akira and Imai Seiichi. Tokyo: Aoki shoten, 1989, 87–128.

Awaya Kentarō and NHK shuzaihan (NHK reporters). *NHK supesharu: Tōkyō saiban e no michi* (The NHK Special: The Road to the Tokyo Trial). Tokyo: Nippon hōsō shuppankai, 1994.

Awaya Kentarō and Utsumi Aiko. "Tōkyō saiban: Nihon no sensō sekinin" (The Tokyo Trial: Japan's War Responsibility). In *Sengo Nihon no genten 1— Senryōshi no genzai* (The Origin of Postwar Japan, Vol. 1—The Current Studies of the Occupation Era), ed. Takemae Eiji and Sodei Rinzaburō. Tokyo: Yūshisha, 1992, 217–92.

Bass, Gary Jonathan. *Stay the Hand of Vengeance: The Politics of War Crimes Tribunals*. Princeton and Oxford: Princeton University Press, 2000.

Bergerud, Eric. *Touched with Fire: The Land War in the South Pacific*. New York: Penguin Books, 1996.

Bix, Herbert P. *Hirohito and the Making of Modern Japan*. New York: Harper-Collins, 2000.

Bose, Sugata, and Ayesha Jalal. *Modern South Asia: History, Culture, and Political Economy*. New York: Routledge, 2001.

Brackman, Arnold C. *The Other Nuremberg: The Untold Story of the Tokyo War Crimes Trials*. New York: William Morrow and Company, 1987.

Bradsher, Greg. *World War II Japanese Records: History of Their Capture, Exploitation, and Disposition*. Forthcoming.

Bradsher, Greg, et al. *Researching Japanese War Crimes Records: Introductory Essays*. Washington, DC: Nazi War Crimes and Japanese Imperial Government Records Interagency Working Group, National Archives and Records Administration, 2006. Available for download at http://www.archives.gov/iwg/japanese-war-crimes/introductory-essays.pdf.

Brook, Timothy. "The Tokyo Judgment and the Rape of Nanking," *Journal of Asian Studies* 60, no. 3 (August 2001): 673–700.

Broomfield, J. M. *Elite Conflict in a Plural Society: Twentieth-Century Bengal*. Berkeley and Los Angeles: University of California Press, 1968.

Buruma, Ian. *The Wages of Guilt: Memories of War in Germany and Japan*. London: Phoenix, 2002.

Cassese, Antonio, Paola Gaeta, and John R. W. D. Jones, eds. *The Rome Statute of the International Criminal Court: A Commentary*. 2 vols. Oxford and New York: Oxford University Press, 2002.

Chang, Iris. *The Rape of Nanking: The Forgotten Holocaust of World War II*. New York: Basic Books, 1997.

Chatterji, Joya. *Bengal Divided: Hindu Communalism and Partition, 1932–1947*. Cambridge, UK: Cambridge University Press, 1994.

Chūgoku kikansha renrakukai (Association of the expatriated soldiers from China), ed. *Sankō: yaki tsukushi, koroshi tsukushi, ubai tsukusu* (Three-All Policy: Burn All, Kill All, and Loot All). Tokyo: Kappa bukkusu, 1957.

———, ed. *Shinryaku: Chūgoku ni okeru Nihon senpan no kokuhaku* (Aggression: Confessions by the Japanese War Criminals in China). Tokyo: Shin doku-shosha, 2002.

Chūgokujin sensō higai baishō seikyū jiken bengodan (Lawyer's association for reparation lawsuits by Chinese victims of war), ed. *Sajō no shōheki: Chūgokujin sengo hoshō saiban 10-nen no kiseki* (Barrier in the Sand: The Ten-Year Trajectory of Postwar Chinese Reparation Trials). Tokyo: Nihon hyōronsha, 2005.

Cohen, David. "Beyond Nuremberg: Individual Responsibility for War Crimes." In *Human Rights in Political Transitions: Gettysburg to Bosnia*, ed. Carla Hesse and Robert Post. New York: Zone Books, 1999, 53–92.

———. "Bureaucracy, Justice, and Collective Responsibility in the World War II War Crimes Trials," *Rechtshistorisches Journal* 18. Frankfurt am Main: Löwenklau Gesellschaft e.V., 1999: 313–42.

Cook, Haruko Taya, and Theodore F. Cook. *Japan at War: An Oral History.* New York: The New Press, 1992.

Dallaire, Roméo. *Shake Hands with the Devil: The Failure of Humanity in Rwanda.* Toronto: Random House Canada, 2003.

Dandō Shigemitsu. "Sensō hanzai no rironteki kaibō" (The Theoretical Anatomy of War Crimes). In *Keihō no kindaiteki tenkai*, by Dandō Shigemitsu. Tokyo: Kōbundō, 1948, 159–84.

Daws, Gavan. *Prisoners of the Japanese: POWs of World War II in the Pacific.* New York: W. Morrow, 1994.

Des Forges, Alison. *Leave None to Tell the Story: Genocide in Rwanda.* 2nd edition. New York, Washington, London, Brussels: Human Rights Watch, 1999.

Douglas, Lawrence. *The Memory of Judgment: Making Law and History in the Trials of the Holocaust.* New Haven, CT and London: Yale University Press, 2000.

Dower, John W. *Embracing Defeat: Japan in the Wake of World War II.* New York: W. W. Norton, 1999.

Duus, Peter. "Remembering the Empire: Postwar interpretations of the Greater East Asia Coprosperity Sphere." *The Woodrow Wilson Center, Asian Program, Occasional Paper*, no. 54 (March 1993).

Eguchi Keiichi. *Jūgonen sensō shōshi* (A Concise History of the Fifteen-Year War). Tokyo: Aoki shoten, 1986.

Fuji Nobuo. *Watakushi no mita Tōkyō saiban* (The Tokyo Trial I Witnessed). 2 vols. Tokyo: Kōdansha, 1988.

Fujita Hisakazu. *Sensō hanzai to wa nanika* (What Is a War Crime). Tokyo: Iwanami shoten, 1995.

———. "Tōkyō saiban no konnichiteki imi" (The Relevance of the Tokyo Trial Today), *Hōritsu jihō* 61, no. 9 (1989): 24–30.

Fujiwara Akira. "'Sankō sakusen' to Kitashina hōmen gun" ("Three-All Policy" and the North China Area Army), 2 installments. *Sensō sekinin kenkyū*, nos. 20 and 21 (Summer and Fall 1998): 21–29 (no. 20), 68–75 (no. 21).

———. "Kainantō ni okeru Nihon kaigun no 'sankō sakusen'" (The Japanese Navy's "Three-All Policy" on Hainan Island). *Sensō sekinin kenkyū*, no. 24 (Summer 1999): 46–54.

Furness, George A. "Tōkyō saiban no butaiura: hiroku" (The Backstage of the Tokyo Trial: A Secret Record). A conversation hosted by Kiyose Ichirō and Yanai Tsuneo. *Bungei shunjū* (May 1952): 50–59.

Gordon, Leonard A. *Bengal: The Nationalist Movement 1876–1940.* New York and London: Columbia University Press, 1974.

Gourevitch, Philip. *We Wish to Inform You That Tomorrow We Will Be Killed with Our Families: Stories from Rwanda.* New York: Picador USA, 1998.

Gushima Kanesaburō. "Tōkyō saiban no rekishiteki igi" (The Historical Significance of the Tokyo Trial). *Rekishi hyōron* 3, no. 6 (1948): 25–32.

———. *Honryū: watashi no aruita michi* (Torrent: The Path I Have Trod). Fuku-oka: Kyūshū daigaku shuppankai, 1981.

Gutman, Roy, and David Rieff, eds. *Crimes of War: What the Public Should Know.* New York and London: W. W. Norton, 1999.

Hankey, Maurice Pascal Alers, Baron, *Politics, Trials and Errors.* Chicago, IL: Henry Regnery Company, 1950.

Harries, Meirion, and Susie Harries. *Sheathing the Sword: The Demilitarization of Postwar Japan.* New York: Macmillan, 1987.

Harris, Sheldon H. *Factories of Death: Japanese Biological Warfare 1932–45 and the American Cover-up.* London and New York: Routledge, 1994.

Hayashi Fusao. *Daitōa sensō kōteiron* (The Affirmation-of-the-Greater-East-Asia-War View). Tokyo: Banchō shobō, 1964.

Hayashi Hirofumi. *BC-kyū senpan saiban* (Class BC War Crimes Trials). Tokyo: Iwanami shoten, 2005.

———. "BC-kyū saiban: Igirisu wa nani o sabaitaka" (Class BC trials: What Britain Prosecuted). In *Nihongun seidoreisei o sabaku 2000-nen josei kokusai senpan hōtei no kiroku* (The Records of the Women's International War Crimes Tribunal to Prosecute Japanese Military's Sexual Slavery, Year 2000), ed. VAWW-NET Japan. Vol. 1. Tokyo: Ryokufū shuppan, 2002, 104–22.

———. *Sabakareta sensō hanzai: Igirisu no tainichi senpan saiban* (The War Crimes Tried: British War Crimes Trials against the Japanese). Tokyo: Iwanami shoten, 1998.

———. *Shingapōru kakyō shukusei* (Liquidation of Ethnic Chinese in Singapore). Tokyo: Kōbunken, 2007.

Higashino Makoto, ed. *Shōwa tennō futatsu no "dokuhaku"* (Emperor Shōwa's Two "Monologues"), annot. Awaya Kentarō and Yoshida Yutaka. Tokyo: Nippon hōsō shuppan kyōkai, 1998.

Higurashi Yoshinobu. "Kyokutō kokusai gunji saibansho kōseikoku no jōken: Indo saibankan ninmei mondai o megutte" (The Conditions for Becoming a Member of the International Military Tribunal for the Far East: Concerning the Appointment of the Indian Judge). *Kokusai seiji*, no. 95 (October 1990): 151–66.

————. "Paru hanketsu saikō: Tōkyō saiban ni okeru bekko iken no kokusai kankyō" (Rethinking Pal's Judgment: The International Environment Surrounding the Separate Opinion at the Tokyo Trial). In *Nihon kindaishi no saikōchiku* (Reconstruction of Modern Japanese History), ed. Itō Takashi. Tokyo: Yamakawa shuppansha, 1993, 384–411.

————. *Tōkyō saiban no kokusai kankei: kokusai seiji ni okeru kenryoku to kihan* (International Relations of the Tokyo Trial: Power and Norms in International Politics). Tokyo: Bokutakusha, 2002.

Honda Katsuichi. *The Nanjing Massacre: A Japanese Journalist Confronts Japan's National Shame*, ed. Frank Gibney, trans. Karen Sandness. Armonk, NY and London, England: M.E. Sharpe. 1999.

Hora Tomio, ed. *Nicchū sensō Nankin daizangyaku jiken shiryōshū* (The China-Japan War: Sources of the Great Nanking Atrocity). 2 vols. Tokyo: Aoki shoten, 1985.

Horwitz, Solis. "The Tokyo Trial." *International Conciliation*, no. 465 (November 1950): 473–584.

Hosoya Chihiro, Andō Nisuke, Ōnuma Yasuaki, and Richard Minear, eds. *The Tokyo War Crimes Trial: An International Symposium*. Tokyo: Kōdansha, 1986.

Ienaga Saburō. "Futatabi Pāru hanketsu ni tsuite: Mainia kyōju ni kotaeru" (On Pal's Judgment for the Second Time: My Response to Professor Minear). In *Rekishi to sekinin*, by Ienaga Saburō. Tokyo: Chūō daigaku shuppanbu, 1979, 114–26.

————. "Bias in the Guise of Objectivity." *Japan Interpreter* 11 (Winter 1977): 271–78.

————. *Ichi rekishi gakusha no ayumi: kyōkasho saiban ni itaru made* (The Path of a Historian: Leading up to the Textbook Trial). Tokyo: Sanseidō, 1967.

————. *Japan's Past, Japan's Future: One Historian's Odyssey*, annot. and trans. Richard H. Minear. Lanham, MD: Rowman & Littlefield Publishers, 2001.

————. "Jūgonen sensō to Pāru hanketsusho" (The Fifteen-Year War and Pal's Judgment). In *Sensō to kyōiku o megutte* (On War and Education), by Ienaga Saburō. Tokyo: Hōsei daigaku shuppankyoku, 1973, 23–43.

————. "Kyokutō saiban ni tsuite no shiron" (A Tentative Essay on the Tokyo trial). In *Sensō to kyōiku o megutte* (On War and Education), by Ienaga Saburō. Tokyo: Hōsei daigaku shuppankyoku, 1973, 3–22.

————. "Kyokutō saiban o dō kangaeru bekika" (How to Think about the Far Eastern Trial). In *Rekishi to sekinin* (History and Responsibility), by Ienaga Saburō. Tokyo: Chūō daigaku shuppanbu, 1979, 101–13.

———. *Sensō sekinin* (Responsibility for War). Tokyo: Iwanami shoten, 1985.

———. *Taiheiyō sensō* (The Pacific War). Tokyo: Iwanami shoten, 2002.

———. *The Pacific War: World War II and the Japanese, 1931–1945.* New York: Pantheon Books, 1978.

Ienaga Saburō and Takashima Nobuyoshi. *Kyōkasho saiban wa tsuzuku* (The Textbook Trials Continue). Booklet. Tokyo: Iwanami shoten, 1998.

Ienaga kyōkasho soshō bengodan (Lawyers' association for the Ienaga textbook lawsuits), ed. *Ienaga kyōkasho saiban: 32-nen ni wataru bengodan katsudō no sōkatsu* (Ienaga Textbook Trials: The Summation of the Thirty-Two-Year Activities of the Lawyers' Association). Tokyo: Nihon hyōronsha, 1998.

Ikeda Tasuku, ed. *Hiroku: Daitōa senshi, 6: Genbaku kokunai Tōkyō saiban hen* (Secret Records of the History of Greater East Asia War, Vol. 6: Atomic Bombs, Home Front, and the Tokyo Trial). Tokyo: Fuji shoen, 1954.

Ikō Toshiya. "Chūgoku kokumin seifu no Nihon senpan shobatsu hōshin no tenkai" (The Trajectory of the Chinese Nationalist Government's Policy for the Punishment of Japanese War Criminals). In *Gendai rekishigaku to Nankin jiken* (Historical Studies Today and the Nanking Incident), ed. Yoshida Yutaka and Kasahara Tokushi. Tokyo: Kashiwa shobō, 2006, 94–124.

Inoue Kiyoshi. "Hō no ronri to rekishi no ronri" (Logic of Law and Logic of History), *Rekishi hyōron* 3, no. 6 (1948): 1–13.

———. *Shōwa tennō no sensō sekinin* (Emperor Shōwa's Responsibility for War). Tokyo: Akashi shoten, 1989.

———. *Tennō no sensō sekinin* (The Emperor's Responsibility for War). Tokyo: Gendai hyōronsha, 1975.

Irie Keishirō. "Tōkyō hanketsu no yōryō to sono shōkai" (A Summary and Explanation of the Tokyo Judgment). *Hōritsu jihō* 21, no. 2 (1949): 29–45, 12.

Ishida Yūji et al., eds. *Chūgoku Kahokushō ni okeru sankō sakusen: gyakusatsu no mura, Hokutan mura* (Three-All Policy in Hopeh Province: Massacre in Beituan Village). Tokyo: Ōtsuki shoten, 2003.

Ishida Yūji and Kasahara Tokushi, eds. *Shiryō: Doitsu gaikōkan no mita Nankin jiken* (Sources: The Nanking Incident as Witnessed by German Diplomats). Tokyo: Ōtsuki shoten, 2001.

Jōhō Yoshio. *Tōkyō saiban to Tōjō Hideki* (The Tokyo Trial and Tōjō Hideki). Tokyo: Fuyō shobō, 1983.

Jones, Dorothy V. *Toward a Just World: The Critical Years in the Search for International Justice.* Chicago and London: University of Chicago Press, 2002.

Kainō Michitaka. "Hōtei gijutsu" (Court Techniques). In *Kainō Michitaka chosakushū 3: saiban* (Kainō Michitaka's Writings, Vol. 3: Trials), ed. and annot. Shiomi Toshitaka. Tokyo: Nihon hyōronsha, 1977, 3–116.

———. "Kyokutō saiban" (The Far Eastern Trial). In *Nihon shihonshugi kōza 1* (Lectures on Japanese Capitalism, Vol. 1) by Kainō Michitaka. Tokyo: Iwanami shoten, 1953, 385–96.

———. "Kyokutō saiban: sono go" (The Far Eastern Trial: Afterwards). In *Kainō Michitaka chosakushū 3: saiban* (Kainō Michitaka's Writings, Vol. 3: Trials), ed. and annot. Shiomi Toshitaka. Tokyo: Nihon hyōronsha, 1977, 275–84.

———. "Sensō saiban no hōritsu riron" (Legal Theory of a War Trial). *Rekishi hyōron* 3, no. 6 (1948): 13–24.

Kainō Michitaka, Maruyama Masao, Takano Yūichi, Tsuji Kiyoaki, and Ukai Nobushige. "Zadankai: Tōkyō saiban no jijitsu to hōri" (Discussion: Facts and Legal Doctrines at the Tokyo Trial). *Hōritsu jihō* 21, no. 2 (1949): 12–28.

Kajii Sumihiro. "Tōkyō saiban ni okeru 'BC-kyū hanzai' tsuikyū" (The Charge of "Class BC Crimes" at the Tokyo Trial). *Ritsumeikan hōgakugakusei ronshū (bessatsu)*, no. 42 (1996): 492–531.

Kasahara Tokushi. "Chūgoku sensen ni okeru Nihongun no seihanzai: Kahoku-shō, Sanseishō no jirei" (Japanese Military Sexual Crimes in the Chinese Theater: Cases of Hopeh and Shansi Provinces). *Sensō sekinin kenkyū* (Report on Japan's War Responsibility) 13 (Fall 1996): 2–11.

———. *Nanking jiken* (The Nanking Incident). Tokyo: Iwanami shoten, 1997.

———. *Nankin jiken to sankō sakusen: mirai ni ikasu sensō no kioku* (The Nanking Incident and Three-All Policy: War Memory for the Future). Tokyo: Ōtsuki shoten, 1999.

———. "Nihongun no zangyaku kōi to seihanzai: Sanseishō Yuiken no jirei" (Japanese Atrocities and Sexual Crimes: The Case of Yuishen, Shansi Province). *Sensō sekinin kenkyū* (Report on Japan's War Responsibility) 17 (Fall 1997): 38–50.

Kido Kōichi. *Kido Kōichi nikki* (The Diary of Kido Kōichi). 2 vols. Tokyo: Tōkyō daigaku shuppankai, 1966.

Kikuchi Kenji. *Nihon o suibō e michibiku "Tōkyō saiban shikan"* (The "Tokyo Trial View of History" That Leads to the Downfall of Japan). Tokyo: Zenbōsha, 1991.

Kiyose Ichirō. *Hiroku: Tōkyō saiban* (A Secret Record of the Tokyo Trial). Tokyo: Yomiuri shinbunsha, 1966.

Kojima Noboru. *Tōkyō saiban* (The Tokyo Trial). 2 vols. Tokyo: Chūō kōronsha, 1982.

Kopelman, Elizabeth. "Ideology and International Law: The Dissent of the Indian Justice at the Tokyo War Crimes Trial." *New York University Journal of International Law and Politics* 28, no. 2 (1991): 373–494.

Kyōkasho kentei soshō o shien suru zenkoku renrakukai (National Support Network for the Textbook Censorship Lawsuits), ed. *Ienaga kyōkasho saiban no subete: 32-nen no undō to korekara* (A Comprehensive Account of Ienaga Textbook Trials: Thirty-Two-Year Activism and Its Future Direction). Tokyo: Minshūsha, 1998.

Lael, Richard L. *The Yamashita Precedent: War Crimes and Command Responsibility.* Wilmington, DE: Scholarly Resources Inc., 1982.

Lee, Roy S., ed. *The International Criminal Court: The Making of the Rome Statute. Issues, Negotiations, Results.* The Hague, London, and Boston: Kluwer Law International, 1999.

MacArthur, Douglas. *Reminiscences.* New York: McGraw Hill, 1964.

Maga, Tim. *Judgment at Tokyo: The Japanese War Crimes Trials.* Lexington, KY: University Press of Kentucky, 2001.

Maruyama Masao. *Gendai seiji no shisō to kōdō* (Thought and Behavior in Modern Japanese Politics). Tokyo: Miraisha, 1964.

————. *Thought and Behaviour in Modern Japanese Politics.* ed. Ivan Morris. London, New York: Oxford University Press, 1963.

Minear, Richard H. "In Defense of Radha Binod Pal." *Japan Interpreter* 11 (Winter 1977): 263–71.

————. *Victors' Justice: The Tokyo War Crimes Trial.* Princeton, NJ: Princeton University Press, 2001.

————. *Tōkyō saiban: shōsha no sabaki* (The Tokyo Trial: Victors' Justice). trans. Andō Nisuke. Tokyo: Fukumura shuppan, 1986.

Morimura Seiichi. *Akuma no hōshoku: "Kantōgun saikinsen butai"* (Devil's Insatiability: The "Bacteriological Unit of the Kwantung Army"). Tokyo: Kōbunsha, 1981.

Mizushima Asaho. *Mirai sōzō to shite no "sengo hoshō": "kako no seisan" o koete* ("Postwar Reparation" for the Making of the Future: Beyond the "Settlement of the Past"). Tokyo: Gendai jinbunsha, 2003.

Naitō Masao. "M. K. Gāndī to Nihonjin: Nicchū sensō o megutte" (M. K. Gandhi, the Japanese People, and the Sino-Japanese War). In *Ajia Afurika gengo bunka kenkyū*, no. 63 (2002): 125–74.

Nagai Hitoshi. "Firipin to Tōkyō saiban: daihyō kenji no kensatsu katsudō o chūshin to shite" (The Philippines and the Tokyo Trial: Centering on the Prosecutorial Activities of the Philippine Prosecutor). *Shien* 57, no. 2 (March 1997): 43–67.

Nakajima Takeshi. *Nakamuraya no Bōsu: Indo dokuritsu undō to kindai Nihon no Ajiashugi* (Bose of the Nakamuraya: The Indian Independence Movement and Asianism in Modern Japan). Tokyo: Hakusuisha, 2005.

———. *Pāru hanji: Tōkyō saiban hihan to zettai heiwashugi* (Justice Pal: Criticism of the Tokyo Trial and Absolute Pacifism). Tokyo: Hakusuisha, 2007.

Nakamura Masanori. *Sengoshi to shōchō tennō* (Postwar History and the Symbol-Emperor System). Tokyo: Iwanami shoten, 1992.

———. *The Japanese Monarchy: Ambassador Joseph Grew and the Making of the "Symbol Emperor System," 1931–1991*, trans. Herbert P. Bix, Jonathan Baker-Bates, and Derek Bowen. Armonk, NY and London, England: M.E. Sharpe, 1992.

Nakane Shintarō. *Kike! Nihon muzai no sakebi: sengo 50-nen ketsugi to hikoku, Murayama Tomiichi* (Listen to the Cry of Japan-Is-Not-Guilty!: Murayama Tomiichi, the Accused, and the Fifty-Year Resolution). Tokyo: Nihon shuppan hōsō kikaku, 1995.

Nandy, Ashis. "The Other Within: The Strange Case of Radhabinod Pal's Judgment on Culpability." *New Literary History: A Journal of Theory and Interpretation* 23, no. 1 (Winter 1992): 45–67.

Nankin jiken chōsa kenkyūkai (Research group on the investigation of the Nanking Incident), ed. *Nankin jiken shiryōshū* (Sources on the Nanking Incident). 2 vols. Tokyo: Aoki shoten, 1992.

Neier, Aryeh. *War Crimes: Brutality, Genocide, Terror, and the Struggle for Justice.* New York: Random House, 1998.

Neuffer, Elizabeth. *The Key to My Neighbor's House: Seeking Justice in Bosnia and Rwanda.* New York: Picador USA, 2001.

Nihon no sensō shiryō sentā kenkyū jimukyoku (Office of the Center for Research and Documentation on Japan's War), ed. "Tōkyō saiban de sabakareta Nihongun 'ianfu' seido" (The Japanese Military "Comfort Women" System Tried at the Tokyo Trial). *Sensō sekinin kenkyū* 56 (Summer 2007): 11–17.

Nozoe Kenji. *Hanaoka jiken to Chūgokujin: daitaichō Ken Tsen no hōki* (The Hanaoka Incident and the Chinese: The Uprising of the Battalion Leader Ken Tsen). Tokyo: San'ichi shobō, 1997.

———. *Hanaoka jiken no hitotachi: Chūgokujin kyōsei renkō no kiroku* (The People Involved in the Hanaoka Incident: A Record of Chinese Forced Deportation). Tokyo: Hyōronsha, 1975.

———. *Kiki aruki Hanaoka jiken* (Inquiring into the Hanaoka Incident). Akita: Mumyōsha shuppan, 1983.

Okabe Makio. *Jūgonen sensōshi ron: gen'in to kekka to sekinin to* (The Fifteen-Year War: The Cause, the Outcome, and Responsibility). Tokyo: Aoki shoten, 1999.

Okuhara Toshio. "Tōkyō saiban ni okeru kyōdō bōgi riron" (The Theory of Conspiracy at the Tokyo Trial). 3 installments. *Kokushikan daigaku seikei ronsō,* no. 5 (September 1966), 155–92; no. 7 (January 1968), 387–413; and no. 12 (June 1970), 181–204.

———. "Shōkai: *Victors' Justice—The Tokyo War Crimes Trial*" (Review: *Victors' Justice—The Tokyo War Crimes Trial*). *Kokushikan daigaku seikei ronsō*, no. 18 (June 1973): 349–63.

Onodera Toshitaka. "Sensō sekinin to sengo hoshō: Yoriyoi mirai o kizukiageru tame ni" (Responsibility for War and Postwar Reparation: To Build a Better Future). *Hō to minshushugi* 284 (December 2003): 3–7.

Ōnuma Yasuaki. *Sensō sekinin josetsu: "heiwa ni taisuru tsumi" no keisei katei ni okeru ideorogī to kōsokusei* (The Introduction to War Responsibility: Ideology and Restrictiveness in the Formulation of "Crimes against Peace"). Tokyo: Tōkyō daigaku shuppankai, 1975.

———. *Tōkyō saiban kara sengo sekinin no shisō e: zōhoban* (From the Tokyo Trial to the Concept of Postwar Responsibility, Expanded Edition). Tokyo: Tōshindō, 1987.

———. "Tōkyō saiban, sensō sekinin, sengo sekinin" (The Tokyo Trial, War Responsibility, Postwar Responsibility). *Shisō*, no. 719 (May 1984): 70–100.

Ōnuma Yasuaki, Hosaka Masayasu, Utsumi Aiko, and Yoshida Yutaka. "Renzoku tōron—sengo sekinin, 1: Tōkyō saiban to sensō sekinin" (Serialized Debates—Responsibility for War, No. 1: The Tokyo Trial and the Responsibility for War). *Sekai*, no. 709 (January 2003): 277–91.

Oppenheim, L. *International Law: A Treatise.* Vol. II: *Disputes, War and Neutrality.* 7th edition, ed. Hersh Lauterpacht. London and New York: Longmans, Green and Co., 1952.

Pal, Radhabinod. "Ajia minzokushugi no shisōteki kiso: hōkai suru sekai bunmei no saiken no tameni" (The Conceptual Foundation of Asianism: For the Reconstruction of the Collapsing World Civilization). *Kaizō* (March 1953): 94–103.

———. *Crimes in International Relations.* Calcutta: University of Calcutta, 1955.

———. *Heiwa no sengen* (The Declaration of Peace), ed. Tanaka Masaaki. Tokyo: Tōzai bunmeisha, 1953.

———. *The Hindu Philosophy of Law.* Calcutta, n.d.

———. *The History of Hindu Law in the Vedic Age and the Post-Vedic Times Down to the Institutes of Manu.* Calcutta, 1959.

———. *In Defense of Japan's Case.* 2 vols., ed. Nakamura Akira. Tokyo: Kenkyusha, 1976.

———. "Paru hanji ooi ni kataru!" (Justice Pal Freely Talks!). A conversation hosted by Shimonaka Yasaburō and Kagawa Toyohiko. *Bungei shunjū* (December 1952): 100–108.

————. *Zen'yaku, Nihon muzairon: kyokutō kokusai gunji saiban Indo daihyō hanji R. Pāru jutsu* (The Complete Translation: The Japan-Is-Not-Guilty View: Written by Justice R. Pal, the Indian Member of the International Military Tribunal for the Far East). Tokyo: Nihon shobō, 1952.

Pāru-Shimonaka kinenkan kensetsu iinkai (Committee for the establishment of the Pal-Shimonaka Memorial), ed. "Pal-Shimonaka Memorial Hall" (The Pal-Shimonaka Memorial Hall). Pamphlet. Tokyo: Heibonsha, 1975.

Piccigallo, Philip R. *The Japanese on Trial: Allied War Crimes Operations in the East, 1945–1951.* Austin and London: University of Texas Press, 1979.

Powell, John. "A Hidden Chapter in History." *Bulletin of the Atomic Scientists* 37, no. 8 (October 1981): 44–53.

————. "Japan's Germ Warfare: The U.S. Cover-Up of a War Crime." *Bulletin of Concerned Asian Scholars* 12, no. 4 (October–December 1980): 2–17.

Rabe, John H. D. *Nankin no shinjitsu: The Diary of John Rabe* (The Truth about Nanking: The Diary of John Rabe), trans. Hirano Kyoko. Tokyo: Kōdansha, 1997.

Pritchard, R. John. "An Overview of the Historical Importance of the Tokyo War Trial." *Nissan Occasional Paper Series*, no. 5 (1987): 1–51.

Reel, A. Frank. *The Case of General Yamashita.* Chicago, IL: University of Chicago Press, 1949.

Robertson, Geoffrey. *Crimes against Humanity: The Struggle for Global Justice.* New York: The New Press, 1999.

Röling, B. V. A. "Tōkyō saiban no gendaishiteki igi" (The Relevance of the Tokyo Trial to Modern History). *Chūō kōron* (August 1983): 190–93.

Röling, B. V. A., and Antonio Cassese. *The Tokyo Trial and Beyond: Reflections of a Peacemonger.* Cambridge, UK: Polity Press, 1993.

Sawanobori Yoshito, Sawanobori Toshio, and Niwayama Hideo. *Keiji soshō hō shi* (The History of Criminal Law). Tokyo: Fūbaisha, 1968.

Schabas, William A. *An Introduction to the International Criminal Court.* Second edition, Cambridge, UK: Cambridge University Press, 2004.

————. *The UN International Criminal Tribunals: The Former Yugoslavia, Rwanda, and Sierra Leone.* Cambridge, UK: Cambridge University Press, 2006.

Shigemitsu Mamoru. "Hikokuseki no kaisō: Kīnan no inshō" (Recollections from the Defendants' Dock: The Impression of Keenan). *Bungei shunjū* (May 1952): 60–61.

Shimanouchi Tatsuoki. *Tōkyō saiban* (The Tokyo Trial). Tokyo: Nihon hyōronsha, 1984.

————. *Tōkyō saiban bengo zatsuroku* (Miscellanies of the Defense at the Tokyo Trial). Tokyo: Tōyō shuppan, 1973.

Sissons, D. C. "Ōsutoraria ni yoru sensō hanzai chōsa to saiban: tennō menseki ni itaru katei" (The Australian War Crimes Trials and Investigations: Leading up to the Exemption of the Emperor from Prosecution). In *Iwanami kōza kindai Nihon to shokuminchi 8: Ajia no reisen to datsu shokuminchika* (Iwanami Lecture Series on Modern Japan and Colonialism, Vol. 8: The Cold War in Asia and Post-Colonialism), ed. Asada Kyōji et al. Tokyo: Iwanami shoten, 1993, 291–314.

Song Zhi-yong. "Shūsen zengo ni okeru Chūgoku no tainichi seisaku" (Chinese Policies toward Japan around the End of World War II: Centering on War Crimes Trials). *Shien* 54, no. 1 (December 1993): 63–80.

Stanton, John. "Canada and War Crimes: Judgment at Tokyo." *International Journal* 55, no. 3 (Summer 2000): 376–400.

Sugawara Yutaka. *Tōkyō saiban no shōtai* (The True Character of the Tokyo Trial). Tokyo: Kokusho kankōkai, 2002.

Sugihara Tōru. *Chūgokujin kyōsei renkō* (The Forced Deportation of the Chinese People). Tokyo: Iwanami shoten, 2002.

Sumitani Takeshi. "Sensō hanzai saiban ron, sensō sekinin ron no dōkō: bunken shōkai o chūshin ni" (The Trends in the Debates on War Crimes Trials and War Responsibility: Centering on the Introduction of Historical Literature). *Shisō*, no. 719 (May 1984): 123–31.

Suzuki Chieko. "Nankin daigyakusatsu o meguru dōkō to kadai" (Trends and Tasks Related to the Nanking Atrocity). *Sensō sekinin kenkyū* (Report on Japan's War Responsibility), no. 46 (Winter 2004): 30–37.

Tabata Shigejirō. "Tōkyō saiban no hōri" (Legal Theory of the Tokyo Trial). *Sekai*, no. 42 (June 1949): 12–20.

Takaki, Ronald. *Strangers from a Different Shore: A History of Asian Americans.* Boston, MA: Little, Brown, 1989.

Takayanagi Kenzō. *The Tokio Trials and International Law: Answer to the Prosecution's Arguments on International Law Delivered at the International Military Tribunal for the Far East on 3 & 4 March 1948.* Tokyo: Yūhikaku, 1948.

———. "Kyokutō hanketsu no hōritsuron" (Legal Theory in the Far Eastern Judgment). *Hōritsu taimuzu* 3, nos. 2 and 3 (1949): 1–11.

———. "Tōkyō hanketsu no hamon" (Repercussions of the Tokyo Judgment). *Hōritsu taimuzu* 3, no. 5 (1949): 44–51.

Takeda Kiyoko. *Tennō kan no sōkoku: 1945-nen zengo* (The Competing Views of the Emperor: Around Year 1945). Tokyo: Iwanami shoten, 1978.

———. *The Dual-Image of the Japanese Emperor.* New York: New York University Press, 1988.

Takemae Eiji. "Shōchō tennōsei e no kiseki" (The Trajectory toward the Symbol-Emperor System). *Chūō kōron* (March 1975): 195–214.

Takemoto Tadao and Ohara Yasuo. *The Alleged "Nanking Massacre": Japan's Rebuttal to China's Forged Claims.* Tokyo: Meiseisha, 2000.

Takigawa Masajirō. *Tōkyō saiban o sabaku* (Judging the Tokyo Trial). 2 vols. Tokyo: Tōwasha, 1953.

Tanaka Masaaki, ed. *Pāru hakase jutsu, shinri no sabaki, Nihon muzai ron* (Truthful Judgment as Told by Dr. Pal: The Japan-Is-Not-Guilty View). Tokyo: Taiheiyō shuppansha, 1952.

———. *Pāru hakase no kotoba: Tōkyō saiban go, rainichi sareta toki no episōdo* (Words of Dr. Pal: Episodes from His Post-Tokyo Trial Visits to Japan). Booklet. Tokyo: Shimonaka kinen zaidan, 1995.

———. *Pāru hakase no Nihon muzai ron* (Japan Is Not Guilty: The View Propounded by Dr. Pal). Kanagawa: Keibunsha, 1963.

Tanaka, Yuki. *Hidden Horrors: Japanese War Crimes in World War II.* Boulder, CO and Oxford: Westview Press, 1996.

———. *Japan's Comfort Women: Sexual Slavery and Prostitution during World War II and the U.S. Occupation.* London and New York: Routledge, 2002.

Taylor, Telford. *The Anatomy of the Nuremberg Trials: A Personal Memoir.* New York: Alfred A. Knopf, 1992.

———. *Final Report to the Secretary of the Army on the Nuremberg War Crimes Trials under Control Council Law No. 10.* Buffalo, NY: William S. Hein & Co., Inc. 1997.

Tōkyō saiban handobukku henshū iinkai (Tokyo trial handbook compilation committee), ed. *Tōkyō saiban handobukku* (The Tokyo Trial Handbook). Tokyo: Aoki shoten, 1989.

Tōkyō saiban kenkyūkai (Tokyo trial research group), ed. *Kyōdō kenkyū: Paru hanketsusho* (Collaborative Research on Pal's Judgment). 2 vols. Tokyo: Tōkyō saiban kankōkai, 1966.

———, ed. *Tōjō Hideki sensei kyōjutsusho* (Tōjō Hideki's Affidavit). Tokyo: Yōyōsha, 1948.

Totani Yuma. "Tōkyō saiban ni okeru sensō hanzai sotsui to hanketsu: Nankin jiken to seidoreisei ni taisuru kokka shidōsha sekinin o chūshin ni" (The Prosecution of War Crimes and the Judgment of the Tokyo Tribunal: Focusing on the Responsibility of State Leaders for the Nanking Incident and Sexual Slavery). In *Gendai rekishigaku to Nankin jiken* (Historical Studies Today and the Nanking Incident), ed. Kasahara Tokushi and Yoshida Yutaka. Tokyo: Kashiwa shobō, 2006, 125–63.

Totsuka Etsurō. *Nihon ga shiranai sensō sekinin: kokuren no jinken katsudō to Nihongun "ianfu" mondai* (The War Crimes Responsibility That Japan Does Not Know: Human Rights Activism at the United Nations and the Japanese Military "Comfort Women" Issue). Tokyo: Gendai jinbunsha, 1999.

Trotter, Ann. "New Zealanders and the International Military Tribunal for the Far East." *New Zealand Journal of History* 23, no. 2 (October 1989): 142–56.

Truman, Harry S. *Memoirs by Harry S. Truman,* Vol. 1: *Year of Decisions.* New York: Doubleday & Company, Inc., 1955.

Tsuneishi Keiichi, trans. and ed. *Hyōteki Ishii: 731-butai to Beigun chōhō katsudō* (Targeting Ishii: Unit 731 and U.S. Military Intelligence Activities). Tokyo: Ōtsuki shoten, 1984.

Ubukata Naokichi. "Tōkyō saiban o meguru shoronten: 'jindō ni taisuru tsumi' to jikō" (Points of Discussion Concerning the Tokyo Trial: "Crimes against Humanity" and the Statute of Limitations). *Shisō,* no. 719 (May 1984): 101–12.

Uchida Rikizō. "Kyokutō saiban no hōrironteki igi: shu to shite Eibei hōgaku no tachiba kara" (Significance of the Far Eastern Trial to Legal Theory: Primarily from the Viewpoint of the Field of Anglo-American Law). *Chōryū* (September 1948): 22–30.

Ushimura Kei. *Beyond the "Judgment of Civilization": The Intellectual Legacy of the Japanese War Crimes Trials, 1946–1949,* Trans. Steven J. Ericson. Tokyo: International House of Japan, 2003.

———. *"Bunmei no sabaki" o koete: tainichi senpan saiban dokkai no kokoromi* (Beyond the "Judgment of Civilization": An Interpretation of War Crimes Trials against the Japanese). Tokyo: Chūō kōronsha, 2000.

———. *"Sensō sekinin" ron no shinjitsu: sengo Nihon no chiteki taiman o danzu* (The Truth about the War Responsibility Debate: The Judgment on Intellectual Laziness in Postwar Japan). Tokyo: PHP kenkyūjo, 2006.

United Nations War Crimes Commission, ed. *History of the United Nations War Crimes Commission and the Development of the Laws of War.* London: His Majesty's Stationery Office, 1948.

———, ed. *Law Reports of Trials of War Criminals.* 15 vols. Selected and prepared by the United Nations War Crimes Commission. Buffalo, NY: William S. Hein & Co., Inc. 1997.

Utsumi Aiko. *Chōsenjin BC-kyū senpan no kiroku* (The Records of the Korean Class BC War Criminals). Tokyo: Keisō shobō, 1982.

———. "Senji seibōryoku to Tōkyō saiban" (Wartime Sexual Violence and the Tokyo Trial). In *Nihongun seidoreisei o sabaku 2000-nen josei kokusai senpan hōtei no kiroku* (The Records of the Women's International War Crimes Tribunal to Prosecute Japanese Military's Sexual Slavery, Year 2000), ed. VAWW-NET Japan. Vol. 1. Tokyo: Ryokufū shuppan, 2002, 58–102.

Van Poelgeest, L. "The Netherlands and the Tokyo Tribunal." *Japan Forum* 4, no. 1 (April 1992): 81–90.

————. *Tōkyō saiban to Oranda* (The Tokyo Trial and the Netherlands), trans. Mizushima Jirō and Tsukahara Tōgo, annot. Awaya Kentarō. Tokyo: Misuzu shobō, 1997.

Vautrin, Minnie. *Nankin Jiken no hibi: Minī Vōtorin no nikki* (The Days of the Nanking Incident: The Diary of Minnie Vautrin), trans. Okada Ryōnosuke and Ihara Yōko, annot. Kasahara Tokushi. Tokyo: Ōtsuki shoten, 1999.

VAWW-NET Japan, ed. *Nihongun seidoreisei o sabaku 2000-nen josei kokusai senpan hōtei no kiroku* (The Records of the Women's International War Crimes Tribunal to Prosecute Japanese Military's Sexual Slavery, Year 2000). 6 vols. Tokyo: Ryokufū shuppan, 2002.

Yamada Akira. *Shōwa tennō no gunji shisō to senryaku* (Military Ideas and Strategies of Emperor Shōwa). Tokyo: Azekura shobō, 2002.

Yamagiwa Akira. "Kenkyū nōto—Chūka minkoku seifu no 'Nipponjin shuyō senpan meibo' ni tsuite: tennō no senpan shimei mondai o chūshin ni" (A Research Note—On the "List of Major Japanese War Criminals" Prepared by the Government of the Republic of China: Centering on the Naming of the Emperor as a War Criminal). *Yokohama shiritsu daigaku ronshū* 41, nos. 1–3 (1990): 179–91.

Yamamoto, Masahiro. *Nanking: Anatomy of an Atrocity*. Westport, CT and London: Praeger, 2000.

Yang, Daqing. "The Malleable and the Contested: The Nanjing Massacre in Postwar China and Japan." In *Perilous Memories: The Asia-Pacific War(s)*, ed. T. Fujitani, Geoffrey M. White, and Lisa Yoneyama. Durham, NC and London: Duke University Press, 2001, 50–86.

Yokota Kisaburō. "Sekai no shinpan: jiei ron o funsai" (The Verdict of the World: The Doctrine of Self-Defense Destroyed). In *Shinbun shiryō ni miru Tōkyō saiban, BC-kyū saiban 1: Tōkyō saiban* (The Tokyo Trial and Class BC Trials Seen in Newspaper Sources, Vol. 1: The Tokyo Trial), ed. Nagai Hitoshi and Utsumi Aiko. Tokyo: Gendai shiryō shuppan, 2000, 346.

————. *Sensō hanzai ron, zōteiban* (A Treatise on War Crimes, Revised Edition). Tokyo: Yūhikaku, 1949.

————. "Tōkyō hanketsu to jiei ron" (The Tokyo Judgment and the Doctrine of Self-Defense). *Hōritsu jihō* 21, no. 2 (1949): 5–12.

Yoshida, Takashi. *The Making of the "Rape of Nanking": History and Memory in Japan, China, and the United States*. Oxford, UK: Oxford University Press, 2006.

Yoshida Yutaka. "Haisen zengo ni okeru kōbunsho no shōkyaku to intoku" (The Burning and Concealment of Government Records before and after the Defeat). In *Gendai rekishigaku to sensō sekinin* (Historical Studies Today and Responsibility for War), by Yoshida Yutaka. Tokyo: Aoki shoten, 1997, 127–41.

———. "Kyokutō kokusai gunji saiban to sensō sekinin mondai" (The International Military Tribunal for the Far East and Matters concerning Responsibility for War). In *Gendai rekishigaku to sensō sekinin* (Historical Studies Today and Responsibility for War), by Yoshida Yutaka. Tokyo: Aoki shoten, 1997, 142–78.

———. "Nankin jiken ronsō to kokusaihō" (The Debate on the Nanking Incident and International Law). In *Gendai rekishigaku to Nankin jiken* (Historical Studies Today and the Nanking Incident), ed. Yoshida Yutaka and Kasahara Tokushi. Tokyo: Kashiwa shobō, 2006, 68–93.

———. *Nihonjin no sensōkan: sengoshi no naka no hen'yō* (The Japanese Perception of War: Its Transformation in Postwar History). Tokyo: Iwanami shoten, 1995.

———. *Shōwa tennō no shūsenshi* (Emperor Shōwa's History of the Termination of War). Tokyo: Iwanami shoten, 1992.

Yoshimi Yoshiaki. *Jūgun ianfu* (Comfort Women). Tokyo: Iwanami shoten, 1995.

———. *Comfort Women: Sexual Slavery in the Japanese Military during World War II*, trans. Suzanne O'Brien. New York: Columbia University Press, 2000.

———. *Dokugasusen to Nihongun* (Poison Gas Warfare and the Japanese Army). Tokyo: Iwanami shoten, 2004.

———, ed. *Jūgun ianfu shiryōshū* (Sources on the Comfort Women). Tokyo: Ōtsuki shoten, 1992.

Yoshimi Yoshiaki and Hayashi Hirofumi, eds. *Kyōdō kenkyū: Nihongun ianfu* (Collaborative Research: Japanese Army's Comfort Women). Tokyo: Ōtsuki shoten, 1995.

Zhang, Kaiyuan, ed. *Eyewitnesses to Massacre: American Missionaries Bear Witness to Japanese Atrocities in Nanjing*. Armonk, NY: M.E. Sharpe, 2001.

Audio-Visual Materials

Hara Kazuo, dir. *Yukiyukite shingun* (The Imperial Army Marches On). Shissō purodakushon, 1987.

Ichikawa Kon, dir. *Nobi*. (Fires on the Plain). Daiei, 1959.

Itō Shun'ya, dir. *Puraido: unmei no toki* (Pride: The Fateful Moment). Tōei, 1998.

NHK supesharu shuzai chīmu (NHK special reporters), dir. *Pāru hanji wa nani o toikaketanoka: Tōkyō saiban shirarezaru kōbō* (What Did Justice Pal Attempt to Ask?: The Tokyo Trial, the Unknown Tug-Of-War). TV documentary. NHK, August 14, 2007.

Bibliographic Guides

Bibliography on the International Military Tribunal for the Far East (Tokyo), comp. Institute of International Studies Library. University of California, October 1964.

The Tokyo Trial: A Bibliographic Guide to English-Language Sources, comp. Jeanie M. Welch. Westport, CT and London: Greenwood Press, 2002.

Uncertain Judgment: A Bibliography of War Crimes Trials, comp. John R. Lewis. Santa Barbara, CA and Oxford, UK: ABC-Clio, 1979.

Index

incidents, the rhetoric of, 81, 92, 242
India, 10, 12, 26, 28, 110, 223, 228, 240
Indian National Army (INA), 223–24
Indian National Congress, 223, 243
indictment, 82–84, 90, 98, 103–5,
  108–9, 184–85
individual criminal liability, 20, 86–87,
  103–5, 107–8, 114, 260; criticisms
  concerning, 84, 182–83, 220, 222,
  236
Indonesia, 12–13, 114, 180, 216, 266*n*15.
  See also Dutch East Indies
Inoue Kiyoshi, 200–204
International Commission of Jurists,
  14
international criminal tribunals, 4,
  78–79, 135, 141, 259–60
international law, the foundational
  idea of, 191–93, 195–96, 207, 210–
  12, 220–21, 227, 259
International Military Tribunal at
  Nuremberg, 1, 12, 20–21, 24, 41,
  106, 115, 266*n*13; as a model of the
  Tokyo trial, 1, 8–10, 22–23, 26, 28,
  67, 265*n*7; as a precedent-setter,
  17, 84–85, 87, 208–9, 236–37, 257;
  the charter of, 21–22, 29–30, 80–
  81, 85, 87, 94, 101–2, 278*n*40; findings made by, 85–87, 89–90, 95,
  139–40, 221, 237; Japanese views
  on, 198, 208, 211–12, 257–58
International Military Tribunal for
  the Far East, 1, 7, 22, 27–28; participants in, 10, 12–13, 269*n*32;
  independence and impartiality of,
  2, 14–17, 30–32, 206; the charter
  of, 28–31, 42, 81, 94, 98, 102, 192,
  269*n*29, 278*n*23, 278*n*40. *See also*
  judgment at Tokyo *and* judges

International Prosecution Section,
  18–19, 23–24, 64, 202, 267*n*27;
  cohesion within, 12, 32–40, 67–
  69, 71–72; the Emperor and, 40,
  55–56, 58; war crimes investigations by, 32–34, 105–8, 110–12, 256;
  prosecutorial priorities of, 68–69,
  96–97, 115–16, 120, 151–60, 162–63,
  172, 174–77, 180–82, 188, 256; substantiation strategies by, 107–8,
  151–52, 157–59, 173–74, 177, 184,
  189; format of presentation by,
  112–15, 152, 155–57, 162, 173–74
internment camps, mistreatment at,
  108–9, 174–76, 184
interpreters, *see* translation
Iraq, 260
Irie Keishirō, 213
Ishii Itarō, 136–38, 140, 148
Ishii Shirō, 60
Itagaki Seishirō, 92, 186, 230
Itō Kiyoshi, 125–26

Jackson, Robert H., 21, 24, 41, 235
Jaranilla, Delfin, 16–17
Japan, 44–45, 52, 80, 99–100, 175,
  228–29; Allied occupation of, 28,
  32, 44, 51, 53, 61–62, 70, 213, 218,
  261; destruction of documents by,
  105–7, 151, 184
Japan-Is-Not-Guilty View, 224, 228,
  232, 240
Japanese courts-martial, 120,127–28,
  143–44, 283*n*4
Japanese Defense Agency, 106–7
Japanese economic elite, the culpability of, 202, 215–16, 250
Japanese domestic law, 100, 137–38,
  148

Harvard East Asian Monographs
(*out-of-print)

48. Paul Richard Bohr, *Famine and the Missionary: Timothy Richard as Relief Administrator and Advocate of National Reform*

49. Endymion Wilkinson, *The History of Imperial China: A Research Guide*

50. Britten Dean, *China and Great Britain: The Diplomacy of Commercial Relations, 1860–1864*

51. Ellsworth C. Carlson, *The Foochow Missionaries, 1847–1880*

52. Yeh-chien Wang, *An Estimate of the Land-Tax Collection in China, 1753 and 1908*

53. Richard M. Pfeffer, *Understanding Business Contracts in China, 1949–1963*

*54. Han-sheng Chuan and Richard Kraus, *Mid-Ching Rice Markets and Trade: An Essay in Price History*

55. Ranbir Vohra, *Lao She and the Chinese Revolution*

56. Liang-lin Hsiao, *China's Foreign Trade Statistics, 1864–1949*

*57. Lee-hsia Hsu Ting, *Government Control of the Press in Modern China, 1900–1949*

*58. Edward W. Wagner, *The Literati Purges: Political Conflict in Early Yi Korea*

*59. Joungwon A. Kim, *Divided Korea: The Politics of Development, 1945–1972*

60. Noriko Kamachi, John K. Fairbank, and Chūzō Ichiko, *Japanese Studies of Modern China Since 1953: A Bibliographical Guide to Historical and Social-Science Research on the Nineteenth and Twentieth Centuries, Supplementary Volume for 1953–1969*

61. Donald A. Gibbs and Yun-chen Li, *A Bibliography of Studies and Translations of Modern Chinese Literature, 1918–1942*

62. Robert H. Silin, *Leadership and Values: The Organization of Large-Scale Taiwanese Enterprises*

63. David Pong, *A Critical Guide to the Kwangtung Provincial Archives Deposited at the Public Record Office of London*

*64. Fred W. Drake, *China Charts the World: Hsu Chi-yü and His Geography of 1848*

*65. William A. Brown and Urgrunge Onon, translators and annotators, *History of the Mongolian People's Republic*

66. Edward L. Farmer, *Early Ming Government: The Evolution of Dual Capitals*

*67. Ralph C. Croizier, *Koxinga and Chinese Nationalism: History, Myth, and the Hero*

*68. William J. Tyler, tr., *The Psychological World of Natsume Sōseki*, by Doi Takeo

69. Eric Widmer, *The Russian Ecclesiastical Mission in Peking During the Eighteenth Century*

*70. Charlton M. Lewis, *Prologue to the Chinese Revolution: The Transformation of Ideas and Institutions in Hunan Province, 1891–1907*

71. Preston Torbert, *The Ching Imperial Household Department: A Study of Its Organization and Principal Functions, 1662–1796*

72. Paul A. Cohen and John E. Schrecker, eds., *Reform in Nineteenth-Century China*

73. Jon Sigurdson, *Rural Industrialism in China*

74. Kang Chao, *The Development of Cotton Textile Production in China*

Harvard East Asian Monographs

Harvard East Asian Monographs

203. Robert S. Ross and Jiang Changbin, eds., *Re-examining the Cold War: U.S.-China Diplomacy, 1954–1973*

204. Guanhua Wang, *In Search of Justice: The 1905–1906 Chinese Anti-American Boycott*

205. David Schaberg, *A Patterned Past: Form and Thought in Early Chinese Historiography*

206. Christine Yano, *Tears of Longing: Nostalgia and the Nation in Japanese Popular Song*

207. Milena Doleželová-Velingerová and Oldřich Král, with Graham Sanders, eds., *The Appropriation of Cultural Capital: China's May Fourth Project*

208. Robert N. Huey, *The Making of 'Shinkokinshū'*

209. Lee Butler, *Emperor and Aristocracy in Japan, 1467–1680: Resilience and Renewal*

210. Suzanne Ogden, *Inklings of Democracy in China*

211. Kenneth J. Ruoff, *The People's Emperor: Democracy and the Japanese Monarchy, 1945–1995*

212. Haun Saussy, *Great Walls of Discourse and Other Adventures in Cultural China*

213. Aviad E. Raz, *Emotions at Work: Normative Control, Organizations, and Culture in Japan and America*

214. Rebecca E. Karl and Peter Zarrow, eds., *Rethinking the 1898 Reform Period: Political and Cultural Change in Late Qing China*

215. Kevin O'Rourke, *The Book of Korean Shijo*

216. Ezra F. Vogel, ed., *The Golden Age of the U.S.-China-Japan Triangle, 1972–1989*

217. Thomas A. Wilson, ed., *On Sacred Grounds: Culture, Society, Politics, and the Formation of the Cult of Confucius* ·

218. Donald S. Sutton, *Steps of Perfection: Exorcistic Performers and Chinese Religion in Twentieth-Century Taiwan*

219. Daqing Yang, *Technology of Empire: Telecommunications and Japanese Expansionism, 1895–1945*

220. Qianshen Bai, *Fu Shan's World: The Transformation of Chinese Calligraphy in the Seventeenth Century*

221. Paul Jakov Smith and Richard von Glahn, eds., *The Song-Yuan-Ming Transition in Chinese History*

222. Rania Huntington, *Alien Kind: Foxes and Late Imperial Chinese Narrative*

223. Jordan Sand, *House and Home in Modern Japan: Architecture, Domestic Space, and Bourgeois Culture, 1880–1930*

224. Karl Gerth, *China Made: Consumer Culture and the Creation of the Nation*

225. Xiaoshan Yang, *Metamorphosis of the Private Sphere: Gardens and Objects in Tang-Song Poetry*

226. Barbara Mittler, *A Newspaper for China? Power, Identity, and Change in Shanghai's News Media, 1872–1912*

227. Joyce A. Madancy, *The Troublesome Legacy of Commissioner Lin: The Opium Trade and Opium Suppression in Fujian Province, 1820s to 1920s*

Harvard East Asian Monographs

Harvard East Asian Monographs